T0184183

Natural Computing Series

Founding Editor

Grzegorz Rozenberg

Series Editors

Thomas Bäck⬤, Natural Computing Group–LIACS, Leiden University, Leiden, The Netherlands

Lila Kari, School of Computer Science, University of Waterloo, Waterloo, ON, Canada

Susan Stepney, Department of Computer Science, University of York, York, UK

Scope

Natural Computing is one of the most exciting developments in computer science, and there is a growing consensus that it will become a major field in this century. This series includes monographs, textbooks, and state-of-the-art collections covering the whole spectrum of Natural Computing and ranging from theory to applications.

Leonardo Vanneschi · Sara Silva

Lectures on Intelligent Systems

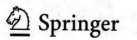 Springer

Leonardo Vanneschi
NOVA Information Management School
Universidade Nova de Lisboa
Lisbon, Portugal

Sara Silva
LASIGE, Departamento de Informática
Faculdade de Ciências
Universidade de Lisboa
Lisbon, Portugal

ISSN 1619-7127
Natural Computing Series
ISBN 978-3-031-17924-2   ISBN 978-3-031-17922-8   (eBook)
https://doi.org/10.1007/978-3-031-17922-8

© Springer Nature Switzerland AG 2023
This work is subject to copyright. All rights are reserved by the Publisher, whether the whole or part of the material is concerned, specifically the rights of translation, reprinting, reuse of illustrations, recitation, broadcasting, reproduction on microfilms or in any other physical way, and transmission or information storage and retrieval, electronic adaptation, computer software, or by similar or dissimilar methodology now known or hereafter developed.
The use of general descriptive names, registered names, trademarks, service marks, etc. in this publication does not imply, even in the absence of a specific statement, that such names are exempt from the relevant protective laws and regulations and therefore free for general use.
The publisher, the authors, and the editors are safe to assume that the advice and information in this book are believed to be true and accurate at the date of publication. Neither the publisher nor the authors or the editors give a warranty, expressed or implied, with respect to the material contained herein or for any errors or omissions that may have been made. The publisher remains neutral with regard to jurisdictional claims in published maps and institutional affiliations.

This Springer imprint is published by the registered company Springer Nature Switzerland AG
The registered company address is: Gewerbestrasse 11, 6330 Cham, Switzerland

To our children Dani, David and Lara.

To our parents Altina, Eurico, Giovanna and Marco.

Leonardo and Sara

To my dad. He would be proud.

Sara

Acknowledgements

My first acknowledgment goes to Marco Tomassini. As my former PhD supervisor, he is the person who introduced me to the area of Computational Intelligence. He has been a central figure for the development of my profession. This book would surely not exist without him.

My second acknowledgment goes to Mauro Castelli. He was an undergraduate student when I first used some of the ideas of this book in my classes. Then he became my Masters student, and later my PhD student. Finally, he is now my colleague and my great friend. His collaboration has been invaluable for at least the past twelve years. It had a tremendous impact on my work and so, indirectly, also on this book.

Then, I would like to thank all the collaborators that I have had from the beginning of my career until today. They are many, so I cannot mention them all, but each one of them has been, in their own way, special and important for my work.

Last but not least, I would like to express my gratitude to my family for their infinite support and for making me grow up in an environment where value was given to studying and education.

Leonardo

First things first, thank you to my family for never having tried to convince me that "scientist of artificial intelligence" was not what a young teenage girl should want to be. In a country where there is still no such thing as a research career, it took (and still takes) a lot of stubbornness on my part, but also a lot of support from many people, to achieve it. I acknowledge every single research grant I have ever received, every travel grant that allowed me to participate in conferences, every research centre that took me in, and everyone who believed in me and respected my wish to take the road less traveled.

Sara

Contents

Chapter 1
Introduction

Computer science is the science that deals with the treatment of information by means of automatic procedures. It has multiple objectives, including the study of computation at a logical level and the several possible practical techniques for its implementation and application in automated electronic systems, i.e., computers. One of the focal points of computer science is *problem solving*, i.e., the act of defining a problem and then developing and implementing a solution. In this context, a *problem* can be defined as a task that has to be fulfilled automatically, and solving a problem typically implies the design and development of an *algorithm*. An algorithm is a process, or method, that solves a problem by means of a finite set of well-defined and unambiguous actions, each of which can be mechanically executed in a finite amount of time. At the bottom of the process stands the implementation, which consists in the development of a computer *program*, i.e., the encoding of an algorithm in a programming language, which can be directly compiled and/or executed on a computer. A problem can typically be expressed by means of a set of data, called *inputs*, that the algorithm, and consequently the program that implements it, can use. The execution of the program on a computer finally produces the solution to the problem, which can be the value of a variable or set of variables, or any other type of information we were looking for, called the *output*.

Example 1.1. Arguably one of the simplest problems that can be solved using a computer is the following one:

   Find the maximum of a finite sequence of numbers.

An algorithm to solve this problem can be described by the following actions:

1. Define a numeric variable called *max*;
2. Assign to *max* the value of the first number in the sequence;
3. For each value x in the sequence:

   3.1. if x is larger than the value currently contained in variable *max*
        then change the value of *max*, so that it becomes equal to x;

4. return the value of variable *max*;

© Springer Nature Switzerland AG 2023
L. Vanneschi and S. Silva, *Lectures on Intelligent Systems*, Natural Computing Series,
https://doi.org/10.1007/978-3-031-17922-8_1

Such an algorithm can be executed manually for small sequences, but it clearly needs automatic computation for large sequences. In order to execute the algorithm automatically on a computer, it needs to be encoded in a programming language. For instance, a possible program that implements the previous algorithm can be represented by the following Java method:

```
public static int findMax(int[] inputSequence) {
    int max = inputSequence[0];
    for (int i = 1; i < inputSequence.length; i++) {
        if (inputSequence[i] > max)
            max = inputSequence[i];
    }
    return max;
}
```

In this example, the input (i.e., the data that characterize the problem) is the given sequence of numbers and the output (i.e., the sought for result) is a value, the maximum of the sequence. Encoding an algorithm into a computer program typically implies a number of implementation choices, such as, in this case, the data types of the numeric values contained in the sequence (integer numbers in the implementation given above), the way of representing the sequence of numbers (an array of integer values, in this case), and the way of receiving inputs and returning outputs (parameter passage of Java methods and return Java statement, respectively).

From this example, it should be clear that, in the context of computer science, a problem is generally not dependent on the particular data, or instance, used, but it is instead a much more general concept, which actually *abstracts* from the data used in the particular instance. The above problem could, in fact, be reformulated as "Develop a method to find the maximum of *any* finite sequence of numbers", and this is exactly what the reported algorithm and program do. In particular, one should remark that the Java method findMax can be used for finding the maximum of *any* array of integer values, independently of its length (provided that it is not longer than the longest sequence that can fit in the memory of the computer we are using) and of the particular values it contains.

Furthermore, it should not be hard to convince oneself that, apart from some implementation choices like the ones discussed above, coding an algorithm into a computer program is broadly a mechanical task. In fact, each particular action, or group of actions, contained in an algorithm has an immediate correspondence to one or more instructions of a programming language. On the other hand, developing an algorithm able to solve a problem is, typically, a very *creative* task, for which no formal rules exist in general. In traditional computer science, the design of an algorithm, which actually corresponds to the development of the "strategy" to solve the problem, is completely manual and assigned to human beings.

1.1 Motivation for Intelligent Systems

Intelligent systems can be broadly defined as systems that have the ability to solve problems autonomously, i.e., with reduced or even no intervention from humans. The motivation for intelligent systems is straightforward: the traditional computational method described previously, where the design of an algorithm is assigned to a human being, fails in many cases. This can happen, depending on the situation, because it is extremely hard, or even impossible, for a human being to conceive an algorithm for a problem, or because the algorithms that we are able to design for particular problems are so inefficient that it is impossible to execute their implementations in a reasonable amount of time, even on the most powerful existing computers. As a first and simple example, one may think of the following problem: assume that you are the owner of a store, and a person enters your store. The problem consists in giving a reliable answer to the following question:

Will that person be a good client?

Or, in other words: will that person buy enough products sold in your store, so that you will achieve a profit? Remembering that an algorithm is a precise sequence of formal actions that allow us to solve a general problem (in other words, the algorithm should potentially work for *any* person entering the store), we challenge the reader to design an algorithm for this problem. We believe that we can state, with a high degree of confidence, that such a design is impossible for a human being.

Let us now consider another example. Given a set of photographs picturing human faces, answer the following question:

Who is the person that is pictured in this photo?

In this case, a human being may possibly imagine an algorithm, mainly based on somatic characteristics of the face, like the color of the hair, the color of the eyes, the distance between the eyes, the position, shape and size of nose and mouth, etc. However, it is clear that it is possible to present to a human being two photos picturing the faces of two different persons with absolutely identical somatic characteristics, and, even in those cases, the human brain is able to distinguish between the two pictured persons. Probably no handmade algorithm will ever have the discernment ability that is typical of the human brain, and so probably none of them will ever solve this problem in a satisfactory way. Indeed, practically the totality of the face recognition systems existing nowadays heavily rely on intelligent systems, instead of traditional computational methods.

Let us consider a third example. The problem consists in answering the following question:

What is the right mix of molecules that can be used to create a new drug?

For instance, we may be interested in creating a new medicine with some particular characteristics, or able to cure a new disease. In this case, it is possible, and arguably even "easy", for a human being to conceive an algorithm. For instance, the algorithm may consist in trying, one by one, all the possible combinations of known molecules and testing them, to see whether they obtain the sought for effect. This algorithm can, in principle, solve the problem perfectly, but it has a major flaw: the number of molecules existing in one cubic centimeter is estimated as being approximately equal to 2.7×10^{19}. Even without dwelling on the calculations required to estimate the number of possible combinations of existing molecules, it should not be hard to convince oneself that testing all these combinations in acceptable time is impossible.

As a fourth example, one may imagine the problem of writing a program able to drive a robot in a 3D space, so that the robot is able to efficiently accomplish complex tasks, independently of the characteristics of the particular space. To fix ideas, one may consider the practical case of self-driving vehicles. Also in this case, it is not hard to convince oneself that the number of possible situations that the robot may have to deal with is so high that any handcrafted algorithm is probably destined to fail. In fact, self-driving vehicles are based on intelligent systems.

The above list of examples could continue indefinitely. For all these problems, either it is impossible for a human being to conceive an algorithm or the algorithms that can be developed are not executable in practice. Generally speaking, none of these problems can be solved using the traditional computational method. At the same time, with today's proliferation of data, these types of problems are becoming more and more numerous and, thanks to improvements in technology, we are every day more and more interested in solving those problems. So, what to do? The idea is to design computational systems that have the ability to autonomously *learn* to solve problems. This is the objective of the area of study, particularly popular and active nowadays, called *Machine Learning*. The idea of building machines able to learn is not new. Alan Turing was probably the first person to describe computer intelligence as "a machine that can learn from experience" in a public lecture in London, in 1947, going as far as stating that "the possibility of letting the machine alter its own instructions provides the mechanism for this". However, these ideas remained unpublished, only to be reinvented later. Early work can be broadly dated back to the studies of Samuel in the late 1950s [Samuel, 1959], later revisited and deepened by Mitchell in the 1990s [Mitchell, 1997]. According to Mitchell, Machine Learning is:

> *"the study of algorithms able to automatically improve by means of experience"*

This definition is significant for at least two reasons. First of all, Mitchell puts the accent on algorithms, actually raising the bar on the objective of overcoming the limitations of traditional computing, which entirely assigns the design of algorithms to humans. Secondly, Mitchell defines the concept of learning as improvement by means of experience. In this way, Mitchell gives a clear idea of the general functioning of a learning computational system: it has to be based on an iterative process in which, at each iteration, either a new entire solution or a piece of an existing solution is proposed, based on the experience gathered in the previous iterations. Key in all this process is, once again, the idea that solutions to complex problems should be built with very limited or even no human intervention. The only task for humans now is to give the system a very precise description of the problem, and no hint on how to solve it, while the solution should be completely generated in an automatic way by the computational system.

1.2 Intelligent Systems and Bioinspired Algorithms

A very large number of techniques that can be considered intelligent exist nowadays, and a significant part of those techniques draw inspiration from the idea that learning is a characteristic that is typical of living beings. So, those techniques are inspired by the biology of some living beings with the objective of, in some way, mimicking their ability to learn. When this happens, we talk about *bioinspired* intelligent systems, or simply bioinspired algorithms. The best known are:

- *Artificial Neural Networks*, which are inspired by the structure of the human brain, and try to simulate, although in an elementary way, its functioning.
- *Evolutionary Algorithms*, which are inspired by the Theory of Evolution of Charles Darwin [Darwin, 1859], and have the objective of evolving solutions using processes that, although simplified, are similar to those that are responsible for the evolution of species.
- *Swarm Intelligence*, which draws inspiration from the collective intelligence arising from the collaboration of animals in groups, like for instance ant colonies, bird flocking, hawks hunting, animal herding, bacterial growth, fish schooling and microbial intelligence.
- *Fuzzy Systems*, which simulate the ability of human beings to deal with concepts such as uncertainty or imprecise information, an ability that is crucial for learning general behaviors.
- *Local Search Systems*, whose biological inspiration can arguably be imagined as coming from their ability to simulate the sense of orientation of living beings.

All these approaches share one important characteristic: they have the ability to return an approximate, or imprecise, solution to problems whenever they are not able to find a perfect one. This characteristic is typical of the set of techniques that are identified with the name *Soft Computing* [Tettamanzi and Tomassini, 2001]. This feature can be very important in many situations for at least the following reasons: first of all, problems exist that are so complex that the idea of finding a perfect solution is purely utopian. In those cases, obviously, it is better to have an approximate solution than to not have any solution at all. Secondly, there are cases in which an approximate solution can be as good as a perfect one. One may, for instance, imagine a problem consisting in driving a robot in a room, following a path from a given starting point A to a given destination B, avoiding obstacles that are positioned in the room. In this context, it is obvious that no particular path is required, as any path that allows the robot to go from A to B avoiding obstacles is exactly as good as all the others that have this characteristic. Last but not least, having the ability to return approximate solutions can be crucial for improving the generalization ability of a system, given that a perfect solution may be affected by *overfitting*, a key concept of Machine Learning discussed in Chapter 5.

This book introduces various bioinspired intelligent systems and also some intelligent systems that are not bioinspired. In particular, we will discuss two types of local search algorithms, Hill Climbing and Simulated Annealing, two types of evolutionary algorithms, Genetic Algorithms and Genetic Programming, one swarm intelligence algorithm, Particle Swarm Optimization, and various types of artificial neural networks. Among the systems that are not bioinspired, we will present Decision Trees, Random Forests, Support Vector Machines, Bayesian Classifiers and others.

1.3 Applications of Intelligent Systems

Intelligent systems are used nowadays in so many applications, both in industry and academia, that listing them all is inconceivable. However, in this section, we try to give an incomplete and limited list of possible applications, just to give the reader an idea of the abundance and breadth of possible areas where intelligent systems are successfully employed.

- *Robotics*. Optimization of paths and movements of robots, treatment of signals coming from sensors and other sources, and many other related applications are nowadays a reality, and they have led, for instance, to the development of self-driving vehicles and autonomous appliances.
- *Engineering*. The automatic synthesis of integrated electronic circuits and the management of mechanical systems, such as appliances, trains or assistance devices, are only few examples of the numerous engineering applications that are nowadays strongly based on intelligent systems.
- *Biology*. From the study of DNA and the human genome, to the modeling of complex biological systems like gene regulatory networks or viruses, and many other applications, intelligent systems have played a central role in recent developments in biology.
- *Chemistry*. The automatization of the drug discovery process, aimed at designing, developing and commercializing new medicines, and the study and the optimization of the 3D structure of molecules and their properties are only a few examples of the numerous applications of chemistry in which intelligent systems have been applied successfully.
- *Medicine*. The analysis and mining of the vast amounts of data that arise in radiomics, genomics, epigenomics and proteomics, together with clinical data and many other forms of data are nowadays analyzed by intelligent systems with the objective of developing predictive models for diagnosis, prognosis and therapy, supporting decision making in medicine.
- *Economics and Business*. Simulation and prediction of stock market trends, risk management, decision support in companies and organizations, and pricing are

only some of the numerous applications in which intelligent systems are applied in economics and business nowadays.

- *Marketing*. Optimization of marketing campaigns, optimization of the placement of goods in the supermarket shelves and design of marketing strategies are performed successfully using intelligent systems in several companies and organizations.
- *Security*. Traffic control, face recognition, identity checking and tracking are tasks that are automated and optimized by means of intelligent systems in many situations nowadays.
- *Computational Security*. Cryptography, identification of malware and protection of computational systems, from large to small scale, by means of intelligent systems are a reality.
- *Society*. Predicting debt problems in families, the school performance of children, or inclination towards gambling addiction, drug addiction or other types of addiction are currently performed by intelligent systems in several situations, facilitating early intervention and social support.
- *Pervasive Computing*. Computers are everywhere nowadays. For instance, houses equipped with domotics, smart appliances and interactive facilities, where intelligent systems obviously play a crucial role.

1.4 Objectives and Limits of This Book

The list of possible applications of intelligent systems presented above could continue indefinitely. The conclusion is straightforward: intelligent systems are general-purpose methods that can be used with success in practically all existing application areas. With this perspective, it is clear that it would be presumptuous, and ultimately impossible, to try to discuss all possible applications in one book. Instead, in this book we have decided to not enter into the details of any application, except for some examples in some specific cases. Instead, the book focuses on computational methods, with the objective of providing readers with the necessary methodological tools and competencies that can hopefully allow them to tackle complex applications in the future.

The book has two ambitions: first, remaining general enough to be independent of any one application, but at the same time concrete enough to promote the future use of intelligent systems in any such application. Second, disseminating to readers, in particular students or young researchers, the message that intelligent systems is still a young area, where many improvements are still possible, and often necessary. Research in this area is, today more than ever, in demand, and this book aims to be an incentive for young, enthusiastic and dynamic minds to express and develop new ideas, to actively contribute to the field.

Of course, being general (i.e., independent of applications) does not have to mean being abstract or insubstantial. The book is supposed to be the backbone of the didactic material of a university course. The numerous examples contained in the book, as well as the necessary practical classes in the course, are the means to maintain an appropriate level of concreteness, in a discipline that is naturally at the frontier of research. However, it is our conviction that, in order to successfully apply intelligent computational methods at an industrial level, a deep expertise is needed which involves not only a "final user" knowledge of the needed technicalities to apply those methods, but also a deep understanding and possession of their inner functioning and dynamics. This is the type of knowledge that this book has the ambition to transfer.

The book will not present any programming language or environment for intelligent systems, for at least two reasons. First, for reasons of space: the book would otherwise become unreasonably long. Second, because the most popular technologies and programming environments evolve and change rapidly, and any one of them would shortly become outdated and would be replaced by others.

1.5 Organization of the Book

In Section 1.1, we identified the main motivation for intelligent systems in relation to complex problems, for which the manual design of an algorithm is either extremely hard or impossible. Many of those problems exist, but undoubtedly a large part of them can be categorized into two main classes of problems that, although strongly interrelated, have important differences: *optimization* problems and *machine learning* problems. The main organization of the book reflects this categorization. The book is, in fact, partitioned into two main parts: Part I, devoted to computational intelligence methods for optimization, and Part II, dedicated to Machine Learning (ML).

Part I is organized as follows:

- Chapter 2 introduces the concept of optimization and optimization problems, discussing some fundamental concepts, and also introducing some computational intelligence algorithms which can be categorized as local search algorithms, such as Hill Climbing and Simulated Annealing.
- Chapter 3 presents a population-based method belonging to the field of evolutionary algorithms, called Genetic Algorithms, deepening its functioning and discussing some advanced topics.
- Chapter 4 tackles another population-based method, belonging to the field of swarm intelligence called Particle Swarm Optimization.

Part II is organized as follows:

- Chapter 5 introduces Machine Learning, with its definitions and general concepts, and presents some simple algorithms.
- Chapter 6 discusses Decision Trees.
- Chapter 7 presents Artificial Neural Networks, and some of their variants for supervised ML.

- Chapter 8 tackles Genetic Programming, the second flavor of evolutionary algorithm discussed in this book.
- Chapter 9 presents Bayesian learning and some of its supervised ML algorithms.
- Chapter 10 introduces Support Vector Machines.
- Chapter 11 discusses Ensemble Methods.
- Finally, Chapter 12 focuses on Unsupervised Machine Learning, introducing some of the best-known clustering algorithms.

Part I
Computational Intelligence for Optimization

Chapter 2
Optimization Problems and Local Search

This chapter introduces optimization problems, one of the largest classes of complex tasks where intelligent systems have become a reality in the last few years. Then, this chapter tackles the first type of algorithms that can be used to approach optimization problems: local search algorithms. Generally speaking, local search algorithms function by "moving" from solution to solution in the space of candidate solutions, by applying *local* changes, until a satisfactory solution is found or a time bound elapses.

2.1 Introduction to Optimization

Optimization [Antoniou and Lu, 2007, Kochenderfer and Wheeler, 2019] is a field of study aimed at developing methods, strategies and algorithms for solving complex optimization problems. In its most general sense, the objective of an optimization problem is to find the best solution(s) to a problem in a (huge) set of possible alternative solutions. Generally speaking, an optimization problem can be approached if we are in possession of at least two pieces of information: we need to know all the possible solutions, or at least to recognize whether an object is a possible solution or not, and we need to know, or at least to be able to measure, the quality of each one of the solutions, in such a way that each one of them can be compared to the others. Furthermore, a general hypothesis of optimization is that the set of all possible solutions is so large that it is impossible to enumerate all of them, looking for the best one(s). And this is why "intelligent" algorithms are generally in demand for solving optimization problems. Just to settle on some ideas, let us consider the following examples of optimization problems:

- Example 1: given a three-dimensional space characterized by a set of paths where a robot can move, find the path that allows the robot to minimize the number of collisions with obstacles during its motion;

© Springer Nature Switzerland AG 2023
L. Vanneschi and S. Silva, *Lectures on Intelligent Systems*, Natural Computing Series, https://doi.org/10.1007/978-3-031-17922-8_2

- Example 2: given a set of photographs of human faces, find the one that most "resembles" a given target face.

Both these examples can be considered optimization problems, because for both of them we know the solutions, or at least we are able to recognize them, and we are able to assess the quality of all the solutions. For instance: in Example 1, solutions are all the possible paths contained in the three-dimensional space at hand, and in order to assess the quality of each one of them, all we have to do is to allow the robot to move along the path, and count the number of obstacles that are hit: the lower this number, the better the quality. Concerning Example 2, the solutions are pictures of human faces and in order to quantify their quality, all we have to do is to define a measure of similarity between pictures: the greater the similarity with the target face, the better the quality.

Several optimization problems are NP-complete [Garey and Johnson, 1990]. This means that optimal solutions cannot be obtained in a "reasonable" amount of time by means of classical, deterministic algorithms (and generally, the time required to solve this type of problem is exponential in the size of the data). This is the main motivation for using Computational Intelligence methods to solve this kind of problem. Optimization problems can usually be specified by means of a set of *instances* of the problem.

Definition 2.1. An instance of an optimization problem is a pair:

$$(S, f)$$

where:

- S is the set of all possible solutions, also called the solution space, or search space;
- f is a function, defined on all elements of S, that associates a real number to each one of them:

$$f : S \rightarrow \mathbb{R}$$

f quantifies the quality of the solutions in S and is called the cost function, or fitness function.

Before continuing, it is important to understand the difference between an optimization problem and an instance of an optimization problem. An instance of an optimization problem is a specification of the problem itself, given by the formal definition of S and f. Defining a particular instance for a given problem is usually a process that forces us to make choices and also to give an interpretation of the problem (an instance of an optimization problem, in fact, cannot be ambiguous). Let us consider again the optimization problem of Example 2, consisting in finding, in a given set of photographs of human faces, the one that most "resembles" a given target face. Let us assume also that the target face is represented in a picture, and let t be that picture. Let $\{\phi_1, \phi_2, ..., \phi_n\}$ be the set of photographs of human faces, among which we have to chose the most similar to t. For that problem, we can imagine, at least, the existence of the following instances:

- Instance 1:

    - $S = \{P_i,\ i = 1, 2, ..., n \mid P_i$ is the matrix of pixels composing picture $\phi_i\}$;
    - $\forall i = 1, 2, ..., n : f(P_i) =$ pixel-to-pixel distance between P_i and the target image t.

- Instance 2: let us assume the existence of an algorithm $\mathscr{A}$ that, given a photograph ϕ representing a face, returns a set of *features* of ϕ; just to fix ideas, one could for instance imagine somatic features, like for instance the position of the nose, of the eyes and of the mouth, the color of the eyes, the hair color, etc.

    - $S = \{\mathscr{A}(\phi_i),\ i = 1, 2, ..., n\}$;
    - $\forall i = 1, 2, ..., n : f(P_i) =$ feature-based distance between $\mathscr{A}(\phi_i)$ and $\mathscr{A}(t)$.

Several things can be observed from the previous examples: first of all, several instances can be defined for the same problem; second, the possible instances can even be extremely different from each other, both in terms of the representation of the solutions in S and in terms of the fitness function f; third, while an optimization problem can be defined in a rather generic way (for instance, if the set of pictures is small enough, it is even possible to solve the problem manually, using a concept of "similarity" between faces that is subjective, and not measurable), an instance of an optimization problem has to be defined formally, and this is a necessary step so that it can be solved using a computer; fourth, to define an instance, we have to interpret and formalize the problem, and this usually implies a set of choices; last but not least, as we will see in the continuation of the book, the algorithms that we will study may have very different performance on different instances of the same problem. So, the choices that we make when we define an instance of an optimization problem are very important, because they may have a direct impact on the functioning of the algorithm. For instance, considering the previous example, it is well known that the distance between image features is more likely to correspond to our idea of "similarity" between the pictures than the pixel-to-pixel distance. For this reason, an algorithm solving Instance 2 will probably return better results than an algorithm solving Instance 1.

An instance of an optimization problem can identify a maximization or a minimization problem.

Definition 2.2. A *minimization problem* consists in finding a solution $o \in S$ such that:

$$f(o) \leq f(i),\ \forall i \in S$$

while a *maximization problem* consists in finding a solution $o \in S$ such that:

$$f(o) \geq f(i),\ \forall i \in S$$

In both cases, the sought for solution o is called a *global optimum* or *globally optimal* solution, $f(o)$ or f_o is called the optimal fitness and the notation S_o is used to indicate the set of the global optima contained in S (remark that, given that in general many solutions can have the same fitness value, global optima are generally not unique).

In the area of optimization, it is typical to talk about several types of problems. In particular, it is frequent to talk about *combinatorial* optimization problems. With this terminology, it is customary to identify a subset of optimization problems where the search space S, although typically huge, is finite. It is not infrequent to also find in the literature the term combinatorial optimization problems associated with optimization problems in which the feasible solutions can be expressed using concepts from combinatorics (such as sets, subsets, combinations or permutations) and/or graph theory (such as vertices, edges, cliques, paths, cycles or cuts). The term "combinatorial" can be understood as a combination of steps chosen from a series/set of possible steps, which will allow us to arrive at the optimum result. Other typical cases of optimization problems are *discrete* and *continuous* optimization problems. These terms are used, once again, to identify the search space S, distinguishing the case in which it is a discrete, or a continuous set, respectively. The definition of optimization problem given so far is general enough to include all these variants.

2.2 Examples of Optimization Problems

Before deepening the study of optimization problems with an important theoretical result and several algorithms to solve them, we present some examples of optimization problems, along with instance definitions.

Example 2.1. (Knapsack Problem). Given a set of *n objects*, each one with a known *weight* and *value*, and a knapsack with a predefined maximum *capacity k*, the objective of this optimization problem is to fill the knapsack with objects with the largest possible total value, such that the total weight of these objects does not surpass the knapsack's capacity. A possible instance for this problem could be defined as follows; let $\{1, 2, ..., n\}$ be the available objects and, for each $i = 1, 2, ..., n$, let *weight*(i) be the weight of object i and *value*(i) be its value. Assuming that, for each $i = 1, 2, ..., n$, *value*(i) and *weight*(i) are positive numbers:

- The search space S can be defined as the set of all possible strings of bits of length equal to n (i.e., the number of available objects);
- Given a solution $\mathbf{z} = \{z_1, z_2, ..., z_n\}$, where for each $i = 1, 2, ..., n, z_i \in \{0, 1\}$, the fitness of $\mathbf{z}$ can be defined as:

$$f(\mathbf{z}) = \begin{cases} \sum_{z_i=1} value(i) & \text{if } \sum_{z_i=1} weight(i) \leq k \\ -1 & \text{otherwise} \end{cases} \qquad (2.1)$$

With this fitness function, the problem is a maximization one: the higher the fitness, the better the solution.

Using this representation, the solutions represent the possible selections of the n available objects. In fact, when a bit z_i is equal to 1, this can be interpreted as the object i being carried inside the knapsack. Analogously, if a bit z_i is equal to 0, then the corresponding object i is not carried inside the knapsack. In other words, with this representation, we are creating two groups, or *clusters* of objects: the ones that are carried inside the knapsack, corresponding to a bit equal to 1, and the ones that are not carried, corresponding to a bit equal to 0. The fitness function distinguishes between admissible solutions, i.e., solutions for which the total weight of the carried objects is not larger than the knapsack's capacity, and nonadmissible ones. For the admissible solutions, the fitness is equal to the sum of the values of the objects carried in the knapsack, while for the nonadmissible solutions it is equal to a negative constant (for instance -1, as in the example). In this way, knowing that all the values are positive, each admissible solution will have a better fitness than any non-admissible solution. The fact that all nonadmissible solutions have the same fitness may be a problem, particularly when these solutions are numerous. For this reason, an improved version of Equation (2.1) may be:

$$f(\mathbf{z}) = \begin{cases} \sum_{z_i=1} value(i) & \text{if } \sum_{z_i=1} weight(i) \le k \\ -\sum_{z_i=1} weight(i) & \text{otherwise} \end{cases} \qquad (2.2)$$

In this way, we identify a *gradient* also in the area of the nonadmissible solutions, which can be useful in some cases for the algorithms that will be studied in the continuation of this book. With the fitness defined in Equation (2.2), the fitness of nonadmissible solutions becomes better and better as the total weight of the carried objects gets closer to the threshold.

Let us now consider a numeric case, characterized by the following data:

- let the number of available objects be $n = 10$;
- let the knapsack's capacity be $k = 165$;
- let the weights of the objects be: 23, 31, 29, 44, 53, 38, 63, 85, 89, 82;
- let the values of the objects be: 92, 57, 49, 68, 60, 43, 67, 84, 87, 72.

Let us now consider solution:

$$\mathbf{z} = 1111010000$$

This object represents the case in which the 1*st*, 2*nd*, 3*rd*, 4*th* and 6*th* objects are carried in the knapsack, while the others are not. The total weight of the carried objects is:

$$\sum_{z_i=1} weight(i) = 23 + 31 + 29 + 44 + 38 = 165$$

Given that the total weight of the carried objects is identical to the knapsack's capacity, the solution $\mathbf{z}$ is admissible, so its fitness is:

$$f(\mathbf{z}) = \sum_{z_i=1} value(i) = 92 + 57 + 49 + 68 + 43 = 309$$

An exhaustive analysis of the search space was done for this particular numeric case, and it showed that this solution represents a global optimum, in other words it is not possible to find another combination of 10 bits corresponding to a better selection of the objects than this one.

The Knapsack Problem has a large number of real-life applications. Just as an example, one may consider the case of a set of investments that can be made on the stock market, for each of which we know the cost and the expected profit. The objective, in that case, would be to select the subsets of investments that allow us to maximize the expected profit, with a total cost that is not larger than our predefined budget.

The Knapsack Problem is a well-known and widely studied optimization problem. The interested reader is referred, for instance, to [Martello and Toth, 1990].

Example 2.2. (Traveling Salesperson Problem). Given a set of cities and distances between each pair of cities, the objective of the Traveling Salesperson Problem (TSP) is to find the shortest possible route that visits each city, returning to the origin city. More specifically, n cities are given and the pairwise distances of all the cities are known. For instance, they can be given in an $n \times n$ matrix D, where the element of indexes p and q ($D_{p,q}$) denotes the distance between the pth and the qth cities. The matrix is, of course, symmetric; in other words $D_{p,q} = D_{q,p}$ for any pair of cities p and q. A cycle is a closed walk that visits each city exactly once. The problem consists in finding a cycle of minimal length. A *permutation* of the n cities could be indicated as:

$$\pi = \{k, \pi(k), \pi^2(k), ..., \pi^{n-1}(k)\}$$

where $k = 1, 2, ..., n$ denotes a city. For each k, $\pi(k)$ denotes the successor of city k, i.e., the city that is visited right after k, and, by definition:

$$\pi^t(k) = \underbrace{\pi(\pi...(\pi(k)))}_{t \text{ times}}$$

in other words $\pi^t(k)$ denotes the city that is visited t steps after k was visited. A *cycle* is a permutation π such that the following properties are respected:

- $\pi^\ell(k) \neq k$, if $\ell = 1, 2, ..., n-2$;
- $\pi^{n-1}(k) = k$

Given this formalization, an instance of the TSP can be defined as:

- $S = \{\pi \mid \pi \text{ is a cycle on the } n \text{ given cities}\}$
- Given any solution $\pi \in S$, the fitness of π can be defined as:

$$f(\pi) = \sum_{i=1}^{n} D_{i,\pi(i)}$$

$f(\pi)$ returns the total length of cycle π.

Let us now apply these concepts to a numeric case. For simplicity, let the number of cities be $n = 4$, and let the matrix of the pairwise distances be:

$$D = \begin{array}{|c|c|c|c|} \hline \times & 7 & 2 & 3 \\ \hline \times & \times & 4 & 1 \\ \hline \times & \times & \times & 8 \\ \hline \times & \times & \times & \times \\ \hline \end{array}$$

This matrix represents the graph shown in Figure 2.1.

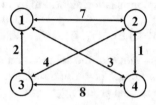

Fig. 2.1 Graph representation of the instance of the TSP discussed in Example 2.2

Let us now consider solution $\pi_1 = \{1, 2, 3, 4, 1\}$ and let us calculate its fitness. We have:

$$f(\pi_1) = D_{1,2} + D_{2,3} + D_{3,4} + D_{4,1} = 7 + 4 + 8 + 3 = 22$$

Let us now consider solution $\pi_2 = \{1, 4, 2, 3, 1\}$ and let us calculate its fitness. We have:

$$f(\pi_2) = D_{1,4} + D_{4,2} + D_{2,3} + D_{3,1} = 3 + 1 + 4 + 2 = 10$$

The TSP has many possible real-life applications, particularly in the field of logistics and transportation. One may think, for instance, of optimizing the itinerary of a person delivering pizza to a set of houses, starting from, and returning to, the same location, which may be the pizzeria. At the same time, it is not difficult to imagine how many concepts of the TSP can be applied to the optimization of a bus itinerary or even to air traffic optimization.

The TSP is a well-known and widely studied optimization problem. The interested reader is referred, for instance, to [Applegate et al., 2007].

2.3 No Free Lunch Theorem

In the continuation of this book, we will study several algorithms to solve optimization problems. These algorithms will generally be called optimization algorithms or, more particularly, *computational intelligence* optimization algorithms, with the objective of distinguishing them from classical, deterministic optimization algorithms. Although very different from each other, these algorithms all share a common structure: they are all iterative algorithms that, at each iteration, return a solution to the problem. In other words, given an instance of an optimization problem (S, f), an execution of an optimization algorithm can be identified by a sequence, or vector, of solutions, each one being returned at the termination of an iteration. Let this vector be $\mathbf{b} = \{s_1, s_2, ..., s_m\}$, where, for all $i = 1, 2, ..., m$, $s_i \in S$. Given that, by definition, the fitness function f must be defined on all the elements of S, for each solution s_i in $\mathbf{b}$, its fitness value $f_i = f(s_i)$ can be calculated. So, instead of using $\mathbf{b}$, one may identify an execution of an optimization algorithm by means of the vector:

$$\mathbf{c} = \{f_1, f_2, ..., f_m\}$$

$\mathbf{c}$ is the vector of the fitness values of the solutions returned at each generation by an optimization algorithm. Let $\mathscr{A}$ be an optimization algorithm, and let us now consider the following conditional probability:

$$P(\mathbf{c} \mid f, m, \mathscr{A})$$

This is the conditional probability that algorithm $\mathscr{A}$, using f as a fitness function, yields exactly vector $\mathbf{c}$ as the sequence of the fitness values of the solutions returned in the first m iterations of its execution. If we think carefully, this conditional probability can be imagined as a generalization of the concept of *performance* of an algorithm. A particular case, in fact, is if for any $i = 1, 2, ..., m$, $f_i = f_o$, in other words if the sequence of solutions returned by $\mathscr{A}$ in its first m iterations contains a globally optimal solution. In that case, this conditional probability can be interpreted as the probability of algorithm $\mathscr{A}$ finding a global optimum in its first m executions, using f as a fitness function. Given that the objective of an optimization problem is to find a globally optimal solution, we can say that, in this particular case, this conditional probability corresponds to our interpretation of the performance of an algorithm, intended as its ability to find a global optimum. In simple terms, we could informally say: the higher the probability of finding a global optimum, the better the performance of the algorithm.

Using this notion, we are now ready to enunciate one of the most general and fundamental results in the field of optimization.

Theorem 2.1. (No Free Lunch Theorem) [Wolpert and Macready, 1997].
Given any sequence of fitness values $\mathbf{c} = \{f_1, f_2, ..., f_m\}$ *and any pair of optimization algorithms* $\mathscr{A}_1$ *and* $\mathscr{A}_2$, *we have:*

$$\sum_f P(\mathbf{c} \mid f, m, \mathscr{A}_1) = \sum_f P(\mathbf{c} \mid f, m, \mathscr{A}_2) \tag{2.3}$$

A formal proof of the No Free Lunch Theorem is beyond the scope of this book; the interested reader is referred to [Wolpert and Macready, 1997] for a proof and a wide discussion of this very important result. Here, we are more interested in discussing the intuitive meaning, and the important consequences, of the No Free Lunch Theorem. In order to understand what this theorem is telling us, we first need to have an intuition of the meaning of summing up $P(\mathbf{c} \mid f, m, \mathscr{A})$ over all possible fitness values f (remark that this is what is happening on both sides of Equation (2.3): the summations run over all possible fitness functions). Informally, we can interpret it as the sum of the performance of an algorithm *over all existing optimization problems*. To convince one self about it, consider a countable[1] space of solutions S. In this situation, for each possible optimization problem, we could rename the existing feasible solutions into solution$_1$, solution$_2$, solution$_3$,... In this way, we could imagine that all optimization problems have the same set of solutions. Given that, as we will understand when we study some optimization algorithms, the fitness function is useful only to compare solutions with each other (so that the best one can be identified), we can also imagine that, once solutions have been sorted from the worst to the best, the fitness values are modified into $1, 2, 3, ...$ (the case of solutions with identical fitness values is also taken into account in [Wolpert and Macready, 1997]). In this way, what makes the difference between one problem and another is the assignment of the fitness values to the solutions, or, if we imagine solutions to always keep the same order, the sorting of the possible fitness values. In this interpretation, a fitness function identifies a possible sorting of fitness values, and all possible ways of sorting the fitness values identify all the possible problems. Under this perspective, a new, and more informal formulation of the No Free Lunch Theorem could be given as follows.

Theorem 2.2. (No Free Lunch Theorem, informal statement). *Given any pair of optimization algorithms $\mathscr{A}_1$ and $\mathscr{A}_2$, $\mathscr{A}_1$ and $\mathscr{A}_2$ have identical average performance, calculated on all existing optimization problems.*

In other words, there cannot exist an algorithm (which we could call a "super" algorithm) that performs better than all the others on all possible existing optimization problems, and if a set of problems exists on which an algorithm $\mathscr{A}_1$ outperforms an algorithm $\mathscr{A}_2$, another set of problems exists on which $\mathscr{A}_2$ outperforms $\mathscr{A}_1$.

This fact has an interesting consequence: every time that we are faced with a particular optimization problem, we have no formal/automatic method to decide what is the best algorithm to solve it. Indeed, if such a method existed, it would be the super algorithm that would contradict the No Free Lunch Theorem. In other words, the choice of an appropriate algorithm to solve a particular problem can only be a heuristic and informal process, typically based on our experience as problem solvers, on our knowledge of the dynamics of the different algorithms, and/or on a set of experiments, aimed at comparing different algorithms. Under this perspective, the No Free Lunch Theorem encourages the study of many different algorithms. As we will study in Chapter 5, the No Free Lunch Theorem can also be extended to Machine Learning [Wolpert, 1996]. So, all these considerations can be extended also to the field of Machine Learning. In conclusion, the No Free Lunch

---

[1] The validity of the No Free Lunch Theorem for continuous optimization, i.e., when S is infinite and not numerable, was questioned in [Auger and Teytaud, 2010], and so that case will not be discussed in this section.

Theorem motivates and paves the way for the existence of several software environments, in which several different Computational Intelligence and Machine Learning techniques are implemented, and a comparison between them is made particularly easy and automatic. Two of the numerous existing software environments with these characteristics are: Weka [Hall et al., 2009] (implemented in Java) and Scikit-learn [Pedregosa et al., 2011] (implemented in Python).

We conclude this section by drawing the attention of the reader to a singular, and possibly counterintuitive, fact. At the beginning of this section, we defined the concept of heuristic optimization algorithm as an iterative algorithm, able to return a solution at the end of each iteration. This definition is general, and it applies regardless of the principle that is used to generate the next solution, which is what distinguishes the different algorithms from each other. The definition is so general that even *random search*, i.e., a rather "naive" algorithm that returns a random solution at each iteration, respects it. Thus, also random search can be considered an optimization algorithm, and so the No Free Lunch Theorem applies also to it. In other words, if averaged on all existing problems, random search performs exactly as well as all the other heuristic optimization algorithms, including the ones that are considered more sophisticated or "intelligent", and, given any such algorithm, a set of problems exists on which random search outperforms it. Although surprising, this fact is true, and in the continuation of this chapter, problems on which random search outperforms all the other algorithms will be studied. Of course, those problems have particular characteristics that make them rather different from real-life applications, where, instead, more sophisticated or "intelligent" methods than random search are often the most appropriate choice.

2.4 Hill Climbing

As studied in the previous section, one of the consequences of the No Free Lunch Theorem is that the choice of an appropriate algorithm to solve a problem can only be a heuristic process, in which our knowledge of the functioning and dynamics of many different algorithms may play a crucial role. Thus, it makes sense to study several optimization algorithms of different natures. This study begins in this section, in which one of the simplest and most naive Computational Intelligence algorithms is presented: *Hill Climbing* [Aarts and Korst, 1989, Russell and Norvig, 2009].

Hill Climbing is possibly the most natural and immediate technique to try to solve an optimization problem, and it consists in an attempt to improve fitness in a stepwise refinement way, by means of the concept of *neighborhood*. The process is so simple that it can be informally described in a few words: let us assume that we are able, for each solution i belonging to the space of solutions S, to generate a subset $N(i)$ of S, where $N(i)$ can be interpreted as the set of "neighbor" solutions of i ($N(i)$ is also called the neighborhood of i). Hill Climbing starts with an initial (typically random) solution i, which is made the current solution, and tries to improve it. In particular, it chooses one solution j from $N(i)$ (for instance, it can be the solution with the best fitness in $N(i)$), and, if the fitness of j is better than the fitness of i, makes j the new current solution i. The process is iterated until the neighborhood of the current solution i does not contain any better solution than i. At that point, the algorithm terminates, returning i as the final result.

This process depends on the fundamental concept of neighborhood structure N, which is discussed here, before the functioning of Hill Climbing is presented with more rigor and details.

Definition 2.3. (Neighborhood Structure) Let (S, f) be an instance of an optimization problem. A neighborhood structure is a mapping:

$$N : S \rightarrow 2^S$$

that associates to each solution $i \in S$ a subset of S, which we denote by $N(i)$, and that we call the neighborhood of i.

Each solution $j \in N(i)$ is called a neighbor of i and in general we assume that, for any pair of solutions $i, j \in S$, $j \in N(i)$ if and only if $i \in N(j)$. Furthermore, we assume the existence of a precise algorithm $\mathscr{A}$ that allows us, given a solution i, to generate its neighborhood $N(i)$, and we assume that, for each solution $i \in S$, $\mathscr{A}$ applied to i terminates and returns a set containing at least one admissible solution $j \in S$.

In general, there are neither restrictions nor rules for defining a neighborhood structure, and any mapping respecting the above properties is, in general, acceptable. However, it is customary to associate the definition of a neighborhood structure either to an operator that transforms solutions, or to a measure of distance between solutions. So, given a solution $i \in S$, we define the neighborhood of i in one of the following ways:

- $N(i) = \{j \in S \mid j = op(i)\}$, for a given operator op.
- $N(i) = \{j \in S \mid d(i, j) \leq k\}$, for a given distance metric d and prefixed constant k.

According to the first definition, the neighborhood of a solution i is the set of solutions that can be obtained by applying an operator op to i. According to the second one, once a distance metric has been chosen, the neighborhood of a solution i is the set of solutions that have a distance to i smaller than or equal to a given prefixed constant k. As we will see in the next examples, these two definitions often coincide, as it is generally possible to define a distance *corresponding* to an operator, and vice versa. In practice, if we apply one of these two definitions, the neighbors of a solution i often end up being solutions that are structurally rather similar to i.

Example 2.3. Let us assume that the feasible solutions are strings of bits of a prefixed length, like in the knapsack problem that we have studied in Example 2.1. For instance, one possible neighborhood could be defined in such a way that two solutions are neighbors if and only if they differ by one bit in a corresponding position. For instance, given a solution:

$$i = 1011011$$

the solution:

$$j = 1011001$$

is a neighbor of i, because all the bits of j are, position by position, identical to the corresponding bits of i, except for the bit in the $6th$ position of the string, which is different. On the other hand, the solution:

$$h = 1000101$$

is *not* a neighbor of i, in fact the bits in the $3rd$, $4th$, $5th$ and $6th$ position of h are different from the corresponding bits of i, and so the number of different bits in corresponding positions is larger than one.

Let us now see how it is possible to define such a neighborhood by means of an operator and by means of a distance. The operator can simply work as follows: choose a position in the string and flip the bit contained in that position, leaving the other bits unchanged. The distance is the Hamming distance [Norouzi et al., 2012] (defined as the number of different bits in corresponding positions), and $k = 1$.

Example 2.4. Let us now assume that feasible solutions are all the permutations of integer numbers in a given range, and let us assume that, as in the TSP studied in Example 2.2, the first and last values in the string are fixed and unchangeable. A possible neighborhood could be obtained by exchanging two values in a solution. For instance, given solution:

$$i = 1234567891$$

a possible neighbor of i could be:

$$j = 1237564891$$

because all the characters in j are identical to the corresponding characters in i, except for 4 and 7, which have been exchanged. The reader is invited to notice that, in order to define this neighborhood, it was natural to use the concept of operator: the operator that swaps two characters, at any pair of positions.

Given an instance of an optimization problem, neighborhoods are generally not unique. On the contrary, a vast number of possible neighborhoods could be chosen. Just as an example, for the problem studied in this example, another possible neighborhood could be obtained using an operator that selects two characters at any pair of positions and exchanges the order of all the characters in between. Using this new definition of neighborhood, a neighbor of individual i could be:

$$h = 1265437891$$

since all characters in h are like the corresponding ones in i except for the characters that appear from the $3rd$ to the $6th$ positions, which appear in the opposite order.

Given an instance of an optimization problem (S, f), and a neighborhood structure N, the pseudocode of Hill Climbing is reported in Algorithm 1. In that algorithm, i represents the variable storing the current solution at each step. The different steps of the algorithm can be explained as follows:

Algorithm 1: Pseudocode of Hill Climbing for an instance of an optimization problem (S, f) and a neighborhood structure N.

1. Initialize a feasible solution i_{start} from the search space S (typically at random);

2. $i := i_{start}$;   // Let the current solution i be equal to i_{start}

3. **repeat**

   3.1. Generate a solution j from $N(i)$;

   3.2. **if** $(f(j)$ is better than or equal to $f(i))$ **then**

       $i := j$;   // Let j become the new current solution i

   end

   until $\forall j \in N(i) : f(j)$ is worse than $f(i)$;

4. **return** i

- In Step 1, an initial solution i_{start} is generated to allow the process to begin. If we have some information about the problem, like for instance that solutions with good fitness should have certain characteristics, that information may be used in this step. But the typical situation is that we do not have this type of information. So, in general, the initial solution is randomly generated[2];

- In Step 2, the variable i, used to store the current solution at each step of the algorithm, is initialized by assigning i_{start} to it;

- Step 3 contains the main cycle of the algorithm, in which we try to improve the fitness of the current solution in a stepwise manner:

  - Step 3.1 consists in the generation of a neighbor j of the current solution i. This can be obtained using the transformation operator that defines the neighborhood structure N. Several different variants of Hill Climbing can exist, corresponding to different possible choices, but the most frequent choice is that j is the best neighbor (in terms of fitness) of i;

  - Step 3.2 consists in a comparison of the fitness of j with the fitness of i. In case the fitness of j is better than or equal to that of i, j becomes the new current solution. In minimization problems, $f(j)$ is better than or equal to $f(i)$ if $f(j) \leq f(i)$, while in maximization problems $f(j)$ is better than or equal to

---

[2] One important point to understand is that, in general, given that we know how the space of solutions S is defined, we are also able to generate a random solution. For instance, consider the case of Example 2.3, where S is the set of all possible strings of bits of a given fixed length n. Generating a random solution, in that case, can be simply done by flipping a coin n times, inserting a 0 in case of a tail and a 1 in case of a head, or vice versa.

$f(i)$ if $f(j) \geq f(i)$. Remark that a variant of the Hill Climbing algorithm also exists in which the current solution is *not* replaced if the generated neighbor has identical fitness to the current solution. In that case, which we call *strict Hill Climbing*, the term "better or equal" in the pseudocode should be replaced with "better".

The cycle terminates when all neighbors of the current solution i are worse in fitness than i. In the case of strict Hill Climbing, the cycle terminates also if the best neighbor of i has a fitness that is identical to that of i.

- Step 4 is executed when the main cycle of the algorithm has terminated, and it consists in returning the current solution i as the final result.

Before we present an example that should clarify the functioning of Hill Climbing, it is important to study the following definition.

Definition 2.4. (Local Optimum). Let (S, f) be an instance of an optimization problem, and let N be a neighborhood structure. A solution $\bar{i} \in S$ is called a local optimum with respect to N if $\bar{i}$ has a fitness that is better than or equal to all the other solutions in its neighborhood. In other words, in minimization problems, $\bar{i}$ is a local optimum with respect to N if:

$$f(\bar{i}) \leq f(j), \forall j \in N(\bar{i})$$

and in maximization problems, $\bar{i}$ is a local optimum with respect to N if:

$$f(\bar{i}) \geq f(j), \forall j \in N(\bar{i})$$

The reader is invited to notice that, by its very definition, the solution returned by Hill Climbing is always a local optimum. In fact, the termination condition of the algorithm exactly corresponds to the definition of local optimum. Furthermore, it should be noticed that *a global optimum is also a local optimum*. In fact, because a global optimum is the best solution among all the feasible ones, it is also the best of its neighborhood. We conclude that Hill Climbing *may* return a global optimum, however we have no guarantee that this will happen. For a given optimization problem instance, the quality of the solution returned by Hill Climbing mainly depends on the initial solution i_{start}, which is typically generated at random, and on the particular neighborhood structure employed, which is a choice we must make when solving the problem.

Example 2.5. (*Execution of Hill Climbing on a Numeric Case*). Let (S, f) be an instance of an optimization problem, where:

- $S = \{i \mid i \in \mathbb{N} \ \& \ 0 \leq i \leq 15\}$;
- $\forall i \in S : f(i) =$ number of bits equal to 1 in the binary code of i (maximization).

Furthermore, consider the following neighborhood structure:

$$\forall i, j \in S : j \in N(i) \iff |j - i| = 1$$

In this "toy" case study, the search space comprises only 16 feasible solutions: the natural numbers between 0 and 15 inclusive. As a fitness function, we use the number of 1s in the binary code. Give that the problem was defined as a maximization one, it is straightforward to understand that the global optimum for this problem is represented by solution 15, given that it is the only natural number between 0 and 15 inclusive that contains four bits equal to 1 (the binary code of 15 is, in fact, 1111). Finally, the neighborhood structure represents, so to say, the "intuitive" neighborhood of natural numbers: for instance, 4 is a neighbor of 3 and 5, 9 is a neighbor of 8 and 10, and so on and so forth.

Let us, now, simulate the execution of Hill Climbing on this problem. The first step consists in the random generation of an initial solution. Let us assume that our random number generator allowed us to obtain 5 as the initial solution. So, $i = 5$ is the first current solution. Given that the binary code of 5 is 101, the fitness of this solution is 2 (two bits are equal to 1 in the binary code). At this point, Hill Climbing is supposed to generate a solution from the neighborhood of 5. Let us assume that, as it is usual, the solution chosen by Hill Climbing is the best in the neighborhood. So, the neighborhood of the current solution is:

$$N(5) = \{4,6\}$$

Given that the fitness of 4 is 1 and the fitness of 6 is 2, the generated neighbor of 5 is $j = 6$. The fitness of j is now compared to the fitness of i and, consistently with the pseudocode of Algorithm 1, given that the two fitness values are identical, the current solution is updated. The new current solution is: $i = 6$. The algorithm now iterates the process by analyzing the neighborhood of 6:

$$N(6) = \{5,7\}$$

Given that the fitness of 5 is 2 and the fitness of 7 is 3, the best neighbor is $j = 7$. Since the fitness of j is better than the fitness of i, the current solution is updated again. The new current solution is $i = 7$. The algorithm iterates again, analyzing now the neighborhood of 7:

$$N(7) = \{6,8\}$$

Given that the fitness of 6 is 2 and the fitness of 8 is 1, the best neighbor is $j = 6$. But since the fitness of the best neighbor j is worse than the fitness of i, it is straightforward to infer that all the solutions in the neighborhood of 7 are worse than 7. Consequently, the algorithm terminates, and 7 is returned as the final solution. It is worth pointing out that 7 is a local optimum, but it is not the global optimum for this problem, since the global optimum, as previously mentioned, is 15.

Before terminating this section, it is worth discussing the pros and cons of Hill Climbing: advantages of Hill Climbing are that it is very simple, and easy to specify, implement and use. A further advantage of this algorithm consists in its flexibility: in fact, it is rather simple to change the configuration of the problem, the neighborhood structure, or even only the initial solution, and run the algorithm again, obtaining a different result. The main disadvantage of Hill Climbing is, of course, that it returns a local optimum, with no guarantee that it corresponds to a global optimum. This is a very important flaw, since a local optimum can even be a very poor solution. So, methods to overcome this disadvantage deserve to be studied. In order to increase the probability of Hill Climbing returning solutions of better quality, one may imagine the following approaches:

- run Hill Climbing multiple times, each time using a different initial solution (possibly all these independent executions can be run in parallel, to save computational time);
- use a more complex neighborhood structure, so that we are able to explore a larger portion of the search space at each iteration;

Unfortunately, both these strategies are, in general, destined to fail. Concerning the first idea, in fact, in real problems the number of local optima can be so high that each agent of parallel Hill Climbing may end up trapped in a different local optimum. On the other hand, although extending the neighborhood may effectively improve exploration ability, in general, in order to significantly increase our confidence that the algorithm returns a global optimum, the neighborhood should become so large as to become unmanageable. Indeed, one of the most widely accepted approaches for improving Hill Climbing consists in accepting, with a given limited probability, a worsening in the fitness of the current solution. This is the idea that is at the basis of Simulated Annealing, which will be studied in Section 2.6. But before we study the Simulated Annealing, the concept of Fitness Landscape is presented in Section 2.5.

2.5 Fitness Landscapes

Let us revisit the optimization problem instance studied in Example 2.5, with the neighborhood considered in the example, and let us now perform the following exercise: let us draw a plot in which in the horizontal direction we arrange all the solutions in the search space, *sorted consistently with the used neighborhood structure*, and on the vertical axis we put fitness. In the particular case of Example 2.5, sorting the solutions consistently with the neighborhood structure is straightforward: we just need to arrange them using the habitual ordering of natural numbers. The obtained graphic is shown in Figure 2.2. Such a plot is called a *fitness landscape*, given that it visually resembles a landscape, with peaks, valleys, plateaux, etc. The behavior of Hill Climbing can be imagined as a "walk" on this landscape, where each single movement is represented by the passage from one current solution to the next. Given that, at every step of the algorithm, the current solution can only be a neighbor of the previous current solution, and given that, in the fitness landscape, neighbor solutions are actually physically "neighbors" in the horizontal direction, so "jumps" are allowed in the landscape. For instance, in the case of Example 2.5, Hill Climbing started its "motion" at abscissa 5 (the randomly generated initial solution

Fig. 2.2 Fitness landscape for the optimization problem instance and neighborhood studied in Example 2.5

was 5), then "moved" to 6, and finally moved to 7, and then stopped, returning 7 as a final solution.

As we can see from this simple example, the behavior of Hill Climbing can be imagined as that of a "mountaineer", devoted to "climbing" the fitness landscape, and that stops every time it reaches a top (peak), whether or not it is the highest one in the landscape. A Fitness Landscape [Stadler, 2002, Pitzer and Affenzeller, 2012] is a classical way of visualizing the relationship between the syntactic structures of the solutions and their fitness. The concept is inherited from Biology, and it can be defined as follows.

Definition 2.5. (*Fitness Landscape*). Given an instance of an optimization problem (S, f) and a neighborhood structure N, a Fitness Landscape (FL) is a plot in which all the solutions in S are represented on the horizontal direction, sorted consistently with N, and, for each solution $i \in S$, the fitness value $f(i)$ is reported on the vertical direction. An FL is completely identified by the triple:

$$(S, f, N)$$

An FL gives visual intuition on the difficulty, or a simplicity, with which a problem instance can be solved using a configuration of an optimization algorithm. In particular, we can imagine the existence of at least the following cases:

- a "smooth" landscape, with one, or very few, peaks;
- a "rugged" landscape, with several different steep peaks.

The former scenario typically corresponds to an easy problem that can often be solved by many algorithms, including Hill Climbing. The latter case generally corresponds to a hard problem that is difficult to solve not only by Hill Climbing, but also by any of the other existing algorithms, which often get stuck in one of the numerous local optima. Besides these two cases, one could also mention neutral landscapes, i.e., FLs in which a large number of neighbors have the same, or approximately the same, fitness values. This scenario corresponds to the presence of plateaux on the landscape. Although no gradient can be identified in flat portions of the landscape, the usefulness of the presence of neutrality in FLs is still controversial. Smooth, rugged and neutral FLs and their implications for the performance of optimization algorithms are discussed in [Vassilev et al., 2003].

Although the concept of FL is in general very useful for understanding the difficulty of a problem, it is generally impossible to draw an FL (even though significant steps forward are proposed in [McCandlish, 2011]), at least for the following reasons:

- the vast magnitude of the search space;
- the large dimensionality of the neighborhood.

The former point makes it generally impossible to arrange all the feasible solutions on the horizontal direction of a plot. The latter one turns the plot into a multidimensional one, which makes it hard to draw it. The difficulty represented by the latter point can be mitigated by representing the FL in the following way: let d be the distance that is associated with the used neighborhood structure (see the second definition of neighborhood on page 23); an FL can be represented using a graph, where each vertex represents a solution, and it is labelled with the fitness of the solution it represents, and each edge joining a solution i_1 to a solution i_2 is labeled with the value of the distance $d(i_1, i_2)$. An execution of Hill Climbing defines a walk on this graph. To make the representation more "visual", one may imagine "leaning" the graph on a horizontal plane, arranging the solutions in such a way that the distance between each pair of solutions i_1 and i_2 on the plane is directly proportional to $d(i_1, i_2)$, and fitness could be given by a projection of each vertex in the third dimension. This three-dimensional plot can give a visual idea of the ruggedness of a landscape even in the presence of high-dimensional neighborhoods, but still it cannot be drawn in general, due to the vast magnitude of the search space. Nevertheless, in many real cases, it is possible to imagine the shape of the FL, for instance starting from some points of known fitness, and this can be useful to obtain information about the ability of an algorithm to find a global optimum. Let us now consider some examples of fitness landscapes, drawing their shape whenever possible, and trying to imagine it otherwise.

Example 2.6. Let us recall Example 2.5, and let us extend the number of solutions in the search space, by increasing the upper bound of the natural numbers to 1023 in the definition of S. In other words, we have the following optimization problem instance:

- $S = \{i \mid i \in \mathbb{N} \ \& \ 0 \leq i \leq 1023\}$;
- $\forall i \in S : f(i) =$ number of bits equal to 1 in the binary code of i (maximization).

And the following neighborhood structure:

$$\forall i, j \in S : j \in N(i) \iff |j - i| = 1$$

Analogously to the case of Example 2.5, it is easy to see that the global optimum is represented by solution 1023, which can be represented by a chain of 10 bits, each of which equals 1, while all other numbers between 0 and 1022 can be represented using 10 bits, but all of them contain at least one bit equal to 0. Given that the neighborhood is two-dimensional, we can still draw the FL using a two-dimensional plot as in Figure 2.3. As we can see, this landscape is very rugged. The reader is

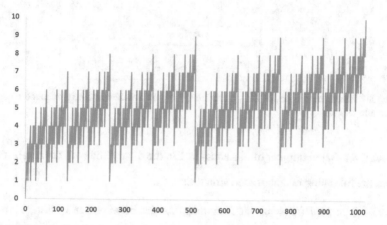

Fig. 2.3 Fitness landscape for the optimization problem instance and neighborhood studied in Example 2.6

invited to implement Hill Climbing and try to use it to solve this problem. It will quickly be observed that very often Hill Climbing will not be able to return the global optimum.

Example 2.7. Let us now consider the following optimization problem instance:

- $S = \{i \mid i \in \mathbb{N} \ \& \ 0 \le i \le 1023\}$;
- $\forall i \in S : f(i) = i^2$ (maximization).

And the following neighborhood structure:

$$\forall i, j \in S : j \in N(i) \iff |j - i| = 1$$

As we can see, the only difference between this case and the one studied in Example 2.6 consists in a different fitness function. The FL, in this case, is represented in Figure 2.4. The landscape is clearly smooth, with no local optimum, except for the unique global optimum, represented, again, by solution 1023. This corresponds to the typical configuration of a problem that is easy to solve. The interested reader is invited, once again, to implement this simple problem and try to solve it with Hill Climbing. It will immediately be observed that Hill Climbing will always be able to return the global optimum.

Example 2.8. Let us now consider the following optimization problem instance:

- $S = \{i \mid i \in \mathbb{N} \ \& \ 0 \le i \le 1023\}$;

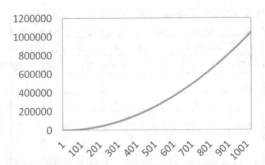

Fig. 2.4 Fitness landscape for the optimization problem instance and neighborhood studied in Example 2.7

- $\forall i \in S : f(i) =$ number of bits equal to 1 in the binary code of i (maximization).

And the following neighborhood structure:

$$\forall i, j \in S : j \in N(i) \iff \text{ the Hamming distance between } i \text{ and } j \text{ is equal to } 1.$$

As we can see, the only difference between this case and the one studied in Example 2.6 consists in a different neighborhood structure. This time, two solutions are neighbors if they differ by just one bit. As an attentive reader will agree, given that all solutions in S can be represented by strings of 10 bits, each solution now has 10 neighbors. In other words, the neighborhood, in this case, is 10-dimensional. This makes it very hard to draw the fitness landscape. Nevertheless, it should not be too hard to imagine what its shape should be: if a solution is not the global optimum (which, once again, is represented by solution 1023, whose binary code is 1111111111), it will have at least one bit equal to 0 in its binary code. And thus, changing that 0 into a 1, we will be able to obtain a better neighbor. Consequently, all the solutions in S, except for the global optimum, have at least one neighbor that is better than them. We conclude that, in this case, the FL is smooth, with no local optima, except for the unique global optimum. Once again, this can be easily confirmed in practice, by implementing Hill Climbing to solve this problem. The reader will observe that, in a worst case of 10 steps, Hill Climbing will always be able to return the global optimum.

From Examples 2.6, 2.7 and 2.8, it is possible to understand that a variation of any of the three elements defining an FL, i.e., S, f and N, may completely change the shape of the FL, and thus the ability of an algorithm to find the global optimum.

We conclude this section with a last example that should represent cause for reflection about the No Free Lunch Theorem (Theorem 2.1).

Example 2.9. Let us consider the two-dimensional FL shown in Figure 2.5, and let the problem be a maximization one. Let us also assume that $B \ll D$, or, in other

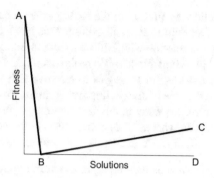

Fig. 2.5 Graphical representation of a deceptive fitness landscape

words, let us assume that the probability that a random number drawn with uniform distribution in $[0, D]$ is smaller than or equal to B is practically equal to zero. In such a situation, it should not be difficult to convince oneself that Hill Climbing has a very poor performance. In fact, with high probability the random initial solution will correspond to an abscissa in $(B, D]$, and given that the algorithm tends to improve fitness at every step, the solution returned by Hill Climbing will often be the one corresponding to abscissa D. This solution is a local optimum, with a fitness equal to C, which is qualitatively much worse than the fitness A of the global optimum. But the fact that a solution of poor quality is returned is only one of the flaws that Hill Climbing has on this type of problem: if we consider the distance d that is associated with the used neighborhood structure (see the second definition of neighborhood on page 23), the returned solution is even the one that is furthest away from the global optimum according to d. In simple terms, Hill Climbing is returning a solution of poor quality that is also very different from the global optimum.

These types of problems are called *deceptive* problems, and they are characterized by the fact that, most of the time, a steady attempt to improve fitness leads the algorithm towards local optima. In other words, the fitness function is misleading, in the sense that it tends to conduct the search towards poor-quality solutions. Even though problems that are deceptive in each part of the search space are hard to find, it is not infrequent in real-life applications to have significant portions of the search space that are deceptive. The existence of problems of this type pushes us to the following reflections:

- On deceptive problems, Random Search (i.e., an optimization algorithm that returns a random solution at each iteration) generally outperforms Hill Climbing. This is a corroboration of the validity of the No Free Lunch Theorem (Theorem 2.1), and of the fact that this theorem holds also for an apparently very naive algorithm such as Random Search. Indeed, surprisingly as it may seem, in the presence of deceptive or partially deceptive problems, Random Search can be a reasonable strategy.

- Always blindly following fitness, in the steady attempt to improve it, can be a losing strategy for an optimization algorithm. This is what Hill Climbing does, and this is one of the reasons why Hill Climbing is not one of the most effective optimization algorithms for real-life problems. Actually, as previously mentioned, one of the most useful strategies to improve Hill Climbing is to release the algorithm from the idea of always improving fitness. In Simulated Annealing, which is the algorithm we study in the next section, in some cases the fitness of the current solution can worsen. This corresponds to the possibility of letting an algorithm go downhill in an FL during its exploration.

Looking again at a case such as the one represented in Figure 2.2, it should not be hard to convince oneself that, if the current solution is any of the solutions corresponding to an abscissa smaller than 12, the only possibility that an agent has of reaching the global optimum (abscissa 15) is accepting some downhill steps during the exploration. Thus, the idea behind Simulated Annealing seems reasonable and promising.

2.6 Simulated Annealing

Simulated Annealing [Kirkpatrick et al., 1983, Černý, 1985, Aarts and Korst, 1989] extends Hill Climbing, taking inspiration from a metallurgy and materials science heat treatment, called annealing [Vlack, 2008]. Annealing is a process that allows us to obtain materials in a solid state, with the lowest possible level of energy. It alters the physical and sometimes chemical properties of the material, and it is used to increase its ductility and reduce its hardness, making it more workable. It involves heating the material above its recrystallization temperature, maintaining a suitable temperature for a suitable amount of time, and then allowing slow cooling.

In simple terms, the annealing process can be summarized as follows: it begins with the material in a solid state i, with energy E_i. Then some chemical bonds are modified, so as to obtain a new solid state j, with energy E_j. At this point, the new current state of the material is chosen, with some probability distribution, between i and j, and the process is iterated until the material stabilizes in a given state. The choice of accepting i or j as the new current state is based on the respective energy values E_i and E_j. In particular, the probability of accepting j is given by $P(\text{accept } j)$, defined in Equation (2.4), while the probability of maintaining i as the current state is $1 - P(\text{accept } j)$. $P(\text{accept } j)$ is defined as:

$$P(\text{accept } j) = \begin{cases} 1 & \text{if } E_j \leq E_i \\ e^{\frac{-|E_j - E_i|}{k_B T}} & \text{otherwise} \end{cases} \tag{2.4}$$

where T is the temperature and k_B is the Boltzmann constant [Fischer, 2019].

The process described so far is a particular case of the Metropolis algorithm [Chib and Greenberg, 1995] and it was shown to be effective in finding the solid state of a material with the lowest level of energy. Its similarities with Hill Climbing are visible, in the sense that we talk of a current state, similarly to how in Hill Climbing we talk of a current solution, and we try to update the current state by applying some transformations that may loosely remind us of the application of an operator to obtain a neighbor. Energy in annealing corresponds to fitness for optimization algorithms, and it is supposed to be minimized. The macroscopic difference from the Hill Climbing is clearly that the energy of the current state can increase with some probability. Simulated Annealing extends Hill Climbing to also envisage the case of a temporary worsening in the fitness of the current solution. This worsening will be accepted with a given probability that is inspired by Equation (2.4).

Given an instance of an optimization problem (S, f) and a current solution $i \in S$, the probability of accepting a new solution $j \in S$ as the new current solution is given by:

$$P(\text{accept } j) = \begin{cases} 1 & \text{if } f(j) \text{ is better than or equal to } f(i) \\ e^{\frac{-|f(j)-f(i)|}{c}} & \text{otherwise} \end{cases} \tag{2.5}$$

where, as usual, in minimization problems $f(j)$ is better than or equal to $f(i)$ if $f(j) \leq f(i)$, while for maximization problems $f(j)$ is better than or equal to $f(i)$ if $f(j) \geq f(i)$. Compared to Equation (2.4), in Equation (2.5) the concept of the energy of a material was replaced by the fitness of a solution. Furthermore, the term $k_B T$ was replaced by a *positive* number c that will be called the *control parameter* of Simulated Annealing and which, as we will see, plays an important role in the dynamics of the algorithm.

Once these similarities are established between Simulated Annealing and the Metropolis algorithm used for annealing, Simulated Annealing can be seen as an iteration of the Metropolis algorithm, using decreasing values of the control parameter c. The idea of beginning the execution with a high value of c and steadily decreasing c during the execution of the algorithm can be motivated if we observe Figure 2.6, reporting the graphical representation of the function $\phi(c) = e^{-\frac{k}{c}}$, where k is a positive constant ($k = 2$ was used in the figure). This plot can be used to study the variation of the probability that Simulated Annealing accepts a worse solution than the current one, as c is modified. As we can observe, if we use a "large" value of c in the early phase of the execution of the algorithm, in this phase we will have a rather "large" probability of accepting fitness deteriorations. Also, if we assume that c is steadily decreased during the execution, we can clearly see that this is equivalent to a steady decrease in the probability of accepting a worse solution than the current one. Finally, if we assume that the algorithm works by decreasing c in such a way that c tends towards zero, without ever arriving at zero[3], it is easy to understand

---

[3] If the value of c is equal to zero and j is a worse solution than i, then $P(\text{accept } j)$ in Equation (2.5) returns an error, due to a denominator equal to zero. This case is avoided by avoiding c ever becoming equal to zero during the execution of Simulated Annealing.

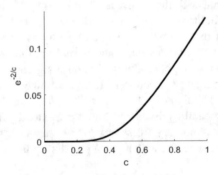

Fig. 2.6 Graphical representation of the function $\phi(c) = e^{-\frac{2}{c}}$, used to understand the contribution of the control parameter c to the probability of accepting a solution with worse fitness, compared to the current one

that this corresponds to a probability of accepting a worsening in fitness that tends towards zero.

From all this, we infer that beginning with a high value of c, and steadily decreasing it in such a way that c tends towards zero without ever reaching zero, is equivalent to beginning the execution of the algorithm in a situation in which the probability of worsening the fitness of the current solution is high, and then steadily decreasing this probability, tending towards a situation that resembles Hill Climbing, i.e., where the probability of accepting fitness deteriorations is very low. The rationale behind this idea is, in simple terms, that at the beginning of its execution the algorithm may be in a difficult area of the search space, characterized by the presence of several local optima. In such a situation, going downhill with reasonably high probability can be useful to step over some hills. On the other hand, as long as the execution proceeds, we are possibly approaching one of the highest hills, and hopefully in the basin of attraction of a global optimum. In that case, we do not have any interest in going downhill. On the other hand, in such a situation, the most effective behavior is climbing up the hill as fast as possible, as Hill Climbing would do.

The pseudocode of Simulated Annealing is reported in Algorithm 2. The algorithm has the objective of navigating the search space by iteratively updating the current solution i. This is done by executing several *transitions*, where a transition of Simulated Annealing is, by definition, a sequence characterized by the generation of a neighbor j of the current solution i, followed by the decision whether or not to accept j as the new current solution, a decision that may depend on the current value of the control parameter c. The algorithm is characterized by two nested loops. The idea of having two loops is that, for each value of the control parameter c, we should give the algorithm a number L of "attempts" before c is modified. Several considerations concerning Algorithm 2 are discussed in the next paragraphs.

Algorithm 2: Pseudocode of Simulated Annealing for an instance of an optimization problem (S, f) and a neighborhood structure N.

---

1. Initialize a feasible solution i_{start} from the search space S (typically at random);

2. $i := i_{start}$;   // Let the current solution i be equal to i_{start}

3. Initialize L and c;
   // L is the number of iterations of the internal loop, c is the control parameter

4. **repeat until** *termination condition*

   4.1. **repeat L times**

      4.1.1. Generate a solution j from $N(i)$;

      4.1.2. **if** $(f(j)$ is better than or equal to $f(i))$ **then**

      $\quad\quad i := j$;   // Let j become the new current solution

      $\quad$**else if** $\left(\text{Rand}[0, 1) < e^{\frac{-|f(j)-f(i)|}{c}}\right)$ **then**

      $\quad\quad i := j$;   // Let j become the new current solution

   end

   4.2. Update c;

   4.3. Update L;

   end

5. **return** the solution with best fitness encountered so far;

---

1. *External Loop and Termination Condition* (point 4). The external loop has a termination condition, which actually corresponds to the stopping criterion of the algorithm, that is usually satisfied when one of these two conditions is satisfied:

   - a "satisfactory" solution has been found, or
   - a previously fixed maximum number of iterations has been executed.

   Concerning the first point: let us assume that the optimal fitness f_o is known[4]. In such a situation, we could define an admissible deviation ε_f from that fitness value. By "satisfactory" solution, here, we mean a solution x whose fitness value f_x is at a distance smaller than or equal to ε_f from f_o. Concerning the second point: the previously chosen maximum number of iterations can be con-

---

[4] The reader should observe that knowing the optimal fitness is rather usual in optimization problems, where the objective is finding a solution with such a fitness. To convince oneself about this, one may consider Example 1 on page 13. In that case, the optimal fitness is equal to zero (no obstacles hit by the robot). Finding a path that allows the robot to hit zero obstacles is the objective of the problem.

sidered a parameter of the algorithm, to be set before beginning the execution. In case f_o is not known, the second point remains the only termination condition.

2. *Internal Loop* (point 4.1). The internal loop of the algorithm is executed for L iterations. The most general situation (the one reported in Algorithm 2), is that the value of L is modified at each iteration of the external loop, but it can be kept as a constant during the whole execution, eliminating point 4.3., and making L a further parameter to be set beforehand.

3. *Generation of the neighbor j* (point 4.1.1). Although the algorithm is general, and any strategy to choose the neighbor can be used, in the case of Simulated Annealing it is customary to consider a *random* neighbor of the current solution. In order to convince oneself about the appropriateness of this choice, the reader is invited to have a look back at the fitness landscape represented in Figure 2.2. Let us assume that the current solution is 7. This solution has two neighbors: 6 and 8. The fitness of 6 is equal to 2, while the fitness of 8 is equal to 1. So, if our choice was to choose the best neighbor, as is customary for Hill Climbing, in such a situation the generated neighbor would be 6. On the other hand, the reader should recognize that, if the current solution is 7, the only hope that the algorithm has to reach the global optimum (that is 15) is to accept 8 as the next solution. Such a situation can be generalized, that is, in some situations, always choosing the best neighbor of the current solution may jeopardize our chances of reaching a global optimum. Besides this, it is also straightforward to understand that, particularly in the presence of large neighborhoods, generating a random neighbor is much faster than finding the best neighbor, which implies an evaluation of all the solutions in the neighborhood.

4. *Probabilistic Acceptance of a Worse Solution* (else branch of point 4.1.2). If the chosen neighbor j has a worse fitness than the current solution i, the event of accepting j as the new current solution is probabilistic. Its implementation in Algorithm 2 uses the primitive $\text{Rand}[0, 1)$, which returns a random number between 0 and 1, drawn with uniform distribution[5]. The reader is invited to reflect on the portion of pseudocode:

$$\textbf{if } (\text{Rand}[0, 1) < e^{\frac{-|f(j)-f(i)|}{c}}) \textbf{ then}$$
$$i := j$$

This can be interpreted as the implementation of the sentence:

j is accepted as the new current solution with a probability given by $e^{\frac{-|f(j)-f(i)|}{c}}$

---

[5] Practically all existing programming languages have such a predefined primitive. For instance, in Java, one may use the method `random()` of the class `Math`.

5. *Update of the Control Parameter* c (point 4.2). As previously discussed, c should be decremented at each iteration, in such a way that it steadily tends towards zero, but without even being equal to zero. In this way, the algorithm should be able to climb over several hills, basins of attraction of local optima, in the first phase of the execution, while it should "resemble" Hill Climbing in the second phase, when the basin of attraction of a global optimum has hopefully been reached. Any way of updating c that respects these principles can generally be used. A simple example is to divide the value of c by a constant that is larger than 1. As we will understand later, it is generally a good idea to have a slow decrement of the value of c. In order to obtain this, for instance, c could be divided by a constant that is "slightly" larger than 1.

Let us now study the functioning of Simulated Annealing on a simple numeric example.

Example 2.10. Let us recall the optimization problem instance (S, f) and neighborhood structure N of Example 2.5, i.e.,

- $S = \{i \mid i \in \mathbb{N} \ \& \ 0 \le i \le 15\}$;
- $\forall i \in S : f(i) =$ number of bits equal to 1 in the binary code of i (maximization);
- $\forall i, j \in S : j \in N(i) \iff |j - i| = 1$.

As we did in Example 2.5, let us assume that the initial random solution is $i = 5$. Given that the binary code of 5 is 101, the fitness of 5 is equal to 2 (since the binary code has two bits equal to 1). Let us also assume that the generation of the neighbor j is random and that $j = 6$. Given that the binary code of 6 is 110, also the fitness of 6 is equal to 2. Although a "strict" version of Simulated Annealing exists, the most common version (and the one reported in Algorithm 2) envisages a replacement of the current solution when the generated neighbor has a fitness that is identical to the current solution. Thus, the new solution is now $i = 6$, and the algorithm is iterated.

Let us assume, now, that the random neighbor of 6 generated by the algorithm is $j = 7$. Given that the binary code of 7 is 111, the fitness of j is equal to 3, i.e., better than the fitness of i. In such a situation, without any further computation, j is accepted as the new current solution. So, now the current solution is $i = 7$.

Let us assume that the generated neighbor of 7 is $j = 8$. The binary code of 8 is 1000, so the fitness of 8 is equal to 1. We are now in a situation in which the generated neighbor has a worse fitness than the current solution. In such a situation, we can accept or not j as the new current solution with a certain probability given by:

$$P(\text{accept } 8) = e^{\frac{-|f(8) - f(7)|}{c}}$$

Let us assume, just for simplicity, that in this moment of the execution of the algorithm the value of the control parameter c is equal to 1. We have:

$$P(\text{accept } 8) = e^{\frac{-|1-3|}{1}} = e^{-2} \approx 0.13$$

In other words, we have a probability approximately equal to 13% of accepting 8 as the new current solution. Just to give the reader an informal understanding of the usual dynamics of Simulated Annealing, it is worth pointing out that this must be considered a significantly *large* probability of accepting the new solution. In fact, over 10 independent attempts in the same situation, the solution should on average be accepted at least once. Although it can be useful in some circumstances, accepting a fitness worsening is generally a rather rare event. When Simulated Annealing encounters a local optimum, it typically remains stuck on it for several iterations before being able to climb over it and begin to explore new regions of the search space.

Contrarily to Hill Climbing, Simulated Annealing has the ability to escape from local optima, while still maintaining some positive characteristics of Hill Climbing, such as simplicity and generality. The convergence speed of the algorithm depends on several factors, including:

- the initial value of the control parameter c;
- the speed at which c is decreased;
- the number of iterations L in which the same value of c is maintained.

Setting these parameters in an appropriate way is generally a hard task, depending on the characteristics and complexity of the problem. Nevertheless, some heuristics can be given, after having studied some theoretical properties of the algorithm.

2.6.1 Theory of Simulated Annealing

The objective of this section is to study the asymptotic convergence behavior of Simulated Annealing. The final result will be presented and commented on in Theorem 2.3. But, as a stepping stone to that result, we first introduce Definition 2.6 and Lemma 2.1.

Definition 2.6. Given an instance of an optimization problem (S, f) and a neighborhood structure N, we say that N is a *completely interconnected* neighborhood if and only if for each pair of solutions $i, j \in S$, a sequence $\ell_0, \ell_1, ..., \ell_p$ exists such that:

- $\forall k = 0, 1, ..., p : \ell_k \in S$;
- $\forall k = 1, 2, ..., p : \ell_k \in N(\ell_{k-1})$;
- $\ell_0 = i$;
- $\ell_p = j$.

In informal terms, a neighborhood structure is completely interconnected if given any pair of solutions i and j it is always possible to obtain j starting from i by means of a sequence of solutions that are pairwise neighbors. Use of a completely interconnected neighborhood structure is a necessary condition for Lemma 2.1 and Theorem 2.3 to hold.

Lemma 2.1. *Let (S, f) be an instance of a minimization problem on which Simulated Annealing is executed using a completely interconnected neighborhood structure. After a "sufficiently large" number of transitions performed using constant c as a control parameter, Simulated Annealing stabilizes on a solution $i \in S$ with a probability equal to:*

$$P\{X = i\} = q_i(c) = \frac{1}{N_0(c)} \; e^{-\frac{f(i)}{c}}$$

where:

$$N_0(c) = \sum_{j \in S} e^{-\frac{f(j)}{c}}$$

$P\{X = i\} = q_i(c)$ is called the *stationary probability*, or *equilibrium distribution*, of Simulated Annealing, for control parameter c. Lemma 2.1 is not proven in this book. The reader interested in a proof of this Lemma, based on Markov Chains, is referred to [Aarts and Korst, 1989]. Lemma 2.1 was enunciated for minimization problems; an analogous result also holds for maximization problems, but will not be discussed in this book. With Theorem 2.3, we are now interested in understanding on what solution(s) Simulated Annealing will stabilize, after a large number of iterations, when c is modified.

Theorem 2.3. (Theorem of Asymptotic Convergence of Simulated Annealing). *Let (S, f) be an instance of a minimization problem, on which Simulated Annealing is executed using a completely interconnected neighborhood structure. Assuming that Simulated Annealing is executed by steadily decreasing the value of the control parameter c in such a way that c tends towards zero, without ever being equal to zero, we have:*

$$\lim_{c \to 0} q_i(c) = \frac{1}{|S_{opt}|} \; \chi_{(S_{opt})}(i)$$

where:

- *S_{opt} is the set of all the globally optimal solutions in the search space[6];*
- *$\chi_{(S_{opt})} : S \to \{0, 1\}$ is a function defined for all the solutions i in the search space, such that:*

$$\chi_{(S_{opt})}(i) = \begin{cases} 1 & \text{if } i \in S_{opt} \\ 0 & \text{otherwise} \end{cases} \qquad (2.6)$$

---

[6] It is worth recalling that globally optimal solutions are not necessarily unique, in fact several solutions can have the same fitness. So, all the solutions that have an optimal fitness are global optima. For this reason, in general, we talk of a set of globally optimal solutions.

Proof. For the sake of simplicity, in this proof we will use a different notation for the exponential function: from now until the end of the proof, for each argument x, e^x will be represented using the notation $exp(x)$. From Lemma 2.1, and applying the limit for c tending towards infinity, we directly obtain:

$$\lim_{c \to 0} q_i(c) = \lim_{c \to 0} \frac{exp(-\frac{f(i)}{c})}{\sum_{j \in S} exp(-\frac{f(j)}{c})} \tag{2.7}$$

Let f_{opt} be the optimal (in this case, minimum) fitness value. Multiplying the numerator and denominator of the right part of Equation (2.7) by $exp(\frac{f_{opt}}{c})$, we obtain:

$$\lim_{c \to 0} q_i(c) = \lim_{c \to 0} \frac{exp(\frac{f_{opt}}{c}) \cdot exp(-\frac{f(i)}{c})}{exp(\frac{f_{opt}}{c}) \cdot \sum_{j \in S} exp(-\frac{f(j)}{c})}$$

from which it is possible to immediately derive:

$$\lim_{c \to 0} q_i(c) = \lim_{c \to 0} \frac{exp(\frac{f_{opt} - f(i)}{c})}{\sum_{j \in S} exp(\frac{f_{opt} - f(j)}{c})} \tag{2.8}$$

Now, in order to complete the proof, we have to use a property according to which:

$$\forall a \le 0 : \lim_{x \to 0} exp(\frac{a}{x}) = \begin{cases} 1 & \text{if } a = 0 \\ 0 & \text{otherwise} \end{cases} \tag{2.9}$$

The interested reader is referred to [Rudin, 1986] for a proof and discussion of this property.

Let us isolate the numerator in the right-hand side of Equation (2.8):

$$\lim_{c \to 0} exp(\frac{f_{opt} - f(i)}{c}) \tag{2.10}$$

As we can observe, Equation (2.10) is rather similar to Equation (2.9): both of them express the limit of an exponential function, in both cases the argument of the exponential is a fraction, and in both cases the denominator of this fraction is the quantity tending towards zero in the limit. Furthermore, given that we are considering a minimization problem, by definition of f_{opt} we have: $\forall i \in S : f_{opt} \le f(i)$. So, the numerator of the fraction, i.e., $f_{opt} - f_i$, is a quantity that is smaller than or equal to zero. We conclude that Equation (2.9) can be used to obtain the result of Equation (2.10): that result will be equal to 1 when $f_{opt} - f_i$ is equal to zero, and equal to zero otherwise. But if $f_{opt} - f_i = 0$, then $f(i) = f_{opt}$, which means that i is a globally optimal solution. In other terms, Equation (2.10) is equal to 1 if $i \in S_{opt}$, and equal to zero otherwise. But this is exactly the definition of $\chi_{(S_{opt})}(i)$ given in Equation (2.6). We conclude that:

$$\lim_{c \to 0} \ exp(\frac{f_{opt} - f(i)}{c}) = \chi_{(S_{opt})}(i) \qquad (2.11)$$

Let us now isolate the denominator in the right-hand side of Equation (2.8):

$$\lim_{c \to 0} \ \sum_{j \in S} exp(\frac{f_{opt} - f(j)}{c}) \qquad (2.12)$$

Applying exactly the same reasoning used previously, we have that, for each $j \in S$, $\lim_{c \to 0} exp(\frac{f_{opt} - f(j)}{c})$ is equal to 1 if $j \in S_{opt}$ and equal to zero otherwise. But given that this quantity is summed up for each $j \in S$, the result of the summation is clearly equal to the number of globally optimal solutions in S. In other terms:

$$\lim_{c \to 0} \ \sum_{j \in S} exp(\frac{f_{opt} - f(j)}{c}) = |S_{opt}| \qquad (2.13)$$

Now, substituting Equation (2.11) and Equation (2.13) into Equation (2.8), we obtain:

$$\lim_{c \to 0} q_i(c) = \frac{1}{|S_{opt}|} \ \chi_{(S_{opt})}(i) \qquad (2.14)$$

But Equation (2.14) is identical to the thesis of the theorem, which allows us to terminate this proof.

$\square$

Theorem 2.3 was enunciated for minimization problems; an analogous result also holds for maximization problems, but will not be studied in this book. In order to understand the intuitive meaning of Theorem 2.3, first of all, we have to remark that, given the functioning of Simulated Annealing (i.e., given the fact that c is steadily decreased, in such a way that it tends towards zero), a limit for c tending towards zero is equivalent to a limit for time tending to infinity. So, Theorem 2.3 gives us information about the properties of Simulated Annealing as the running time tends to infinity (asymptotic properties).

Let us now try to answer the following question: what does the theorem tell us if the search space contains just one global optimum? The answer is straightforward: it says that, as time tends to infinity, Simulated Annealing will tend to stabilize on that global optimum with a probability equal to 1, and on any other solution different from the global optimum with probability zero. Let us now try to understand what the theorem tells us if the search space contains two global optima. Also in this case, it is not difficult to convince oneself that as time tends to infinity, Simulated Annealing will tend to stabilize on one of those global optima with a probability equal to 0.5, on the other global optimum with a probability equal to 0.5, and on any solution that is not a global optimum with probability zero.

Generalizing the previous reasoning, we can conclude that the theorem tells us that, as time tends to infinity, Simulated Annealing tends to stabilize on a global optimum, and the probability is uniformly distributed over all existing global optima. Interestingly, this property holds independently of the problem at hand, and, as such, from the shape of the fitness landscape.

Of course, this property does *not* tell us that Simulated Annealing will find a global optimum in a humanly acceptable time. It actually tells us that it will happen, but it does not say anything about the convergence speed, and thus about the time in which it will happen. As already mentioned above, the optimization speed of the algorithm depends only on the parameter setting, which is a problem-dependent task. In order to maximize our chances of finding a global optimum, all we can do is execute a large number of transitions for each value of the control parameter, and decrease the control parameter slowly, in such a way that the total number of iterations performed is as large as possible. As is intuitively easy to see, this also slows down the running time of the algorithm, and finding a good compromise between efficiency and effectiveness can be a hard task when we decide the values of the parameters.

Before concluding this section, it is worth discussing one point: using the *Law of Large Numbers* [Keane, 1995], one can easily infer that, given a potentially infinite amount of time, Random Search will find a global optimum for any problem. From this consideration, one may start wondering whether there is really a difference in terms of effectiveness between Simulated Annealing[7] and Random Search, which may induce one to mistrust the real usefulness of Simulated Annealing. Indeed, what Theorem 2.3 tells us is much more than the simple application of the Law of Large Numbers for Random Search. Theorem 2.3 tells us that Simulated Annealing tends asymptotically towards a global optimum. From the intuitive meaning of limit [Rudin, 1986], and in informal terms, we could say that this entails that, after a certain amount of computation, Simulated Annealing starts getting closer and closer to a global optimum. So, Simulated Annealing is able to approximate a globally optimal solution, when it is not able to find it. In other words, we could say that an amount of time t spent executing Simulated Annealing is "well spent", because, after this time, we have a significant probability of having found a solution that is better than the initial one, and this probability is generally higher as t gets bigger. On the other hand, nothing like this can be said for Random Search, for which the probability of finding a good solution at any time t is identical to that at time zero. These considerations allow us to conclude that asymptotic convergence towards a global optimum is a very important property, and for an algorithm to be considered "intelligent", such a property should hold.

---

[7] The reasoning proposed here holds also for any other algorithm for which it is possible to prove asymptotic convergence to a globally optimal solution.

Chapter 3
Genetic Algorithms

Genetic Algorithms (GAs) [Holland, 1975, Goldberg, 1989] are a commonly known method belonging to the field of Evolutionary Computation (EC) [Eiben and Smith, 2015]. Like Simulated Annealing, studied previously:

- GAs are a method for searching for optimal solutions in a space of possible alternative solutions;
- GAs do not require an exhaustive analysis of the search space (which would be impractical, given the vast size of the search space);
- GAs begin their search with randomly generated solutions and try to improve their quality in a stepwise refinement fashion, by means of an iterative algorithm.

However, unlike in Simulated Annealing, in GAs:

- the potential solutions (called *individuals* in EC terminology) are normally represented as strings of characters of a previously fixed length, which do not change during the execution of the algorithm;
- multiple solutions that are considered at each iteration (called a *generation* in EC terminology), in fact we talk of a *population* of individuals;
- the principle used as an inspiration is the theory of evolution of Charles Darwin [Darwin, 1859], which characterizes all methods belonging in the area of EC (Evolutionary Algorithms, EAs).

One of the fundamental elements of Darwin's theory of evolution is the idea of *natural selection*, thanks to which living beings have evolved through the millennia from simple unicellular creatures to the vast variety of species that populate Earth today. Natural selection identifies five basic pillars as the main requirements for the evolution of species:

- *Reproduction*, i.e., the fact that parents generate children (or offspring), which allows species to survive.
- *Adaptation*, i.e., the different abilities of individuals to function in their environment, which directly affects their probability of surviving and thus reproducing.

© Springer Nature Switzerland AG 2023
L. Vanneschi and S. Silva, *Lectures on Intelligent Systems*, Natural Computing Series,
https://doi.org/10.1007/978-3-031-17922-8_3

- *Inheritance*, i.e., the fact that some characteristics of the parents are transmitted to their offspring.
- *Variation*, which is, in some sense, in conflict with inheritance, and tells us that some characteristics of the offspring are different from those of their parents, and this potentially allows the species to introduce elements of novelty over generations.
- *Competition*, i.e., the idea that a limited amount of resources exists and, in order to survive, individuals have to compete to obtain them. Typically, the individuals that are better adapted to the surrounding environment have more chances of obtaining resources and thus surviving, while the others are likely to die and, in the long term, their line to be extinguished.

The idea behind EC is to transfer these concepts to computational optimization. GAs use a population of admissible solutions to the problem and function by means of an iterative process in which, at each generation, the solutions with the best fitness are probabilistically selected and genetic operators (typically crossover and mutation) are applied to those solutions, in order to create new and potentially better (in terms of fitness) solutions. The process is visualized in Figure 3.1. At a high level of

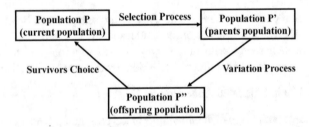

Fig. 3.1 Graphical representation of the general functioning of a GA

abstraction, the GA process can be seen as the iteration of three phases of transformation of a population of solutions: selection phase, variation phase and survivors choice. The three transformed populations are usually called the current population (P), which is typically initialized with random solutions at the beginning of the process, parents population (P') and offspring population (P''). Even though several variants exist, in the most standard version of GAs these three populations all have the same size N (i.e., they contain the same number N of individuals).

- The *selection process* mimics the principles of ability of adaptation to the environment and competition of Darwin's theory of evolution. In simple words, solutions are chosen from P, based on their fitness, and copied into P'. No modification is applied to the solutions in this phase. The process is implemented as an iteration of N independent executions of a *selection algorithm*. The objective of a selection algorithm is to probabilistically choose one solution from the current population and insert it into the parents population. Some of the most well-known selection algorithms are presented in Section 3.1. Iterating this process N times allows us to obtain a population of N parents.

- The *variation process* mimics the principles of reproduction, inheritance and variation of Darwin's theory of evolution. It consists in the application of genetic operators to the individuals in the parents population, in order to modify them and generate new solutions. The individuals resulting from the application of the genetic operators are then inserted into the offspring population P''. Typical genetic operators are *crossover* and *mutation*, which mimic the homonymous biological processes, and are discussed in Section 3.2. The variation phase allows GAs to explore the search space.

- The *survivors choice* is the phase in which the new current population is created, in order to begin the next generation. The choice of the N individuals that will form the current population in the next generation is usually made by choosing from the union of the $2N$ individuals that are in the offspring population and in the old current population. Various options are possible: from choosing the best N individuals (in terms of fitness) from $P'' \cup P$, to applying the selection algorithms discussed in Section 3.1 to choose the N individuals, or even a simple random choice. One of the most-used types of survivors choice, and the one used in this book from now on, is the so-called *generational* choice of survivors, which consists simply in replacing the current population with the offspring population. In other words, with the generational choice of survivors, the old current population is removed and the new current population becomes the offspring population ($P := P''$).

Before we take a global look at the functioning of GAs in Section 3.3, it is appropriate to understand the main blocks that compose the algorithm, i.e., the selection algorithms, presented in Section 3.1, and the genetic operators, presented in Section 3.2. The main difference between these two basic components of GAs is that, as in nature, selection acts on the *phenotype*, while genetic operators act on the *genotype* of individuals. In other words, selection is based on fitness (or a function of it), and it is completely independent of the syntactic structure of the individuals. On the other hand, genetic operators act on the structure of the individuals, normally in a way that is totally independent of (or agnostic to) fitness.

3.1 Selection Algorithms

Genetic operators are not applied to all the individuals in the population, but only to those that have been selected, according to the Darwinian principles of degree of adaption to the environment and competition. Selection algorithms enforce those principles, by choosing one individual from the current population. Several different selection algorithms exist, but all of them usually respect the following general properties:

1. Selection is probabilistic, in the sense that if the choice is repeated several times in exactly the same conditions, the outcome (i.e., the selected individual) in all these different experiments could change;

2. Selection has to be based on fitness, in the sense that given any two individuals i and j in the current population, if i has a better fitness than j, then i must have a higher probability than j of being selected;

3. All individuals in the population, even the worst ones, should have a probability different from zero of being selected. This allows the algorithm to maintain a certain degree of randomness that is observable also in nature, where it is possible for an individual to survive not only because of its adaptation to the environment, but also due to purely fortuitous events;

4. Assuming that a selection algorithm is executed multiple times at differ-ent time intervals $1, 2, ..., N$, if an individual i has been selected at a given instant $t < N$, i remains in the current population also for the executions that will be performed at times $t+1, t+2, ..., N$. In other words, all the executions are per-formed using the same current population P, and, after each execution, what is inserted in the parents population P' is a copy of the individual selected from P.

The previous principles are rather general, and one may imagine several different possible algorithms to implement them. The most-used selection algorithms of GAs are:

- Fitness proportionate selection (or "roulette wheel");
- Ranking selection;
- Tournament selection.

These three algorithms are presented next.

3.1.1 Fitness Proportionate Selection (or "Roulette Wheel")

Let N be the number of individuals in population P (population size) and let $F = \{f_1, f_2, ..., f_N\}$ be the set of their fitness values. For any individual $i \in P$, the proba-bility of selecting i, for maximization problems, is:

$$P(\text{sel } i) = p_i = \frac{f_i}{\sum_{j=1}^{N} f_j} \tag{3.1}$$

Given that the denominator is the same for all individuals (it is the sum of all the fitness values of the individuals in P), it is clear that, the bigger f_i, the higher the probability of selecting i, so this selection algorithm respects Point 2 of the selection algorithms general principles discussed above. In some cases, in order to apply fitness proportionate selection, fitness values may need some rescaling. For instance, looking at Equation 3.1 it is straightforward to understand that if f_i is negative, then p_i is not a probability. If negative values exist in F, one may imagine, for instance, rescaling all fitness values by summing to each one a quantity greater than or equal to $f_{min} + 1$, where f_{min} is the minimum value in F, and using the rescaled values to calculate p_i in Equation 3.1. At the same time, it is easy to convince oneself that if for some i we have $f_i = 0$, then Point 3 of the selection algorithms principles is not respected. If one wants this principle to be respected, one may simply rescale all values in F by summing the same positive constant to each one of them. Last but not least, in order to extend this algorithm to minimization problems, one may simply consider $1/p_i$, instead of p_i, as the probability of selecting an individual i.

Once we have established the probability of each solution P being selected, implementing the selection is straightforward[1]. One simple way of simulating the algorithm is to consider a roulette wheel and partition it into N segments $\{s_1, s_2, ..., s_N\}$, one for each individual in the population, where the area of each s_i is directly proportional to f_i. When an individual needs to be selected, all we have to do is "play" a roulette game, letting a ball roll on the wheel. The selected individual will be the one corresponding to the segment in which the ball will terminate its trajectory. In other words, if the ball stops in segment s_k, k will be the selected individual. In this way, it is clear that fitter individuals have a higher probability of being selected, because they are associated to a larger segment of the wheel (Point 2), but if all the individuals are associated to a segment, none of them has a probability equal to zero of being selected (Point 3). Executing the algorithm one more time is straightforward: it is enough to play another roulette game, letting the ball roll on the same wheel. In the new execution, the probabilities are the same (because we use the same wheel), but the outcome may be different (Point 4).

Example 3.1. Let us assume that we are trying to solve a maximization problem and we have a population $P = \{i_1, i_2, i_3\}$, where the fitness values are:

- $f_1 = 4$
- $f_2 = 12$
- $f_3 = 2$

The probabilities of selecting the various individuals are:

$$P(\text{sel } i_1) = 4/18 \approx 0.22$$
$$P(\text{sel } i_2) = 12/18 \approx 0.67$$
$$P(\text{sel } i_3) = 2/18 \approx 0.11$$

---

[1] The reader is referred to pages 38 and 53 for a discussion on how to implement a certain action with a given probability.

3.1.2 Ranking Selection

In this case, the selection algorithm begins by sorting the individuals in the population on the basis of their fitness, typically from the worst to the best. For each individual i, the selection probability is a function ϕ of the position occupied by i in the ranking. In principle, any monotonically growing function ϕ can be used. Typical cases are linear, logarithmic and exponential functions.

Example 3.2. Let us recall the case of Example 3.1. The ranking from the worst to the best is:

1. i_3
2. i_1
3. i_2

An example of the probability of selecting individual i_1, in case a simple linear function is used, is:
$$P(\text{sel } i_1) = 2/6 \approx 0.33$$

To calculate this probability, we have used the position occupied by i_1 in the ranking, divided by the sum of the ranking indexes of all the individuals.

The major difference between fitness proportionate selection and ranking selection should be clear to the reader: fitness proportionate selection is sensitive to the differences in fitness, while ranking selection is not: in ranking selection, only the position in the ranking matters. To convince oneself, one may consider the fitness values of the individuals in Example 3.1 and Example 3.2, and then change drastically the fitness values, without altering the ranking. The selection probabilities are likely to change for fitness proportionate selection, but remain the same for ranking selection. For instance, starting from the fitness values in Example 3.1, let us consider that the fitness value of i_2 is now equal to 1200, instead of 12. Let us now recalculate the probabilities of selecting the various individuals with fitness proportionate selection, and we will see that not only does the probability of selecting i_2 become much larger compared to Example 3.1, but consequently also the probabilities of selecting the other two individuals become much smaller. At the same time, and with the same fitness modification, the probabilities of selecting the individuals with ranking selection remains as in Example 3.2.

3.1.3 Tournament Selection

With this technique, to select one individual, we do not have to evaluate the fitness of all the individuals in the population, but only a part of them. Every time that an individual has to be selected, a number k of individuals are chosen randomly, with uniform distribution, from the current population. The selected individual is the best, in terms of fitness, among these k. The method is divided into two parts: the first part is completely independent of fitness and completely random (the choice of the k individuals taking part in the tournament), while the second part is completely deterministic and based on fitness (the selection of the best, among those k individuals).

Point 1 (at page 48) of the selection algorithms principles is clearly respected, because the first part gives randomness to the technique. Point 2 is respected because of the second part, which uses fitness to ratify the winner of the tournament. Point 3 can be respected if we imagine that we execute the random choice of the k individuals with repetition, so that multiple copies of the same individual can participate in the tournament. In this case, all individuals, including the worst one in the population, have a positive probability of being selected. In fact, if the tournament comprises k copies of the worst individual, it is the worst individual that will be selected. Finally, in order to iterate the method when the next individual needs to be selected, it is important to keep in mind that the *whole* algorithm needs to be repeated, including the generation of a new pool of k individuals, randomly chosen from the current population. This allows the different executions of the algorithm to be completely independent of one another.

Constant k is called the *tournament size*, and it is an important parameter to establish the selection pressure, i.e., to establish how strong is the probability of the best individuals to be selected, at the expense of the others. A small value of k causes a low selection pressure; a large value of k causes a high selection pressure. All in all, tournament selection is an interesting algorithm for at least the following two reasons:

- In some conditions, it may be more efficient than the other studied selection algorithms, since it may relieve us of the burden of having to evaluate all the individuals in the population (but this is not the case if elitism is used, as explained in Section 3.3);
- It allows us to tune the selection pressure in a very simple way, i.e., by modifying a single number (the tournament size). It is interesting to point out that tuning the selection pressure is harder in ranking selection (where it can be changed by modifying a function, like ϕ, instead of a number), while it cannot be tuned at all in fitness proportionate selection.

3.2 Genetic Operators

When the selection phase is terminated, the parents population (P' in Figure 3.1) is inhabited by individuals that have been chosen as apt for mating. In the variation phase, they are modified, in order to generate new individuals. This modification is implemented by applying genetic operators. In the standard formulation of GAs [Holland, 1975, Goldberg, 1989], two genetic operators exist: *crossover* and *mutation*. Crossover exchanges some syntactic characteristics of a set of (usually two) individuals, in order to generate offspring individuals that are a recombination of their parents. Mutation creates a new individual by modifying (typically at random) a small portion of the syntactic structure of an existing individual. Mutation is usually identified as an *innovation* operator, since it introduces into the population new genetic material, while crossover is a *conservation* operator, since it uses already existing genetic material and works by recombining it in new ways.

As discussed previously, while selection is based on the phenotype of individuals, genetic operators are based on their genotype, i.e., on their syntactic structure. So, while it was possible to present the selection algorithms without even mentioning what representation the individuals have, and using only fitness, to discuss the genetic operators, we need to define the structure of the individuals. As mentioned at page 45, in GAs the individuals are normally represented as strings of characters of a previously fixed length. Characters are normally chosen from a predefined *alphabet*, which can be, according to different situations, finite, infinite, discrete, continuous, etc. In the next examples, we will limit ourselves to the simple, but very important[2], case of *binary* strings, i.e., strings whose characters belong to the set $\{0, 1\}$.

The first thing we have to learn about GA genetic operators is that a vast amount of possible varieties of crossovers and mutations have been defined so far. At least in this very first approach to the algorithm, we will define and discuss only the standard versions of these operators, i.e., the ones originally proposed by J. Holland in his pioneering book [Holland, 1975] and later widely studied by D. Goldberg [Goldberg, 1989].

Standard crossover

Standard crossover of GAs works by taking as input two individuals (the *parents*), selecting at random a position (called the *crossover point*) between two consecutive characters in the string (the point has to be the same for both individuals) and exchanging the substrings that are at the left and at the right of this position, thus generating two new individuals (the *offspring*). This process implements a very simple model of biological crossover, in which the offspring's DNA is formed by a part of the DNA of one parent, and the remaining part of the other parent.

Example 3.3. Let us consider the following two parents, where the different font in the two strings is used only to distinguish them more easily:

$$x = \mathbf{011000110}$$
$$y = 000111101$$

Let us assume that the randomly chosen crossover point is in position 4. In this case, the crossover between x and y generates the following offspring:

---

[2] A vast set of real-world optimization problems can be solved using binary representation. Just as an example, one could consider the representation used for the knapsack problem and its numerous practical applications, discussed in Example 2.1 at page 16.

$$z = 0\,1\,1\,0\,1\,1\,1\,0\,1$$
$$w = 0\,0\,0\,1\,0\,0\,1\,1\,0$$

As we can observe, child z inherited the left substring from parent x and the right substring from parent y, while child w inherited the left substring from parent y and the right substring from parent x.

Standard mutation

Standard mutation of GAs works by considering one individual as input, and by iterating on all the positions in the string (also called *genes*, inheriting the terminology of biological evolution). For each gene, the current character is replaced with another randomly chosen possible character, with a given probability p_m, called the *mutation rate*. Obviously, the higher p_m, the more disruptive the mutation, which can, as a limit case, even modify the entire string representing the individual. Given that, usually, we do not want mutation to be very disruptive, it is typical to use very small values of the mutation rate, as happens also in nature, where mutation is generally a rather rare event.

Example 3.4. Let us assume that we want to mutate the following individual:

$$x = 1\,0\,0\,0\,1\,0$$

Potentially, any individual could be generated by the mutation of individual x. Let us assume, for instance, that we are using a mutation rate $p_m = 0.33$ (which, generally speaking, has to be considered a very high value). In this case, we may expect that, on average, two of the six characters that form x will be modified (this is, of course, a probabilistic event, and something totally different may happen). Let us assume, for instance, that the event of modifying the gene is verified only for the third and the fifth character. In this case, the mutation of x generates the individual:

$$x = 1\,0\,1\,0\,0\,0$$

where the modified characters have been written in bold for the sake of visibility.

Before moving on with a discussion of the general functioning of GAs, it is worth spending some more minutes reflecting on what a probabilistic event is, and how it can be implemented. As already discussed on page 38, the following sentence:

Perform an action $\mathscr{A}$ with probability $\mathscr{P}$

can be rewritten, in terms that are "closer" to an algorithmic implementation, as:

If a random number, extracted with uniform probability from $[0, 1)$,
is smaller than $\mathscr{P}$, **then** perform action $\mathscr{A}$, **else** do not perform action $\mathscr{A}$

If we try to execute such an event several times, in some cases we might perform action $\mathscr{A}$, and in some cases we might not perform it. In fact, the event depends on the value of a random number that is, by definition, not predictable *a priori*[3].

All this considered, a realistic implementation of the standard mutation of an individual x, represented as a string of characters of length ℓ, and using a mutation rate equal to p_m, could be given by the pseudocode of Algorithm 3, where $\text{Rand}[0, 1)$ is a random number extracted with uniform probability from $[0, 1)$.

Algorithm 3: Implementation of standard GA mutation of an individual x, represented as a string of characters of length ℓ, using a mutation rate equal to p_m.

```
for each i from 1 to ℓ do
    if Rand[0, 1) < pₘ then
        Replace the iᵗʰ character of individual x with a random admissible character;
    end
end
```

Probabilities of the Operators and Replication

As we have seen, mutation has an associated probability p_m. It corresponds to the probability of modifying each gene in the string that represents an individual, and it bestows on the operator some stochasticity, in the sense that if we apply the operator several times in the same conditions, the outcome can be different. Actually, all the genetic operators of GAs are stochastic. This reinforces the analogy between the genetic operators of GAs and the corresponding biological operators and, generally speaking, improves the exploration ability of the algorithm.

Under this perspective, also a probability associated to crossover exists, the *crossover rate* p_c. The crossover rate represents the probability of applying crossover to two parents. In case this probabilistic event does not happen, another operator is applied to those two individuals, called *replication* (also known as *reproduction*). Replication is simply copying of the parents, unchanged, into the offspring population. Thanks to replication, individuals of different "ages" can coexist in the same population, and possibly mate in the next generations. Replication is one possible way of enforcing elitism, a concept that will be explained in the next section. Crossover rate p_c and mutation rate p_m are two of the numerous parameters of GAs that will also be discussed later in this chapter.

---

[3] Given that probabilistic events are discussed in many parts of this book (modifying one gene in GAs' mutation is just an example of it), the reader is invited to spend some more time trying to convince herself about this concept before reading any further.

Other Types of Crossover and Mutation

Besides the basic genetic operators of crossover and mutation presented so far, many others have been defined. The number of existing genetic operators nowadays is, indeed, so high that the idea of describing them all would be purely utopian. The interested reader is referred to [Katoch et al., 2021] for a rather complete survey. Here, we limit ourselves to citing multiple-point crossover [De Jong and Spears, 1992], where more than one crossover point can be selected for remixing the genetic material of the parents, as a natural and very popular extension of the one-point crossover presented so far. Several variants of the basic mutation introduced so far also exist [Bhandari et al., 1994]. For instance, instead of changing the value of each allele in the chromosome with a given probability, one could imagine changing just one of them, or a subset, thus obtaining one-point mutation (also called bit flip, in the case of a binary chromosome) or multiple-point mutation. Finally, it is worth mentioning that standard crossover and mutation can be ineffective in some situations, and in that case it may be appropriate to define "ad hoc" operators. Some of these situations are discussed later in the book, for instance in Section 3.5.2 and in Section 3.7.

3.3 General Functioning of Genetic Algorithms

The pseudocode of the standard version of GAs [Holland, 1975, Goldberg, 1989] is shown in Algorithm 4. Before analyzing this algorithm in detail, it is worth recalling that this is only one of the possible existing variants of GAs that can be found in the numerous existing bibliographic references. For instance, as is clear from Point 2.4 of the pseudocode, this algorithm uses generational choice of survivors (in other words, it describes generational GAs), which, as we have already discussed, is only one of the possible existing processes for creating a new population, joining the old current population and the offspring population. Alternatively, a *steady-state* approach could be adopted. In steady-state GA, only a small number of offspring are created in each generation (for example, only the two offspring of crossover) and then immediately replace individuals that are currently in the population. The removed individuals are often the ones with worst fitness, but they can also be the parents of the new offspring, or simply randomly selected individuals. After the new offspring have been inserted into the population, a new iteration/generation begins. This approach results in a much smoother evolution of the population, since only a very small number of individuals change in each generation.

Looking at Algorithm 4, and comparing it with the schema represented in Figure 3.1, one major difference can be seen: in Figure 3.1, three populations (P, P' and P'') appear, while only two populations (P and P') are used in Algorithm 4. The reader is invited to reflect on the fact that, in spite of this difference, Algorithm 4 and the schema of Figure 3.1 are functionally completely equivalent. In fact, the process represented in Figure 3.1 assumes that once the parents are selected, they are stored in a population P', and only later used to apply the genetic operators and

---

Algorithm 4: The pseudocode of standard generational GAs.

---

1. Create an initial population P of N individuals (typically generated at random);

2. **repeat until** (termination condition)

   2.1. Calculate the fitness of each individual in P;   // can be avoided in some cases

   2.2. Create an empty population P';

   2.3. **repeat until** (population P' contains N individuals)

      2.3.1. Choose a genetic operator between *crossover* (with probability p_c) and *replication* (with probability $1 - p_c$);

      2.3.2. Select two individuals from P, using a *selection* algorithm;

      2.3.3. Apply the genetic operator chosen at Point 2.3.1 to the individuals selected at Point 2.3.2 ;

      2.3.4. Apply *mutation* to the individuals obtained at Point 2.3.3;

      2.3.5. Insert the individuals obtained at Point 2.3.4 into population P';
      end

   2.4. $P := P'$;   // Replace population P with P' (generational choice of survivors)

   end

3. **return** the best individual in P;

---

generate the offspring. The role of population P' in Figure 3.1 is "passive": P' is only a "container", where individuals that already existed are copied, waiting to be used later. In Algorithm 4, instead, once parents are selected, genetic operators are immediately applied. There is no storage of the parents. So, Algorithm 4 allows us to save the memory space needed to store a population (and given that, in real cases, populations usually contain numerous individuals, this saving can be significant). The schema in Figure 3.1 was useful to conceptually separate the phases of selection and variation, but when GAs have to be implemented, it is generally more efficient to follow Algorithm 4.

The pseudocode in Algorithm 4 works for an even population size (i.e., when N is an even number), since it inserts a pair of individuals into P' at each generation. When the population size is odd, some care is needed to allow the algorithm to fill P' with N individuals. Several variants exist, including: selecting one individual, mutating it and inserting it into P' without applying crossover; in one application of crossover, just inserting one child into the population instead of both (for instance, the better of the two in terms of fitness, or a child picked at random); inserting into P' one random individual, etc. Algorithm 4 has a potential flaw, since it allows the best individual to be "lost" from the population, if none of the offspring is better than this previous best. This problem can be avoided by copying, at each iteration, the best individual(s) into the next population, unchanged. This process is called *elitism*, a very common practice in GAs, in particular when the population is reasonably large. Elitism can be applied as soon as all the individuals have been assigned a fitness value, or during the survival phase before the beginning of the next iteration. For these elite individuals, the processes of selection are *de facto* bypassed, be it selection for breeding or selection for survival. Either way, their presence in the next generation is guaranteed. By contrast, another type of elitism mentioned earlier, that is the replication of individuals instead of submitting them to the genetic operators, does not guarantee that these replicated individuals are the best, or that they actually make it into the next iteration. Note that when elitism is mentioned without any further specification, it means the main type of elitism, not this "softer" type related to the replication rate.

When we try to solve a problem using GAs, first of all we have to find a representation for the solutions, using strings of characters of fixed length. After that, the following *parameters* need to be set:

- Length of the strings representing the individuals;
- Population size;
- Selection algorithm;
- Elitism and size of elite;
- Crossover rate p_c;
- Mutation rate p_m;
- Maximum number of generations.

Even though there are no rules for an optimal setting of these parameters, and appropriate values are strongly problem dependent, the following informal guidelines can be identified:

- The length of the strings representing the individuals is usually not a choice that we have, but it is part of the definition of the problem. For instance, the reader is invited to consider the Knapsack problem, discussed in Example 2.1 at page 16, where the length of the string is equal to the total number of available objects, or the Travelling Salesperson problem, discussed in Example 2.2 on page 18, where the length of the string is equal to the number of cities to visit. In other words, when we have defined an appropriate representation for the individuals, this is usually a parameter that does not concern us further.

- For the population size, it is clear that one basic rule of thumb exists: the larger the population, the better the exploration power of the algorithm. Nevertheless, experimental evidence also tells us that a threshold exists, beyond which keeping adding individuals to the population does not compensate for the increment in the computational effort. Finding that limit, by means of a set of preliminary experiments, can be a good practice for appropriately setting this parameter.

- No golden rule exists for choosing the most appropriate selection algorithm, and all the existing ones have their pros and cons. However, tournament selection presents a set of advantages that could make it our first bet: if no elitism is used, the choice of tournament selection may allow us to avoid evaluating the fitness of all the individuals in the population at each generation (in other words, if we use tournament selection and no elitism, then it is possible to avoid executing Point 2.1 in Algorithm 4). Furthermore, tournament selection allows us to tune the selection pressure by modifying one simple number, the tournament size (which becomes a further parameter to set, in case tournament is the chosen selection algorithm).

- Although Algorithm 4 does not use it, elitism is a common option in GAs. The size of the elite, i.e., the number of best individuals to which survival in the next generation is guaranteed, is normally a low value, and the most common choice is to ensure the survival of only the one best individual. Using elites larger than this may cause loss of diversity in the population, since the next best individuals are normally very similar (or even equal) to the best. Likewise, the replication rate, which represents the "softer" type of elitism, should also not be high (normally not higher than 0.1).

- Concerning the crossover and mutation rate, it is customary to work with high values of p_c (say from 0.8 to 1) and low values of p_m (say from 0 to 0.2). This is similar to what happens in nature, where crossover is an event with much higher probability than mutation. This is also the configuration that allows GAs to obtain the best results most of the time. However, it is not infrequent, as we will see in the continuation of this chapter, to have problems where crossover is much less effective than mutation. In such cases, the rates of these two operators may be inverted.

- Last but not least, for the maximum number of generations, similar considerations can be made to those that we made for the population size. Also in this case, in general, the more we let the algorithm evolve, the more likely it will be to find good-quality solutions. However, also in this case, experimental evidence tells us that there is a point beyond which evolving for more generations does not compensate, in terms of the quality of the solutions, for the computational effort it requires. Once again, an experimental investigation of this threshold can be a good practice for appropriately setting this parameter.

When setting the parameters of GAs, it can be appropriate to consider that the evolution of the algorithm can often be partitioned into two, ideally distinct, phases: *exploration* and *exploitation*. In exploration, the algorithm is searching for new solutions, exploring different regions of the search space, while in exploitation it focuses on a particular region of the search space in which particularly promising solutions have been found during exploration, using already existing solutions and making refinements to further improve their fitness. For this reason, having dynamic parameters that change during the course of the evolution can be an appropriate strategy.

Example 3.5. (Functioning of GAs). Let us consider the simple problem of maximizing the function $f(x) = x^2$, with $x \in \mathbb{N}$ & $0 \le x \le 31$. As usual in GAs, the first step is to decide a representation for all admissible solutions as strings of fixed length. In this case, the admissible solutions are the natural numbers between 0 and 31 inclusive. In order to represent these numbers in binary, we need up to a maximum of 5 bits. So, completing the numbers that need a smaller number of bits with zeros at the left, we can represent all solutions using strings of bits of size 5.

Let us assume, for simplicity, that we use a population of size equal to 4, fitness proportionate selection, p_c equal to 1 and p_m equal to 0, no elitism and generational choice of survivors. The first step is the random generation of an initial population. In the case of binary representation, like in this example, creating an initial population of randomly generated individuals is straightforward: to create four strings of bits of length 5, we simply flip a coin 20 times, using bit 1 if the outcome is heads and 0 if it is tails for each one of the bits that have to be initialized. Let us assume, for instance, that the randomly generated population is: $P = \{01101, 11000, 01000, 10011\}$.

Table 3.1 Initial population for Example 3.5. The first column contains an identifier for each individual, the second one the binary representation, the third one the decimal representation, the fourth one the fitness and the fifth one the probability of selection

Individual	Binary	Decimal	Fitness	Probability of selection
x_1	01101	13	169	0.14
x_2	11000	24	576	0.49
x_3	01000	8	64	0.06
x_4	10011	19	361	0.31

Table 3.1 reports the decimal value and the fitness for each individual in P, along with an approximation of the value of the probability of selection. For each solution, the fitness is given by the square of the value it represents, while, given that we are using fitness proportionate selection, the probability of selection is given by the fitness divided by the sum of all the fitnesses of all the individuals in the population. For instance, for the case of x_1, we have:

$$P(\text{sel } x_1) = \frac{169}{169 + 576 + 64 + 361} \approx 0.14$$

Both from the fitness values and the selection probabilities, we can clearly see that x_2 is the best individual in P, while x_3 is the worse one. As expected, all individuals including x_3 have a probability different from zero of being selected. Figure 3.2 reports a representation of a roulette wheel that could be used for simulating the selection process in this case. The reader is invited to consider the areas of the different slices of the wheel proportional to the fitness of the individual they have been assigned to. Let us now assume that, at the first roulette game, the ball stops in the area assigned to individual x_1, and at the second one it stops in the area of individual x_2. Then, these two individuals are the first pair that is selected as parents. Given that p_c is equal to 1, crossover between x_1 and x_2 has to be performed. This

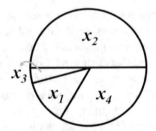

Fig. 3.2 Roulette wheel used for the initial population of Example 3.5

implies alignment of the two strings representing the individuals, random choice of a common crossover point, and swapping of substrings, in order to generate two new individuals. If we assume that the crossover point is point number 4, the application of the crossover is reported in Figure 3.3. As the figure shows, this crossover has

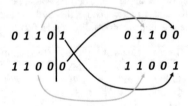

Fig. 3.3 A possible crossover (using the fourth crossover point) between individuals x_1 and x_2 of Example 3.5

generated individuals:

$$x_5 = 01100$$
$$x_6 = 11001$$

Given that p_m is equal to 0, we do not apply mutation, and so we insert x_5 and x_6 into the new population P'. So, P' now has two individuals. Two further individuals are needed to reach the target population size of 4. So, two further parents need to be selected. Using again the roulette wheel of Figure 3.2, and playing two further games, let us assume that the first time the ball stops in the area of x_2 and the second time it stops in the area of x_4. So, x_2 and x_4 will be the parents of a new crossover. Assuming that the randomly chosen crossover point this time is point number two[4], the result of this crossover is shown in Figure 3.4. The individuals generated by this crossover are:

$$x_7 = 11011$$
$$x_8 = 10000$$

---

[4] Remark that the crossover point is randomly generated at each crossover event, so it is likely to be different from the one that was used previously.

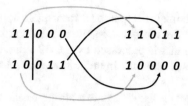

Fig. 3.4 A possible crossover (using the second crossover point) between individuals x_2 and x_4 of Example 3.5

Given that p_m is equal to 0, once again no mutation is applied and these individuals are inserted into P', which now contains four individuals. This allows us to terminate the first generation of the algorithm, allowing P' to become the new current population P. Before analyzing this new population, let us observe the behavior of selection in the first generation. We can see that:

- the individual with the best fitness (i.e., x_2) was selected twice for mating;
- the worst individual (i.e., x_3) was never selected, and so it got extinguished.

Even though these events are probabilistic, and so if we run the same experiment in the same conditions different events may happen, this situation is rather typical: the fittest individuals in the population, being the ones with the highest selection probabilities, usually have several possibilities of engaging in a crossover, while the worst individuals in the population are likely to have very few, or even no chances of mating. Let us now visualize the new population, in Table 3.2. Comparing the

Table 3.2 The second population in Example 3.5. The first column contains an identifier for each individual, the second one the binary representation, the third one the decimal representation and the fourth one the fitness

Individual	Binary	Decimal	Fitness
x_5	01100	12	144
x_6	11001	25	625
x_7	11011	27	729
x_8	10000	16	256

second population with the first one, reported in Table 3.1, we can notice that, in this case, both the best fitness and the average fitness in the population, after one generation, have improved.

3.4 Theory of Genetic Algorithms

Observing the evolutionary process of GAs, an important question arises naturally: are GAs a good optimization algorithm? In other words: will this process allow us to find a globally optimal solution, or a reasonable approximation, for a given problem? In order to answer this question, other questions need to be answered first: what is the information that is processed by a GA? What does a GAs' population contain generation after generation? In order to answer these questions, we need to deeply understand how GAs work.

One of the basic hypothesis of GAs is a strong relationship between genotype and phenotype. Putting it in simple terms, we hypothesize that if an individual is good, i.e., it has a good fitness, then it has some structural/syntactic characteristics that make it good. We can also imagine that, potentially, several different structural characteristics can have a beneficial effect on fitness. So, assume we select two individuals with good fitness: x_1 and x_2. If x_1 is good because it possesses a beneficial characteristic a and x_2 is good because it has another beneficial characteristic b, then we hope that if we remix the structures of x_1 and x_2 by means of crossover, the offspring will contain *both* characteristics a and b, and thus it will have a better fitness than both x_1 and x_2. At the same time, what we expect from mutation is that it acts on those parts of the chromosome of an individual that are not beneficial, in order to improve them. This leads to yet another question: how can we define a structural/syntactic characteristic of an individual? The first step to answer this question is to analyze data from some examples. This will allow us to formulate a hypothesis, that later will be proven.

Let us recall the initial population of Example 3.5, represented in Table 3.1. Observing this population, for instance, one may hypothesize that having a bit equal to 1 in the leftmost position of the string can be a beneficial characteristic. Indeed, also considering larger samples, it is possible to observe that individuals with a 1 in the leftmost position always have a better fitness than individuals having a 0 in the leftmost position. So, now let us ask to ourselves: how can we represent this characteristic with a formal notation that can be useful? One possible answer was given by Holland in his book [Holland, 1975], by means of the introduction of the concept of *schema*. For instance, the characteristic of *having a 1 in the leftmost position* can be represented as:

$$1 * * * *$$

In informal terms, the above notation can be interpreted as having a 1 in the leftmost position, independently of the information that appears in the other positions. The general definition of schema is as follows.

Definition 3.1. (*Schema*). A schema is a set of individuals that share the fact of having the same characters in some positions.

A rather simple way of representing a schema is by means of a string, where the characters come from the same alphabet used to build the individuals, plus one further "special" symbol, called the *don't care* symbol, and represented by a $*$. So, in the case of individuals that are represented as binary strings, schemata can be represented as strings where each symbol comes from the alphabet $\{0, 1, *\}$. The meaning of the concept of schema can be better understood if we think of it as a *pattern-matching tool*: in the case of binary representation, an individual "matches" a schema (or, in other words, an individual belongs to a schema) if, in each corresponding position, a 1 matches a 1, a 0 matches a 0, and a $*$ matches either a 1 or a 0.

Example 3.6. Schema $*0000$ represents the set of individuals $\{00000, 10000\}$. In other terms, we can write:

$$*0000 = \{00000, 10000\}$$

Both individuals 00000 and 10000, in fact, match schema $*0000$. In fact, whenever in the schema there is a character different from $*$, the individuals have the same character in the same position. If the binary alphabet is used to represent the individuals, then the reader is invited to agree that no other individual different from 00000 and 10000 matches schema $*0000$. A schema represents the set containing all and only the individuals that match it. Analogously, we have, for instance:

$$*111* = \{01110, 01111, 11110, 11111\}$$

The larger the number of $*$ symbols in the schema, the larger the cardinality of the set of individuals it represents (i.e., the number of strings that match the schema).

Remark that $*$ is just a metasymbol: it is not explicitly used by GAs. However, we hypothesize that, implicitly, GAs also work on schemata. In the next pages, we are interested in trying to understand what is the effect of a GA on schemata. But before doing that, let us first perform some simple "exercises", that can help us acquire familiarity with the concept of schema.

- *Question.* If individuals can be represented as binary strings of length ℓ, how many possible schemata exist?
  Answer. The number of existing schemata is 3^ℓ, in fact the schemata are all the possible length ℓ strings that can be built from the "extended" alphabet $\{0, 1, *\}$.

- *Question.* To how many different schemata does an individual belong?
  Answer. Each binary string x is member of 2^ℓ different schemata. In fact, in each position of the string can have the value of the bit that actually appears in x in that position, or the $*$ symbol. For instance, string 111 belongs to the following schemata: $\{111, *11, 1*1, 11*, **1, 1**, *1*, ***\}$, corresponding to all the length 3 strings from the alphabet $\{0, 1, *\}$ that have, in each position, either 1 or $*$. Notice that a string without any *don't care* symbol can also be considered a schema, containing only one individual.

- *Question.* Let us consider a population of n individuals, each of which, as in the previous questions, is represented as a string of bits of length ℓ. How many different schemata can the population (implicitly) contain? In order to answer this question, one has to keep in mind that, by definition, we say that a population "contains" a schema if it contains at least one individual belonging to that schema.
  Answer. The population can contain a number of schemata between 2^ℓ

and $(n \times 2^\ell)$ inclusive, depending on the *diversity* of the population: if all the n individuals in the population are identical to each other, then the population contains only 2^ℓ schemata, which are the ones matching a single string, as we have seen in the previous question. On the other hand, if all the individuals in the population are different from each other, then the population can contain up to a maximum of $(n \times 2^\ell)$, i.e., 2^ℓ schemata for each one of the different strings in the population. Of course, this is just an upper bound on the possible number of schemata, since, given two individuals x and y in the population, generally the set of schemata matching x and the one matching y have a nonempty intersection.

Before investigating how the concept of schema can be important in understanding the dynamics of GAs, let us define two important concepts related to schemata.

Definition 3.2. *(Order of a Schema)* The *order* of a schema H, denoted $o(H)$, is the number of symbols different from $*$ that appear in H.

Example 3.7. For instance, we have:
$$o(011*1**) = 4$$
$$o(**0**1*) = 2$$

Definition 3.3. *(Length of a Schema)* The *length* of a schema H, denoted $\delta(H)$, is the distance between the leftmost and the rightmost positions that contain a symbol different from $*$ in H.

Example 3.8. Considering the same schemata as in the previous example, we have:
$$\delta(011*1**) = 5 - 1 = 4$$
$$\delta(**0**1*) = 6 - 3 = 3$$

In order to answer the questions that we asked at the beginning of this section, we now ask other questions: of the schemata that are (implicitly) contained in a population, how many and which ones will be used by the GA, and how? How many of them will survive in the next generation? What is the modification in the number of individuals in the population matching a given schema, from one generation to the next? Answering these questions will be insightful for understanding the functioning of GAs.

In order to answer these questions, one may consider that the GA process is nothing but an iteration of a set of selection-crossover-mutation events. For this reason, it could be useful to study the effect of selection, crossover and mutation on the number and type of schemata that are contained in a population from one generation to the next. In particular, we are interested in understanding how many, and which ones, of the schemata will be represented by a steadily growing number of individuals, and which ones will disappear from the population during the evolution. One interesting point is that, in GAs, selection, crossover and mutation are independent events. For this reason, the effect of these three events on the schemata can be studied separately, and then it will be straightforward to obtain their combined effect.

Effect of Selection on the Schemata of a Population

In this section, we study the effect of *fitness proportionate selection* on the schemata of a population[5]. Focusing, without loss of generality, on maximization problems, we are interested in studying the *expected value* of the number of individuals belonging to a schema H in the population, at a given generation t. We indicate by $m(H,t)$ that expected value, and we want to study how this value changes with t. We have:

$$m(H,t+1) \;=\; m(H,t) \cdot n \cdot \frac{f(H)}{\sum_j f_j} \tag{3.2}$$

where $f(H)$ is the average fitness of the individuals matching H and belonging to the population; n is the population size; for each individual j, f_j is the fitness of j and the summation in the term $\sum_j f_j$ runs over all the individuals in the population.

In order to give an intuitive interpretation of Equation (3.2), let us begin with and attempt to understand the following term:

$$\frac{f(H)}{\sum_j f_j} \tag{3.3}$$

Knowing that, for each individual i in the population, the probability of selecting i with fitness proportionate selection is equal to $\frac{f_i}{\sum_j f_j}$, the term in Equation (3.3) is the average probability of selecting an individual that matches H, with *one step* of the selection algorithm. However, to generate the parents population, the algorithm has to be repeated for n independent executions. This is why the term in Equation (3.3) is multiplied by n in Equation (3.2). So, the term:

$$n \cdot \frac{f(H)}{\sum_j f_j}$$

represents the average probability of selecting an individual that matches H in one generation. If we multiply this term by the expected value of the number of individuals matching H in the population at time t, what we obtain is the same expected value at time $t+1$, *assuming that only selection is applied* (remember that we are now considering only the effect of selection on the schemata of a population. The effect of the genetic operators will be studied later).

Equation (3.2) does not seem to give us much information. However, it is possible to develop that equation further, in order to turn it into a more insightful form. Let us begin by defining the average fitness of the individuals in the population $\tilde{f}$, that is, straightforwardly:

---

[5] Analogous results exist also for other types of selection algorithms, but they are out of the scope of this book.

$$\tilde{f} = \frac{\sum_j f_j}{n}$$

From which it immediately follows that:

$$\frac{n}{\sum_j f_j} = \frac{1}{\tilde{f}} \qquad (3.4)$$

Now, substituting Equation (3.4) in Equation (3.2), we obtain a new form for Equation (3.2), given by Equation (3.5):

$$m(H, t+1) \;=\; m(H, t) \cdot \frac{f(H)}{\tilde{f}} \qquad (3.5)$$

Equation (3.5) is more informative than Equation (3.2). In particular, from Equation (3.5), we can understand that the expected value of the number of individuals matching a schema H in the population *increases* if the average fitness of the individuals matching H is larger than the average fitness of all the individuals in the population, and *decreases* if it is smaller. In other words, schemata with an average fitness larger than the average of the population "grow" from one generation to the next (i.e., increase their number of representatives in the population), while the others "shrink", eventually tending towards extinction. If on the one hand, it could have been intuitive to imagine that schemata with a good average fitness would grow and the others would shrink, it was not so intuitive *a priori* to say that the threshold between the two types of schemata is given by the average fitness of the individuals in the population.

We are now interested in understanding *at what speed* the good schemata increase in number, while the others decrease. To obtain this information, let us assume that a schema H has an average fitness larger than the average population fitness by a quantity equal to $c \cdot \tilde{f}$, where c is a constant. In other words, let us assume that:

$$f(H) = \tilde{f} + c \cdot \tilde{f} \qquad (3.6)$$

Substituting Equation (3.6) in Equation (3.5), we obtain:

$$m(H, t+1) \;=\; m(H, t) \cdot \frac{\tilde{f} + c \cdot \tilde{f}}{\tilde{f}} \;=\; (1+c) \cdot m(H, t) \qquad (3.7)$$

Starting from $t = 0$, and assuming a stationary value of c, we have:

$$
\begin{aligned}
m(H,1) &= m(H,0) \cdot (1+c) \\
m(H,2) &= m(H,1) \cdot (1+c) = m(H,0) \cdot (1+c) \cdot (1+c) = m(H,0) \cdot (1+c)^2 \\
m(H,3) &= m(H,2) \cdot (1+c) = m(H,0) \cdot (1+c)^2 \cdot (1+c) = m(H,0) \cdot (1+c)^3 \\
&\ldots
\end{aligned}
$$

Extending the process to a generic time t, we have:

$$m(H,t) \;=\; m(H,0) \cdot (1+c)^t \tag{3.8}$$

Equation (3.8) clearly tells us that the growing speed of good schemata (as well as the shrinking speed of bad schemata) is exponential. In other words, selection allocates an exponentially increasing amount of individuals to schemata with larger average fitness than the average of the population, and an exponentially decreasing amount of individuals to schemata with smaller average fitness than the average of the population. It is clear that, in this way, bad schemata (i.e., those with smaller average fitness than the average of the population) will rapidly tend to be extinguished.

Effect of Crossover on the Schemata of a Population

Selection alone does not do anything to promote exploration of new areas of the search space, since it does not produce any new individuals inside the population. On the other hand, crossover creates new individuals by remixing structures that were already part of the population. To have a simple intuition on the effect of standard GA crossover on schemata, let us consider a simple binary string A of length ℓ equal to 7, and two schemata H_1 and H_2 that are matched by this string:

$$
\begin{aligned}
A &= 0111000 \\
H_1 &= *1****0 \\
H_2 &= ***10**
\end{aligned}
$$

Let us assume that the individual represented by string A has been selected for mating. Given that the length of the string ℓ is equal to 7, there are 6 existing crossover points (i.e., points between two consecutive bits that can be chosen as the break point, to decompose the string into two substrings that will be exchanged). Let us suppose that we use a completely balanced die to decide the crossover point. Let us assume, for instance, that the die gives, as outcome, crossover point number 3. So, the strings will be partitioned into the substring until the third digit, and the rest of the string, as follows:

$$
\begin{aligned}
A &= 011|1000 \\
H_1 &= *1*|***0 \\
H_2 &= ***|10**
\end{aligned}
$$

As we can see, if we ignore the event of choosing a partner of A that matches one of the two substrings of H_1, H_1 will be "destroyed" by this crossover event. In fact, this crossover will create a child that has a bit equal to 1 in the second position, but does not have a bit equal to 0 in the seventh position, and a child that has a bit equal to 0 in the seventh position but does not have a bit equal to 1 in the second position.

In other words, none of the offspring will match H_1. The situation is different for schema H_2: H_2 will survive this crossover event, because one of the two children will have both a bit equal to 1 in the fourth position and a bit equal to 0 in the fifth position.

Even though in the previous example we have used one particular crossover point, it is not hard to convince oneself that in general it is less probable that H_1 will survive crossover, compared to H_2. In order to quantify this intuition, let us count the number of crossover points that will destroy H_1. Unless the lucky event in which crossover point number 1 is chosen, in all other cases the two characters different from * will be separated by crossover. So, the probability of destroying H_1 is:

$$P(\text{destr } H_1) = \frac{5}{6} \tag{3.9}$$

We now point out that 5 (i.e., the number of crossover points that, if chosen, cause the destruction of H_1) is equal to the length of H_1 (see Definition 3.3), while 6 is the number of possible crossover points, which is equal to the number of characters minus one. So, we hypothesize that Equation (3.9) can be generalized by:

$$P(\text{destr } H_1) = \frac{\delta(H_1)}{\ell - 1}$$

Of course, from the probability of destroying H_1, it is immediate to obtain the probability of H_1 surviving crossover:

$$P(\text{surv } H_1) = 1 - \frac{\delta(H_1)}{\ell - 1} = \frac{1}{6}$$

Once again, it is worth mentioning that this probability has been calculated disregarding the event of a "lucky" crossover, in which H_1 survives thanks to the partner of A.

If we now consider schema H_2, we can see that the only way of destroying it is by choosing the fourth crossover point. In all other cases, H_2 will survive crossover. So:

$$P(\text{destr } H_2) = \frac{1}{6}$$

Once again, the length of H_2 is equal to 1 (see Definition 3.3), so we can write:

$$P(\text{destr } H_2) = \frac{\delta(H_2)}{\ell - 1}$$

The probability of H_2 surviving crossover is:

$$P(\text{surv } H_2) = 1 - \frac{\delta(H_2)}{\ell - 1} = \frac{5}{6}$$

The observations made so far can be generalized: if crossover is performed with a probability equal to p_c, the probability of any schema H to survive crossover can be expressed by the following lower limit:

$$P(\text{surv } H) \geq 1 - p_c \frac{\delta(H)}{\ell - 1} \tag{3.10}$$

Equation (3.10) is a generalization of the previous ones, and it is expressed as a lower limit because the right side of the equation takes into account only one crossover event (and schema H may survive also because of other crossover events in the same generation) and because, as we already mentioned, it does not take into account "lucky" crossovers, where the schema survives thanks to the genetic material made available by the partner. We also point out that the right side of Equation (3.10) becomes like the previous equations if $p_c = 1$.

Given that we can assume that selection and crossover are two mutually independent events, we can obtain the combined effect of selection and crossover on the schemata of a population by simply multiplying the two single effects, obtaining:

$$m(H, t+1) \geq m(H, t) \cdot \frac{f(H)}{\tilde{f}} \left[1 - p_c \frac{\delta(H)}{\ell - 1}\right] \tag{3.11}$$

With this new expression, we can notice that, if only selection and crossover are used, the factors that influence the growth (respectively, the shrinking) of a given schema in the population are whether the average fitness is larger (respectively, smaller) than the population average and whether the schema has a small (respectively, large) length. More specifically, schemata with:

- superior average fitness than the population average;
- small length

will steadily increase the number of representatives in the population from one generation to the next. In the multiplicative factor that estimates the probability of survival of a schema after crossover, there is no expression of time t. So, crossover does not change the fact that the increase in the number of representatives has an exponential speed.

Effect of Mutation on the Schemata of a Population

Standard GAs mutation consists in the random perturbation of each and every character in a string, with a given (and typically low) probability p_m. For a schema to survive a mutation event, it is necessary that all the positions with a character different from $*$ do *not* change. By definition (see Definition 3.2), the number of positions containing a character different from $*$ is the order of the schema. Given that each character in the string survives with a probability equal to $1 - p_m$, and given that the event of mutating a character is, in general, independent of the mutation of the others in the string, the probability that a schema H will survive a mutation event is:

$$P(\text{surv } H) = \underbrace{(1 - p_m)\,(1 - p_m) \cdots (1 - p_m)}_{o(H)\ \text{times}} = (1 - p_m)^{o(H)}$$

If $p_m \ll 1$, which is typical in GAs, this probability can be reasonably approximated by:

$$P(\text{surv } H) = 1 - o(H)\,p_m$$

Intuitively, this equation is telling us that schemata with small order have a higher probability of surviving a mutation event than large-order ones.

Schema Theorem

Joining together the effect on schemata of selection, crossover and mutation, which can be considered mutually independent events, we have that a generic schema H receives an expected number of representative individuals in the next generation of a GA given by:

$$m(H, t+1) \geq m(H, t) \cdot \frac{f(H)}{\bar{f}}\,\Big[1 - p_c\,\frac{\delta(H)}{\ell - 1}\Big]\,[1 - o(H)\,p_m] \qquad (3.12)$$

For simplicity, Equation (3.12) can be rewritten as:

$$m(H, t+1) \geq m(H, t) \cdot \frac{f(H)}{\bar{f}}\,\Big[1 - p_c\,\frac{\delta(H)}{\ell - 1} - o(H)\,p_m\Big] \qquad (3.13)$$

where the term $\big(p_c \cdot p_m \cdot \frac{\delta(H)}{\ell - 1} \cdot o(H)\big)$ was ignored, because it is considered to be very small.

Intuitively, what Equation (3.13) is telling us is that, in GAs, schemata that are:

- short;
- of low order; and
- with an average fitness better than the average of the population

receive an exponentially growing number of representatives in the population, from one generation to the next. The information these schemata contain is commonly called *building blocks*. Building blocks can be imagined as short and compact sequences of characters (different from ∗), such that the presence of those characters in those specific positions in an individual brings a benefit to the individual in terms of fitness. So, in a nutshell, the schema theorem tells us that GAs work by maintaining and proliferating building blocks in the population.

At the same time, Equation (3.13) also tells us that schemata that are:

- long;
- of high order; and
- with an average fitness worse than the average of the population

receive an exponentially decreasing number of representatives in the population, from one generation to the next, until they are eventually extinguished.

Example 3.9. (An empirical validation of the Schema Theorem).

Let us recall the case of Example 3.5. In other words, let us consider the problem of maximizing the function $f(x) = x^2$, with $x \in \mathbb{N}$ & $0 \le x \le 31$. As we might remember from Example 3.5, the initial (randomly generated) population was:

$$x_1 : 01101$$
$$x_2 : 11000$$
$$x_3 : 01000$$
$$x_4 : 10011$$

Let us now consider the following three schemata:

$$H_1 = 1****$$
$$H_2 = *10**$$
$$H_3 = 0***1$$

From Example 3.5, we should also remember that individual x_2 was selected twice, individuals x_1 and x_4 were selected once, while individual x_3 was never selected, and that the population at the second generation was:

$$x_5 : 01100$$
$$x_6 : 11001$$
$$x_7 : 11011$$
$$x_8 : 10000$$

Let us consider first schema H_1. Strings x_2 and x_4 in the initial population belong to this schema. In other words:

$$m(H_1, 0) = 2$$

After selection, three individuals belong to H_1 (two copies of x_2, plus one copy of x_4). Let us check whether this is confirmed by the Schema Theorem. If we take into account only selection, we have:

$$m(H_1, 1) = m(H_1, 0) \frac{f(H_1)}{\tilde{f}} = 3.20$$

This is a substantial confirmation of the fact that, with some approximation, the Schema Theorem is able to predict the number of representatives of H_1 after selection. Let us now consider crossover and mutation. Given that $\delta(H_1) = 0$, the probability that crossover destroys H_1 is equal to zero. In other terms, crossover does not affect H_1. Also, in the example we considered a mutation rate $p_m = 0$, so also mutation has no effect on H_1. As a conclusion, the Schema Theorem predicts that, at generation 2, the number of representatives of schema H_1 in the population should be 3. Indeed, three individuals in the second population, namely x_6, x_7 and x_8, belong to schema H_1.

Let us now consider schema H_2. There are two individuals belonging to H_2 in the initial population and two individual belonging to H_2 in the second population. Applying the Schema Theorem, we have that, after selection:

$$m(H_2, 1) \approx 2.18$$

The probability of survival of H_2 after crossover is:

$$P(\text{surv } H_2) = 1 - p_c \frac{\delta(H_2)}{\ell - 1} = 1 - 1 \frac{1}{5-1} = 0.75$$

So, the expected number of individuals matching H_2 after selection and crossover is:

$$m(H_2, 1) = 2.18 \times 0.75 = 1.64$$

which is still a good approximation of the observed result (two individuals belong to H_2 in the second population).

Finally, let us consider schema H_3. In the initial population, there is one individual belonging to H_3, while in the second population there is no individual belonging to H_3. This is confirmed by the Schema Theorem. In fact, the probability of schema H_3 surviving after crossover is:

$$P(\text{surv } H_3) = 1 - p_c \frac{\delta(H_3)}{\ell - 1} = 1 - 1 \frac{4}{5-1} = 0$$

In other words, crossover will surely destroy this schema. So, the number of expected representatives of H_3 in the second population is:

$$m(H_3, 1) = m(H_3, 0) \times \frac{f(H_3)}{\tilde{f}} \times 0 = 0$$

Building Blocks Hypothesis

The Schema Theorem tells us that GAs allocate an exponentially growing number of representatives to schemata that are short, of low order, and with average fitness better than the population's average. In other words, the building blocks. The Building Blocks Hypothesis says that allocating an exponentially growing number of representatives to the building blocks is *useful* to solve an optimization problem. In other words, it is beneficial in the process of searching for a globally optimal solution. There are fundamentally two ways of giving evidence of the truth of this hypothesis. The first one was shown by J. Holland [Holland, 1975]; it is rather complex and only a superficial intuition will be shown in this book. The second one is more intuitive and will be presented later in an example.

Let us now concentrate on Holland's empirical demonstration of the Building Blocks Hypothesis. This is based on a well-known game theory problem, called the *k-armed bandit problem*. In synthesis, the problem can be formulated as follows: n slot machines are given. For each $j = 1, 2, ..., n$, we assume that slot machine j has a known number of arms, that we call K_j. We assume that we have played t times and, for each one of these games, we assume that we know: the slot machine on which the game was played and the outcome of the game, which can only win or defeat. The problem consists in answering the following question: at which slot machines should we allocate the next games/trials, in order to maximize our probability of winning?

Before further discussing this problem, and investigating the consequences for GAs, let us fix some terminology. Given a slot machine j, let S_j be the probability of obtaining a winning game on slot machine j, calculated on the basis of the t games that have been played until present. In other words:

$$S_j = \frac{\#\text{winning games using slot machine } j}{\#\text{games played using } j}$$

An important result concerning the k-armed bandit problem can be proven. In the continuation of this book, this result will be stated informally, and the proof will not be given. The interested reader is referred to [Holland, 1975].

Theorem 3.1. *(Informal Statement).*

   If *in the next games we allocate an exponentially growing number of trials to slot machines j such that:*

- S_j *is larger than the average calculated over all the slot machines. In other words:*

$$S_j > \frac{\sum_{i=1}^{n} S_i}{n}$$

- *j has a "small" number of arms*

   Then:

- *The probability of winning is maximal;*
- *The probability of winning tends to 1 as the number of future trials tends to infinity.*

Based on this result, Holland was able to demonstrate an important result on GAs. In simple terms, Holland's way of reasoning was to formalize the k-armed bandit problem and GAs, establishing the following correspondences:

k-armed bandit	GAs
slot machine	schema
number of arms of a slot machine	order and length of a schema
probability of winning of a slot machine (calculated on the previous t trials)	average fitness of the schema
winning in the future trials	finding a globally optimal solution
allocating a future trial to one arm of a slot machine	inserting in the next population an individual belonging to a schema

From Theorem 3.1, and from this correspondence between the two systems, it is possible to deduce that maintaining in a GA's population an exponentially growing number of schemata with average fitness better than the population's average and small order and length maximizes the probability of finding a globally optimal solution and this probability tends to 1 as the number of generations of the GA tends to infinity. On the other hand, the Schema Theorem tells us that maintaining in the population an exponentially growing number of schemata with average fitness better than the population's average and small order and length is exactly what GAs do. As a consequence, the following result can be asserted.

Theorem 3.2. *(Theorem of Asymptotic Convergence of Genetic Algorithms). Let $i(t)$ be the best solution in a GA's population at generation t, and let S_{opt} be the set of globally optimal solutions in the search space, then:*

$$\lim_{t\to\infty} P\big(i(t) \in S_{opt}\big) = 1$$

From Theorem 3.2, it immediately follows that the succession $[i(0), i(1), ..., i(t), ...]$ tends towards a solution $o \in S_{opt}$. Besides Holland's heuristic reasoning, Theorem 3.2 can also be formally proven, in the case of elitism, using the concept of Markov chains. The interested reader is referred to [Rudolph, 1997] for this proof.

As already mentioned, the Building Blocks Hypothesis can also have an intuitive justification. In order to discuss it, let us recall Example 3.5, consisting in the problem of maximizing the function $f(x) = x^2$, with $x \in \mathbb{N}$ & $0 \le x \le 31$. The graphical representation of this function is shown in Figure 3.5(a). The idea is that, since individuals can be seen as points on the abscissa of that plot, schemata can be seen as "areas". For instance, schema $H_1 = 1****$ contains all the individuals represented by a numeric value larger than 15. So, H_1 can be represented by the area highlighted in gray in Figure 3.5(b). Similarly, schema $H_2 = 10***$ can be represented by the area in Figure 3.5(c), and schema $H_3 = **1*1$ can be represented by the area in Figure 3.5(d). From these examples, we can notice that:

- The higher the average fitness of a schema, the "closer" the area that represents the schema is to the global optimum (which, in this example, corresponds to number 31).
- The smaller the order of the schema, the smaller the area that represents it.

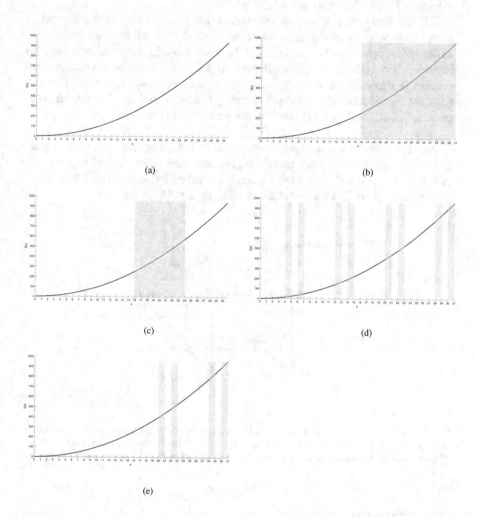

Fig. 3.5 Plot (a): graphical representation of the function $f(x) = x^2$, with $x \in \mathbb{N}$ & $0 \leq x \leq 31$, used in Example 3.5. Plot (b): area represented by schema $1****$. Plot (c): area represented by schema $10***$. Plot (d): area represented by schema $**1*1$. Plot (e): area represented by schema $1*1*1$

From a graphical viewpoint, a crossover between two schemata H_i and H_j that does not destroy either H_i nor H_j can be seen as the *intersection* of the areas representing H_i and H_j. For instance, given the schemata $H_1 = 1****$ and $H_3 = **1*1$, if position 1 is chosen as the crossover point, then crossover does not destroy either H_1

nor H_3, and one of the resulting schemata is $H_4 = 1 * 1 * 1$, which is represented by the area highlighted in gray in Figure 3.5(e).

All this considered, it easy to understand that crossover between schemata of good fitness and small order gives rise to schemata represented by small areas, close to the global optimum. So, maintaining these schemata in the population (and the Schema Theorem tells us that this is what GAs do), and iterating the evolutionary process, it is possible to progressively get closer to the global optimum. The area representing the schemata in the population gets smaller and smaller and, for some of those schemata, closer and closer to the global optimum.

Another possible geometrical interpretation of GAs is by means of a hypercube. Let us consider, for simplicity, individuals represented by bit strings of length $\ell = 3$. In this case, the search space can be seen as a cube of side equal to 1 in a three-dimensional space, like the one represented in Figure 3.6. In this cube:

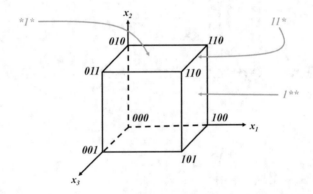

Fig. 3.6 Graphical representation of a GA in which individuals are represented as bit strings of length $\ell = 3$. The search space can be represented as a cube where individuals are vertexes, schemata with one character equal to * are edges and schemata with two characters equal to * are faces

- the vertexes represent the individuals;
- the edges represent schemata with one character equal to *;
- the vertexes of one side α represent the individuals matching the schema represented by α;
- the faces represent schemata with two characters equal to *;
- the vertexes of one face β represent the individuals matching the schema represented by β;
- the intersection edge of two faces β_1 and β_2 can be interpreted as a crossover between the schemata represented by β_1 and β_2.

If the length of the strings representing the individuals is larger than 3, these ideas still hold, even though the search space (represented now by a hypercube) cannot be graphically represented.

3.5 Advanced Methods for Genetic Algorithms

As we have studied in the previous section, GAs converge asymptotically towards global optima. However, the Theorem of Asymptotic Convergence of GAs does not say anything about the speed with which a GA will approximate globally optimal solutions in real scenarios, and empirical evidence tells us that, in several cases, neither globally optimal solutions, nor reasonable approximations of those solutions, can be found in "reasonable" time by standard GAs[6]. For this reason, in the last three decades, effort was dedicated by researchers to the attempt to define improvements for GAs, able to accelerate the process of convergence towards good-quality solutions. The amount of produced work is so vast that to even imagine covering all of it in this book would be utopian. Nevertheless, it is worth discussing some of the most popular approaches. In particular, this section will be organized by identifying a number of possible drawbacks of the standard formulation of GAs which may prevent them from finding good-quality solutions in reasonable time. Then, possible workarounds for those problems will be discussed, thus defining a set of advanced GA methods that can potentially improve them. The problems of standard GAs that will be discussed in this section are:

- Premature convergence, or lack of diversity;
- Position problem of standard crossover;
- Uniqueness of the fitness function.

After defining each one of these potential issues, solutions that have been proposed in the literature will be discussed. In particular, the premature convergence problem will be defined in Section 3.5.1, and workarounds presented for this problem will be fitness sharing, in Section 3.5.1.1, restricted mating, in Section 3.5.1.2, and diploid chromosomes, in Section 3.5.1.3; the position problem of standard crossover will be presented in Section 3.5.2 and, in order to counteract this problem, we will discuss inversion and reordering operators in Section 3.5.2.1 and two new types of crossover, namely partially matched crossover and cycle crossover, in Section 3.5.2.2; finally, the uniqueness of the fitness function will be discussed in Section 3.5.3, and the solution to this issue that will be discussed is multiobjective optimization, in Section 3.5.3.1.

3.5.1 Premature Convergence

The problem of premature convergence, or loss of diversity, is one of the most studied, and most visible, problems of evolutionary algorithms. It can be explained in very simple terms: during evolution, standard GAs tend to create populations in

---

[6] From now on, we will use the term standard GAs to indicate the version of GAs introduced in [Holland, 1975, Goldberg, 1989], studied in Sections 3.1, 3.2, 3.3 and 3.4 and represented by the pseudocode given in Algorithm 4.

which all the individuals are very similar to each other. In such a situation, typically the population contains few blocks of information, and these are shared among all the individuals. It is intuitive that, if these blocks of information differ significantly from the characteristics of globally optimal solutions, the genetic operators will have difficulty in improving the quality of the individuals in the population.

To counteract this issue, several different strategies were developed by researchers through the years. Before studying some of them, however, it is important to define some measures that can allow us to quantify the diversity of a population, so that, using those measures, we are able to monitor and eventually prevent premature convergence. Even though several different measures of diversity exist, the two most employed measures are probably *entropy* and *variance*. Furthermore, both these measures can be used to quantify *phenotypic* diversity (i.e., the diversity in the fitness values, or functions of them) or *genotypic* diversity (i.e., diversity in the syntactic structures of the individuals). Let us begin with presenting entropy. The entropy of a population P is defined as:

$$H(P) = \sum_{j=1}^{N} F_j \log(F_j) \tag{3.14}$$

If phenotypic entropy is considered, F_j is the fraction n_j/N of individuals in P having a certain fitness value, where N is the total number of fitness values in P. To define genotypic entropy, two different techniques can be used: for the first one, F_j is defined as the fraction of individuals in population P having a certain genotype, and N is the total number of genotypes in P. The second technique consists in defining a distance measure between individual genotypes; in this case, F_j is the fraction of individuals having a certain distance value to a previously fixed individual (often called the "origin"), and N is the total number of distance values to the origin appearing in P. Experimental evidence indicates that this measure, at least qualitatively, is not strongly dependent on the choice of the particular individual used as the origin. The logarithm in Equation (3.14) is normally used with base equal to 2, even though the choice of the base usually does not qualitatively affect the measurement of the diversity.

The variance of a population P is defined as:

$$V(P) = \frac{1}{n-1} \sum_{i=1}^{n} (x_i - \bar{x})^2 \tag{3.15}$$

If phenotypic variance is considered, $\bar{x}$ is the average fitness of the individuals in P, x_i is the fitness of the ith individual in P and n is the total number of individuals in P (i.e., the population size). To define genotypic variance, only the notion of distance is normally used. In this case, $\bar{x}$ is the average of all the individual distances to the origin, x_i is the distance of the ith individual in the population to the origin and, again, n is the total number of individuals in P.

Given that both genotypic entropy and phenotypic variance may need the notion of distance between individuals, it is a good idea to discuss a particular, and popular, measure commonly employed in GAs. Even though many other different measures can exist, and given that GA individuals are represented as strings of characters of a prefixed length, in GAs it is typical to use Hamming distance in the case of a discrete alphabet and Euclidean distance in the case of a continuous alphabet. Hamming distance between two strings x_1 and x_2, to be used if the characters in the strings are taken from a discrete alphabet, is defined as follows:

$$d_H(x_1, x_2) = \sum_{i=1}^{\ell} \Psi(x_1[i], x_2[i])$$

where, for each pair of characters a and b from the alphabet:

$$\Psi(a,b) = \begin{cases} 1 & \text{if } a \neq b \\ 0 & \text{otherwise} \end{cases}$$

and where, for each string x, $x[i]$ represents the *ith* character of x and ℓ is the string length.

Euclidean distance between two strings x_1 and x_2, to be used if the characters in the strings are taken from a continuous alphabet (typically, they are floating-point numbers), is defined as follows:

$$d_E(x_1, x_2) = \sqrt{\sum_{i=1}^{n} (x_1[i] - x_2[i])^2}$$

Before presenting sophisticated methods to counteract premature convergence, it is worth noticing that a very simple method can be employed. It is called *novelty search*, and it simply consists in replacing the fitness with a measure of the "novelty" of an individual in the population (for instance, one could quantify how many times the individual was part of the population during the evolution, and/or how many generations ago). This method is called *novelty search* [Lehman and Stanley, 2011] and, despite its simplicity, it has been demonstrated to be very effective in several practical domains.

3.5.1.1 Fitness Sharing

Fitness sharing is a method aimed at maintaining diversity in a population. The basic idea is to modify fitness in such a way that individuals that are more diverse, compared to the rest of the population, receive a "reward", while individuals that are similar to the majority of the others in the population receive a "penalty". Given a measure of distance between individuals, and assuming that we are solving a maximization problem, fitness sharing can be applied to update the fitness of an individual x by performing the following steps:

1. Calculate the distance of x to all the other individuals in the population;
2. Normalize all distances in the $[0, 1]$ range (let $d_N(x, y)$ be the normalized distance of x to another individual y);

3. Apply a steadily decreasing function, called the *sharing function S*, to the distances, so that sharing is large when the distance is small and vice versa.
4. Calculate the *sharing coefficient* of x as follows:

$$\mathscr{S}(x) = \sum_{y \in P, y \neq x} S(d_N(x,y))$$

5. Redefine the fitness of x as follows:

$$f_S(x) = \frac{f(x)}{\mathscr{S}(x)}$$

By applying this process, it is clear that when $\mathscr{S}(x)$ is large (i.e., when x is rather similar to the majority of the other individuals in the population) f_S receives a "penalty", while when $\mathscr{S}(x)$ is small, f_S receives a "reward". A simple way of implementing point 2 (normalization of the distances) when Hamming distance is the chosen metric is to define all distances by the string length. Analogously, a simple way of implementing point 3 (calculation of the sharing, by "inverting" the distance) is by using a simple linear sharing function like: $S(k) = 1 - k$.

It is clear that, if fitness sharing is applied, individuals that are different from the majority gain a better fitness than they would have if fitness sharing was not applied. This automatically gives those individuals a higher probability of being selected for mating, keeping a higher diversity in the population. The use of fitness sharing induces different population dynamics compared to standard GAs. This different behavior is idealized in Figure 3.7. Plot (a) of Figure 3.7 shows the typical

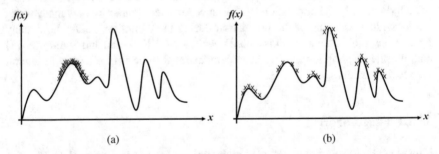

Fig. 3.7 Plot (a): idealized search of a GAs population over a fitness landscape when fitness sharing is *not* used. Plot (b): typical population dynamics on the same fitness landscape when fitness sharing is used. The crosses indicate the positions in the fitness landscape assumed by the individuals in the population

population dynamics, expecially in an advanced stage of the search, when fitness sharing is not used. All individuals often tend to cluster around one single peak of the fitness landscape. On the other hand, Figure 3.7(b) shows the idealized dynamics induced by the use of fitness sharing: the individuals in the population are supposed to distribute more uniformly around the different peaks of the fitness landscape. The better exploration power bestowed by fitness sharing is paid for in the larger computational cost of the algorithm. In fact, with fitness sharing, in order to evaluate the individuals, we have to calculate pairwise distances among all the individuals in the population.

3.5.1.2 Restricted Mating

As we can see from Figure 3.7, fitness sharing implicitly partitions the GAs population into *niches*. An intuition of the reason why, in some cases, organizing a population into niches can be beneficial can be given by observing the simple bidimensional fitness landscape represented in Figure 3.8. Assuming that the represented

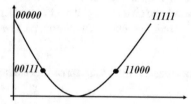

Fig. 3.8 Graphical representation of a simple fitness landscape for a maximization problem. Good-quality individuals, in this case, have either a lot of 0s or a lot of 1s in their genotype

problem is a maximization one, it is straightforward to remark that good-quality individuals have either many bits equal to 0, or many bits equal to 1. If we allow a good individual "with many 0s" to mate with a good individual "with many 1s", the offspring will have a hybrid chromosome that will probably be less fit than their parents. For reasons like this, in many applications, it is appropriate to partition the population into niches, or species, promoting crossover between individuals in the same niche and discouraging crossover between individuals coming from different niches. Similar dynamics, obviously, exist also in biological populations and are believed to promote population diversity.

In order to foster the formation of niches in the population, methods imposing some mating restrictions have been proposed so far. One of the first contributions in this direction was proposed by Hollstien [Goldberg, 1989], who introduced a model in which crossover is allowed between two individuals i and j if and only if $d(i, j) < k$, where d is a chosen distance metric and k a fixed threshold value. In Hollstien's model, only if the average population fitness does not improve for some generations is crossover between individuals that are further apart from each other (and so belonging to different niches) allowed.

A different model was later introduced by Brooker [Goldberg, 1989]. In Brooker's model each individual is represented using two substrings, which are usually called the *template part* and the *functional part*. The functional part contains the usual representation of the individual, as imposed by the definition of the problem. On the other hand, the template part is a schema (see Definition 3.1, on page 62). Intuitively, we could say that the template part of an individual x encodes in x's genome the "sexual tastes" of x, containing some characteristics of potential crossover partners of x. In order to know whether two individuals can mate, we will compare the template part of one of them with the functional part of the other, and vice versa. Brooker defined the following three models:

- *Bidirectional match.* In this model, two individuals i and j are allowed to mate if the template part of i matches the functional part of j *and* the template part of j matches the functional part of i.
- *Unidirectional match.* In this model, two individuals i and j are allowed to mate if the template part of i matches the functional part of j *or* the template part of j matches the functional part of i.
- *Best partial match.* In this model, selection is modified in such a way that when an individual i is selected, the crossover partner of i is selected by choosing one of the individuals in the population whose functional part best matches the template part of i.

Example 3.10. Let us consider the following three individuals:

<Individual's ID>	<Template>	<Functional>
a	*10*	1010
b	*01*	1101
c	*00*	0000

In this case, we could informally say that "a is sexually attracted to b". In fact, the functional part of b matches the template of a. But we can also say that the attraction of a is "reciprocated" by b, or that also "b is sexually attracted to a". In fact, also the functional part of a matches the template of b. The conclusion is that individuals a and b are allowed to mate under any of the models presented above. On the other hand, neither of the other individuals is attracted to c. However, it should be noted that the functional part of c matches the template part of c itself. So, if the implementation allows it, a crossover between two copies of c can take place.

In Brooker's model, fitness is calculated using only the functional part (we could say that the functional part corresponds to the representation of an individual in standard GAs, and so it contains the information that is needed to calculate the fitness). On the other hand, before applying crossover and mutation, the template and functional part are concatenated, to obtain a single string of double length. Then, crossover and mutation are applied to these longer strings. We could say that each individual is evolving its sexual preferences as a part of its genome. Under this viewpoint, as it is easy to hypothesize that it may happen also in natural populations, sexual preferences evolve (and thus change) with time.

3.5.1.3 Diploid Chromosome

Some organisms in nature are characterized by chromosomes that can be represented by means of a single string. This type of chromosome, called a *haploid* chromosome, is typical of rather simple living beings. The chromosomes of more complex living beings, instead, can be represented by means of two strings of characters, and they are called *diploid* chromosomes. A diploid chromosome can be represented as in the following simple example:

$$A \; b \; C \; D \; e$$
$$a \; B \; C \; d \; e$$

As we can see, the two strings representing the chromosome have identical lengths and can be imagined, in some sense, to be "aligned". The characters that appear in the same position in the two strings represent two alternative features for a particular genetic trait. For instance, character *B* could represent the fact that the individual has brown eyes, while character *b* could represent the fact that the individual has blue eyes. Given that an individual cannot have these two traits at the same time, nature has developed a choice mechanism, called *dominance*. In Biology, we say that in a particular *locus* (i.e., a position in a string), an *allele* (i.e., a character) dominates another allele. The former is called a *dominant* allele, while the latter is a *recessive* allele. Assuming by convention that the dominant characters are written with an uppercase letter, the chromosome of the previous example could be transcribed as:

$$A \; B \; C \; D \; e$$

In other words, the dominant characters are always chosen, compared to the recessive ones. A recessive character can only be chosen if it does not have a dominant character in the corresponding position.

At this point, a question naturally arises: why do the most complex species have diploid chromosomes? The answer to this question is, in large part, still the object of scientific research, however the most accredited hypothesis is that a diploid chromosome allows the species to better adapt to environmental variations. For instance, in the case of climate change, with a significant lowering of the temperature, an animal possessing an allele that corresponds to long hair will probably have better ability to adapt to the new environment. Furthermore, it is an observed fact that a diploid chromosome fosters greater population diversity, which allows for better adaptability.

The idea of a diploid chromosome has been transferred to GAs by several researchers. One of the first models to be developed was Bagley's model, in which each character of a string has an associated dominance value. Genetic operators are applied to both strings composing the chromosome, and then the character with higher dominance in each position is chosen, to generate a single string used to calculate fitness. The flaw of Bagley's model is that dominance values are fixed in advance, and genetic operators do not modify those values. In this way, after several generations, selection pressure causes few dominance values to survive in the population, thus eliminating the usefulness of having a diploid chromosome.

Another interesting model is the Hollstien-Holland model. In this model, each locus contains a pair of characters. In case of a binary encoding, the first character comes from the alphabet $\{0,1\}$, while in general the second character comes from the alphabet $\{m,M\}$. The chromosome is diploid, in the sense that it is characterized by two strings, each of which contains this pair of characters at each locus. The string resulting from the dominance application, i.e., the string used to calculate fitness, in case of a binary encoding, is a binary string obtained by applying to each locus a mapping given by a previously fixed dominance table. This model was later updated by a diploid chromosome in which, in case of a binary encoding, the two strings are formed by characters coming from the augmented alphabet $\{0,1,2\}$. In this second Hollstien-Holland model, genetic operators act on these two strings, and a dominance table is used to transform the two strings into a single binary string, used to calculate fitness. This table associates to each pair of characters in $\{0,1,2\}$ a character in $\{0,1\}$. Experimental results confirm that this second model, also called the *triallelic* model given that three characters are used in the chromosome, allows for a larger population diversity compared to the two previously discussed models. Furthermore, using schema theory, it is also possible to prove that, under some specific hypotheses, the triallelic model has better performance than the previously discussed models and also better than standard GAs [Goldberg, 1989].

3.5.2 Position Problem of Standard Crossover

The position problem of standard crossover can be explained in very simple terms: let us assume that, for some unknown reasons inherent to the faced problem, individuals with good fitness must have a certain allele x in a string locus i that is close to the left end of the string, and a certain allele y in a locus j close to the right end, as represented here:

It is clear that, in such a situation, standard crossover has a high probability of destroying good-quality individuals. In fact, it is highly probable that the randomly chosen crossover point falls between alleles x and y. In this way, without a lucky contribution of the crossover partner, one offspring will contain allele x in locus i, but not allele y in locus j, while the other will contain allele y in locus j, but not allele x in locus i. If the feature that makes fitness good is to have *both* allele x in locus i *and* allele y in locus j, both offspring will have worse fitness than the parent.

Using the schema theory terminology, we could say that, in GAs, building blocks do not have to necessarily be compact pieces of information, contained in contiguous loci. In some situations, a useful building block could also be composed of pieces of information that are spread across the string, distributed in loci that are far apart from each other. Destroying those building blocks could be deleterious. Obviously, if we were able to:

- change the order of the characters in the string, so that positions i and j get close to each other;
- apply crossover;
- reorder the string;

the problem would be solved. But, unfortunately, we are in general not able to do this, because the information on how to change the order of the characters in the string is not known. In the following sections, workarounds to limit this problem are proposed.

3.5.2.1 Inversion and Reordering Operators

A first attempt to counteract the position problem of standard crossover was made by Bagley. In his model, at each locus in the string, a value and an index are associated. In other words, initially, individuals have the following aspect:

$$\begin{matrix} 1\ 2\ 3\ 4\ 5\ 6\ 7\ 8 \\ \begin{bmatrix} 1\ 0\ 1\ 1\ 1\ 0\ 1\ 1 \end{bmatrix} \end{matrix}$$

In Bagley's model, a new operator, called the inversion operator, was defined, allowing two randomly chosen alleles to be swapped. For instance, applying inversion to the previous individual, it would be possible to obtain:

$$\begin{matrix} 1\ 2\ 6\ 4\ 5\ 3\ 7\ 8 \\ \begin{bmatrix} 1\ 0\ 0\ 1\ 1\ 1\ 1\ 1 \end{bmatrix} \end{matrix}$$

where alleles 3 and 6 have been swapped. This operator can be applied once, or multiple times, according to the level of reshuffling we want to obtain. Crossover and mutation are applied to the string after the inversion, and before calculating fitness the string needs to be reordered. Of course, this method has the obvious problem of how to handle crossover between two strings in which indexes are not in the same positions. These strings are called *nonhomologous*. For instance, consider a standard crossover between the following individuals:

$$\begin{matrix} 1\ 2\ 3\ 4\ |\ 5\ 6\ 7\ 8 \\ \begin{bmatrix} 1\ 0\ 1\ 1\ |\ 1\ 0\ 1\ 1 \end{bmatrix} \end{matrix}$$

$$\begin{matrix} 1\ 2\ 6\ 5\ |\ 4\ 3\ 7\ 8 \\ \begin{bmatrix} 1\ 0\ 0\ 1\ |\ 1\ 1\ 1\ 1 \end{bmatrix} \end{matrix}$$

Using the fourth crossover point, the offspring would be:

$$
\begin{array}{cccccccc}
1 & 2 & 3 & 4 & 4 & 3 & 7 & 8
\end{array}
$$
$$
\begin{bmatrix} 1 & 0 & 1 & 1 & 1 & 1 & 1 & 1 \end{bmatrix}
$$

$$
\begin{array}{cccccccc}
1 & 2 & 6 & 5 & 5 & 6 & 7 & 8
\end{array}
$$
$$
\begin{bmatrix} 1 & 0 & 0 & 1 & 1 & 0 & 1 & 1 \end{bmatrix}
$$

But clearly these strings cannot be reordered because some indexes are missing and some appear more than once. The method proposed in Bagley's model simply consists in prohibiting crossover between pairs of nonhomologous strings. This solves the problem, but strongly limits the power of crossover. A possible alternative was suggested by Frantz [Goldberg, 1989], presenting several operators of inversion and mating. The inversion operators proposed by Frantz are:

- Linear Inversion. This is the inversion we have seen so far: two loci are chosen randomly and swapped.

- Linear+end inversion. In this type of inversion, linear inversion is applied with a given probability. If linear inversion has been applied, the algorithm terminates. Otherwise, with uniform probability, the left or the right extreme of the string is chosen, and then exchanged with a point chosen at random among all the points that have at least $\ell/2$ characters of distance from the chosen extreme, where ℓ is the string length.

With linear+end inversion, Frantz aimed at minimizing the tendency of linear inversion to swap alleles that are close to the central part of the string. Both these inversions can be applied with one of the following modalities:

- Modality of continuous inversion. Inversion is applied with a given probability p_i to each individual in the population.

- Modality of mass inversion. Once the new population is generated and evaluated, half of the individuals are randomly chosen, and the same inversion is applied to all of them.

The rationale beyond mass inversion is that it should tend to limit the cases of nonhomologous strings. After applying inversion, Frantz proposed four types of mating:

- Mating between homologous strings. This is the same idea proposed by Bagley: crossover is allowed only among homologous strings.

- Viability mating. Crossover is allowed also if the parent strings are not homologous, but if the offspring do not contain all the indexes, they are disregarded and not inserted in the population.

- Any-pattern mating. One of the two parents is randomly chosen as the primary parent. The indexes of the other parent are changed, and they become identical to the ones of the primary parent. In this way, the two strings are forced to become homologous, and crossover can be applied.

- Best-pattern mating. Works like any-pattern, but the primary individual is always the one with better fitness among the two parents.

Some studies [Bethke, 1980] have shown that Frantz's operators of inversion and mating can be useful for improving the performance of GAs on particularly hard problems. However, empirical evidence also shows that inversion is more powerful if it is applied multiple times, and in different ways for the different individuals in the population, causing *de facto* a different random reshuffling of each string. A consequence of this strong inversion is that nonhomologous strings become very frequent in the population, and Frantz's models become ineffective. Having a random reshuffling of individuals before applying crossover calls for the definition of recombination operators that are different from standard crossover. The next section presents two types of crossover that can be applied to nonhomologous strings and, independently of the order of the indexes in the parent strings, by construction generate offspring containing all the indexes once and only once, in such a way that reordering is possible.

3.5.2.2 Partially Matched and Cycle Crossover

These two types of crossover, introduced in [Goldberg, 1989], can be applied to nonhomologous individuals, independently of the type of inversion that has been applied to them, and both of them generate offspring that are a recombination of the chromosomes of the parents and contain all the indexes. Let us begin by discussing *partially matched* crossover. The two parents that have been selected for mating (with any of the selection algorithms studied in Section 3.1) are aligned, and two crossover points are chosen randomly, like in the following example:

$$9 \ 8 \ 4 \ | \ 5 \ 6 \ 7 \ | \ 1 \ 3 \ 2 \ 10$$
$$[1 \ 0 \ 1 \ | \ 1 \ 0 \ 1 \ | \ 0 \ 0 \ 0 \ 1]$$

$$8 \ 7 \ 1 \ | \ 2 \ 3 \ 10 \ | \ 9 \ 5 \ 4 \ 6$$
$$[0 \ 0 \ 1 \ | \ 0 \ 1 \ 1 \ | \ 1 \ 1 \ 0 \ 0]$$

The area of the string between the two crossover points in called a *window*. The algorithm starts by constructing the first offspring, in the following way: for each locus of the first parent (where loci are analyzed one by one, from left to right, in the order they appear in the string), if the index is not in the window, then the locus is copied in the corresponding position of the offspring. Otherwise, if the index belongs to the window in one of the two parents, the locus that is copied in the offspring is the corresponding one in the other parent. It is worth reinforcing that a locus is, by definition, a pair composed of an index and a character from the alphabet. So, when a locus is inherited by the offspring, both its index and its content are inherited. Following this process, the first offspring generated by the crossover between the two previous parents is:

$$9 \ 8 \ 4 \ \big| 2 \ 3 \ 10 \ \big| 1 \ 6 \ 5 \ 7$$
$$\begin{bmatrix} 1 \ 0 \ 1 \ \big| 0 \ 1 \ 1 \ \big| 0 \ 0 \ 1 \ 1 \end{bmatrix}$$

The reader is invited to notice that not only the loci inside the window have been exchanged, but also the three rightmost loci of the first parent. In fact, the indexes of those three loci also belong to the window, even though the window of the second parent, and so they have been exchanged with the loci in corresponding positions from the first parent. As we can see, the first offspring contains all the indexes, and each one appears once and only once. So, the string can be reordered and the individual inserted in the new population in a straightforward way. In order to construct the second offspring, the same method is applied, but this time the loci of the second parent are analyzed one by one. In the considered example, this allows us to create the following second offspring:

$$8 \ 10 \ 1 \ \big| 5 \ 6 \ 7 \ \big| 9 \ 2 \ 4 \ 3$$
$$\begin{bmatrix} 0 \ 1 \ 1 \ \big| 1 \ 0 \ 1 \ \big| 1 \ 0 \ 0 \ 1 \end{bmatrix}$$

The reader is invited to remark that, also in this case, not only the loci inside the window have been exchanged, but also the loci in the 2nd, 8th and 10th positions, since their indexes belong to the window in the first parent.

Let us now present *cycle* crossover, and also in this case, let us discuss it with an example. For instance, let us consider the following parents, both of which have undergone inversion:

$$9 \ 8 \ 2 \ 1 \ 7 \ 4 \ 5 \ 10 \ 6 \ 3$$
$$\begin{bmatrix} 1 \ 0 \ 1 \ 1 \ 0 \ 1 \ 0 \ 0 \ 0 \ 1 \end{bmatrix}$$

$$1 \ 2 \ 3 \ 4 \ 5 \ 6 \ 7 \ 8 \ 9 \ 10$$
$$\begin{bmatrix} 0 \ 0 \ 1 \ 0 \ 1 \ 1 \ 1 \ 1 \ 0 \ 0 \end{bmatrix}$$

Let us start by building the first offspring. The algorithm starts by selecting a random locus from a random parent, and copying it into the corresponding position of the offspring. For simplicity, in this case, let us assume that the chosen locus is the first one of the first parent. So, the offspring that was built so far is:

$$9$$
$$\begin{bmatrix} 1 \ - \ - \ - \ - \ - \ - \ - \ - \ - \end{bmatrix}$$

As we can see, only the first locus of the first parent was copied into the offspring, so far. All the rest of the offspring is, up to now, "empty", in the sense that all the other loci are still to be defined. Let us now take a further step. What makes us perform the next step is the following reasoning: given that locus with index equal to 9 has been inherited from the first parent, also the locus with index equal to 1 has to be inherited from the first parent. In fact, let us assume that the locus with index 1 was inherited from the second parent. If we accept that loci have to be copied in the offspring in the same positions in which they appear in the parents, we simply could not copy that locus into the offspring. In fact, the locus with index 1 appears in the first position of the string of the second parent. So, it should be copied into the first position of the offspring. But the first position of the offspring is already occupied. Obviously, the only remaining option is to inherit also the locus of index 1 from the first parent. So, now the part of offspring built so far is:

$$\overset{9}{\underset{}{}}\quad\overset{1}{\underset{}{}}$$
$$\left[1 - - 1 - - - - - -\right]$$

Now, if we repeat the same reasoning, given that the locus with index 1 was inherited from the first parent, also the locus with index 4 has to be inherited from the first parent. In fact, the locus with index 4 appears in the second parent in the same position as the locus with index 1 in the first parent. So, adding the locus with index 4 from the first parent, the part of the offspring that was built so far is:

$$\overset{9}{}\quad\overset{1}{}\quad\overset{4}{}$$
$$\left[1 - - 1 - 1 - - - -\right]$$

Once again, the fact of having inherited the locus with index 4 from the first parent "forces" the offspring to inherit also the locus with index 6 from the first parent, and so the construction of the offspring becomes:

$$\overset{9}{}\quad\overset{1}{}\quad\overset{4}{}\quad\overset{6}{}$$
$$\left[1 - - 1 - 1 - - 0 -\right]$$

Iterating the reasoning, and observing that the locus with index 9 appears in the second parent in the same position as the locus with index 6 in the first parent, now we could say that the fact of having inherited the locus with index 6 from the first parent induces the offspring to also inherit the locus with index 9 from the first parent. But, as we can observe, the locus with index 9 was already inherited from the first parent and it already appears in the offspring. This event allows us to terminate a cycle (hence the name *cycle* crossover) that has allowed us to decide which loci the offspring should inherit from the first parent. The offspring is now completed by simply inheriting all the missing loci from the second parent. So, the final string representing the offspring is:

$$9\ ②\ ③\ 1\ ⑤\ 4\ ⑦\ ⑧\ 6\ ⑩$$
$$[1\ ⓪\ ①\ 1\ ①\ 1\ ①\ ①\ 0\ ⓪]$$

where, for the sake of readability, loci inherited from the second parent have been highlighted by a circle. As the reader can easily observe, the first offspring has all the indexes, each of which appears once, and thus the string can be reordered straightforwardly. At this point, building the second offspring is simple: in each string position, the second offspring simply inherits the locus from the parent that did not pass the locus to the first offspring. So, in this example, the second offspring is simply:

$$①\ 8\ 2\ ④\ 7\ ⑥\ 5\ 10\ ⑨\ 3$$
$$[⓪\ 0\ 1\ ⓪\ 0\ ①\ 0\ 0\ ⓪\ 1]$$

As we can see, also the second offspring has all the indexes, and each one of them appears once, and so its string can be reordered. This property is general, in the sense that, as for the partially matched crossover, also cycle crossover is able to build offspring recombining parents' loci in such a way that the offspring always have all the indexes. One event that can happen is that, during the construction of the first offspring, the cycle that allows us to inherit the loci from the first parent only terminates when all the loci have been inherited. In that case, cycle crossover generates offspring that are identical to the parents. Given that this is rather rare, particularly for long strings, this event is normally accepted, with no further controls or restrictions. Partially matched crossover and cycle crossover have been successful in several applications, in particular when dealing with hard problems.

3.5.3 Uniqueness of the Fitness Function

This issue, shared also by all the other optimization algorithms studied so far, consists in the fact that, in standard GAs, the fitness function is unique. So, only one criterion at a time can be optimized. However, the real world is full of cases in which, at the same time, we have to optimize more than one, in some cases many, criteria at the time. One may think, for instance, of the simple problem of buying a new car: it is typical to look for a car that has some qualities, like power, speed, or comfort, but also that has a contained cost. In many cases, like this one, the criteria that have to be optimized are conflicting: cars with many qualities are typically expensive, while cheap cars usually do not have many qualities.

Intuitively, one simple way to deal with this problem is to have several functions, able to quantify the different criteria to be optimized, and to define statistics over all these measurements, like for instance the average or the median, in order to unify all criteria in one single fitness function. If, on the one hand, this strategy has the advantage of being simple, and allows us to use GAs without any modification, on the other hand, it may create a number of new issues that may be very hard, or even impossible, to solve in practical cases. First of all, in order for a statistic, like the average, to be a realistic expression of all the criteria, the different measurements should have the same scale. For instance, optimizing the average between a measurement α and a measurement β, where α takes values in $[0, 1]$ and β in $[0, 1000]$, would clearly advantage the optimization of β, making any improvement in the optimization of α almost irrelevant. Even though normalization methods exist, in many cases normalizing measures of different natures can be tricky, and lead to misleading results. Also, calculating statistics over the different criteria may imply the necessity of defining appropriate values for the weights of each one of the criteria, which may be an extremely hard task. For this reason, in the continuation of this section, we present methods that do not try, in any way, to join different criteria together in a unique fitness function. Instead, each criterion will define its own fitness function, and several different fitness functions will be optimized together.

A first attempt to integrate concepts of multiobjective optimization in GAs was proposed in [Schaffer, 1985], where an environment called Vector Evaluated Genetic Algorithm (VEGA) was presented. In VEGA, given a population of n individuals and given k optimization criteria, selection allows us to choose n/k individuals using each one of the k criteria. Then, crossover and mutation are performed as usual on the whole population, with the rationale of integrating genetic material coming from the optimization of the different criteria. This method has the advantage of being simple, but the proposed selection mechanism tends to allow survival only of individuals that excel in one criterion, but are inadequate in all the others. However, in multiobjective optimization, we are often interested in solutions that represent a good compromise between all the existing criteria. This drawback is overcome by Pareto multiobjective optimization, discussed in the continuation.

3.5.3.1 Pareto Multiobjective Optimization in Genetic Algorithms

In multiobjective optimization, several fitness functions exist that need to be optimized at the same time. In such a context, the concept of optimal solution is not obvious. One of the most used concepts is that of *Pareto optimal*. Let us assume, for instance, that we want to build a product, to optimize at the same time the average number of accidents caused by that product and its prize. In this model, the fitness of a particular product x can be seen as a pair:

$$f(x) = (\text{cost}, \text{average number of accidents})$$

For instance, let is assume that we have five products, A, B, C, D and E, with the following fitness values:

$$A = (2, 10)$$
$$B = (4, 6)$$
$$C = (8, 4)$$
$$D = (9, 5)$$
$$E = (7, 8)$$

Which one of these products can be considered to be "the best"? To help us answer this question, it can be useful to notice that the fitness values of the different products can be seen as points in a bidimensional space. So, it can be useful to plot those points in a Cartesian plane, like in Figure 3.9. At a first observation, we can imme-

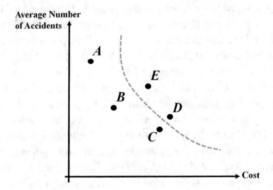

Fig. 3.9 Five solutions and the Pareto front, separating dominated from non-dominated ones (dashed gray line)

diately notice that there is an important difference between points A, B and C and the others: these three points have the property that no other solution is better on all optimization criteria. A, B and C are called *nondominated* solutions. Concerning D and E, we can, instead, observe that they are dominated. In fact, C is better than D on both criteria (we say that C dominates D) and B dominates E. So, instead of answering with a single solution, we can answer the previous question with a set of solutions: $\{A, B, C\}$. This is the set of nondominated solutions, also called the *Pareto optimal set*. The gray dashed line in Figure 3.9 is called the *Pareto front*, and it is a line separating the nondominated solutions from the dominated ones.

Actually, in multiobjective optimization it is typical to have a set of optimal solutions, instead of a single one. In order to decide which one among A, B and C is best, we either need to give weights to the criteria, or we can imagine calculating a distance from an ideal "super optimal" point. This point is a theoretical (and often nonexistent) solution that joins the best known values on all criteria. For the previous example, it is represented in Figure 3.10, where it is indicated as α. If Euclidean distance was used, in this case we can observe that B would be the closest solution to α among the ones belonging to the Pareto optimal set.

A method to integrate the concept of Pareto optimal inside the functioning of GAs was proposed by [Baker, 1985] The method consists in sorting the indi-

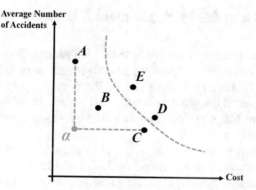

Fig. 3.10 Same solutions as in Figure 3.9, where also the ideal "super-solution" is shown. It consists in point α, which has the best known values for both criteria

viduals in a population on the basis of nondominance and then applying selection, based on this ranking. The functioning of the method can be summarized by the pseudocode in Algorithm 5. Baker applied this technique to multiobjective prob-

---

Algorithm 5: The pseudocode for applying selection in Pareto-based multiobjective GAs, according to Baker's method.

---

1. Insert all the individuals in the population into a set S;

2. *currentFlagValue* := 1;

3. **repeat until** (S is empty)

    3.1. Assign a flag equal to *currentFlagValue* to the nondominated solutions in S;

    3.2. Remove the nondominated solutions from S;

    3.3. *currentFlagValue* := *currentFlagValue* + 1;

  end

4. Assign to each individual in the population a selection probability that is *inversely* proportional to its flag value;

---

lems, in conjunction with methods to maintain diversity in the population, reporting very interesting experimental results. This method was later extended, to give birth to more sophisticated and efficient algorithms, such as NSGA-II and SPEA. A presentation of these algorithms is beyond the scope of this book, and the interested reader is referred to [Deb et al., 2002] and [Zitzler and Thiele, 1999], respectively. For a rather complete discussion of methods for multiobjective evolutionary algorithms, the reader is referred to [Coello Coello et al., 2006].

3.6 How to Organize an Experimental Comparison

One of the consequences of the No Free Lunch Theorem (Section 2.3) is that no formal method can exist to choose the best algorithm, or even the best algorithm configuration, to solve a particular problem. For this reason, on many different occasions, experimental comparisons are the only option. In this section, we discuss how two, or more, different algorithms, or configurations of algorithms, can be compared with each other.

Before entering into the details of the discussion, it is worth saying what, in general, an experimental comparison should *not* look like, thus revealing one of the most frequent and serious mistakes when dealing with metaheuristic optimization algorithms. If we want to compare the performance of two algorithm configurations on a given problem, we should *not* execute both configurations once and choose the one that returned the best result. In fact, all the algorithms that we have studied so far, and also the majority of the algorithms we will study later in this book, are *nondeterministic*. In other words, they are based on random events and, in general, if we run the same configuration twice, we will obtain two different results. So, the outcome of a single run is not significant, since it may have been produced by fortuitous events. To perform a fair comparison, what is needed is to execute the algorithms for a number of runs much larger than one, and base the comparison on statistics, calculated on the outcomes of those runs. The continuation of this section discusses how to organize such experiments, distinguishing between two cases:

- comparison of performance *against iterations*;
- comparison of performance *against computational effort*.

Comparison against iterations is the simpler of the two, and can be used *only* when the configurations we are comparing are executed for the same number of iterations and, at each iteration, they perform a comparable amount of computational effort. This type of comparison is discussed in Section 3.6.1. When a comparison against iterations cannot be made, the alternative is a comparison against computational effort, which is discussed in Section 3.6.2.

3.6.1 Comparison Against Iterations

As previously mentioned, this type of comparison can only be used when the configurations we are comparing are executed for the same number of iterations and, at each iteration, they perform a comparable amount of computational effort. In metaheuristic optimization algorithms, like the ones studied so far, it is a typical and reliable approximation to estimate the amount of computational effort spent in one iteration using the number of fitness evaluations that have been performed in that iteration. In fact, fitness evaluation is usually the most computationally expensive activity of those algorithms, and the other actions performed by the algorithm usually have a negligible effect on computational effort, compared to it. For instance,

Simulated Annealing usually performs one fitness evaluation per iteration (the solution that is evaluated is the chosen neighbor, which has to be compared with the current solution), while GAs perform n fitness evaluations per iteration, where n is the population size. So, for instance, two different configurations of Simulated Annealing, executed for the same number of iterations, can be compared with each other against iterations. Analogously, two different GA configurations, both using the same population size and left to evolve for the same number of generations, can be compared against iterations. A configuration of Particle Swarm Optimization (this algorithm will be studied in Chapter 4) and a GA configuration, using the same population size and left to evolve for the same number of generations, can also be compared against iterations. On the other hand, as we will clarify in the first part of Section 3.6.2, it is *incorrect* to compare against iterations, for instance, a configuration of Simulated Annealing executed for m iterations with a GA configuration with population size equal to $n > 1$, left to evolve for m generations. Analogously, it is incorrect to compare against iterations two GA configurations left to evolve for the same number of generations, but using two different population sizes.

To fix the ideas and discuss how a comparison of performance against iterations can be organized, let us assume from now on, just as a matter of example, that we are interested in comparing two different GA configurations $\mathscr{A}$ and $\mathscr{B}$, which use the same population size and are left to evolve for the same number of generations. For instance, $\mathscr{A}$ and $\mathscr{B}$ could differ from each other in using two different types of crossover, or two different rates of the genetic operators.

Let us assume that both $\mathscr{A}$ and $\mathscr{B}$ are left to evolve for four generations, and, in both cases, the experiment is repeated in three independent runs[7]. Let us assume that we are facing a minimization problem, where the globally optimal fitness value is equal to 0. For each one of the three runs of configuration $\mathscr{A}$, we report, at each iteration, the value of the fitness of the best individual in the population. Let us assume that the obtained results are the ones reported in Figure 3.11, where each of the tables reports the outcome of a different run.

Generations	Best Fitness
1	20
2	15
3	10
4	5

Generations	Best Fitness
1	18
2	13
3	12
4	10

Generations	Best Fitness
1	15
2	10
3	5
4	0

Fig. 3.11 Results obtained in three different independent runs by configuration $\mathscr{A}$ of the example used in this section. Each table reports the results obtained in a single run. For each generation, the best fitness value in the population is reported

---

[7] It is crucial, for the understanding of this section, that the reader clearly understands the difference between the concept of run and the concept of generation: a generation is an iteration of the GA, aimed at building a new population. A run indicates a complete execution of a GA evolution, from the moment at which the population is initialized, to the moment at which the process terminates and a final solution is returned. Obviously, the numbers used in this example (four generations and three runs) are toy quantities, which have been used only for the sake of simplicity; both need to be much larger in real experiments.

Let us now repeat the same set of experiments for configuration $\mathscr{B}$, and let us assume that the obtained results are the ones reported in Figure 3.12.

Generations	Best Fitness	Generations	Best Fitness	Generations	Best Fitness
1	18	1	20	1	10
2	17	2	10	2	5
3	16	3	3	3	2
4	12	4	0	4	0

Fig. 3.12 Results obtained in three different independent runs by configuration $\mathscr{B}$ of the example used in this section. Each table reports the results obtained in a single run. For each generation, the best fitness value in the population is reported

To compare the results of configurations $\mathscr{A}$ and $\mathscr{B}$, we can now calculate, for each generation of each run, a measure called the Average Best Fitness (ABF). It simply consists in computing the average of the best fitness obtained at a given generation, over all performed runs. The ABF results for configuration $\mathscr{A}$ are reported in Table 3.3. What is reported in Table 3.3 can be interpreted, in some senses, as a sort

Table 3.3 Using the data of Figure 3.11, we can obtain the ABF results for configuration $\mathscr{A}$ reported here

Generations	ABF
1	$\frac{20+18+15}{3} \approx 17.667$
2	$\frac{15+13+10}{3} \approx 12.667$
3	$\frac{10+12+5}{3} = 9$
4	$\frac{5+10+0}{3} = 5$

of "average run". The table has, in fact, the same dimensions as each one of the tables reporting the outcome of a single run, shown in Figure 3.11. The reader is invited to remark that, in order to obtain the results of Table 3.3, no calculation was performed using data coming from the same run, but only using data coming from different runs. The analogous ABF results for configuration $\mathscr{B}$ are reported in Table 3.4. At this point, the comparison between configurations $\mathscr{A}$ and $\mathscr{B}$ can be done in a visual way, by plotting in the same diagram the ABF of the two configurations for each generation, as in Figure 3.13. In some situations, it can be convenient to report the Median Best Fitness (MBF), instead of the ABF, because the median is more resistant to outliers than the average. Given that the plot of configuration $\mathscr{B}$ stands steadily below the plot of configuration $\mathscr{A}$, and given that we are facing a

Table 3.4 Using the data of Figure 3.12, we can obtain the ABF results for configuration $\mathscr{B}$ reported here

Generations	ABF
1	$\frac{18+20+10}{3} = 16$
2	$\frac{17+10+5}{3} \approx 10.67$
3	$\frac{16+3+2}{3} \approx 7$
4	$\frac{12+0+0}{3} = 4$

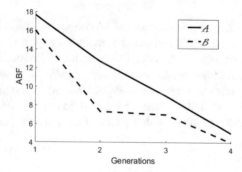

Fig. 3.13 A plot of the data of Table 3.3 and Table 3.4

minimization problem, the indication we receive from Figure 3.13 is that configuration $\mathscr{B}$ seems to outperform configuration $\mathscr{A}$.

However, in such a situation, it is *mandatory* to assess the statistical significance of the results. What we want is to understand whether the differences between the results obtained by the two configurations are statistically significant or not. This can be obtained using several different statistical tests. Furthermore, in principle, single different tests can be performed at each generation, even though it is typical to run the tests only at termination (i.e., at the last performed generation). The first test that should be executed is aimed at understanding whether the data are normally distributed or not. This can be done, for instance, using the Kolmogorov-Smirnov test [Massey, 1951, Dodge, 2008]. If the data are normally distributed, a parametric test such as the Student's t-test can be used. In the opposite situation, i.e., when data are not normally distributed, which is also the most frequent situation when analyzing experimental results coming from a set of independent runs, it is mandatory to use nonparametric tests, such as, for instance, the Mann-Whitney test, the Kruskal-Wallis test, the Friedman test or, most typically, the Wilcoxon rank-sum test for pairwise data comparison [Rey and Neuhäuser, 2011]. An explanation of these tests is beyond the scope of this book, but the interested reader is referred, for instance, to [Lovric, 2011] for a deep introduction. In addition, a plot like the one in Figure 3.13 could be equipped with standard deviations at each generation, if the ABF is reported, or with boxplots [Benjamini, 1988] at termination, if the MBF is reported.

The ABF and MBF give a visual understanding of the performance of an algorithm, or algorithm configuration, in a "typical" run, but do not say anything about the ability to find globally optimal solutions, or reasonable approximations to them. On the other hand, in many situations, this is interesting information. This information can be captured by another measure, called the Success Rate (SR), which can be studied in conjunction with ABF and MBF, to give a more complete picture of the experimental results. SR is defined as follows:

$$SR = \frac{\#\text{successful runs}}{\#\text{performed runs}} \tag{3.16}$$

where, according to the situation, a run can be considered successful if the global optimum has been found, or if a solution that reasonably approximates a global optimum has been found. In the latter case, the maximum difference between a fitness value and the optimal fitness needed to consider a solution a "reasonable" approximation to a global optimum must be defined beforehand. In the previous example, assuming that 0 is the globally optimal fitness and that a run is successful only if a global optimum was found, if we apply Equation (3.16) to configurations $\mathscr{A}$ and $\mathscr{B}$, we obtain:

$$SR(\mathscr{A}) = \frac{1}{3}$$

$$SR(\mathscr{B}) = \frac{2}{3}$$

When, as in this example, a configuration, like $\mathscr{B}$, is better than another configuration, like $\mathscr{A}$, both using ABF or MBF and SR, we can confidently conclude that $\mathscr{B}$ is preferable to $\mathscr{A}$. However, these measures do not necessarily return consistent results, and if not, the choice of the best configuration can be not trivial. Finally, it worth pointing out that it is not always possible to calculate SR, because a globally optimal solution, or any reasonable approximation, may never be found in any of the performed runs.

3.6.2 Comparison Against Computational Effort

Let us consider, now, a comparison between two configurations of GAs $\mathscr{A}$ and $\mathscr{B}$ that use two different population sizes. This is just one of the numerous examples in which the comparison cannot be done against the number of generations. In fact, it is clear that the computational cost of performing one generation is bigger for the model that uses the larger population. Just to fix the ideas, let us assume that model $\mathscr{A}$ uses a population size of six individuals, while model $\mathscr{B}$ uses a population size of three individuals. If we consider the number of fitness evaluations as an appropriate surrogate of the computational effort, which is customary for optimization metaheuristics, it is clear that performing one generation of model $\mathscr{A}$ costs twice as much as performing one generation of model $\mathscr{B}$. In fact, the population of model $\mathscr{A}$ contains twice as many individuals as the population of model $\mathscr{B}$.

To fairly compare the performance of model $\mathscr{A}$ and model $\mathscr{B}$, all we have to do is to store, at each run and for each generation, together with the generation number and the ABF, also the cumulative number of fitness evaluations that the model has executed until that generation. Considering that the number of fitness evaluations at each generation is, with a few exceptions that can be ignored, equal to the number of individuals in the population, we simply have to add the population size to this cumulative counter, at each generation. Also, the two models have to be executed for a number of generations that allows us to obtain the same number of fitness evaluations at the end. So, in our case, model $\mathscr{B}$ has to be executed for twice as many generations as model $\mathscr{A}$.

Let us give a numeric example that should clarify the issue. Let us assume, again, that we are solving a minimization problem where the globally optimal fitness is equal to zero. Also, let us assume that we execute the two models for three runs each. Finally, let us assume that model $\mathscr{A}$ is evolved for three generations[8]. Let the results obtained by model $\mathscr{A}$ be the ones stored in the tables in Figure 3.14. Remark

Generations	Best Fitness	# Fit. Eval.
1	20	6
2	15	12
3	10	18

Generations	Best Fitness	# Fit. Eval.
1	18	6
2	13	12
3	12	18

Generations	Best Fitness	# Fit. Eval.
1	15	6
2	10	12
3	5	18

Fig. 3.14 Results obtained in three independent runs of configuration $\mathscr{A}$ of the example used in this Section 3.6.2. Each table reports the results obtained in a single run

the third column of these tables: it contains the cumulative number of fitness evaluations, and it is obtained simply by adding the population size at each generation.

Now, let the results obtained by model $\mathscr{B}$ be the ones stored in the tables of Figure 3.15. Remark, once again, that model $\mathscr{B}$ was executed for a number of generations that is twice that of model $\mathscr{A}$, which allows us to terminate with the same cumulative number of fitness evaluations.

---

[8] Once again, these are just toy values used for the sake of simplicity in this example. Much larger numbers have to be employed in real experiments.

Generations	Best Fitness	# Fit. Eval.
1	22	3
2	18	6
3	15	9
4	13	12
5	11	15
6	9	18

Generations	Best Fitness	# Fit. Eval.
1	19	3
2	16	6
3	14	9
4	13	12
5	12	15
6	11	18

Generations	Best Fitness	# Fit. Eval.
1	18	3
2	12	6
3	10	9
4	7	12
5	4	15
6	2	18

Fig. 3.15 Results obtained in three independent runs of configuration $\mathcal{B}$ of the example used in this Section 3.6.2. Each table reports the results obtained in a single run

Now, for both models, we calculate the averages of the second and third columns at each generation. For model $\mathcal{A}$ we have the results reported in Table 3.5, and for model $\mathcal{B}$ we have the results reported in Table 3.6.

Table 3.5 Using the data of Figure 3.14, we can obtain the average results for configuration $\mathcal{A}$ reported here.

Generations	ABF	# Fit. Eval.
1	$\frac{20+18+15}{3} \approx 17.667$	6
2	$\frac{15+13+10}{3} \approx 12.667$	12
3	$\frac{10+12+5}{3} = 9$	18

Finally, to draw the curves of the ABF, instead of plotting the first column against the second, we simply plot the third column against the second. In other words, we report the cumulative number of fitness evaluations on the horizontal axis, and the ABF on the vertical axis. The curves are reported in Figure 3.16. Notice that, for the sake of clarity, only the part in which both curves are present, i.e., for the number of evaluations between 6 and 18, has been reported in the figure. Also, it is important to remark that, if the same number of generations had been performed for both models, say three generations, and the results were reported against generations, the model with the better performance would have appeared to be $\mathcal{A}$. In fact, model $\mathcal{A}$ obtained a better (i.e., smaller) ABF in the first three generations. But this compari-

Table 3.6 Using the data of Figure 3.15, we can obtain the average results for configuration $\mathscr{B}$ reported here

Generations	ABF	# Fit. Eval.
1	$\frac{22+19+18}{3} \approx 19.67$	3
2	$\frac{18+16+12}{3} \approx 15.33$	6
3	$\frac{15+14+10}{3} = 13$	9
4	$\frac{13+13+7}{3} = 11$	12
5	$\frac{11+12+4}{3} = 9$	15
6	$\frac{9+11+2}{3} \approx 7.33$	18

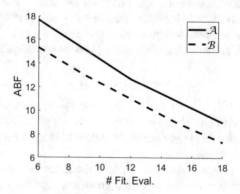

Fig. 3.16 A plot of the data of Table 3.5 and Table 3.6

son would have been *wrong*. The correct comparison of ABF against computational effort tells us, instead, that model $\mathscr{B}$ outperforms model $\mathscr{A}$.

Before terminating this section, it is important to point out that also a comparison between a population-based approach like GAs and Simulated Annealing[9] needs to be done against computational effort. In fact, Simulated Annealing processes one solution at each iteration, and so performs one fitness evaluation at each iteration. So, if we want to produce tables like the ones in Figure 3.15 for Simulated Annealing, the third column has to be increment by just one unit at each iteration. Also, if Simulated Annealing is compared, say, to a GA that evolves a population of p individuals for g generations, Simulated Annealing must be executed for $p \times g$ iterations, in order to have the same cumulative number of fitness evaluations at the end.

---

[9] The same reasoning holds for all comparisons between any population-based metaheuristic and any metaheuristic that does not use a population, and processes one solution at each iteration.

3.7 Genetic Algorithms for Continuous Optimization

Continuous optimization is a very frequent class of problems, with numerous real-life applications. Just as an example, one may consider the optimization of the parameters of a device, or even the parameters of another algorithm. Even though several of the concepts studied so far in this chapter apply also to continuous optimization, some of the methods and examples were specific for discrete optimization, i.e., for the case in which the individuals are strings of characters extracted from a discrete alphabet. Some characteristics of GAs can to be changed/improved when the possible set of values of the alleles are extracted from a continuous set (like for instance the set of the real numbers $\mathbb{R}$). Specifically, more effective genetic operators can be defined. In fact, it is not hard to imagine that standard GA crossover may be particularly weak when it comes to continuous optimization: by just swapping substrings, it is not able to generate new values for the alleles, and this largely limits the exploration ability of the algorithm. Before studying more effective operators, let us first define the continuous optimization problem.

In continuous optimization, individuals (i.e., feasible solutions) are vectors of the following shape:

$$\mathbf{x} = [x_1, x_2, ..., x_m]$$

where, for each $i = 1, 2, ..., m$, $x_i \in \mathbb{R}$ and $x_i \in [\alpha_i, \beta_i]$. In other words, the value of each allele has a well-defined and *a priory* known range of variation. It is worth pointing out that, under these hypotheses, an individual can be interpreted as a point in m-dimensional Cartesian space.

Several types of genetic operators can be defined for continuous optimization. Possibly, the best known are the so-called geometric operators [Moraglio, 2008]. Geometric crossover works as follows: given two parents $[x_1, x_2, ..., x_m]$ and $[y_1, y_2, ..., y_m]$, it generates only one offspring, defined as:

$$[r_1 x_1 + (1 - r_1) y_1, \ r_2 x_2 + (1 - r_2) y_2, \ ..., \ r_m x_m + (1 - r_m) y_m]$$

where, for each $i = 1, 2, ..., m$, r_i is a random number extracted with uniform distribution from the interval $[0, 1]$. The reason why this operator is called "geometric" is that, if individuals are interpreted as points in Cartesian space, the offspring has precise geometric characteristics compared to the parents. More specifically, in the particular case in which all the r_is are identical to each other, the offspring stands in the segment joining the parents. This geometric property has an important consequence: if fitness (to be minimized) is directly proportional to the distance to a global optimum, then the offspring cannot be worse than the worst of the parents. This is shown by the example in Figure 3.17, where $m = 2$ for simplicity, and where we can clearly see that the offspring is closer to the reported global optimum than Parent 1.

Geometric semantic mutation (also called ball mutation or box mutation) works as follows: given an individual $[x_1, x_2, ..., x_m]$, it generates an individual defined as:

$$[x_1 + r_1, \ x_2 + r_2, \ ..., \ x_m + r_m]$$

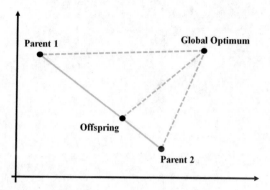

Fig. 3.17 A graphical representation of the effect of geometric crossover, in the simple two-dimensional case

where, for each $i = 1, 2, ..., m$, r_i is a random number drawn with uniform distribution from the interval $[-ms, ms]$, where ms is a parameter of the algorithm called the *mutation step*. In simple terms, geometric mutation consists in a (usually small) random perturbation of the values of the alleles of an individual, where the importance of this perturbation can be tuned by means of a parameter. As Figure 3.18 shows for $m = 2$, geometric mutation can generate any point inside a "box" centered at $[x_1, x_2, ..., x_m]$. Since the offspring can appear in any position inside the box,

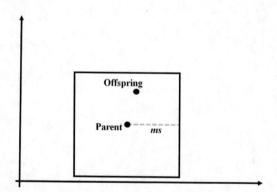

Fig. 3.18 A graphical representation of the effect of geometric mutation (box mutation), in the simple two-dimensional case

it is always possible that geometric mutation generates an offspring that is closer to a global optimum compared to the parent. This implies that, if fitness (to be minimized) is directly proportional to the distance to a global optimum, geometric mutation induces a unimodal fitness landscape (i.e., a fitness landscape of no local optima, except for the global ones).

Chapter 4
Particle Swarm Optimization

Particle Swarm Optimization (PSO) [Kennedy, 2010, Kennedy and Eberhart, 1995] is an optimization algorithm designed for continuous optimization. Like GAs, it is a population-based stochastic method, but unlike GAs it does not take its inspiration from the Theory of Evolution of Darwin, but from the social behavior of bird flocking or fish schooling [Reynolds, 1987]. For instance, one may imagine a flock of birds flying over an area, to find a point to land. In such a situation, defining where the whole swarm should land is a complex problem, since it depends on many pieces of information, such as, for instance, maximizing the availability of food or minimizing the risk of existence of predators. In this context, one can interpret the movement of the birds as a sort of choreography: the birds synchronically move for a period until the best place to land is defined and all the flock lands at once. Given this natural inspiration, PSO is usually not categorized as belonging to the field of Evolutionary Computation, but to the field of Swarm Intelligence.

4.1 The Algorithm

PSO shares many similarities with Evolutionary Computation techniques, such as GAs. For instance, the system is initialized with a population of random solutions and searches for optimal solutions by updating iterations. However, unlike GAs, PSO is not based on the concept of natural selection and does not explore the search space using operators such as crossover and mutation. In PSO, we can imagine that the potential solutions, called particles, "move" through the problem space, mimicking the dynamics of a flock of birds. Several studies have indicated that all birds of a flock searching for a good point to land have a memory of previous points they visited and tend to follow the lead of one of the flock's members. In other words, each member of the flock balances its individual and its swarm knowledge experience, known as social knowledge. While in the natural scenario the quality of a point for the birds to land is quantified by an estimation of the probability of survival, in PSO all solutions have a quality value that is given by the fitness function to be optimized.

© Springer Nature Switzerland AG 2023
L. Vanneschi and S. Silva, *Lectures on Intelligent Systems*, Natural Computing Series,
https://doi.org/10.1007/978-3-031-17922-8_4

Furthermore, PSO uses the concept of velocity, which directs the movement of the particles. Each PSO solution iteratively updates its position, influenced by its "best so far" achieved position and the swarm's current best position. In order to better understand the process, let us first fix some basic concepts and terminology.

- Following the definition of continuous optimization problem given on page 102, individuals of PSO (also called *particles*) are m-dimensional vectors of real numbers.
- A population (also called a *swarm*) is an n-dimensional vector of particles.
- For each $i = 1, 2, ..., n$ we use the notation $\mathbf{x}_i$ to indicate the ith particle of the swarm.
- For each $i = 1, 2, ..., n$ and for each $j = 1, 2, ..., m$, we use the notation x_{ij} to indicate the jth coordinate of the ith particle of the swarm.
- For each $i = 1, 2, ..., n$ we use the notation $\mathbf{v}_i$ to indicate the velocity of the ith particle of the swarm.
- For each $i = 1, 2, ..., n$ and for each $j = 1, 2, ..., m$, we use the notation v_{ij} to indicate the jth coordinate of the velocity of the ith particle of the swarm.
- For each $i = 1, 2, ..., n$ we use the notation $\mathbf{b}_i$ to indicate the best position (i.e., the position with the best fitness) ever reached by the ith particle of the swarm since the beginning of the execution of the algorithm. This position is also called the *local best* of the ith particle of the swarm.
- For each $i = 1, 2, ..., n$ and for each $j = 1, 2, ..., m$, we use the notation b_{ij} to indicate the jth coordinate of the local best of the ith particle of the swarm.
- We use the notation $\mathbf{g}$ to indicate the best position ever reached by any particle of the swarm, since the beginning of the execution of the algorithm. This position is also called the *global best*.
- For each $j = 1, 2, ..., m$, we use the notation g_j to indicate the jth coordinate of the best position ever reached by any particle of the swarm.

We have that:

$$\forall i = 1, 2, ..., n : \mathbf{x}_i \in \mathbb{R}^m \text{ (particle)}, \ \mathbf{v}_i \in \mathbb{R}^m \text{ (velocity)}, \ \mathbf{b}_i \in \mathbb{R}^m \text{ (local best)}$$

Furthermore:

$$\mathbf{g} \in \mathbb{R}^m \text{ (global best)}$$

Finally, the fitness function f returns a real number for each particle, so:

$$f : \mathbb{R}^m \to \mathbb{R}$$

With this in mind, we are now ready to study the general functioning of PSO. Algorithm 6 presents the pseudocode of PSO for the case of minimization problems. In that algorithm:

- w is a parameter, called the *inertia constant*;

Algorithm 6: The pseudocode for Particle Swarm Optimization, in the case of a minimization problem.

---

1. $\forall i = 1, 2, ..., n$: initialize $\mathbf{x}_i$ and $\mathbf{v}_i$;
2. $\forall i = 1, 2, ..., n$: $\mathbf{b}_i := \mathbf{x}_i$;
3. $\mathbf{g} = \operatorname{argmin}_{\mathbf{x}_i} f(\mathbf{x}_i)$, $\forall i = 1, 2, ..., n$;
4. **repeat until** (termination condition)

    4.1. **for** each $i = 1, 2, ..., n$ **do**
        4.1.1. $\mathbf{x}_i := \mathbf{x}_i + \mathbf{v}_i$;
        4.1.2. $\mathbf{v}_i := w\,\mathbf{v}_i \; + \; c_1\,\mathbf{r}_1 \circ (\mathbf{b}_i - \mathbf{x}_i) \; + \; c_2\,\mathbf{r}_2 \circ (\mathbf{g} - \mathbf{x}_i)$;
        4.1.3. **if** $(f(\mathbf{x}_i) < f(\mathbf{b}_i))$ **then** $\mathbf{b}_i := \mathbf{x}_i$;
        4.1.4. **if** $(f(\mathbf{x}_i) < f(\mathbf{g}))$ **then** $\mathbf{g} := \mathbf{x}_i$;
        end

  end

5. **return g;**

- c_1 and c_2 are two parameters, called the *cognitive component* and *social component*, respectively;
- $\mathbf{r}_1$ and $\mathbf{r}_2$ are two m-dimensional vectors of random numbers drawn at every different velocity update event, uniformly from the $[0, 1]$ interval;
- the symbol $\circ$ represents the operator of element by element multiplication between two vectors.

Let us now comment on the pseudocode line by line, in order to understand every detail. Lines 1, 2 and 3 initialize the main employed structures. In particular, line 1 initializes the positions and the velocities of all the particles in the swarm. Generally, the particle positions $\mathbf{x}_i$ are initialized randomly. More precisely, for each $i = 1, 2, ..., n$ and for each $j = 1, 2, ..., m$, x_{ij} is initialized with a random number drawn with uniform probability from interval $[\alpha_j, \beta_j]$[1]. Also, it is customary to initialize all the velocities at zero ($\mathbf{v}_i := \mathbf{0}$). Line 2 initializes the local best of each particle to the current position (which is also the only position that the particle has occupied so far), while line 3 initializes the global best to the particle with the best fitness in the initial swarm. Lines 4 and 4.1 represent the beginning of the main loops that characterize the algorithm. Line 4 represents the beginning of the external loop, which is repeated until a termination condition is achieved. As is customary in optimization metaheuristics, usually the termination condition is that a global optimum (or a reasonable approximation of it) has been found, or a previously fixed maximum number of iterations has been executed. Line 4.1 represents the beginning of the internal loop, indicating a repetition of the same actions for each particle in the swarm. The actions that are executed are represented by lines 4.1.1 to 4.1.4. Line 4.1.1 modifies the position of each particle, by simply adding the current value

---

[1] Following the definition of continuous optimization problem given on page 102, usually each coordinate j of the position vectors of the particles has an *a priori* known range of variation $[\alpha_j, \beta_j]$.

of its velocity. This step is useless the first time if the velocity is initialized to zero. Line 4.1.2 modifies the velocity, and it is probably the hardest point to understand in this algorithm. Basically, the new velocity is determined by the sum of three components:

- $w\,\mathbf{v}_i$: this term tends to maintain the movement of the particle in the same direction as in the previous iteration;
- $c_1\,\mathbf{r}_1 \circ (\mathbf{b}_i - \mathbf{x}_i)$: this term tends to let the particle move towards the position of its own local best (cognitive term);
- $c_2\,\mathbf{r}_2 \circ (\mathbf{g} - \mathbf{x}_i)$: this term tends to let the particle move towards the position of the global best of the swarm (social term).

The respective importance of these three terms can be tuned by setting the three parameters w, c_1 and c_2. However, it should be noticed that both the cognitive and the social term have a random component, which can potentially be different for each one of the coordinates, and which bestows stochasticity on the algorithm. Finally, points 4.1.3 and 4.1.4 update the local best and the global best, respectively, if better solutions than the current ones were found. The final step of the algorithm, point 5, returns the current global best as the final result of the search.

The reader should notice that the algorithm is highly parallelizable. In particular, loop 4.1 executes the same action for all the particles independently, and with only one point of synchronization when it comes to updating the global best (point 4.1.4). All the other actions, including the update of the position, the update of the velocity and the calculation of the fitness of the new position (which is typically the most expensive operation, in terms of computational resources) can be run in parallel for each particle, since no synchronization is needed. Furthermore, the parallelism grain can even be finer, i.e., at the level of the single vector coordinates. In fact, the position and velocity update are vectorial operations that can be executed coordinate by coordinate independently. In other words, loop 4.1 could be rewritten as:

> **for** each $i = 1, 2, ..., n$ **do**
>   **for** each $j = 1, 2, ..., m$ **do**
> $x_{ij} := x_{ij} + v_{ij}$;
> $v_{ij} := w\,v_{ij} \;+\; c_1\,r_1\,(b_{ij} - x_{ij}) \;+\; c_2\,r_2\,(g_j - x_{ij})$;
>   **end**
>   **if** $(f(\mathbf{x}_i) < f(\mathbf{b}_i))$ **then**
>   **for** each $j = 1, 2, ..., m$ **do** $b_{ij} := x_{ij}$;
>   **if** $(f(\mathbf{x}_i) < f(\mathbf{g}))$ **then**
>   **for** each $j = 1, 2, ..., m$ **do** $g_j := x_{ij}$;
> **end**

where r_1 and r_2 are random numbers (scalars) extracted with uniform distribution from the $[0, 1]$ interval. The possibility of parallelizing PSO both at the particle level and at the coordinate level makes the algorithm potentially very efficient. Given that the calculations are mostly vectorial operations, PSO is particularly suitable for implementation using Graphic Processing Units (GPUs), which typically makes the algorithm even faster.

As is typical of all the techniques discussed in this book, the pseudocode in Algorithm 6 has to be interpreted just as a general guideline, and several extensions and specifications need to be added when it comes to actually implementing the method. For instance, one has to decide a strategy to "force" the algorithm to respect the limitation of the values of each coordinate position j to the predefined range $[\alpha_j, \beta_j]$. A possibility, whenever Equation 4.1.1 of Algorithm 6 tends to exceed a margin, is to set the value of the coordinate to the margin itself and to invert the sign of the velocity, or reinitialize it to zero, or to a random number. Reinitialization of the position coordinate with a random number in $[\alpha_j, \beta_j]$ is also an option. For instance, if the strategy of setting the coordinate to the margin and inverting the sign of the velocity is adopted, the previous portion of pseudocode could be extended to:

> **for** each $i = 1, 2, ..., n$ **do**
>   **for** each $j = 1, 2, ..., m$ **do**
> $x_{ij} := x_{ij} + v_{ij}$;
>   **if** $x_{ij} < \alpha_j$ **then**
> $x_{ij} := \alpha_j$;
> $v_{ij} := -v_{ij}$;
>   **else if** $x_{ij} > \beta_j$ **then**
> $x_{ij} := \beta_j$;
> $v_{ij} := -v_{ij}$;
>   **else**
> $v_{ij} := w\, v_{ij} + c_1\, r_1\, (b_{ij} - x_{ij}) + c_2\, r_2\, (g_j - x_{ij})$;
>   **end**
>   **end**
>   **if** $(f(\mathbf{x}_i) < f(\mathbf{b}_i))$ **then**
>   **for** each $j = 1, 2, ..., m$ **do** $b_{ij} := x_{ij}$;
>   **if** $(f(\mathbf{x}_i) < f(\mathbf{g}))$ **then**
>   **for** each $j = 1, 2, ..., m$ **do** $g_j := x_{ij}$;
> **end**

4.2 Parameter Setting

The choice of PSO parameters can have a large impact on optimization effectiveness. Choosing appropriate parameter values is a complex task that has been the subject of much research. The PSO parameters can be tuned by using another optimization algorithm, or fine-tuned before or during the optimization. Like for any other optimization metaheuristics, appropriate PSO parameter values are highly problem dependent. However, some simple rules of thumb can be discussed. These guidelines have to be interpreted only as suggestions to practitioners, and can by no means replace parameter tuning. While the dimensions of the particles (m in the previous section) and the range of the different coordinates are usually determined by the problem, concerning the swarm size (i.e., the number of employed particles), it is typical to have significantly smaller values compared to GA populations. A typical range may be 20 to 40 particles, even though for simple problems even smaller values, like for instance 10 particles, can be large enough to get good results, and for some difficult or special problems, one may need larger values, like 100 or 200 particles. The other side of the coin is that in PSO, it is typical to run the algorithm for a larger number of iterations, compared to GAs: from several thousands of iterations to even millions of iterations in the case of parallel and GPU-based implementations.

The learning factors (c_1 and c_2) and inertia weight (w) are probably the hardest parameters to set. A common practice is to start the tuning by using values equal (or "close") to 2 for c_1 and c_2 and close to 1 for w, values that have been shown to be appropriate for several applications. However, other settings were also used in different papers. Even though exceptions can exist, appropriate values for c_1 and c_2 typically range from 0 to 4. Furthermore, it is possible to also introduce another parameter, which is the maximum possible velocity. This can be an appropriate practice in some cases, to avoid too-large "jumps" of the positions of the particles in the search space. When it is used, a typical value for the maximum velocity for each coordinate j is the magnitude of the variation of the position in that dimension. In other words, if the particle position has a variation range in $[\alpha_j, \beta_j]$ for coordinate j, one may set the maximum velocity for that coordinate to $\beta_j - \alpha_j$. A method to force the algorithm to respect this limitation, for instance, can consist in resetting a coordinate of the velocity to zero whenever Equation 4.1.2 in Algorithm 6 tends to exceed the maximum velocity, or to choose a random value between 0 to the maximum velocity.

4.3 Variants

Several variants of the basic PSO algorithm are possible [Cagnoni et al., 2008], and some of them have already been discussed in the previous section. For instance, one may imagine that each method employed to force the algorithm to respect the interval of variation of the position coordinates or to remain within the maximum possible velocity is, in itself, a variant. Besides this, given the clear analogies between PSO and GAs, a lot of effort has been dedicated by researchers to the idea of generating hybrid versions, integrating PSO and GAs into a unique algorithm. If, on the one hand, the update of the position of the particles can be seen as a particular type of mutation, on the other hand it is clear that selection and crossover are completely absent in PSO. The idea of enriching PSO with selection and crossover has been explored, for instance, in [Miranda and Fonseca, 2002, Garg, 2016]. Furthermore, attempts to integrate PSO with other optimization algorithms have been presented, for instance, in [Krink and Løvbjerg, 2002, Niknam and Amiri, 2010, Zhang and Xie, 2003]. Other research trends consist in using multiple swarms [Vanneschi et al., 2011, Cheung et al., 2014] and multiobjective optimization [Nobile et al., 2012].

Various simplified variants of PSO have been presented, for instance in [Bratton and Blackwell, 2008, Pedersen and Chipperfield, 2010]. Last but not least, PSO has been extended to discrete optimization. A commonly used method is to map the discrete search space to a continuous domain, to apply a classical PSO, and then to demap the result. Such a mapping can be very simple (for example by just using rounded values) or more sophisticated [Roy et al., 2011]. Different approaches for using PSO for discrete optimization were presented, for instance, in [Kennedy and Eberhart, 1997, Clerc, 2004, Jarboui et al., 2008, Chen et al., 2010].

Part II
Machine Learning

Chapter 5
Introduction to Machine Learning

As already discussed in Chapter 1, Machine Learning (ML) [Mitchell, 1997, Shalev-Shwartz and Ben-David, 2014] is a field of study whose objective is to program computers to automatically learn to solve a problem, or accomplish a task. ML is useful when manually programming a computer to carry out a task is either impractical or infeasible. Typical cases are either problems that are so complex that they are beyond human capabilities, like those characterized by vast amounts of data, or tasks that living beings perform routinely, but our introspection on how we do it is not sufficiently elaborated to allow us to extract a well-defined algorithm, for instance driving, speech recognition, image understanding or client categorization. Other tasks where ML is useful are those where adaptability to changes in the environment is a necessary requirement, for instance time series forecasting, handwritten text decoding or spam detection. In its most accepted definition:

> "Machine Learning is the study of algorithms that automatically improve by means of experience" [Mitchell, 1997].

In this definition, *learning* is intended as *improving by means of experience*. Even though the term "learning" can have several meanings and interpretations, we believe that "improving by means of experience" is one of the most intuitive and is close to our everyday experience. For instance, it includes the idea of "trial and error", which is very often implemented by many living beings when they are about to learn how to solve new tasks: learning often implies numerous consecutive attempts (or trials) to solve the task. If a trial gives a positive result, it will be rewarded by similar future trials; on the other hand, if a trial gives a negative result, it is customary to identify it with an erroneous behavior, and thus not repeat it in the future attempts. Iterating the process, the trials should become more and more effective with time, until the task gets solved. A simple example consists in the method rats use to select food: when rats encounter a food item with a new look and smell, they will first eat a small amount of it. According to the flavor and the physiological effect of the food, the rats will later decide whether they eat more or not. If the food produces an ill effect, that food will be associated with illness, and not eaten again. If it tastes good and does not produce any negative effect on the health of the rat, it

© Springer Nature Switzerland AG 2023
L. Vanneschi and S. Silva, *Lectures on Intelligent Systems*, Natural Computing Series,
https://doi.org/10.1007/978-3-031-17922-8_5

will probably be eaten again. Also human beings often use trial and error to learn tasks. For instance, a person that is learning how to play tennis will probably try to hit the ball by performing particular movements of the arms, shoulders and legs. Those movements will be identified as effective or erroneous, according to the result of the shot, and this result will affect the next attempts to hit the ball. As a last example of how much trial and error is used by humans for learning new tasks, students that have recently attended an introductory programming course surely agree that many wrong attempts, with subsequent mistake identifications and adaptations, were needed before they became able to write correct computer programs.

This process is what has inspired the introduction of the field of ML. But what exactly do we want machines to learn? Even though it is impossible to give general definitions to cover such a vast field as ML, we believe that we can cover the large majority of the situations by saying that one of the most frequent objectives of ML is *learning a function*. In many such situations, ML is dealing with a problem that can be defined as follows. Given a set of data pairs:

$$D = \{(\mathbf{x}_1, y_1), (\mathbf{x}_2, y_2), ..., (\mathbf{x}_n, y_n)\},$$

the objective is to find (or approximate) a function (or relation) ϕ, such that:

$$\forall i = 1, 2, ..., n : \phi(\mathbf{x}_i) = y_i$$

In the most general definition, $\mathbf{x}_i$ and y_i can be *any* kind of object (numbers, vectors, matrices, expressions, images, movies, sentences, other objects from the real world, etc.), however the most typical situation is the one in which the $\mathbf{x}_i$ are m-dimensional vectors of objects of any type (including, but not necessarily, numbers), while the y_i are scalar values. This can be represented in a matrix as:

$$D = \begin{bmatrix} x_{11} & x_{12} & ... & x_{1m} & y_1 \\ x_{21} & x_{22} & ... & x_{2m} & y_2 \\ ... & ... & ... & ... & ... \\ x_{n1} & x_{n2} & ... & x_{nm} & y_n \end{bmatrix}$$

Before having a closer look at the problem of learning, it is useful to fix some terminology:

- D is called a *dataset*;
- For each $i = 1, 2, ..., n$, line $\{x_{i1}, x_{i2}, ..., x_{im}\}$ is an input vector, *instance*, *observation*, sample point or just *sample*, and y_i is the corresponding *target*;
- For each $j = 1, 2, ..., m$, column $\{x_{1j}, x_{2j}, ..., x_{nj}\}$ represents a *feature*, corresponding to an *independent variable*, and for each $i = 1, 2, ..., n$, element x_{ij} is a feature value; column $\{y_1, y_2, ..., y_n\}$ is the target vector, corresponding to the *dependent variable*;
- the sought for function ϕ, i.e., the function that perfectly matches all possible data in the input domain to the corresponding targets, is called the *target function*;
- *learning* is a process that allows us to obtain a function f that approximates the target function ϕ;

- function f, i.e., the function obtained as a result of the learning process, is called a *data model*, or simply *model*;
- finally, we will talk of *supervised* learning (and supervised dataset) if the target values $\{y_1, y_2, ..., y_n\}$ are known for each observation, and *unsupervised* learning (and unsupervised dataset) otherwise; a supervised dataset may also be called a *labeled* dataset.

Last but not least, we will say that model f has a good *generalization ability* if f behaves like the target function ϕ also for data that do not belong to D. Understanding whether a model has a good generalization ability can be a hard task, because, of course, in general the target function ϕ is not known *a priori* and cannot be extrapolated by simply looking at the data. Actually, in some senses, we could even say that ϕ is not even an existing function, but more the *concept*, the *logic*, or the *underlying knowledge* that allowed a given entity (a person, a device, etc.) to generate the data (Example 5.2 should clarify this). Furthermore, in some cases, several different functions can perfectly match the known data, and in such a situation, deciding which one is the target function is impossible, unless further data are provided. However, the concept of generalization is crucial to ML, and it is one of the major elements of distinction between ML and optimization: many ML algorithms, in fact, can be seen as optimization methods, given that they look for a model searching the space of all possible functions matching data from the input to the output domain. A fitness function may be considered as any measure quantifying how well a function approximates the target function ϕ on the known data D. However, ML has a further, strong, requirement: models must be general, i.e., work reasonably not only for data in D, but also for other data. The following examples should clarify the issue.

Example 5.1. (A "Toy" Numeric Example). Let us consider the following simple numeric dataset, where x_1 and x_2 are the features and y is the target vector:

$$D = \begin{array}{cc|c} x_1 & x_2 & y \\ \hline 1 & 8 & 9 \\ 3 & 2 & 5 \\ 4 & 1 & 5 \\ 7 & 3 & 10 \end{array}$$

And now we want to answer the question: "What is the target function?" Any attempt to answer this question in a formal way can only lead to the answer "I don't know", given that one may imagine several functions matching the data in D, and no information is given on how to choose among them. However, given the simplicity of this example, one could easily hypothesize that, in this case, the target function is the function that sums two numbers, in other words: $\phi(x_1, x_2) = x_1 + x_2$.

Now, let us assume that an ML system is able to find a model like:

$$f(x_1, x_2) = x_1 + x_2$$

It is obvious that now we can apply f to *any* pair of numbers, and not only the ones in D, and the result will be the sum of those numbers; for instance $f(2,6) = 8$. Let us, instead, assume that our ML system finds a model like:

$$g(x_1, x_2) = \begin{aligned} &\textbf{if } ((x_1 == 1) \ \& \ (x_2 == 8)) \textbf{ then return } 9; \\ &\textbf{else if } ((x_1 == 3) \ \& \ (x_2 == 2)) \textbf{ then return } 5; \\ &\textbf{else if } ((x_1 == 4) \ \& \ (x_2 == 1)) \textbf{ then return } 5; \qquad (5.1) \\ &\textbf{else if } ((x_1 == 7) \ \& \ (x_2 == 3)) \textbf{ then return } 10; \\ &\textbf{else return } \text{a random value}; \end{aligned}$$

If one looks at these two models f and g, it is not difficult to convince oneself that *both* of them work perfectly on the data in D, but (still in the hypothesis that $\phi(x_1, x_2) = x_1 + x_2$ is the target function) f is a perfect approximation of ϕ also for data that are not in D, while g has a completely different behavior: for each pair of input values that are not in D, the output of g will be identical/similar to the output of ϕ only in extremely rare and lucky cases. This is a typical situation in which we can say that f has a good generalization ability, while g does not. Furthermore, it is reasonably clear that the reason why g is not able to generalize seems to be *overfitting* (a concept that will be discussed more deeply later): g is clearly too "specialized" for the data in D, and thus lacks generality.

In general, we could say that the difference between having a good generalization ability and overfitting (which is the difference between f and g in this example) consists in the difference between inducing the knowledge that is hidden in the data (and coding that knowledge in the data model) and just mimicking/mocking what is written in the dataset. It is clearly the former behavior that we want our machines to have: using the data examples to create knowledge that goes beyond (i.e., is more general than) the examples themselves. In other words, we want our ML systems to *learn by examples* and not *learn the examples*.

On the opposite side of overfitting we have the less common *underfitting*, which happens when the model is so far from representing the data that it cannot even provide good predictions for the learning examples. In the example data above, over-simplistic models like $f(x_1, x_2) = x_1$ or $f(x_1, x_2) = 5$ would be underfitted[1]. A lack of generalization ability can be caused by either underfitting or overfitting.

Example 5.2. (A "Real-Life" Example). In this example, we discuss a real-life ML application, consisting in predicting the *toxicity* of a candidate new drug, a step that is an important part of the *drug discovery* process, i.e., the process of discovering and synthesizing a new drug. Studies of this application can be found in several bibliographic references, including, for instance, [Archetti et al., 2007]. Let us consider a dataset:

$$D = \{(\mathbf{x}_1, y_1), (\mathbf{x}_2, y_2), ..., (\mathbf{x}_n, y_n)\},$$

---

[1] Notice that a model of the data does not have to use all its features.

where, for each $i = 1, 2, ..., n$, vector $\mathbf{x}_i = \{x_{i1}, x_{i2}, ..., x_{im}\}$ represents a molecular compound that is a candidate to become a new drug, represented by means of its *molecular descriptors*, and y_i represents the corresponding value of the toxicity of that molecular compound.

Estimating the toxicity of a molecular compound is generally a very expensive and error-prone process. It is done by feeding a sample of test animals with incremental doses of the compound. The amount of compound that has been given when half of the subjects have died is one of the most used measures of toxicity, called the Median Lethal Dose (LD50). Imagine that this is the process that has been applied to create a dataset like D (for each molecular compound $i = 1, 2, ..., n$, 50% of the test animals have been killed in order to estimate the target value y_i!). The objective of ML is now to learn the hidden relationship (assuming it exists) between the molecular descriptors and the level of toxicity, coding it in a data model. In this way, whenever in the future there is the need to estimate the toxicity of a new molecular compound, we can simply apply the model to its molecular descriptors, thus not having to sacrifice any more test animals. At this point, two observations can be made:

1. The toxicity of new molecular compounds is unknown. As such, we have no way of verifying the correctness of the prediction of the model on those new data. The prediction made by the model needs to be *trusted*.

2. Generalization is not just important, it is the only thing that matters. Generating a solution that is able to predict the toxicity only for the compounds that are in the dataset is totally useless: we already know the toxicity of those compounds. What matters is that the model is able to generalize and return a reliable estimation for new compounds that are not in D.

Both these observations are not limited to the specific problem discussed in this example, but can be extended to practically all ML problems. The reader is particularly invited to reflect about the importance of Point 1. Pharmaceutical companies usually invest large amounts of money in the drug discovery process. If we want ML models to be *trusted*, we need to find a way to learn so that generalization is likely, or at least we need to be able to *test* the generalization ability of our models (this issue will be looked at more deeply later).

The ML process, at least in its most basic formulation, is illustrated in Figure 5.1. The process of applying an ML system to induce a model from a dataset is called the *learning* or *training* phase, while the process of applying the model on new data is called the *generalization* or *prediction* phase. The main objective of the next chapters of this book is to "open the box" named Machine Learning System, by studying several different ML algorithms. This is a crucial step, since the *No Free Lunch Theorem* (studied in Section 2.3, on page 19) also holds for ML and for generalization [Wolpert, 1996]. This allows us to "export" many of the consequences of this theorem (that we have already discussed for optimization) also to ML. In particular:

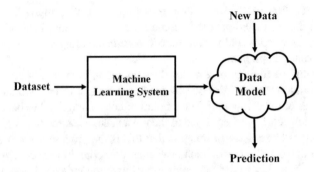

Fig. 5.1 Illustration of a simple ML process, in the case of supervised learning

- If averaged on all possible problems, all ML methods have the same generalization ability;

- There cannot exist a sort of "super ML method", that outperforms all the others on all the problems;

- Every time that we are faced with a new problem, the process of choosing the most appropriate method is a challenge;

- There cannot exist an automatic/formal way of choosing the most appropriate ML method to solve a problem, and thus the only way of making this choice is by means of heuristic/informal processes, typically based on our knowledge of the algorithms (and this is why it is important to know as many of them as possible), on a set of preliminary experiments, etc.

The learning problem discussed so far has two significant particular cases:

- *Classification*, in which the target values $y_1, y_2, ..., y_n$ have a discrete and "limited" codomain, and are called *labels* or *classes*;

- *Regression*, in which the target values $y_1, y_2, ..., y_n$ have a continuous, or "vast", codomain[2], and are called *expected outputs*.

Both these types of problems will be studied in this book, beginning with classification. In this case, the target values can be interpreted as classes, or groups, and the learning problem can be interpreted as the task of partitioning data into groups. Simple examples of classification problems can be, for instance: partitioning a set of images portraying faces into men and women, partitioning a text into English, French, Portuguese or Italian language, partitioning a set of numbers into small, medium and large, etc.

---

[2] The distinction between classification and regression can be fuzzy in some cases, and this is why we have deliberately based the definition on informal terms such as "limited" and "vast".

Partitioning data into groups can be a supervised or an unsupervised task. As mentioned earlier, in supervised learning the target values $y_1, y_2, ..., y_n$ are known and the objective is to find a function that maps the input data to those values. On the other hand, in unsupervised learning no target value is known, and thus the objective of the partitioning is to discover mutual similarities between objects, in such a way that similar data are categorized in the same group, while different data are categorized in different groups. These two approaches differ from each other also in the way new data are treated: in the case of supervised learning, the learned model f is applied to the new data, and the result is interpreted as a prediction (supervised learning is usually employed to generate *predictive models*). On the other hand, when the learning is unsupervised, the new datum is inserted in the group that contains the elements that are most similar to it (unsupervised learning is usually employed to generate *descriptive models*). These two approaches are so different from each other that different names exist to indicate them: when the learning is supervised, the problem of partitioning data into groups is called *classification*, while when it is unsupervised it is called *clustering*. In this chapter, only supervised learning will be studied, starting with classification. Clustering will be studied in Chapter 12.

Focusing on supervised learning, it is important to reassert that the generalization ability of our predictive models is an essential condition. For this reason, methods to experimentally verify the performance of predictive models on data that have not been used during training are much in demand. As we will see in the next section, in order to be reliable and fair, these methods can be very complex in some situations. However, all of them are based on a rather simple idea that can be summarized by the following steps:

- instead of learning (i.e., generating a model) using all available data D, do it using only a part of the available data; let $J \subset D$ be the subset of D used for learning.
- Use the remaining set of data $D - J$ to test the generated model. In other words:

  - evaluate the model on the input data of $D - J$;
  - compare the output obtained on the observations of $D - J$ with the corresponding target values.

In such a situation, any measure of error, dispersion or dissimilarity between calculated outputs and corresponding targets on $D - J$ may be interpreted as a measure of the generalization of the model. Put in simple terms, we are pretending that J is the only available set for learning, and we are treating the data in $D - J$ as data that are not available at learning time and for which the expected output is unknown; for instance, data that will be produced later, once the model has been obtained, and on which the model should be used to make predictions. However, the expected output of the observations of $D - J$ is actually known, and it is used to verify the performance of the model, after it has been generated. In other words, we say that J is used for *training* the model, while $D - J$ is used for *testing* it. In such a situation, the reader should not have any difficulty in understanding one basic and golden rule:

*There must be no intersection between the data used for learning the model
and the data used for testing it.*

Any exception to this golden rule always represents a serious mistake that has to
be interpreted as the developers either cheating or making fools of themselves, and
leads to completely irrelevant and unreliable results.

This idea of splitting the available data into different sets, in order to be able to
test the generality of the learned models, can be implemented in several ways. In the
next section, we provide an overview of the complete ML process that produces a
predictive model from a dataset. It is followed by other sections dedicated to specific
aspects of this process, and the chapter closes with the description of a few simple
yet powerful ML methods, for both classification and regression.

5.1 From Data to Model

Several steps are required from the moment we have a dataset until the point at
which we have a model that will perform predictions on related but unseen data
with a known expected error. These steps are divided into five main groups:

(1) Preprocessing the data
(2) Choosing the method and parameters
(3) Estimating the predictive error
(4) Inducing the final model
(5) Testing the final model

These five groups are not independent from one another. They may not even
be perfectly sequential. Figure 5.2 shows the steps, with an indication of the
group(s) that each step belongs to. While each step may belong to more than one
group, not all groups must always be part of the process. Some may be skipped for
various reasons, including lack of sufficient data, lack of time, or simply because
there is no demand for the complete process. For example, the goal may be simply
to estimate the predictive error of a hypothetical model of the data, without the need
for the model itself, in which case groups (4) and (5) would disappear, as well as
the steps belonging to them (**a**, **e**, **f** and **g1**); or, the method and its parameters may
already be defined, in which case group (2) would disappear, along with the steps
that only belong to this group (only step **b3**, while steps **b3i** and **b3ii** would remain
active). Naturally, some groups make no sense without others; for example, we do
not test (step **f**) or return (step **g1**) the final model unless we induce it (step **e**). There
is only one group without which the entire ML process becomes pointless: (3)
Estimating the predictive error. This estimation is a measure of the generalization
ability, and therefore the most important element in ML.

Before we continue, we clarify the terminology we adopt for the different sets
of data that are used in the ML process. Figure 5.3 illustrates the different data
partitions, linking them to the different steps of Figure 5.2. The entire initial dataset

a. Split reference data into learning data + test data (5)

b. **Repeat**
b1. Split the learning data into training data + validation data (1) (2)
b2. Select and process features in training data (1)
b3. **Repeat** for each method and set of parameters (2)
b3i. Fit a model to training data (1) (2)
b3ii. Measure error on validation data (1) (2)

c. Fix settings that minimize the average validation error (1) (2)

d. **Repeat**
d1. Split learning data into training data + validation data (3)
d2. Fit a model to training data using fixed settings (3)
d3. Measure error on validation data (3)

e. Fit a final model to the learning data using fixed settings (4)
f. Measure error of final model on test data (5)

g. **Return**
g1. Final model (4)
g2. Error estimate (3)

Fig. 5.2 Steps of an ML system, from the data to the final model. Each step belongs to one or more of the groups: (1) Preprocessing the data; (2) Choosing the method and parameters; (3) Estimating the predictive error; (4) Inducing the final model; (5) Testing the final model

is called the reference data. Step **a** of the ML process splits this dataset into learning data and test data, where the test data is meant to validate the final model, while the learning data is meant to be used for everything else. This learning data is further split into training and validation data, in steps **b1** and **d1**. The training part is always used for fitting a model, while the validation part is always used for measuring its error.

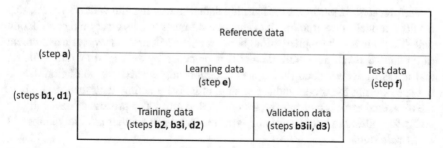

Fig. 5.3 Illustration of the data partitions to be used in the different steps of the ML process (Figure 5.2)

The reader should be aware that there is no full agreement in the literature regarding this terminology, or even regarding the correct sequence and nesting of steps of the ML process itself. For instance, it is common to find works in which the terms test data and validation data are exchanged compared to our terminology. Further-more, in most works the term learning data is not used. In those cases, often the learning set is identified as the training set, or outer training set, while different terminologies can be used to identify the equivalent to our training data, including the expression inner training set. In an ideal world of endless data, a different set of data would be used each time a model is induced and each time its error is measured, with all these sets being disjoint from each other. However, data is not endless, par-ticularly labeled data, which means that decisions must be taken on how to get the best predictive model from a limited set. The message to retain is that our decisions are not the only correct ones, and different decisions from ours are not necessarily wrong.

For the remainder of this section we will go through all the steps, briefly describ-ing their role in the context of their associated group(s), and providing pointers to the subsequent sections that address the most important aspects in further detail. We begin with the most important task: estimating the error.

5.1.1 Estimating the Predictive Error

Even if there is no need to provide a final predictive model, there is always the need to estimate the error of the *hypothetical* model that can be induced from the data. If this is the only task we want to perform, the entire ML process includes only steps **d**, **d1**, **d2**, **d3** and **g2**. In any case, even though this concept has already been presented in the previous section, it is worth reasserting that the most important rule to retain is:

> *The data used for measuring the error of a model cannot be the same data that was used for inducing the model.*

Therefore, step **d1** partitions the learning data into training and validation data, step **d2** fits a model to the training data and step **d3** measures its error on the validation data. This rule is to be applied throughout the entire ML process: every measurement of predictive error (steps **b3ii**, **d3** and **f**) is preceded by data splitting (steps **b1**, **d1** and **a**, respectively). Each time a new data partition is used, the validation data is not seen during the model induction step, effectively acting as unseen data where the measured error represents the generalization error. The process of data splitting and model fitting in one dataset and error measuring in another is widely known as *cross-validation*.

Cross-validation normally involves a number of repetitions, and the error re-ported in step **g2** is normally the average and standard deviation, or median and interquartile range, of the several measurements made in each repetition of step **d3**. Instead of reporting the error, step **g2** may report any other measure of the quality of the model (several of these measures are discussed later in this chapter). Section 5.2 provides more details on how to perform data splitting and Section 5.3 describes different types of cross-validation. Section 5.4 describes different ways of reporting the quality of a classifier, and Section 5.6 explains how to use regularization methods to improve the generalization ability of the induced models.

5.1.2 Choosing Method and Parameters

The previous description assumed that the method used for fitting a model to the training data was already chosen, as well as its running parameters (often called hyperparameters). However, this is seldom the case. With so many ML methods available, it is normally the case that different methods must be tried, with different parameters, in order to decide which one is able to provide the most adequate models, given the available data. Most adequate does not necessarily mean most accurate. It may be acceptable to use a method that induces simple models that can be easily interpreted, even if a higher accuracy could be obtained by a computationally expensive method that returns uninterpretable models. It all depends on the initial motivation for inducing a predictive model. Either way, any choice that is made regarding the method and its parameters is simply that: a choice. Hopefully, an informed one, rather than a blind one, but nevertheless just a choice, which we cannot guarantee to be the best one for future predictions. Therefore, the cycle for choosing the method and its parameters (steps **b**, **b1**, **b3**, **b3i** and **b3ii**, followed by step **c**) does not have to be very exhaustive.

The choice of the method is a high-level choice that mostly determines the type of model that will be achieved. Given the demands that some methods impose on the amount of data and/or computational power required, frequently the choice is only among a small set of possibilities. Among these, the simplest and fastest methods should be tried first, before moving to more complex ones. Regarding the parameters, each method has its own set, and may be more or less dependent on their "correct" settings. Finding appropriate settings for a method is normally called the *tuning* phase. It is absolutely normal that the best settings are different for each training/validation partition, and this is why the choice must be based, once again, on cross-validation results of several different partitions. Therefore, the process involves a nested cycle where, for each partition (step **b1**), different methods and/or parameters are tried (step **b3**), and each combination induces a model on the training set (step **b3i**) and measures its error on the validation set (step **b3ii**). In the end, each combination will have achieved a certain average error, and the one that minimizes this error is fixed (step **c**) as the method and/or parameters to be used in the remaining steps. A growing body of work has been developed in recent years on automated ways for choosing the method and its parameters [Hutter et al., 2019].

The error estimation described in Section 5.1.1 should then be performed using the settings fixed herein. However, if time for additional estimates is limited, and the error measurements obtained in step **b3ii** did not vary much between different validation sets (i.e., had a small variance), then it is acceptable to skip all the **d** cycle and report in step **g2** the estimate based on the results obtained in step **b3ii** (instead of **d3**) for the chosen method and parameters.

5.1.3 Inducing and Testing the Final Model

If there is the need to actually obtain a final model for performing predictions on new data (i.e., if we are using ML in the "real world" and not just performing an academic exercise) then this model should be induced on the complete learning data, and reported together with its estimated error in steps **g1** and **g2**. Besides the error estimation provided in step **g2** (calculated in the **d** cycle), an additional quality assessment of this final model should still be performed. "Any modeling decisions based upon experiments on the training set, even cross validation estimates, are suspect, until independently verified" [Rao and Fung, 2008]. Of course, this requires an initial splitting of the reference data into learning and test data (step **a**), meaning that the learning data available for everything else will be fewer than were initially available in the reference dataset. If data are scarce, this initial splitting and consequent reduction of the amount of data may compromise the remaining steps. In that case, it may be advisable not to do this splitting, and instead use the entire reference dataset as learning data.

If there is the need for a final predictive model but the available data are not enough for a test set, the final model can still be trusted, since it was induced by the same method, with the same parameters, and on the same data (although a larger amount), as the different models used for estimating the error. This is particularly true if the estimated error does not reveal a wide dispersion of values. If, on the other hand, the dispersion of values is high, then we may decide that no single model is trustworthy, and instead provide as final model an ensemble of the different models used for estimating the error (since all of them were independently validated), where each prediction of the ensemble is an average or a vote on the predictions of the different models that compose it. This has the potential to narrow the interval of expected errors, but the disadvantage of reducing the interpretability of the final model. Ensemble ML methods will be studied in Chapter 11.

If, on the other hand, there are enough data to perform an independent validation on a test set, and the interpretability of the model is not an issue, given enough time we may even want to repeat the whole process several times, using different learning and test sets, and in the end provide as final model the ensemble of models obtained in the different learning sets. Whatever is the preferred approach, we should keep in mind that the error measured for the final model is meant as an internal check, and must necessarily be very close to, or fall within, the estimated expected error reported in step **g2**. If this does not happen, then the final model cannot be trusted for predicting unseen data, and a careful analysis of the reference dataset must be performed, as well as a detailed review of the entire process, as it certainly failed at some point.

5.1.4 Preprocessing the Data

Depending on the data available for the ML process, we may want to perform some normalization, clean errors, get rid of outliers, deal with missing values, and/or apply feature selection and/or extraction, in order to obtain data that will make it easier to induce good predictive models. Some of these actions can be performed on the reference set, but only if the decision to perform them is based on prior external knowledge about the data, for example, the knowledge that some of the data features are useless and therefore should be removed from any further analysis. Any decision regarding a preprocessing action that requires looking at an actual dataset can only be based on the training data (step **b2**). Then, the chosen data transformations are applied to the training set before fitting the model (step **b3i**) and to the validation set before measuring the error (step **b3ii**).

Indeed, this is an important point to emphasize: when measuring the error of a model on unseen data, whatever preprocessing this data suffers, it must have been decided beforehand, based solely on information gathered from the training set. A simple example is the normalization of the data. It is common to normalize the training set, and then to normalize the unseen dataset before measuring the error. However, the normalization of the unseen data must use the same scaling that was determined from the training data. Using a scaling determined from observation of the unseen dataset is incorrect. Each observation of unseen data should be handled separately from the other unseen observations, using only the preprocessing that was decided on the training set. These decisions regarding preprocessing are part of the settings that are fixed (step **c**) before the next steps, based on the cross-validation error, just like the decisions regarding the model and its parameters (Section 5.1.2).

The following steps should therefore use the exact same preprocessing settings, without any further tuning, so that the estimation of the error (Section 5.1.1) is not overly optimistic and the final model (Section 5.1.3) is faithful to this estimate. This option, of not tuning the preprocessing to the dataset in which the final model is induced, is certainly debatable. Take feature selection, for example (Section 5.5 focuses on feature selection and extraction). The decision that is fixed in step **c** regarding this preprocessing can be either 'which method of feature selection to use', or 'which specific features to use'. In other words, we either allow that the selected features are tuned to the learning data, or we do not allow it. Can we obtain a better model by tuning the preprocessing to the learning data? Maybe, but then we will not know how much the error of this model may deviate from the calculated estimate. What if the process of estimating the error (the **d** cycle) also allows this tuning of preprocessing to each and every training set? Then the preprocessing can be seen as being part of the model induction process. In fact, some preprocessing actions cannot be detached from the process of fitting the model itself, for example, the embedded methods for feature extraction (see Section 5.5). With important and potentially disruptive decisions to make, like the one to remove features from the data, it is even more important to be able to test the final model in an independent test set (Section 5.1.3).

Whatever option is taken, the most important characteristic of the final predictive model, the one that is going to be used in the real world, is that its expected error is *known*, so that the model can be *trusted*. Even if it may not be the best model we could ever achieve.

5.2 Data Splitting

In Figure 5.2, data splitting is performed several times in different steps, but the same general rules apply to all the splitting actions. Let

$$D = \{(\mathbf{x}_1, y_1), (\mathbf{x}_2, y_2), ..., (\mathbf{x}_n, y_n)\}$$

be a supervised dataset. Let j be the number of observations, with $j < n$, to select and insert in a new set J. Even though, in general, the choice of the instances to be inserted in J is made at random, let us assume for simplicity that the first j observations in D are inserted in J,[3] in other words:

$$J = \{(\mathbf{x}_1, y_1), (\mathbf{x}_2, y_2), ..., (\mathbf{x}_j, y_j)\}$$

Learning a model is performed using only the data in J. Let g be the model obtained as the result of this learning phase. Then the set:

$$D - J = \{(\mathbf{x}_{j+1}, y_{j+1}), (\mathbf{x}_{j+2}, y_{j+2}), ..., (\mathbf{x}_n, y_n)\}$$

can be used to test the generalization ability of g, since it contains only data that was not seen during the learning phase. This can be done by evaluating g on the input data $\mathbf{x}_{j+1}, \mathbf{x}_{j+2}, ..., \mathbf{x}_n$ and comparing the predicted outputs with the respective expected outputs $y_{j+1}, y_{j+2}, ..., y_n$. Any error measure can be used to make this comparison. For instance, if we assume that we use the absolute error, a measure of the generalization ability of our ML system can be:

$$E = \sum_{i=j+1}^{n} |g(\mathbf{x}_i) - y_i| \tag{5.2}$$

The sets D, J and $D - J$ can be the reference, learning and test sets in Figure 5.3, respectively, or they can be the learning, training and validation sets, respectively. Regardless of the particular case, it is generally accepted to use "training" set to refer to where the model is induced, and "test" set to where the model is evaluated, and we also use these terms freely whenever it is not important to specify exactly which dataset is being split.

No rules exist for deciding on the number of instances j that are selected for training, but this should depend on the amount and distribution of the data available

---

[3] The reader should notice that the same effect as selecting j instances at random from D can be obtained by first shuffling at random the instances in D, and then selecting the first j.

in D, which should also influence the type of cross-validation that is going to be performed (next section). The test set $D - J$ should be large, as large as possible, to ensure that the induced model is evaluated on a representative sample of data. However, due to the lack of sufficient labeled data, normally most of the data is needed for learning the model, and then the evaluation is performed on a much smaller sample than the one used for learning. In other words, the test set is normally much smaller than the training set, although it should be the other way around.

Data splitting has the advantage of being very simple, but this lack of sufficient labeled data causes an important drawback: the resulting evaluation of the model depends on the particular set that was used for learning. In other words, if we repeat the fitting and evaluation using a different splitting, the results may be (and in many circumstances actually are significantly) different. Avoiding any kind of logical "choice" when we select the training instances is a first advisable step to counteract this issue (for instance, it is generally not recommended to select the first j instances in the order in which they appear in D, even if no apparent logic exists in the way the observations are sorted). This is why it is common practice to select the training instances randomly. However, this is generally not enough to avoid bias given by the particular training set used. To limit this problem, it is common practice to repeat the process several times, using different data splits. The particular way in which this is done gives rise to different types of cross-validation, the theme of the next section.

5.3 Cross-Validation

The most common type of cross-validation is called *k-fold* cross-validation. The dataset is partitioned into k subsets[4], or *folds*, and data splitting is repeated k times. Each time, one of the folds is used as test set, while the $k - 1$ remaining folds form the training set. At the end of the k iterations, each one of the k partitions has been used exactly once as test set. Let $\{E_1, E_2, ..., E_k\}$ be the errors obtained in each one of the k iterations. A measure of the generalization ability of the ML system can be given, for instance, by:

$$\overline{E} = \frac{1}{k} \sum_{i=1}^{k} E_i \tag{5.3}$$

which corresponds to the average error obtained in the different iterations. Section 5.4 describes different ways of evaluating the performance of classifiers.

The advantage of doing several iterations in cross-validation is that it allows us to obtain an error estimate that is not dependent on a single data splitting and a particular choice of the training data. The drawback is that it requires training to be performed k times, thus taking an amount of time that is approximately k times longer than what is required for a single data splitting. Furthermore, in general, the

---

[4] We recall that, by definition, a partition of a set is a grouping of its elements into nonempty subsets, in such a way that every element is included in exactly one subset.

variance associated to $\overline{E}$ should get smaller as k gets larger. So, in order to have a small variance in the results of different iterations, the number of iterations should be large, which contributes to slow down the process even more.

The reader may have noticed that k-fold cross-validation enforces the formation of test sets that are much smaller than the training sets, and they get proportionally even smaller as k increases. Traditionally, k is 2, 5 or 10, which means the test sets contain 50%, 20% or 10% of the samples available before splitting. In the limit, $k = n$, the total number of available samples, and this is called *leave-one-out* cross-validation, where each test set has only one sample and the process is exhaustively repeated as many times as the number of available samples. This is obviously unfeasible for large datasets. As for datasets of modest size, it presents advantages and disadvantages. On the one hand, leave-one-out uses training sets that are very similar to the unsplit dataset (except for one sample), which means that the error estimation is based on models trained on practically the same data as the final model will be, and therefore it should be a reliable estimate. On the other hand, the different training sets are so similar to each other (once again, except for one sample) that the estimate is probably biased to the particularities of the dataset. There is an active debate in the ML community regarding the merits and weaknesses of the leave-one-out approach, with conflicting views, intuitions and conclusions. We maintain that the amount and distribution of available data should be a paramount factor in deciding the relative sizes of the training and test sets. Besides leave-one-out, other exhaustive approaches may be adopted, like *leave-p-out* cross-validation, that uses as test sets every possible combination of p elements from the dataset.

Another type of cross-validation is called *repeated random subsampling*, also called *Monte Carlo* cross-validation [Dubitzky et al., 2006]. This method simply creates random splits of the data. The advantage is that the proportion of the two parts is not dependent on the number of iterations (i.e., the number of times we repeat the splitting, fitting and evaluation process). Another related advantage is that it does not require the *a priori* decision of how many iterations will be done. We can repeat a minimum acceptable number of times and then observe the variance, i.e., the dispersion of results. If the dispersion is very low, then it is probably useless to keep repeating the process, as the estimate is already reliable; however, if the dispersion is high, it is easy to add many more iterations without the need to go back to the beginning and redo everything with new folds, as k-fold cross-validation would require. The disadvantage of Monte Carlo cross-validation is that some observations may never be selected for the test set, while others will be selected more than once. However, it this proves to be a problem, it can be circumvented by applying a probabilistic instead of a completely random splitting of the data, promoting that every observation is used as unseen data the same number of times as the others.

Since in Monte Carlo cross-validation the relative sizes of the training and test sets do not depend on the number of iterations, it is possible to form larger test sets and still run a decent number of iterations. Indeed, it is common to find studies in the literature in which the training set contains (approximately) 70% of the instances in D, while the test set contains the remaining 30%.

It is not mandatory to use the same type of cross-validation in all the phases of the ML process. For example, it may make sense to use 5-fold or 10-fold cross-validation for choosing the method and parameters (group (2) in Section 5.1) and/or for making decisions regarding data preprocessing (group (1)), and then use Monte Carlo repeated random subsampling cross-validation for performing a thorough estimation of the error (group (3)).

5.4 Measures of Performance of a Classifier

The discussion of the previous section is general, in the sense that it holds both for classification and regression problems. In this section, we focus on classification. The simplest and most popular measure to quantify the predictive ability of a classification model is the *number of correctly classified instances*. To calculate this measure, we simply have to count the number of instances for which the predicted class label is identical to the class label that appears in the supervised dataset. The number of correctly classified instances is a measure that depends on the number of instances. In order to make the measure comparable when used on datasets of different sizes, it is typical to normalize this measure, so as to obtain another measure called *accuracy*, defined as:

$$\text{Accuracy} = \frac{\text{number of correctly classified instances}}{\text{total number of instances}}$$

Using a measure like the number of correctly classified instances, or the accuracy, may not be sufficient to understand the behavior of a classifier. Often, more sophisticated measures of performance are needed for classifiers. For instance, we may need measures that express the quality of a classification *for each class*, and not just one single general number. To convince oneself about the importance of having a measure that expresses a different value for each class, one may imagine, for instance, a binary classification problem where the objective is to categorize a set of patients into one of the two possible classes Healthy or Sick. It is clear that, in some cases, misclassifying a sick patient can have more serious consequences than misclassifying a healthy patient. Starting by saying that both misclassifications are mistakes, and, as such, both of them have serious consequences, treating a healthy patient as a sick one, among other consequences, may cause the patient to undertake unnecessary treatments or to get uselessly worried. On the other hand, treating sick patients as healthy ones may cause these patients to not undertake treatments that may be crucial to save their lives. In such an application, it is clear that information like the number of misclassifications made by the system is not sufficient. On what class those misclassifications happened is also needed information.

Two of the most known and employed measures to quantify the performance of a classifier are *precision* and *recall*. Given a class C in a dataset, these measures are defined as follows:

$$\text{Precision}(C) = \frac{\text{\#instances belonging to } C, \text{ classified as } C}{\text{\#instances classified as } C} \tag{5.4}$$

$$\text{Recall}(C) = \frac{\text{\#instances belonging to } C, \text{ classified as } C}{\text{\#instances belonging to } C} \tag{5.5}$$

As we can see, the measures share the same numerator, consisting of the intersection between the observations labeled as C in the given dataset and the observations that the model has categorized as belonging to class C (in other words, the numerator contains the number of instances that the classifier has categorized correctly as class C). The two measures differ because of the denominator: for precision, the denominator tells us about the work done by the classifier, while for recall, it tells us about the true classes, what is called the *ground truth*. From this perspective, one may have an intuition on the meaning of precision and recall by comparing them to concepts such as correctness and completeness, respectively.

To have a better understanding of how to calculate precision and recall, consider the example shown in Figure 5.4. In this example, three classes are given: C_1, C_2

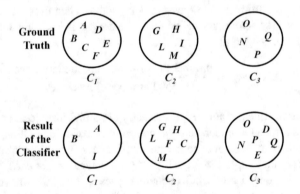

Fig. 5.4 Example used to explain the concepts of precision and recall. The upper line shows how data are really partitioned into three classes C_1, C_2 and C_3 in the given dataset. The lower line shows how a classification model has categorized the same objects in the same classes

and C_3. The upper line of the figure shows how 15 objects (observations) are partitioned into these three classes in the given dataset. The lower line, instead, shows how those objects have been categorized by an ML model. Precision and recall for the different classes are:

$$\text{Precision}(C_1) = \frac{2}{3} \approx 0.66, \quad \text{Recall}(C_1) = \frac{2}{6} \approx 0.33$$

$$\text{Precision}(C_2) = \frac{4}{6} \approx 0.66, \quad \text{Recall}(C_2) = \frac{4}{5} = 0.8$$

$$\text{Precision}(C_3) = \frac{4}{6} \approx 0.66, \quad \text{Recall}(C_3) = \frac{4}{4} = 1$$

Both precision and recall are numbers included in $[0, 1]$, where 1 represents the best value and 0 is the worst one. An ideal model, i.e., one that classifies each observation correctly, has both precision and recall equal to 1. Models that have only one among precision and recall equal to 1 deserve a discussion. One may be tempted to consider such models as good ones, but this can be very misleading. Consider, for instance, the case of C_3 in the previous example. The recall of C_3 is equal to 1 because the classifier has categorized as C_3 all the instances that are really in C_3, plus others. If we take this situation to extremes, even a "naïve" model that blindly categorizes all existing observations in C_3 can have a recall equal to 1. However, this model has clearly not learned anything. A similar argument also holds for precision: any model that categorizes in a class only a subset of the objects that actually belong to that class has a precision equal to 1 for that class. But this argument also holds if many objects belong to the class and, say, only one is categorized in it. For instance, given the objects A, B, C, D, E, F that belong to class C_1, a model that categorizes object A as the only member of class C_1 has a precision equal to 1. However, also in this case, the amount of information that this model has learned is poor. In conclusion, it does not make much sense to study only one among precision and recall, without studying the other. These measures give us two different pieces of information, each of which is incomplete without the other. Only studying them together makes sense.

Other popular measures of performance of a classifier are *true positives* (TP), *true negatives* (TN), *false positives* (FP) and *false negatives* (FN). Given a class C, these measures are defined as follows:

- $\text{TP}(C) = \#$ instances belonging to C, classified as C
- $\text{TN}(C) = \#$ instances that do *not* belong to C, that have *not* been classified as C
- $\text{FP}(C) = \#$ instances that do *not* belong to C, classified as C
- $\text{FN}(C) = \#$ instances belonging to C, that have *not* been classified as C

When the first word is *true*, the measure quantifies a correct behavior of the model: true positives quantify the number of times an object of C has been correctly categorized as C, while true negatives quantify the number of times that an object has been correctly identified as not belonging to C. Analogously, when the first word is *false*, the measure quantifies errors of the model: false positives count the number of times the model has erroneously categorized an object as C, while false negatives count the number of times an object should have been categorized as C but was not.

Knowing the values of TP, FP and FN, it is possible to immediately obtain the precision and the recall. In fact, directly from the definition of precision and recall, we have that, for each class C:

$$\text{Precision}(C) = \frac{\text{TP}(C)}{\text{TP}(C) + \text{FP}(C)}$$

$$\text{Recall}(C) = \frac{\text{TP}(C)}{\text{TP}(C) + \text{FN}(C)}$$

Another important measure that joins precision and recall into one single number for each class is the *F-measure* (also called *F-score* or *F1-score*), defined as:

$$\text{F-measure}(C) = \frac{2 * \text{Precision}(C) * \text{Recall}(C)}{\text{Precision}(C) + \text{Recall}(C)}$$

The F-measure is often preferred over the accuracy in the case of *unbalanced datasets*. Let us consider, for instance, a binary classification problem, i.e., a problem that consists in categorizing observations into one of the two possible classes C_1 and C_2. Let us assume, without loss of generality, that, in our dataset, numerous observations labeled with class C_1 are available, while only a negligible number of observations are labeled with class C_2. It is clear that a "naive" model that blindly categorizes all observations as belonging to class C_1 has an excellent accuracy. If the ML system is guided by accuracy, as a performance measure to choose among the candidate solutions, it is clear that such a model is likely to be the preferred one, even though it has learned none of the information available in the data. On the other hand, given that such a model has poor precision and recall on class C_2, its F-measure is also poor. In order to have a good F-measure in the case of unbalanced datasets, the ML system is forced to learn the information that allows us to distinguish between the different classes.

In some cases, it is useful to understand how much better or worse our classifier is, compared to a random classifier. By random classifier, we mean an algorithm that, for each possible instance, returns a random class, chosen with uniform distribution among all the possible existing alternatives. This can be quantified, for instance, by the *K measure* [Landis and Koch, 1977] that some ML packages have implemented, including Weka [Hall et al., 2009]. This measure is defined as:

$$K = \frac{\text{Accuracy} - P(E)}{1 - P(E)}$$

where $P(E)$ is the probability that the random classifier correctly classifies all elements in the considered dataset. It is clear that K gets closer to the ideal value of 1 as also the accuracy gets closer to its ideal value of 1. When stratifying the results by class is not a requirement, the K measure can give some interesting information that may be integrated with the information given by the accuracy, and/or with statistics calculated over other measures such as precision, recall and the F-measure.

We conclude this presentation of measures of performance of classifiers with the discussion of a measure that is very popular, but can be used only for binary classification, and only if the classifier works with a *threshold* mechanism. Imagine, for instance, the two classes of a binary classification problem to be represented by labels 0 and 1. Given an observation, the ML model could work by generating a number x, which is then transformed into either 0 or 1. The typical case is: if x is smaller than 0.5, then return 0, else return 1. In this case, a threshold equal to 0.5 is used. This is the typical functioning, for instance, of supervised artificial neural networks, discussed in Chapter 7. In such a situation, the performance of the model can be represented by a plot, called a *Receiver Operating Characteristic* (ROC) curve. The plot is created by reporting the values of the true positive rate (TPR) against the false positive rate (FPR) for various different values of the threshold. TPR and FPR are defined as follows:

$$TPR = \frac{TP}{TP+FN}, \quad FPR = \frac{FP}{FP+TN}$$

TPR is identical to recall, and it is also known as *sensitivity* or *probability of detection*. FPR is also known as *fall-out* or *probability of false alarm*. In some references, it is also possible to find the term *specificity*, where:

$$\text{specificity} = 1 - FPR$$

Let us consider the frequent case in which the output of the model is a number in $[0, 1]$. In this case, to combine the FPR and the TPR into a single metric, we first compute the two former measures with a set of different threshold values (like, for instance, $0.00, 0.01, 0.02, ..., 1.00$). Then we plot them on a single graph, with the FPR values on the abscissa and the TPR values on the ordinate. The resulting curve is the ROC curve, and the metric we consider is the area under the curve (AUC), also called AUROC. An example of a ROC curve is reported in Figure 5.5. In this figure, the blue area corresponds to the AUROC. The dashed line is the diagonal, and it represents the ROC curve of a random predictor: it has an AUROC equal to 0.5. The random predictor is commonly used as a baseline to compare with the model. The value of the AUROC is always included in $[0, 1]$. The best possible prediction method would yield a point in the upper left corner (coordinate $(0, 1)$) of the ROC space, representing 100% specificity (i.e., no false positives). The point $(0, 1)$ is also called a perfect classification. A completely random guess would give a point along the diagonal (also called the line of no discrimination) from the bottom left to the top right corner.

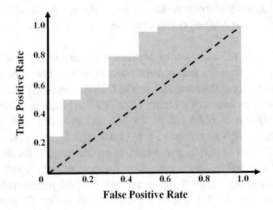

Fig. 5.5 Example of a ROC curve. The AUROC is represented in light blue

5.5 Feature Processing

A feature is a characteristic of the objects that have to be classified or, more generally, for which a prediction is needed. Therefore, datasets are usually a collection of values (or instances) of features. In the case of classification, features are appropriate or useful if they allow us to distinguish between one class (or more) and the others. This is why an appropriate choice of the features is often crucial in supervised ML. Let us consider, for instance, the following toy dataset, whose objective is to classify each animal as Rooster or Dog:

	# feet	# eyes	has crest	body fat	weight	target
animal 1	2	2	True	7%	5.70	Rooster
animal 2	4	2	False	18%	40.38	Dog
animal 3	4	2	False	22%	14.60	Dog
animal 4	2	2	True	10%	2.01	Rooster

This dataset contains four observations, each one representing a different animal. Each animal is represented by five features: *number of feet* and *number of eyes*, which are integer numbers, *has crest*, a Boolean value, *body fat*, which is a percentage, and *weight*, which is a floating-point number. Observing this dataset, we can immediately notice that:

- Number of feet and has crest are *good* features: they clearly allow us to tell dogs from roosters.
- Number of eyes is a totally useless feature: its value is the same for both classes, and so the feature is constant in the whole dataset.

- Body fat and weight may help to make the classification, but if we use these two features the classification may be harder than if we simply use one among number of feet and has crest.

Examples of models that allow us to make a perfect classification for each instance in the dataset are:

> **if** (has crest)
> > **then** Rooster
> > **else** Dog

or:

> **if** (number of feet == 2)
> > **then** Rooster
> > **else if** (number of feet == 4)
> > > **then** Dog

Both these models use a restricted number of features, compared to the total number of features that appear in the dataset. Removing several features from the dataset, possibly leaving only number of feet and/or has crest, may significantly help the work of a classifier. The presence of useless features, or features which make the classification harder, in fact, enlarges the search space and makes it harder to obtain a good model.

Feature selection is the process of choosing the features that are useful for making the prediction, disregarding all the others. It is often a hard task, and it can, in principle, be based on previous knowledge of the problem, or on mathematical relationships between data. *Feature extraction*, also called *feature induction*, *feature construction*, *feature learning* and *feature discovery*, among others[5], is part of the general concept of *feature engineering*, and consist in the process of combining one or more existing features to create a (usually) smaller number of more insightful features. Contrarily to feature selection, in feature extraction features are typically not chosen or disregarded, but only combined. Both feature selection and feature extraction, or only one of them, can be used. Reducing the dimensionality of the feature space can be a crucial task to improve the generalization ability of an ML system, so choosing or creating appropriate features is a fundamental step on which the performance of the whole system can depend. This type of feature processing is normally applied before beginning the learning process, and for this reason it is usually integrated in a so-called *data preprocessing* phase. Data preprocessing also includes a step of data cleaning, aimed at removing mistakes, imperfections or noise from the data, as well as a data normalization step that may be crucial for the success of some ML methods.

---

[5] There may be differences in what each term means exactly, but there is no consensus in the ML community regarding the correct term for each case, and therefore we do not distinguish between them.

Modern datasets have hundreds to tens of thousands of variables or features. Feature selection and extraction, which we will now call simply feature processing, have three main objectives:

- improving the prediction performance of models,
- providing faster and more cost effective predictors, and
- providing a better understanding of the underlying process that generated the data.

Besides this, there are many other potential benefits of feature processing: facilitating data visualization and data understanding, reducing the measurement and storage requirements, reducing training time, etc. Methods for feature processing can essentially be partitioned into:

- Filters;
- Wrappers;
- Embedded methods.

Filters select subsets of variables independently of the chosen predictor. Wrappers use the ML method of interest as a black box to score subsets of variables according to their predictive power. Embedded methods perform variable processing in the process of training and are usually specific to particular ML methods.

The most popular kinds of filters (although by far not the only ones known) are:

- Correlation-based methods;
- Information Theory-based methods.

Both these methods have the objective of ranking the features according to their "usefulness" in helping prediction, so that only the q top-ranked ones are used for generating the predictive model. The intuition is that if a feature is independent of the target, it is uninformative for predicting it. Of course, these methods introduce a new parameter q that can have a crucial influence on the performance of the system, and that can only be set by means of experimental comparisons.

The idea of correlation-based feature selection is simple: calculate the correlation between all features and the target, and then rank the features according to this correlation value. One of the best-known measures is the Pearson correlation coefficient. For a particular feature, given the vector of all the feature values $\mathbf{x} = x_1, x_2, ..., x_n$ and the vector of the target values $\mathbf{y} = y_1, y_2, ..., y_n$, the Pearson correlation between X and Y is:

$$Corr = \frac{cov(\mathbf{x}, \mathbf{y})}{\sqrt{var(\mathbf{x})\ var(\mathbf{y})}}$$

where cov is the covariance of two vectors and var is the variance of one vector, so:

$$Corr = \frac{\sum_{i=1}^{n}(x_i - \bar{x}) \cdot (y_i - \bar{y})}{\sqrt{\sum_{i=1}^{n}(x_i - \bar{x})^2 \cdot \sum_{i=1}^{n}(y_i - \bar{y})^2}}$$

where $\bar{x}$ is the average of the elements of vector **x**. By definition, *Corr* is a value in $[-1,1]$. Usually, the measure that is used to perform the ranking is $Corr^2$, because a negative correlation can be useful (it is enough to consider the feature with a negative sign in the model). One possible drawback of correlation criteria is that they can only detect linear dependencies between features and target. A simple way of lifting this restriction is to make a nonlinear fit of the target with single variables and rank according to the goodness of that fit.

Concerning information theory-based feature selection, the ranking of features is done using mutual information between features and the target:

$$Inf = \sum_{x_i}\sum_{y_i} P(X = x_i, Y = y_i) \cdot log \frac{P(X = x_i, Y = y_i)}{P(X = x_i) \cdot P(Y = y_i)}$$

This measure is appropriate if the features are discrete variables. The case of continuous variables (and possibly continuous targets) is harder and one can consider discretizing the variables.

Besides correlation and information theory, another possible measure to rank the features is the χ^2 between features and targets, which also aims at quantifying the dependence between features and target.

One common criticism of variable ranking is that it may lead to the selection of a redundant subset. The same performance could possibly be achieved with a smaller subset of complementary variables. Still, one may wonder whether adding presumably redundant variables can result in a performance gain. Actually, it is an empirically observed fact that, in classification, better class separation may be obtained by adding variables that are presumably redundant. More precisely, perfectly correlated variables are truly redundant in the sense that no additional information is gained by adding them; but very high variable correlation (or anticorrelation) does not mean absence of variable complementarity. Furthermore, experimental evidence tells us that a variable that is completely useless by itself can provide a significant performance improvement when taken with others, and two variables that are useless by themselves can be useful together. These last two observations led the scientific community to the idea that filters can have important limitations, and they can be overcome by means of, for instance, wrappers or embedded methods.

As we can see, the objective of data preprocessing is usually to generate a new dataset that is generally smaller, cleaner and possibly more informative than the original one. This step is often crucial to facilitate the work of the ML system and often allows us to generate better models.

5.6 Regularization

As we have seen earlier in this chapter, one of the major concerns when training an ML model is avoiding overfitting. Overfitting typically happens because the model is trying to capture the noise in the training dataset, i.e., the points that do not really represent the true properties of the data, but random chance. Statistics and information theory tell us that there are three important characteristics of an ML model that affect its propensity to overfit: *bias*, *variance* and *complexity*. Although these terms have already been freely used throughout the chapter, we now define them informally as follows:

- Bias refers to the error that is introduced by approximating a real-life problem, which may be extremely complex, by means of a simpler model. For instance, algorithms such as linear regression, or logistic regression, make a simplistic assumption on the shape of the model that is unlikely to be able to capture all the information in the data. No matter how many observations we have, it is impossible to produce an accurate prediction if we are using such restrictive/simple algorithms, when the true relation is highly complex.

- Variance refers to the amount by which the accuracy of a method changes if we learn using different training data sets. Since the training set is used to fit the statistical learning method, different training data sets will result in different estimations. But ideally the estimate should not vary too much between training sets. If a method has high variance, then small changes in the training data can result in large changes in the performance of the model.

- The complexity of a model can be defined in several different ways. For instance, the number of variables that it uses, its size or its functional complexity, which can be estimated, for instance, as a measure of its degree of curvature.

The way in which these three elements usually affect the error on unseen data can be ideally represented as in Figure 5.6. Learning unavoidably has the effect of augmenting the complexity of the model. At the same time, the more you learn, the more bias is reduced. In fact, the more you learn, the more the algorithm will try to fit training data with more and more precision, incorporating in the model more and more details. Finally, learning also has the intuitive effect of increasing variance: in order to fit training data with more precision, incorporating more and more details, the model gets clearly more and more dependent on the particular training set that is being used. The trends shown in Figure 5.6 can be confirmed using Statistics [James, 2003], but they can also be observed experimentally in several real-life scenarios. It is a fact that any ML algorithm, including for instance linear and logistic regression, would place us on the right-hand side of the picture, i.e., would tend to generate a model with high complexity and variance, albeit with low bias, which is far from optimal. The objective of regularization is to artificially intervene to balance this trend, lowering the variance at the cost of incrementing bias, thus moving left on the plot, towards the optimum.

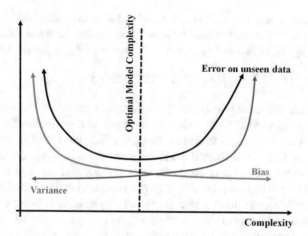

Fig. 5.6 Idealized relationship between complexity, bias, variance and unseen error

5.6.1 Ridge Regression

From the discussion so far, we have understood the importance of decreasing the model complexity. Let us consider a method that generates a model that is a combination of the input variables, weighted with some coefficients. Linear and logistic regression work like this, but, as we will see later in the book, also several other ML algorithms work like this, for instance Artificial Neural Networks and Support Vector Machines. In that case, a simple way of assessing complexity can be given by the number of predictors, i.e., the number of variables used by the model. From this perspective, feature selection, performed in a preprocessing phase, clearly contributes to complexity reduction. However, it is not able to tell us anything about the removed variables' effect on the response. On the other hand, removing predictors from the model can be seen as setting their coefficients (weights) to zero. Instead of forcing them to be exactly zero, it is often appropriate to penalize them if they are too far from zero, thus enforcing them to be small in a continuous way. Doing so, we decrease model complexity while keeping all selected variables in the model. This is, basically, the idea behind Ridge Regression.

In Ridge Regression, the loss function is extended by adding a further term. In this way, the loss function not only minimizes the error, but also penalizes large values of the parameters, in order to shrink them towards zero. Taking as an example linear regression (but analogous formulations can be used for any other algorithm that generates models that are weighted combinations of the variables), the loss function is now defined as:

$$L_{\text{ridge}}(\beta) = \sum_{i=1}^{n}(\mathbf{x_i}\beta - y_i)^2 + \lambda \sum_{i=0}^{m} \beta_i^2 = ||\mathbf{X}\beta - \mathbf{y}||^2 + \lambda ||\beta||^2$$

Minimizing this function should automatically tend to minimize both its terms, including the second one, and thus should tend to minimize the magnitude of the coefficients $\beta_0, \beta_1, \beta_2, ..., \beta_m$. Solving this for β gives the ridge regression estimates:

$$\beta = (\mathbf{X}^T\mathbf{X} + \lambda\mathbf{I})^{-1}(\mathbf{X}^T\mathbf{Y})$$

where $\mathbf{I}$ denotes the identity matrix. The λ parameter is called the *regularization penalty*. If λ is equal to zero, then there is no regularization, and so the traditional ML method is applied. As λ tends to infinity, coefficients β tend to zero. So, setting λ to zero is the same as using the original method, without regularization, while the larger its value, the stronger the coefficients penalization. As λ grows, the variance decreases, and the bias increases. This poses a question: how much bias are we willing to accept in order to decrease the variance? Or, in other words: what is the optimal value for λ? There are two ways to answer this question. One can decide to choose λ in such a way that some information criterion is optimized, or one can perform cross-validation and select the value of λ that minimizes the cross-validated error. The former approach emphasizes the model's fit to the data, while the latter is more focused on its predictive performance.

5.6.2 Lasso Regression

Least Absolute Shrinkage and Selection Operator (lasso) is conceptually similar to ridge regression. The only difference is given by the way in which the coefficients are penalized: while ridge uses the sum of squared coefficients (also called the L2 penalty), lasso penalizes the sum of their absolute values (L1 penalty). As a result, for high values of λ, many coefficients are exactly or approximately equal to zero under lasso, which is usually not the case for ridge. So, in some cases, lasso can perform a real feature selection, *de facto* excluding some variables from the model. The loss function for lasso regression is defined as:

$$L_{\text{lasso}}(\beta) = \sum_{i=1}^{n}(\mathbf{x_i}\beta - y_i)^2 + \lambda \sum_{i=0}^{m}|\beta_i|$$

Concerning how to set parameter λ, similar factors can be considered to those for ridge: it is possible to use the value of λ that optimizes some information criterion, or it is possible to find the appropriate value of λ experimentally, for instance by means of cross-validation. An important difference in the behavior of lasso, compared to ridge, is that, in ridge, the coefficients of correlated variables are usually rather similar to each other. On the other hand, in lasso, one of the correlated variables usually has a larger coefficient, while the others are nearly zeroed. As an intuitive consequence, lasso tends have high performance when only a few variables actually influence the target. On the other hand, ridge usually works well when most variables have a significant impact on the response. Of course, in practical situations, we do not know *a priori* how many of the variables are informative, so the choice between lasso and ridge is usually made as the result of an experimental phase, where the two regularization strategies are compared with each other. A possible alternative, instead of choosing between the two, is to combine them; this is the idea behind elastic net, discussed next.

5.6.3 Elastic Net

Elastic net combines the penalties of ridge regression and lasso, with the objective of getting the best from both techniques. The loss function of elastic net is:

$$L_{enet}(\beta) = \sum_{i=1}^{n}(\mathbf{x_i}\beta - y_i)^2 + \lambda((1-\alpha)\sum_{i=0}^{m}\beta_i^2 + \alpha\sum_{i=0}^{m}|\beta_i|)$$

where $\alpha \in [0,1]$ is a further parameter, called the *mixing* parameter between ridge and lasso. Indeed, elastic net corresponds to ridge if $\alpha = 0$ and it corresponds to lasso if $\alpha = 1$. If on one hand, elastic net is a more general technique, incorporating ridge and lasso as special cases, on the other hand parameter tuning can be harder for elastic net, because now the parameters to optimize are two: λ and α.

5.7 Some Simple Machine Learning Methods

5.7.1 K-Nearest Neighbors

K-Nearest Neighbors (KNN) is one of the simplest ML algorithms, and can be used both for regression and for classification. Let us assume that we have a supervised training set T and an unseen instance $\mathbf{x}$ on which we want to calculate the output (prediction). KNN simply works by considering the k observations in T that are closest to $\mathbf{x}$, using a given distance metric, where k is a parameter of the algorithm. Then, the output for those k training observations is considered, and, using those k output values, the predicted output for unseen observation $\mathbf{x}$ is calculated as follows:

- If it is a regression problem, the predicted output value will be the average of the k selected training outputs;

- If it is a classification problem, the predicted class label will be obtained by a majority vote using those k training outputs; in other words, the class label that appears the largest number of times among the selected k training observations is the one that is returned as prediction.

Both for classification and regression, a useful technique can be to assign weights to the contributions of the neighbors, so that the nearer neighbors contribute more to the average than the more distant ones. For example, a common weighting scheme consists in giving each neighbor a weight of $1/d$, where d is the distance to the neighbor.

As the reader can notice, in this algorithm there is not, properly speaking, a training phase. As such, KNN also does not generate a model, if by model we intend a function, or a program, that can be evaluated on unseen observations to make a prediction. In [Cohen et al., 2018], there is an interesting discussion about the difference between *memorization* and *learning*, where it is said that KNN is a memorization algorithm, as opposed to several other algorithms that will be discussed later in the book, that are learning algorithms. Alternatively, we could say that the model simply consists in the training set itself, which is needed every time a prediction on an unseen instance is needed.

Despite its simplicity, KNN has been very successful in many application areas, returning results that are competitive with or even better than other, more sophisticated methods in terms of generalization ability. However, KNN also has the following potential drawbacks:

- The choice of the parameter k can be crucial. The optimal value for this parameter is strongly dependent on the problem and no guidelines exist to help make this choice. So, the only way to make an appropriate choice is by means of time-consuming experimental attempts.

- The choice of the distance measure used to calculate the k nearest training observations can also be crucial, and the optimal choice is also very often dependent on the problem. For numeric data, one can use the Euclidean distance or, possibly more appropriately when data dispersion is high, the Mahalanobis distance [De Maesschalck et al., 2000]. For discrete variables, such as for text classification, Hamming distance can be used. In several applications, KNN has been employed with correlation coefficients, such as Pearson and Spearman, as a metric.

- Having to "carry on" the training set for evaluating unseen instances can be an unbearable computational burden, in particular when the training set is large, such as in Big Data applications.

- For classification problems, when there is a rough balance between class labels in the selected k nearest training observations, the majority vote can fail to give a reliable result.

- For regression problems, where the variance of the outputs of the selected k nearest training observations is high, returning their average can fail to give a reliable result.

5.7.2 Linear Regression

Linear regression assumes a linear relationship between input values and targets, and aims at finding the coefficients of the linear relationship that minimize a pre-defined error (or loss) measure. More particularly, let:

$$D = \begin{bmatrix} x_{11} & x_{12} & ... & x_{1m} & y_1 \\ x_{21} & x_{22} & ... & x_{2m} & y_2 \\ ... & ... & ... & ... & ... \\ x_{n1} & x_{n2} & ... & x_{nm} & y_n \end{bmatrix}$$

be the given training set, and assume that the error we aim at minimizing is the squared error. Then, the objective of linear regression is to find the vector of coefficients $\beta = \{\beta_0, \beta_1, \beta_2, ..., \beta_m\}$ such that the following quantity is minimized:

$$E = \sum_{i=1}^{n} (\beta_0 + \beta_1 x_{i1} + \beta_2 x_{i2} + ... + \beta_m x_{im} - y_i)^2 \tag{5.6}$$

Once those coefficients that minimize the loss E have been found, let us assume that we want to calculate the output (prediction) on an unseen instance $\mathbf{u} = \{u_1, u_2, ..., u_m\}$; all we have to do is to calculate:

$$\text{prediction } = \beta_0 + \beta_1 u_1 + \beta_2 u_2 + ... + \beta_m u_m$$

So, now the problem is how to find the vector of coefficients β that minimizes E. This is clearly an optimization problem, like the ones that have been discussed in Part I of the book. As such, all the optimization algorithms studied in Part I can potentially be used (and have been used in the literature) to solve this minimization problem. However, historically, linear regression uses a different optimization algorithm called *least squares estimation*. In order to understand the functioning of this algorithm, let us define an artificial output value $x_0 = 1$. This allows us to rewrite Equation (5.6) as:

$$E = \sum_{i=1}^{n} (\beta_0 x_{i0} + \beta_1 x_{i1} + \beta_2 x_{i2} + ... + \beta_m x_{im} - y_i)^2$$

which, using a more compact matrix notation, and indicating the squared error as $||.||^2$, can be rewritten as:

$$E = ||\mathbf{X}\beta - \mathbf{y}||^2 \tag{5.7}$$

where $\mathbf{X}$ is an $n \times m$ matrix, β is an m-dimensional vector and $\mathbf{y}$ is an n-dimensional vector. Developing Equation (5.7), we obtain:

$$E = (\mathbf{X}\beta - \mathbf{y})^T (\mathbf{X}\beta - \mathbf{y}) = \mathbf{y}^T \mathbf{y} - \mathbf{y}^T \mathbf{X}\beta - \beta^T \mathbf{X}^T \mathbf{y} + \beta^T \mathbf{X}^T \mathbf{X}\beta \tag{5.8}$$

As the loss E is convex, the optimum solution lies at gradient zero. The gradient of E is (using Denominator layout convention):

$$\frac{\partial E}{\partial \beta} = \frac{\partial (\mathbf{y}^T \mathbf{y} - \mathbf{y}^T \mathbf{X}\beta - \beta^T \mathbf{X}^T \mathbf{y} + \beta^T \mathbf{X}^T \mathbf{X} \beta)}{\partial \beta} = -2\mathbf{y}^T \mathbf{X} + 2\beta^T \mathbf{X}^T \mathbf{X} \quad (5.9)$$

Now, setting the right part of Equation (5.7) to zero, we obtain:

$$-2\mathbf{y}^T \mathbf{X} + 2\beta^T \mathbf{X}^T \mathbf{X} = 0$$
$$\Rightarrow \mathbf{y}^T \mathbf{X} = \beta^T \mathbf{X}^T \mathbf{X}$$
$$\Rightarrow \mathbf{X}^T \mathbf{y} = \mathbf{X}^T \mathbf{X} \beta$$

From which we obtain:

$$\beta = (\mathbf{X}^T \mathbf{X})^{-1} \mathbf{X}^T \mathbf{y} \quad (5.10)$$

Equation (5.10) gives a formula for the optimal vector β. The term $(\mathbf{X}^T \mathbf{X})^{-1} \mathbf{X}^T$ is called the Moore-Penrose inverse, or *pseudoinverse*, of matrix $\mathbf{X}$. It is possible to prove that the pseudoinverse is defined and unique for all matrices whose entries are real or complex numbers. Furthermore, the pseudoinverse can be computed using a method called *singular value decomposition*. A discussion of this method is beyond the scope of this book. The interested reader is referred to [Golub and Reinsch, 1970, Klema and Laub, 1980].

5.7.3 Logistic Regression

Despite the name, logistic regression is generally used for tackling *classification* problems. The reason why linear regression is not an appropriate method for classification problems is, indeed, intuitive. Let us, for instance, consider a binary classification problem, whose class labels are identified with 0 and 1. One may try to develop a linear model that approximates an output equal to 0 for all the observations belonging to one class and that approximates an output equal to 1 for all the observations belonging to the other class. All the output values that are different from 0 and different from 1 could, for instance, be interpreted as the probability of the observation belonging to one of the two classes. Unfortunately, such a model has several drawbacks, the most important of which is arguably the fact that the outputs of the linear model could, for some observations, assume values that are smaller than 0 or larger than 1. Thus, interpreting this output as a probability would be impossible. To have a visual intuition of this issue, let us consider a simple binary classification problem, whose objective is to categorize persons into women (represented as 1) or men (represented as 0), based on their weight. Using real data from 190 Californian persons who responded to a survey of U.S. licensed drivers, it is possible to generate a linear model. The data points and the model are represented in Figure 5.7(a) (image taken from [Berger, 2017]), where on the horizontal axis we report the body weight of the respondent (expressed in pounds), and on the vertical axis the model's output. As we can notice, the linear model has a very weak ability

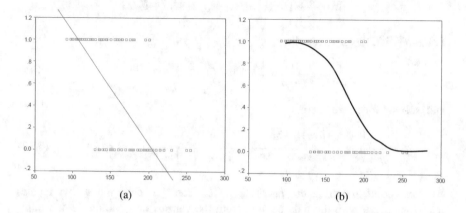

(a)   (b)

Fig. 5.7 Plot (a): linear model for a simple binary classification task; plot (b): logistic model for the same task. Images taken from [Berger, 2017]

to match the data. For someone who weighs 150 pounds, the predicted value for the gender is 0.557. Naively, one might interpret the predicted gender as the probability that the person is a female. However, the model can give predicted values that exceed 1 and/or are smaller than 0, so the predicted values are not probabilities. The linear regression model is clearly not appropriate for this problem. As shown in Figure 5.7(b) (image taken from [Berger, 2017]), a model that would fit the data much better corresponds to a curved line. This is what a logistic regression model looks like. It clearly fits the data better than a straight line when the target variable takes on only two values.

Logistic regression forms its model using a logistic function. Central to logistic regression is the concept of *odds*, or *likelihood*. The odds are simply the ratio of the proportions for the two possible outcomes. If p is the proportion for one outcome, say $p = P(y = 1)$, then $1 - p$ is the proportion for the second outcome, i.e., $1 - p = P(y = 0)$. The odds are defined as:

$$\text{odds} = \frac{p}{1 - p}$$

Logistic regression works with odds rather than proportions, and, to induce a model that is a logistic function, it introduces a new dependent (target) variable, called *logit(p)*, defined as the natural logarithm of the odds:

$$\text{logit}(p) = \ln\left(\frac{p}{1 - p}\right)$$

Now, as we did for linear regression, we define the model as a linear function of the explanatory (target) variable, remembering that this time the target variable is $\text{logit}(p)$. So, we have:

$$\ln\left(\frac{p}{1-p}\right) = \beta_0 + \beta_1 x_1 + \beta_2 x_2 + \ldots + \beta_m x_m$$

Equation (5.7.3) can be rewritten as:

$$\frac{p}{1-p} = e^{\beta_0 + \beta_1 x_1 + \beta_2 x_2 + \ldots + \beta_m x_m} \tag{5.11}$$

and, solving for p, we obtain:

$$p = \frac{e^{\beta_0 + \beta_1 x_1 + \beta_2 x_2 + \ldots + \beta_m x_m}}{1 + e^{\beta_0 + \beta_1 x_1 + \beta_2 x_2 + \ldots + \beta_m x_m}} = \frac{1}{1 + e^{-(\beta_0 + \beta_1 x_1 + \beta_2 x_2 + \ldots + \beta_m x_m)}} \tag{5.12}$$

At this point, coefficients $\beta_0, \beta_1, \beta_2, \ldots, \beta_m$ can be determined by replacing $x_1, x_2, \ldots, x_m$ with the data coming from the various observations in the training set and using *maximum likelihood* procedures to minimize loss compared to the corresponding target values. When this is done, Equation (5.12) can be used to calculate p for an unseen observation, simply using the coefficients $\beta_0, \beta_1, \beta_2, \ldots, \beta_m$ that have been found, and replacing $x_1, x_2, \ldots, x_m$ with the data coming from the unseen observation. If $p > 0.5$ then the observation is categorized as belonging to class 1, otherwise to class 0. The mathematics used for determining $\beta_0, \beta_1, \beta_2, \ldots, \beta_m$ is beyond the scope of the book. The interested reader is referred to [Albert and Andreson, 1984, Czepiel, 2002].

Chapter 6
Decision Tree Learning

Given a training set, Decision Trees (DTs) [Quinlan, 1986] are predictive models represented as trees where each vertex represents a feature, or attribute, and each edge represents a possible value of that attribute. Leaves contain target values and a path from the root to a leaf allows us to make a prediction. Although DTs can be used for a wide variety of tasks [Rokach and Maimon, 2014], we will focus only on classification and regression.

As a simple example, the reader is invited to observe the "toy" training set represented in Table 6.1. It refers to a binary classification problem where all the attributes are categorical. The objective of the problem is to predict whether a person will play tennis in a given day, using meteorological information relative to the day.

Table 6.1 A training set used as an example to explain the functioning of DTs. Each observation corresponds to a day. Input features are four meteorological characteristics that have been observed for that day. The expected output (target) is binary information (Yes or No), revealing whether a given person has played tennis that day. This training set can be used to induce a model able to predict whether the person will play tennis, by making explicit the hidden relationships that may exist between the input features and the target

Day	Outlook	Temperature	Humidity	Wind	PlayTennis
D1	Sunny	Hot	High	Weak	No
D2	Sunny	Hot	High	Strong	No
D3	Overcast	Hot	High	Weak	Yes
D4	Rain	Mild	High	Weak	Yes
D5	Rain	Cool	Normal	Weak	Yes
D6	Rain	Cool	Normal	Strong	No
D7	Overcast	Cool	Normal	Strong	Yes
D8	Sunny	Mild	High	Weak	No
D9	Sunny	Cool	Normal	Weak	Yes
D10	Rain	Mild	Normal	Weak	Yes
D11	Sunny	Mild	Normal	Strong	Yes
D12	Overcast	Mild	High	Strong	Yes
D13	Overcast	Hot	Normal	Weak	Yes
D14	Rain	Mild	High	Strong	No

© Springer Nature Switzerland AG 2023

L. Vanneschi and S. Silva, *Lectures on Intelligent Systems*, Natural Computing Series,
https://doi.org/10.1007/978-3-031-17922-8_6

One may imagine that the training set contains a set of historical observations: each observation represents a past day, for which some meteorological characteristics have been observed and stored, together with binary information (Yes or No) revealing whether the person has played tennis or not on that day. Input data (features, or attributes) are Outlook, Temperature, Humidity and Wind, while PlayTennis represents the binary dependent variable (target). Each one of the features can assume a number of possible values. In particular, Outlook can have three possible values: Sunny, Overcast or Rain; Temperature can have three possible values: Hot, Mild or Cool; Humidity can have two possible values: High or Normal; and Wind can have two possible values: Weak or Strong.

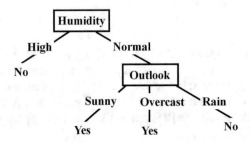

Fig. 6.1 An example of a DT for the training set reported in Table 6.1

Let us now observe a possible DT for this problem, represented in Figure 6.1. This tree, as with any DT, can be interpreted as a model consisting in an *if-then-else* cascade. More specifically, it can be interpreted as:

if (Humidity == High)
    then PlayTennis = No;
    else if (Humidity == Normal)
        then if (Outlook == Sunny)
            then PlayTennis = Yes;
            else if (Outlook == Overcast)
                then PlayTennis = Yes;
                else if (Outlook == Rain)
                    then PlayTennis = No;

The leaves of the tree contain class labels and each path from the root to a leaf allows us to take a decision. Table 6.2 contains an evaluation of this DT on all the observations of the training set of Table 6.1.

The reader is invited to verify each result in the column "Predicted value" coming from the evaluation of the DT on each training observation. As an example, let us consider the seventh observation (D7 in the table). The first attribute that has to be checked is Humidity, because it is the attribute placed at the root of the tree. Since the value of Humidity in observation D7 is Normal, we navigate the right

Table 6.2 The outputs predicted by the DT in Figure 6.1 on the training set of Table 6.1, against the expected outputs. Correct predictions are highlighted in bold

Day	Predicted Value	Expected Value
D1	**No**	No
D2	**No**	No
D3	No	Yes
D4	No	Yes
D5	No	Yes
D6	**No**	No
D7	**Yes**	Yes
D8	**No**	No
D9	**Yes**	Yes
D10	No	Yes
D11	**Yes**	Yes
D12	No	Yes
D13	**Yes**	Yes
D14	**No**	No

branch of the tree, forgetting for this particular observation the left subtree of the root. Navigating the right subtree of the root, the next attribute we find is Outlook. Since in D7 the value of Outlook is Overcast, we follow the connection labeled with Overcast (second child of the node Outlook), ending up in the terminal node Yes, which allows us to make the prediction. As we can see in Table 6.2, this prediction is correct. If we look at all the training observations, the DT represented in Figure 6.1 makes nine correct predictions and five wrong predictions (accuracy on training data equal to $9/14 \approx 0.64$).

As one can imagine, given a dataset, a (generally very) large number of DTs can be built for it. In general, any combination of the features with all their possible outcomes, arranged in a tree, is a possible DT. So, how to choose the one that best allows us to classify? This is the subject of DT learning. Several algorithms to learn DTs have been developed so far, most of them variations of the original ID3 algorithm (Iterative Dichotomiser 3) [Quinlan, 1986].

Before dedicating our attention to DT learning algorithms, the reader is invited to take a look back at the DT represented in Figure 6.1 and observe that it is not using all the features that are in the training set. This is a normal characteristic of DT learning: learning algorithms will tend to let DTs have the most important features in the high levels of the tree (with the most important one at the root). If all the ramifications coming from the most important features terminate with a leaf, and thus allow us to take a decision, the other features are not needed.

The next section describes the application of the ID3 algorithm to the binary classification problem presented before. It is followed by another section describing how simple modifications of different elements of this algorithm allow the induction of DTs for classification problems involving continuous features, and for regression problems involving the prediction of a continuous target.

6.1 ID3 Algorithm

The ID3 algorithm builds a tree top-down (i.e., starting from the root, down to the leaves). The beginning is the attempt to answer the question: "Which attribute should be tested at the root of the tree?" Or, in other words: "Which attribute is the best classifier?" Once the root node of the tree is chosen, the other nodes are chosen using the same strategy, until we reach the leaves of the tree. We would like to choose, as the first attribute, the one that is most useful for classifying the instances (i.e., the attribute that, by itself, allows us to make the largest possible number of correct classifications or at least helps us as much as possible to make the largest possible number of classifications). To do that, we have to find a measure to quantify the usefulness of an attribute. The ID3 algorithm uses a measure that is called *Information Gain* (IG). Before talking about IG, we need to review the concept of entropy, on which IG is based. This concept has previously been studied in this book, but it deserves a new discussion here. Given an attribute A that can have c possible values, and given a collection S that contains some instances of this attribute, the entropy of that attribute is defined as:

$$Entropy(A, S) = \sum_{i=1}^{c} -p_i \, log_2 p_i \qquad (6.1)$$

Notice that the summation is Equation (6.1) has as many terms as the possible values of attribute A in S and, given the *ith* of those possible values, p_i is the fraction of observations in S in which A has that value. As an example, let us consider again the simple training set of Table 6.1, and let us call that training set S, for convenience, from now on. Let us consider attribute Wind. The entropy of that attribute is:

$$
\begin{aligned}
Entropy(Wind, S) &= -\frac{6}{14} \, log_2 \frac{6}{14} - \frac{8}{14} \, log_2 \frac{8}{14} \\
&\approx -0.4286 \, log_2 \, 0.4286 - 0.5714 \, log_2 \, 0.5714 \\
&\approx 0.4286 \cdot 1.2223 + 0.5714 \cdot 0.8074 \\
&\approx 0.5239 + 0.4613 = 0.9852
\end{aligned}
$$

In fact, among the 14 total observations in S, on six observations attribute Wind has one value (i.e., Strong) and, on the remaining eight observations, it has another value (i.e., Weak). Given that attribute Wind only has two possible values in S, the summation is composed by only two terms. Notice that the logarithm of a number in $[0, 1)$ is a negative number, which allows us to simplify the negative signs in Equation (6.1), obtaining a positive result.

What, intuitively, is this number telling us? Even though this intuition is controversial and may be imprecise [Styer, 2019], in this context it is useful to interpret entropy as a measure of the "predictability" of the value of a variable. For instance, two simple cases can be imagined: if all instances of the attribute have the same value, then the entropy is 0 (minimum); in this case, the value of the variable is very predictable: given that it was always the same in all the observations, we can only conclude that it will have the same value also in the future. On the other hand, if half the instances of a given attribute have a particular value, and the other half another value, then the entropy is 1 (which is the maximum entropy value, in the particular case in which the variable can assume only two possible values). In this case, the value of the variable is hard to predict, since this prediction can only be done by random guessing, where both possible outcomes (the possible values of the variable) have 50% probability (coin tossing). In general, we can informally imagine that the bigger the entropy of a variable, the less predictive the variable is.

Let us now repeat the same exercise (calculation of the entropy of a variable), but this time let us consider the dependent variable (target) PlayTennis. Before making the calculations, let us also slightly update the notation that we have used so far: when an attribute A is the target value of a set of data S, the entropy of A in S will not be indicated as $Entropy(A, S)$, but simply as $Entropy(S)$. In other words, when the attribute is omitted, it is clear that it is the entropy of the dependent variable that is calculated. Given that, over the 14 observations of the training set of Table 6.1, nine observations have the variable PlayTennis equal to Yes, and the remaining five observations have PlayTennis equal to No, we have:

$$Entropy(S) = -\frac{9}{14} \; log_2 \frac{9}{14} - \frac{5}{14} \; log_2 \frac{5}{14}$$
$$\approx 0.6429 \cdot 0.6373 + 0.3571 \cdot 1.4856$$
$$\approx 0.4097 + 0.5305 \approx 0.9402 \quad (6.2)$$

We are now ready to introduce and discuss the concept of Information Gain (IG). As previously mentioned, IG is the measure of usefulness of an attribute used by the ID3 algorithm, and it is based on the concept of entropy. Informally, the IG of an attribute A is the expected *reduction* in the entropy of the target variable caused by partitioning the examples according to A. Remembering that, informally speaking, to reduce entropy means to increase predictability, the IG of an attribute A quantifies the increase in the predictability of the target value when the value of A is known.

More particularly, consider all the subsets of the dataset for which the attribute has a particular value, calculate the entropy of the target for each one of these subsets and sum them up (normalizing each one of them by the size of the subset). The IG is a quantification of how much the entropy is reduced, compared to the entropy of the target calculated on the whole dataset. Formally, the IG of an attribute A on a set of data S is defined as:

$$IG(S,A) = Entropy(S) - \sum_{v \in Values(A)} \frac{|S_v|}{|S|} Entropy(S_v) \quad (6.3)$$

where:

- S is the entire training set;
- $Values(A)$ is the set of all possible values of attribute A in the training set;

- S_v is the portion of the training set composed only of the observations in which the value of A is equal to v. In other words: $S_v = \{s \in S \mid A(s) = v\}$;
- for any set of data U, $|U|$ represents the number of observations in U.
- $Entropy(S_v)$ is the entropy of the target, calculated on the portion of the data S_v.

The term in Equation (6.3):

$$\sum_{v \in Values(A)} \frac{|S_v|}{|S|} Entropy(S_v)$$

is the expected value of the entropy after S has been partitioned using the possible values of attribute A. Thus, $IG(S,A)$ can be interpreted as the expected reduction in entropy caused by knowing the value of attribute A. In other words, $IG(S,A)$ is the information provided about the target value, given the value of attribute A.

As an example, let us now calculate the IG of the attribute Wind in the training set of Table 6.1. Developing Equation (6.3) with the particular values that Wind can have in the training set, we have:

$$IG(S,Wind) = Entropy(S) - \sum_{v \in \{Weak, Strong\}} \frac{|S_v|}{|S|} Entropy(S_v)$$

$$= Entropy(S) - \frac{|S_{Weak}|}{|S|} Entropy(S_{Weak}) - \frac{|S_{Strong}|}{|S|} Entropy(S_{Strong}) \quad (6.4)$$

Let us now calculate the single terms of Equation (6.4). We have:

- $Entropy(S) \approx 0.94$ (this value has already been calculated in Equation (6.2));
- $|S_{Weak}| = 8$, because there are eight observations where the value of attribute Wind is equal to Weak;
- $|S_{Strong}| = 6$, because there are six observations where the value of attribute Wind is equal to Strong;
- $|S| = 14$, because there are 14 total observations in the training set;
- $Entropy(S_{Weak}) = -\frac{2}{8} log_2 \frac{2}{8} - \frac{6}{8} log_2 \frac{6}{8} \approx 0.811$, because over the eight observations in which Wind is Weak, PlayTennis (i.e., the target) is equal to No in two observations (i.e., D_1 and D_8) and it is equal to Yes in six observations (i.e., D_3, D_4, D_5, D_9, D_{10}, D_{13}).
- $Entropy(S_{Weak}) = -\frac{3}{6} log_2 \frac{3}{6} - \frac{3}{6} log_2 \frac{3}{6} = 1$, because over the six observations in which Wind is Strong, PlayTennis is equal to No in three observations and it is equal to Yes in three observations.

Now, we can substitute all these values in Equation (6.4), and we can obtain the result:

$$IG(S,Wind) = 0.94 - \frac{8}{14} \cdot 0.811 - \frac{6}{14} \cdot 1 \approx 0.048$$

Repeating the same computations for all the other attributes in the training set, we have:

- $IG(S, Outlook) \approx 0.246$
- $IG(S, Humidity) \approx 0.151$
- $IG(S, Wind) \approx 0.048$
- $IG(S, Temperature) \approx 0.029$

According to these values, the attribute that provides the best prediction of the target is Outlook, given that it is the attribute with the highest IG. For this reason, Outlook is chosen by the ID3 algorithm as the root of the DT. We are now able to start building the DT, as in Figure 6.2. As we can see, the portion of the tree that was built consists of the root, labeled with Outlook, plus three ramifications starting from it, and labeled with the three possible values of attribute Outlook. At this point, the ID3 algorithm proceeds in an iterative way, trying to discover what is the attribute that has to be placed at the termination of each one of the ramifications that have been created in Figure 6.2.

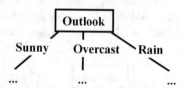

Fig. 6.2 The root of the DT built by the ID3 algorithm for the training set reported in Table 6.1, with its first ramification

As an example, let us try to understand what attribute should be at the root of the leftmost subtree, i.e., at the end of the connection labeled with Sunny. In order to answer this question, we have to iterate the process described so far, but using only the subset of the observations in which the value of Outlook is Sunny, i.e., S_{Sunny}. This portion of the training set is represented in Table 6.3. Using these observations, and calculating the IG of all the attributes except Outlook, we obtain:

Table 6.3 The portion of the training set of Table 6.1 in which the value of the attribute Outlook is equal to Sunny

Day	Outlook	Temperature	Humidity	Wind	PlayTennis
D1	Sunny	Hot	High	Weak	No
D2	Sunny	Hot	High	Strong	No
D8	Sunny	Mild	High	Weak	No
D9	Sunny	Cool	Normal	Weak	Yes
D11	Sunny	Mild	Normal	Strong	Yes

- $IG(S_{Sunny}, Humidity) \approx 0.970$
- $IG(S_{Sunny}, Wind) \approx 0.019$
- $IG(S_{Sunny}, Temperature) \approx 0.570$

Given that Humidity is the attribute with the highest IG, Humidity will be the attribute that will be placed in that point of the tree. Interestingly, looking back at the data in S_{Sunny} (Table 6.3), we can also notice that the choice of Humidity as the leftmost child of Outlook also allows us to terminate that branch of the tree. In fact, in S_{Sunny}, whenever the value of Humidity is High, the value of PlayTennis is No and whenever the value of Humidity is Normal, the value of PlayTennis is Yes. In other words, the attribute Humidity perfectly explains the target in that part of the training set. As a consequence, the node labeled with Humidity will have a branch labeled with High and terminated by No and a branch labeled with Normal and terminated by Yes.

Iterating this process for all the missing nodes, until each branch is terminated by a target value, we obtain the final DT represented in Figure 6.3. If we evaluate this DT on all the lines of the training set of Table 6.1, we can see that this DT performs the correct prediction for each one of the instances (in other words, its accuracy on the training data is equal to 1). Anyway, the reader should be aware that the ID3 algorithm is not guaranteed to find an optimal solution in general.

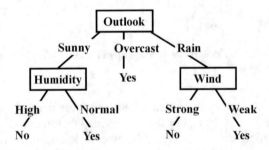

Fig. 6.3 The complete DT built by the ID3 algorithm for the training set reported in Table 6.1

ID3 is a greedy strategy: it selects the locally best attribute to split the dataset at each iteration. The algorithm's optimality can be improved by using backtracking during the search, at the cost of having a slower learning algorithm. Furthermore, ID3 can overfit the training data. To avoid overfitting, smaller DTs are usually preferred over larger ones. Last but not least, as it is clear from the example studied in this section, the ID3 algorithm expects discrete attributes. The next section describes simple modifications to allow the induction of DTs that can deal with continuous attributes and targets.

6.2 Continuous Attributes and Targets

From the original ID3 algorithm many variants have been developed, such as the C4.5 [Quinlan, 1993] and CART [Breiman et al., 1984] algorithms, among many others [Rokach and Maimon, 2014]. The C4.5 algorithm can handle continuous attributes by finding the best binary split of each continuous attribute each time a decision node is to be added to the tree. An efficient way to do this is to sort the observations by the attribute value and then try as many splitting values as the class changes observed in the target. Table 6.4 shows a variant of the same training set as before, with the observations now sorted by the Humidity percentage, which is now a continuous attribute. Two binary splits should be considered, namely split Humidity<72%, where 72% is the middle point of a class change occurring from D5 (70%) to D6 (74%), and split Humidity<81%, where 81% is the middle point of a class change occurring from D8 (80%) to D12 (82%).

Table 6.4 Training set similar to Table 6.1, now with Humidity as a continuous attribute. The observations are sorted by the Humidity value. The target variable PlayTennis changes (from Yes to No or the other way around) at two points: between D5 and D6; between D8 and D12. Decision nodes using the Humidity attribute will use the middle values 72% and/or 81%

Day	Outlook	Temperature	Humidity	Wind	PlayTennis
D9	Sunny	Cool	62%	Weak	Yes
D11	Sunny	Mild	64%	Strong	Yes
D10	Rain	Mild	68%	Weak	Yes
D13	Overcast	Hot	68%	Weak	Yes
D7	Overcast	Cool	69%	Strong	Yes
D5	Rain	Cool	70%	Weak	Yes
D6	Rain	Cool	74%	Strong	No
D1	Sunny	Hot	75%	Weak	No
D2	Sunny	Hot	76%	Strong	No
D14	Rain	Mild	78%	Strong	No
D8	Sunny	Mild	80%	Weak	No
D12	Overcast	Mild	82%	Strong	Yes
D3	Overcast	Hot	85%	Weak	Yes
D4	Rain	Mild	86%	Weak	Yes

Besides dealing with continuous attributes, the C4.5 algorithm can also handle missing values. It also performs pruning of the trees, removing branches (replacing them with leaves) that do not contribute to the accuracy of the tree. The C4.5 algorithm uses the Gain Ratio [Quinlan, 1993] as splitting criterion, which is a normalized form of the IG. Other splitting criteria are popular for inducing DTs, such as the Gini Index used in CART, among others [Rokach and Maimon, 2014].

Regarding the CART algorithm [Breiman et al., 1984], the trees it induces are always binary, meaning that each decision node only has two possible directions, even when it refers to an attribute with more than two categories. When inducing a tree, CART can take into consideration misclassification costs and *a priori* proba-

Table 6.5 Training set similar to Tables 6.1 and 6.4, now with percentage of Humidity as the only attribute, and a continuous target PlayTennis indicating how many minutes were played

Day	Humidity	PlayTennis
D1	75%	0m
D2	76%	0m
D3	85%	30m
D4	86%	60m
D5	70%	90m
D6	74%	0m
D7	69%	120m
D8	80%	0m
D9	62%	90m
D10	68%	90m
D11	64%	120m
D12	82%	60m
D13	68%	75m
D14	78%	0m

bilities, and it also prunes the trees after induction. However, the major novelty of CART is the possibility of inducing regression trees to predict a continuous target, as opposed to the classification trees that have been the only type of DTs described so far.

Table 6.5 shows another variant of the same training set as before, now with a continuous target PlayTennis that indicates how many minutes the person played tennis in each day (0 minutes means the person did not play tennis that day). To induce a regression tree from this data, the splitting criterion must be a measure of the distance between the values predicted by the tree and the expected values, such as the Mean Squared Error (MSE). Unlike in classification trees, where each terminal node predicts the class that is most common among the samples that fell into that node, in regression trees each terminal node predicts the value that is the mean target of all the samples that fell into that node.

Suppose we induce a regression tree for the data in Table 6.5. Figure 6.4 shows a plot of the data, where the dotted lines indicate splitting points and the thick horizontal lines indicate the predicted target for each region of the feature space (97.5m for Humidity<72%; 0m for 72%≤Humidity<81%; 50m for 81%≤Humidity). In the same way that in classification trees some terminal nodes are pure while others are mixed, in regression trees some parts of the function will be accurately predicted while others will be only roughly approximated.

The DTs described here are very simple, but powerful enough to solve many problems. Still today, improvements are being made on both the type of trees and the algorithms to induce them. However, the simplest ones are still the most popular. They are also the preferred predictors for building ensemble models, as will be described in Chapter 11.

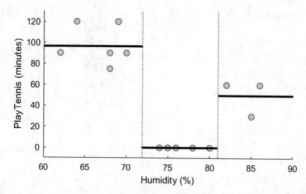

Fig. 6.4 Scatter plot of Humidity (%) versus PlayTennis (minutes) as in Table 6.5. The dotted vertical lines indicate split points of a possible regression tree induced from the data, while the thick horizontal lines indicate its predicted values for each region of the feature space

Chapter 7
Artificial Neural Networks

Artificial Neural Networks (ANNs) are computational methods that belong to the field of Machine Learning [Mitchell, 1997, Kelleher et al., 2015, Gabriel, 2016]. The aim of ANNs is to implement a very simplified model of the human brain. In this way, ANNs try to learn tasks (to solve problems) mimicking the behavior of the brain. The brain is composed of a large set of specialized cells, called *neurons*. Each single neuron is, in itself, a very simple entity, and the power of the brain is given by the fact that neurons are numerous and strongly interconnected, by means of connections called *synapses*. The brain learns because neurons are able to communicate with each other. A picture of a biological neuron and its synapses is shown in Figure 7.1. Biological neurons can receive stimuli and, as a consequence, emit (electric) signals, which can stimulate other neurons. When a biological neuron emits its signal, we say that it "fires".

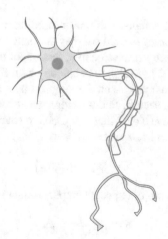

Fig. 7.1 Illustration of a biological neuron and its synapse

© Springer Nature Switzerland AG 2023
L. Vanneschi and S. Silva, *Lectures on Intelligent Systems*, Natural Computing Series,
https://doi.org/10.1007/978-3-031-17922-8_7

In analogy with the human brain, ANNs are computational methods that use a large set of elementary computational units, themselves called (artificial) neurons. ANNs gain their power due to the numerous interconnections between neurons. Each neuron is only able to perform very simple tasks and ANNs are able to perform complex calculations because they are typically composed of many artificial neurons, strongly interconnected with each other and communicating with each other. Before studying complex ANNs that are able to solve large-scale real-life problems, we must understand how single neurons and simple networks work. For this reason, we begin the study of ANNs with a very simple kind of network, called a *Perceptron*.

7.1 Perceptron

A Perceptron [Rosenblatt, 1958, Demuth et al., 2014, Rashid, 2016] is a simple ANN that can be composed of one single neuron, or several neurons arranged *in a single layer*. In the continuation of this chapter, we will study the important concept of "layers" in ANNs and we will be able to understand why ANNs that are composed of more than one layer may be more powerful than ANNs composed of a single layer, like the Perceptron. Another limitation of the Perceptron, compared to some other kinds of networks, is that in the Perceptron the flow of the information is unidirectional (from input to outputs). For this reason, the Perceptron is also called a *Feedforward ANN*.

7.1.1 Single Neuron Perceptron

A Perceptron ANN can be composed of one or more neurons, each of which directly forms the output of the network (and so, they are called output neurons). Furthermore, each neuron is directly connected to several input units by means of connections that are characterized by weights. In analogy with Biology, these connections are called synapses. Let us begin with the simplest possible Perceptron ANN: the one composed of just one neuron. In this section, as in Section 7.2, we will assume that the objective is to solve a classification problem characterized by a supervised training set composed of m input vectors (observations):

$$\mathbf{X} = \{\mathbf{x}_1, \mathbf{x}_2, ..., \mathbf{x}_m\}$$

and the corresponding vector of expected outputs (target values):

$$\mathbf{d} = \{d_1, d_2, ..., d_m\}$$

For each observation $i = 1, 2, ..., m$, the target value d_i generally has the appearance of a class label, or, in some cases, of a numeric value that has been appropriately chosen to represent the class label. Furthermore, for each $i = 1, 2, ..., m$, input vector

$\mathbf{x}_i$ is an n dimensional vector of input values (or feature values), which, in general, will be represented as: $\mathbf{x}_i = \{x_{i1}, x_{i2}, ..., x_{in}\}$. However, the reader is invited to notice that, for the sake of simplicity, when the index i of an observation will be "clear from the context", or "not relevant to the context", a generic input vector may simply be represented using the notation:

$$\mathbf{x} = \{x_1, x_2, ..., x_n\}$$

and, in this case, the target value that is contained in the training set, and that represents the expected output corresponding to observation $\mathbf{x}$, will simply be represented as d. This notation will be updated in Section 7.3, where more complex ANNs will be studied.

The structure of a Single Neuron Perceptron can be represented as in Figure 7.2. The architecture of this elementary ANN is characterized by:

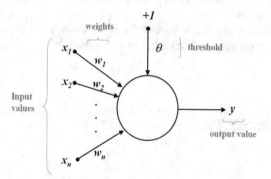

Fig. 7.2 Single Neuron Perceptron

- A set of input units, of the same cardinality as the number of input variables (features), from which input values are fed into the network. As mentioned above, let $\mathbf{x} = \{x_1, x_2, ..., x_n\}$ be a generic observation, taken from the training set, and fed into the ANN;
- a set of weights $w_1, w_2, ..., w_n$, one for each synapse joining an input unit to the neuron. These weights quantify the "importance" of the input signals entering the ANN;
- a particular connection, called the *threshold* connection, whose weight is θ, and whose input value is constantly equal to 1.
- an output y, which is the result of the computation of the ANN.

The output y is calculated as follows:

$$y = f(\sum_{i=1}^{n} w_i x_i + \theta) \tag{7.1}$$

The function f is called the *activation function*, and it is the function that determines the output of the neuron. One of the simplest activation functions is the so-called *threshold* (or "step") function:

$$f(s) = \begin{cases} 1 & \text{if } s > 0 \\ -1 & \text{otherwise} \end{cases}$$

This activation function is particularly useful when we want to solve classification problems. For instance, the Single Neuron Perceptron with this activation function can be used to classify a set of input vectors into one of two possible classes C_1 and C_2 (binary classification). In such a situation, for instance, the Single Neuron Perceptron classifies an input vector into class C_1 if its output is equal to 1 and into class C_2 if its output is equal to -1. If this activation function is used, it should not be difficult to understand the motivation for the presence of the threshold connection: the weight θ of this connection can shift the threshold point that differentiates input values between the two classes.

As an alternative to the step activation function, there are other possible activation functions that are commonly used. Simple examples are:

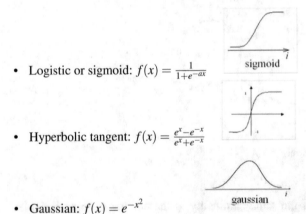

- Logistic or sigmoid: $f(x) = \frac{1}{1+e^{-ax}}$

- Hyperbolic tangent: $f(x) = \frac{e^x - e^{-x}}{e^x + e^{-x}}$

- Gaussian: $f(x) = e^{-x^2}$

Besides these activation functions, several others exist, such as, for instance, the Rectified Linear Units (ReLU) function [Agarap, 2018] and the SoftMax function [Kagalkar and Raghuram, 2020]. The ReLU and SoftMax functions are particularly relevant in Deep Learning, which is not a topic directly tackled in this book. On the other hand, the sigmoid activation function will be particularly relevant in the next sections. The interested reader is referred to [Sharma et al., 2020] for a discussion of different existing activation functions.

For the sake of simplicity, it is often useful to rename the weight of the threshold connection and its input, using the same notation as for the other connections and inputs. In other words, often the weight of the threshold connection is called w_0, and its input x_0. Using this notation, and remembering that x_0 is constantly equal to 1, Equation (7.1) can be rewritten in the following, simpler, form:

$$y = f(\sum_{i=0}^{n} w_i x_i) \qquad (7.2)$$

ANNs are characterized by a learning (or training) phase, in which the network "learns" to solve the given task by modifying, if needed, the weights of its connections. Once the learning phase is complete, the ANN is ready to be used on new data (generalization phase). Predicted outputs on new input data can be calculated using Equation (7.2), employing the final weights obtained at the end of the learning phase. During the training phase, the Single Neuron Perceptron receives in input a training set formed by m vectors of data $\{\mathbf{x}_1, \mathbf{x}_2, ..., \mathbf{x}_m\}$, the training observations, plus a class label (for instance, C_1 or C_2) for each one of them (i.e., the class in which the input observations must be categorized). During the learning, the Perceptron modifies the weights of its synapses (with an algorithm called a *learning rule*) in such a way that it is able to classify, if possible, all the vectors $\mathbf{x}_1, \mathbf{x}_2, ..., \mathbf{x}_m$ into the correct class (C_1 or C_2). The pseudocode of the algorithm used by the Perceptron to modify the weights (i.e., to learn), called the *Perceptron Learning Rule*, is shown in Algorithm 7. The algorithm terminates when all the vectors in the training set are classified in a correct way, or after a previously fixed number of iterations.

Algorithm 7: Perceptron Learning Rule, for ANNs composed of one neuron.

---

1. Initialize all the weights $w_0, w_1, ..., w_n$ with random values;

2. Select an input vector $\mathbf{x}$ from the training set, and calculate the output value y of the neuron for this input value, using Equation (7.2). Let d be the expected output (target), that is associated to $\mathbf{x}$ in the training set;

3. **if** $(y \neq d)$ (i.e., if the output calculated by the Perceptron is wrong) **then**

   for all $i = 0, 1, .., n$, modify the weight w_i as follows:

   - if $y > d$ $w_i := w_i - \eta x_i$
   - if $y < d$ $w_i := w_i + \eta x_i$

   end

4. Go to Point 2.

The following points should be remarked:

- Also the weight of the threshold connection must be modified, together with all the other weights. Thus, from now on, the threshold connection will often be treated like any other connection, with the particularity that the input x_0 of this connection is always equal to 1.

- η is a parameter of the algorithm, and it is called the *learning rate*. It is used to influence the learning speed and it can be a constant, or it can dynamically change during the execution of the algorithm. In any case, it has, by definition, always a positive value. More details about the importance of this parameter, and how to set its value, will be given in Section 7.3.

Let us now consider one of the simplest possible cases: the case in which the Single Neuron Perceptron has only two input units. In this case, once the learning phase is terminated, the values of the weights w_1 and w_2 and of the threshold θ will have been determined. In this situation, it is possible to identify a straight line (it would be a hyperplane in the general case, i.e., when the number of inputs is larger than two):

$$w_1 x_1 + w_2 x_2 + \theta = 0$$

or:

$$x_2 = -\frac{w_1}{w_2} x_1 - \frac{\theta}{w_2}$$

If the training of this network was successful, this straight line allows us to graphically *separate* the two classes C_1 and C_2. This straight line has the following properties:

- All the points that belong to class C_1 are "above" the straight line and all the ones that belong to C_2 are "below" (or vice versa).
- The weights vector $\mathbf{w} = [w_1, w_2]$ is perpendicular to the straight line.
- θ allows us to calculate the distance of the straight line to the origin.

These concepts are shown graphically in Figure 7.3. We point out that, in general,

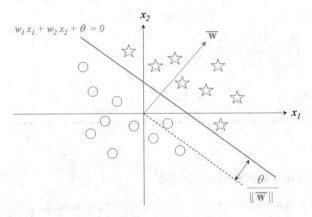

Fig. 7.3 A straight line separating points belonging to two classes

the distance of the straight line to the origin is $\frac{|\theta|}{\|\mathbf{w}\|}$, however, as will be shown later in the section, it is always possible to normalize the weight vector in such a way that $||\mathbf{w}|| = 1$. In that case, the distance of the straight line to the origin is simply given by the magnitude of the weight θ of the threshold connection.

Before considering a simple numeric example that should clarify the functioning of Algorithm 7 and many of the concepts discussed so far, let us present an important property of the Perceptron Learning Rule.

Theorem 7.1. (Perceptron Convergence Theorem). *If a weight vector* $\mathbf{w}^*$ *that allows us to obtain* $y = d$ *for all training instances exists, then the Perceptron converges to a solution (which can be equal to* $\mathbf{w}^*$ *or not) in a finite number of steps, independently of the initial choice of the weights.*

If such a weight vector exists, then we say that the classes are *linearly separable*, which means that a linear function exists that is able to separate the classes, as in Figure 7.3. In the continuation of this chapter, we will also discover two further important properties:

- If a problem is *not* linearly separable (in other words, if a linear function able to correctly separate the classes does *not* exist), then the Perceptron is *not* able to correctly classify all the instances of that problem.
- In order to correctly classify nonlinearly separable problems, ANNs with at least one layer of *hidden neurons* are needed.

By hidden neurons, here, we mean neurons whose outputs are not a part of the output of the network, but are, instead, used as inputs for other neurons. If we consider a network with hidden neurons, it is not hard to understand that the structure of that network can be imagined as organized in *layers*. In this sense, the second point of the previous list can be rewritten by saying that nonlinearly separable problems can be correctly solved only by multilayer ANNs. Multilayer ANNs can be considered to be more general systems than the simple Perceptron and, as we will see in the continuation, they have, in general, the ability to solve any type of problem, independently of the shape of the function separating the classes. For this reason, particular attention will be dedicated to multilayer ANNs, which will be studied in depth in the second part of this chapter.

Example of Application of the Perceptron Learning Rule

Let us now consider a very simple numeric example that should help us clarify the functioning of the Perceptron Learning Rule and many of the concepts discussed so far. Let us consider the following "toy" training set:

(x_1, x_2)	d
$(-2, 6)$	1
$(6, 2)$	1
$(-4, 1)$	-1
$(-10, 4)$	-1

In such a situation, the Perceptron is supposed to classify input data $(-2, 6)$ and $(6, 2)$ into one class and $(-4, 1)$ and $(-10, 4)$ into the other. Target values 1 and -1 have been substituted for the class labels, because those are the possible output values of the "step" activation function that will be used in this example. Following Algorithm 7, the first action that needs to be taken is the random initialization of the weights. Let us assume, for instance, that the generator of random numbers of our programming language has generated the following values for the initial weights:

$$w_1 = 1, \quad w_2 = 2, \quad w_0 = -12$$

Furthermore, let us suppose that we keep the learning rate η constantly equal to 1 for the entire execution of the learning rule (this value has been chosen only to make the calculations in this example simpler). Let us draw the points of the training set (using two different symbols for the points that must be classified into the two different classes) and the straight line:

$$x_1 + 2x_2 - 12 = 0$$

This graphical representation is shown in Figure 7.4. From this graphical representation, it is clear that the straight line *does not* separate the points $(-2, 6)$ and $(6, 2)$ from $(-4, 1)$ and $(-10, 4)$, thus it is necessary to modify the weights in such a way that also the position of the straight line will be modified.

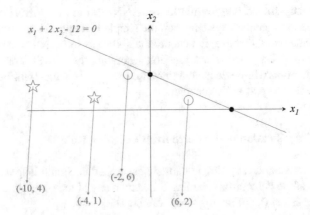

Fig. 7.4 The points of the example, and the straight line obtained using the initial random weights

Let us begin the execution of the Perceptron learning rule in order to modify the weights. The next step that needs to be taken is the choice of an input vector **x** from the training set. In Algorithm 7, no particular rule is given for the choice of the input vector. In fact, the algorithm is general, and any method to choose the input vector can be used, including selecting it at random at every step. However, for simplicity, in this example we assume that the first chosen input vector is the first point in the training set, i.e.: $\mathbf{x} = (-2, 6)$. Let us now calculate the output of the Perceptron for this point:

$$y = f(-2 + 12 - 12) = f(-2) = -1$$

We can observe that the Perceptron's classification does of this point is *not* correct: the calculated output $y = -1$ is different from the target value $d = 1$ that appears in the training set in correspondence with the observation that we are considering. Thus, as it was already expected observing Figure 7.4, it is necessary to modify the weights. Given that $y < d$, the Perceptron learning rule makes those modifications like this:

$$w_0 = w_0 + \eta x_0 = -12 + (1 \cdot 1) = -11$$
$$w_1 = w_1 + \eta x_1 = 1 + 1 \cdot (-2) = -1$$
$$w_2 = w_2 + \eta x_2 = 2 + (1 \cdot 6) = 8$$

We are now supposed to iterate the process, by selecting a new input observation. Let us consider, for instance, the second point in the training set, and let us calculate the output of the Perceptron, using the new weights (it is worth pointing out that, once the values of the weights have been updated, the old values are never used anymore). The point is $\mathbf{x} = (6, 2)$ and the output calculated by the Perceptron is:

$$y = f(-6 + 16 - 11) = f(-1) = -1$$

Also in this case, the classification is *not* correct: the output, $y = -1$, calculated by the Perceptron is different from the target, $d = 1$, that is associated with the point $(6, 2)$ in the training set. Given that the classification is not correct, once again it is necessary to modify the weights. Given that $y < d$, we have:

$$w_0 = w_0 + \eta x_0 = -11 + (1 \cdot 1) = -10$$
$$w_1 = w_1 + \eta x_1 = -1 + 1 \cdot 6 = 5$$
$$w_2 = w_2 + \eta x_2 = 8 + (1 \cdot 2) = 10$$

Let us now consider, for instance, the third point in the training set: $\mathbf{x} = (-4, 1)$. The output calculated by the Perceptron is:

$$y = f(-20 + 10 - 10) = f(-20) = -1$$

In this case, the classification is correct (the output calculated by the Perceptron is equal to the expected output that is associated with the point $(-4, 1)$ in the training set). So, applying Algorithm 7, the weights do not have to be modified, and the algorithm should continue with the selection of another input observation from the training set.

Let us consider the fourth point in the training set: $\mathbf{x} = (-10, 4)$. The output calculated by the Perceptron for this point is:

$$y = f(-50 + 40 - 10) = f(0) = -1$$

Also in this case, the classification is correct, so the weights do not have to be modified.

At this point, we must iterate once again considering all the points in the training set since the last modification of the weights, because the termination condition of the learning algorithm says that the algorithm terminates only when the Perceptron correctly classifies all the training instances. Let us consider, for instance, the first point in the training set: $(-2, 6)$. We have:

$$y = f(-10 + 60 - 10) = f(40) = 1$$

The classification is correct, thus we do not modify the weights. Finally, let us consider the second point in the training set: $(6, 2)$. We have:

$$y = f(30 + 20 - 10) = f(40) = 1$$

Also in this case the classification is correct, and so we do not modify the weights. The third and the fourth vector of the training set have already been tested with the current values of the weights and they have returned a correct classification. So now the algorithm terminates, returning the following, final, values of the weights:

$$w_0 = -10, \; w_1 = 5, \; w_2 = 10$$

With these weights, the Perceptron is able to correctly classify all the input observations in the training set.

Let us now draw the points of the training set and the straight line with the new weights vector, i.e.:

$$5x_1 + 10x_2 - 10 = 0$$

This graphical representation is shown in Figure 7.5. It is clear that now, as expected, the straight line correctly separates the points. Furthermore, it is possible to observe that the weights vector $(w_1, w_2) = (5, 10)$ is perpendicular to the straight line. In fact, the straight line can be expressed as follows:

$$x_2 = -\frac{1}{2}x_1 + 1$$

and thus its slope is: $m_1 = -\frac{1}{2}$. The straight line that extends the weights vector is a straight line that passes through the origin and the point $(5, 10)$, so we can write this straight line as:

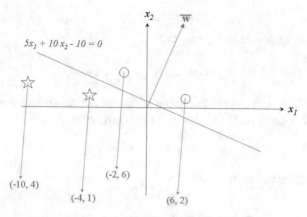

Fig. 7.5 The points of the example, and the straight line obtained using the final weights returned by the Perceptron learning rule

$$\frac{x_1 - 5}{-5} = \frac{x_2 - 10}{-10}$$

$$-\frac{x_1}{5} + 1 = -\frac{x_2}{10} + 1$$

$$x_2 = 2x_1$$

Its slope is: $m_2 = 2$. The condition for two straight lines with slopes m_1 and m_2 to be perpendicular is that: $m_2 = -\frac{1}{m_1}$. So, the two straight lines are indeed perpendicular. Finally, let us calculate the distance to the origin of the straight line:

$$5x_1 + 10x_2 - 10 = 0$$

We recall that the formula of the distance of a point (x_1, y_1) to a straight line:

$$w_1 x + w_2 y + w_0 = 0$$

is given by:

$$d = \frac{|w_1 x_1 + w_2 y_1 + w_0|}{\sqrt{w_1^2 + w_2^2}}$$

In the case in which (x_1, y_1) is the origin, the previous formula becomes:

$$d = \frac{|w_0|}{\sqrt{w_1^2 + w_2^2}}$$

or:

$$d = \frac{|\theta|}{\|\mathbf{w}\|}$$

The straight line:

$$w_1 x_1 + w_2 x_2 + w_0 = 0$$

can always be written in such a way that:

$$\|\mathbf{w}\| = \sqrt{w_1^2 + w_2^2} = 1$$

To obtain this, it is enough to divide the parameters of the straight line by a given constant k. For instance, in the case of the previous straight line:

$$5x_1 + 10x_2 - 10 = 0$$

it can be transformed into:

$$x_1 + 2x_2 - 2 = 0$$

to calculate the constant k all we have to do is:

$$\sqrt{\frac{1}{k^2} + \frac{4}{k^2}} = 1 \quad \Longrightarrow \quad \frac{\sqrt{5}}{k} = 1 \quad \Longrightarrow \quad k = \sqrt{5}$$

So, if we write the straight line in the following form:

$$\frac{1}{\sqrt{5}} x_1 + \frac{2}{\sqrt{5}} x_2 - \frac{2}{\sqrt{5}} = 0$$

we have:

$$\|\mathbf{w}\| = 1$$

This means that $\|\mathbf{w}\|$ can always be considered equal to 1 without loss of generality, and in that case, the distance of the straight line to the origin is given by the absolute value of the weight θ (or w_0) of the threshold connection.

7.1.2 Multiclass Classification and Multineuron, Single-Layer Perceptron

So far, we have considered problems in which data have to be partitioned into *two* classes (*binary classification*). But what happens if data have to be partitioned into *more* than two classes (*multiclass classification*)? Given a problem in which data must be classified into more than two classes, more than two neurons have to be combined into a network. The Perceptron, by its very definition, can have only one layer of neurons, so, for instance, a Perceptron with m neurons will have a structure like the one shown in Figure 7.6. This Perceptron can separate data into 2^m distinct classes, depending on its binary output. In other words, $y_1, y_2, ..., y_m$ can be interpreted as a binary number, which "encodes" one of the labels of the classes into which the data have to be partitioned. During the learning phase, each single neuron is trained independently with the Perceptron Learning Rule that we have studied so far. So, at the end of this phase, we find a weight vector for each neuron. Using

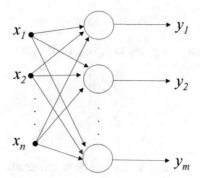

Fig. 7.6 Single-layer Perceptron with m output neurons

this vector, it is possible (in general) to define a *hyperplane*. If the network has two inputs, the weights of each neuron identify a straight line. These straight lines can be represented on a Cartesian plane and, at the end of the learning phase, if this phase was successful, they separate the points that belong to the different classes, as in the example shown in Figure 7.7. Given that all the separating functions are

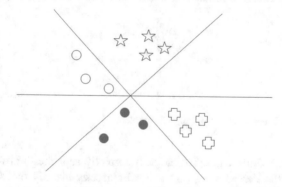

Fig. 7.7 Graphical representation of two straight lines able to separate points from four different classes

linear, also in the case of a (single-layer) Perceptron with more than one neuron, the Perceptron is able to correctly solve a classification problem with m different classes $C_1, C_2, ..., C_m$ *if and only if* these classes are *linearly separable*.

7.1.3 Nonlinearly Separable Problems. An Example

One of the best-known nonlinearly separable problems is the XOR problem. The XOR function is a Boolean function that has two input arguments:

$$y = x_1 \; XOR \; x_2$$

and whose value is expressed by the following truth table:

x_1	x_2	y
-1	-1	-1
-1	1	1
1	-1	1
1	1	-1

On a Cartesian plane, the XOR function can be represented as in Figure 7.8. Clearly,

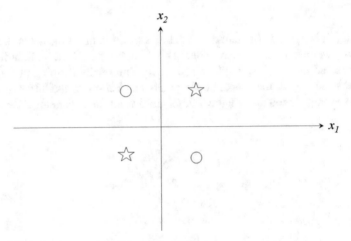

Fig. 7.8 Graphical representation of the XOR problem

no set of straight lines can exist that will correctly separate the two classes. Let us prove that the Perceptron is not able to correctly classify the XOR problem. Given that the problem consists in a binary classification of data which are vectors of cardinality equal to 2, we can consider the case of the Perceptron with two inputs and one single neuron. Let us assume, for a contradiction, that this Perceptron is able to correctly classify the XOR problem. Then, we admit that a vector of weights $[w_0, w_1, w_2]$ exists such that the following system of inequalities holds:

$$
\begin{aligned}
-w_1 - w_2 + w_0 &\leq 0 & \text{(i)} \\
w_1 - w_2 + w_0 &> 0 & \text{(ii)} \\
-w_1 + w_2 + w_0 &> 0 & \text{(iii)} \\
w_1 + w_2 + w_0 &\leq 0 & \text{(iv)}
\end{aligned}
$$

Adding Equation (ii) to Equation (iii) in the previous system, we obtain:

$$2w_0 > 0, \quad \text{i.e.,} \quad w_0 > 0 \qquad \text{(v)}$$

Equation (i) can be transformed into $-w_1 - w_2 \leq -w_0$, and, by using the information coming from Equation (v), this allows us to conclude that $-w_1 - w_2$ is less than or equal to a quantity that is *strictly negative*, and for this reason, it is also strictly negative. In other words:

$$-w_1 - w_2 < 0 \qquad\qquad (vi)$$

Also, Equation (iv) can be transformed into $w_1 + w_2 \leq -w_0$, and, using the information coming from Equation (v), we can conclude that $w_1 + w_2$ is less than or equal to a strictly negative quantity, and thus:

$$w_1 + w_2 < 0 \quad \longrightarrow \quad -w_1 - w_2 > 0 \qquad (vii)$$

Inequalities (vi) and (vii) create a contradiction, which allows us to terminate the proof.

We observe that an ANN composed of *two layers* of neurons (one neuron for each layer) solves the XOR problem. This network, with already the final values of the weights, is represented in Figure 7.9.

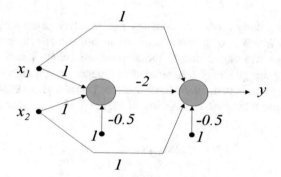

Fig. 7.9 A two-layer ANN able to correctly classify all the instances of the XOR problem

In order to show that the network represented in Figure 7.9 solves the XOR problem, let g be the output of the leftmost neuron, i.e.:

$$g = f(x_1 + x_2 - 0.5)$$

where f is the threshold (or step) activation function. Then, the output of the entire network (which corresponds to the output of the rightmost neuron) is:

$$y = f(x_1 + x_2 - 2g - 0.5)$$

For the different input data, we have:

$$(x_1,x_2) = (-1,-1) \longrightarrow g = f(-2.5) = -1 \longrightarrow y = f(-0.5) = -1$$
$$(x_1,x_2) = (-1,1) \quad \longrightarrow g = f(-0.5) = -1 \longrightarrow y = f(1.5) = 1$$
$$(x_1,x_2) = (1,-1) \quad \longrightarrow g = f(-0.5) = -1 \longrightarrow y = f(1.5) = 1$$
$$(x_1,x_2) = (1,1) \qquad \longrightarrow g = f(1.5) = 1 \qquad \longrightarrow y = f(-0.5) = -1$$

The property that we have just proven for a simple test case, the XOR function, is indeed general and can be enunciated as follows [Minsky and Papert, 1988].

Theorem 7.2. *Nonlinearly separable problems can be solved correctly using ANNs only if those ANNs contain at least one layer of hidden units.*

In other words, ANNs with hidden neurons, also called multilayer ANNs, are more general than single-layer ANNs, and thus they deserve to be studied in depth. The next section introduces this type of ANN.

7.1.4 Nonlinearly Separable Problems and Multilayer ANNs

In general, nonlinearly separable problems can be solved using *multilayer* ANNs, i.e., ANNs in which one or more neurons do not directly form the output of the network (as mentioned above, these units are called *hidden neurons*, and given that they are generally organized into layers, we call these layers *hidden layers*) [Minsky and Papert, 1988, Rashid, 2016, Demuth et al., 2014]. A possible structure of a multilayer ANN is shown in Figure 7.10. This network is called a

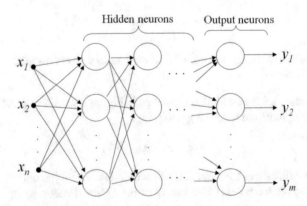

Fig. 7.10 Feedforward, multilayer ANN

Feedforward ANN and its main characteristics are:

- The neurons in a given layer receive as input the outputs of the neurons of the previous layer.

- There are no connections between neurons of the same layer (intralayer connections).
- All possible interlayer connections exist between a layer and the subsequent layer.

The motivation for the name we give to these networks (Feedforward ANNs) resides in the direction of the flux of information circulating in the network while the network is working: we can imagine that, in the graphical representation of Figure 7.10, the information always goes from left to right. In other words, inputs $x_1, x_2, ..., x_n$ are propagated *forward* into the network in order to produce the outputs $y_1, y_2, ..., y_m$. This implies that Feedforward Neural Networks, by their very definition, do *not* contain cycles, or, which is equivalent, do not contain any connection from a neuron to the neuron itself, or from a neuron to any neuron of a previous layer. Even though, by its most accepted definition, a Perceptron is characterized by one single layer of neurons, in some references a feedforward multilayer ANN is also called a *Multilayer Perceptron* (a terminology that is not used in this book).

Typically, feedforward multilayer ANNs are trained using the Backpropagation learning rule, which is the subject of Section 7.3. Backpropagation is a generalization of another, older and simpler, learning rule called the Delta Rule. The Delta Rule was originally defined for single-layer ANNs, or even ANNs composed of only one neuron. Backpropagation can be seen as an extension of the Delta Rule to multilayer ANNs. From this perspective, in order to understand the functioning of Backpropagation, it is a necessary precondition to understand the functioning of the Delta Rule. For this reason, in the next section we present the Delta Rule, and later in this document we present Backpropagation. In general, Backpropagation can be applied to networks with any number of layers, but the following property holds [Hartman et al., 1990, Hornik et al., 1989].

Theorem 7.3. (Universal Approximation Theorem). *One level of hidden neurons is sufficient to approximate any function (with a finite number of discontinuities) with arbitrary precision, provided that the activation functions of the hidden neurons are nonlinear.*

This is one of the reasons why one of the most used configurations of a feedforward multilayer ANN is with only one layer of hidden units, which use a sigmoid activation function, i.e.: $f(x) = \frac{1}{1+e^{-x}}$. This function is not linear, and thus, if we use it as an activation function, the theorem holds. This function will be used in Section 7.2 and in Section 7.3. In Section 7.3, we will also discover another interesting property of the sigmoid activation function: it will allow us to significantly simplify the mathematical steps by which we derive the Backpropagation algorithm.

7.2 Adaptive Linear Element (ADALINE) and Delta Rule

ADALINE is a Neural Network that has an architecture very similar to that of the Perceptron, studied in Section 7.1. The learning algorithm used by ADALINE, called the *Delta Rule* [Haykin, 1998], can be seen as a generalization and/or variation of the Perceptron learning rule. The difference between the Delta Rule and the Perceptron learning rule consists in the way the output is managed. The Perceptron uses as output the result of an activation function (for instance the threshold activation function) to learn. The Delta Rule uses the result of the summation of the inputs (weighted using the weights of the synapses), to which an activation function may or may not be applied:

$$y = \sum_{i=1}^{m} w_i x_i + \theta \quad or \quad y = f(\sum_{i=1}^{m} w_i x_i + \theta) \tag{7.3}$$

In the continuation of this document, an activation function will always be used, but, for reasons that will be clearer later, the used function will not return either 1 or -1, but continuous values. The main difference between the Perceptron learning rule and the Delta Rule is that the Delta Rule compares this calculated output to the desired output, or target, by using an *error*, which is usually quantified by means of the distance between calculated outputs and targets (any distance metric can be used for this aim). Contrarily to the functioning of the Perceptron learning rule, the Delta Rule uses this error as the basis for learning. Given the importance of the concept of error between outputs and targets, the architecture of ADALINE is often represented as in Figure 7.11. The reader is invited to compare this architecture to that of the Perceptron (Figure 7.2), and remark the presence of an error function applied to the output y of the neuron, which is not present in the architecture of the Perceptron.

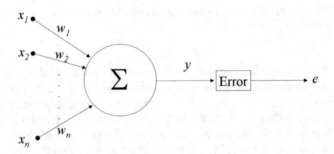

Fig. 7.11 Architectural structure of ADALINE

Let us assume that we want to map a set of input vectors $\{x_1, x_2, ..., x_m\}$ into a set of known expected output values $\{d_1, d_2, ..., d_m\}$. Let $\{y_1, y_2, ..., y_m\}$ be the values respectively calculated by ADALINE for each one of these input vectors. Several error measures can be used to calculate the deviation of the calculated outputs from the expected ones. Typical cases are:

$$E = \frac{1}{m} \sum_{i=1}^{m} (d_i - y_i)^2$$

and in this case the error is commonly called the *mean square error*; or:

$$E = \sum_{i=1}^{m} |d_i - y_i|$$

and in this case the error is commonly called the *absolute error*.

The Delta Rule looks for the vector of weights **w** that *minimizes* the error function, using a method called *gradient descent* [Haykin, 1998]. This method will be defined shortly. So far, it is important to notice that the learning of the ANN becomes an optimization problem, where the cost function, to be minimized, is the error E, and the different possible solutions for this optimization problem are the different possible existing vectors of weights. If we imagine plotting all the possible values of the weights on a horizontal map, and the error made by the ANN using those weights in the vertical direction, the graphical representation of function E can be seen as a multidimensional surface that we call the *error surface*. The objective is to find the point (i.e., the vector of weights) at which this surface has its minimum value. From this perspective, the dynamics of the Delta Rule can be seen as a navigation strategy in this surface, a strategy that, typically starting from a random point, is able to move towards the minimum.

Before studying the functioning of the Delta Rule, the reader is invited to become aware of the existence of the following theoretical result, one of the consequences of which represents one of the most important limitations of the Delta Rule itself.

Theorem 7.4. *If the problem is linearly separable, then the surface of the E function is unimodal, i.e., it contains only one global minimum and no other local minima.*

The functioning of the Delta Rule is simply an iterative modification of the weights that has the objective of decreasing the value of E at each step. Thus, it is easy to understand that, if the problem is not linearly separable and thus the error surface is not guaranteed to be unimodal, it is possible that ADALINE gets trapped in a local minimum different from the global one. On the other hand, for linearly separable problems, as for the Perceptron, also ADALINE is in general an appropriate method to find an optimal solution and thus solve the problem in a satisfactory way.

To decrease the error E at each step, the Delta Rule uses the gradient descent method. In other terms, the Delta Rule functions in a stepwise fashion, by, at each step, modifying the weights as follows:

$$\mathbf{w} = \mathbf{w} + \Delta\mathbf{w}$$

where $\Delta\mathbf{w}$ is *proportional to the derivative* of E, with a negative proportionality constant, i.e.:

$$\Delta\mathbf{w} = -\eta \frac{\partial E}{\partial \mathbf{w}} \tag{7.4}$$

where η is a parameter called the learning rate that has an analogous role to the learning rate in the Perceptron learning rule. We say that, in this way, the weights are modified *in the negative direction of the gradient of E*. Of course, when the minimum of function E is reached, its derivative is equal to zero, thus weights are no longer modified and the algorithm terminates.

Equation (7.4) can be solved independently for each coordinate of vector $\mathbf{w}$. In other words, solving Equation (7.4) is equivalent to solving, for each $i = 1, 2, ..., n$, the following equation:

$$\Delta w_i = -\eta \frac{\partial E}{\partial w_i} \tag{7.5}$$

Let us now assume that:

- E is the mean square error;
- the activation function used by the neuron is the sigmoid, i.e.: $f(x) = \frac{1}{1+e^{-x}}$

Under these hypotheses, given a generic input observation $\mathbf{x}_j = \{x_1, x_2, ..., x_n\}$, with $j = 1, 2, ..., m$, and considering the corresponding output value y_j calculated by the ANN and the corresponding expected output d_j, with some mathematical simplifications Equation (7.5) can be transformed into:

$$\Delta w_i = \eta (d_j - y_j) y_j (1 - y_j) x_i \tag{7.6}$$

In other words, given any input observation, the modification of the weight of a synapse can be expressed as a simple function of the calculated and expected outputs for that observation, and the input entering the network through that synapse.

This calculation is exactly the same as the one used for updating the weights of the output layer in the Backpropagation learning rule. In other words, in Backpropagation, the weights of the connections in the output layer are updated using the Delta Rule. So, the interested reader is referred to Section 7.3.1 for a detailed discussion of the mathematical steps that allow us to transform Equation (7.5) into Equation (7.6). Using Equation (7.6), we are now able to write the pseudocode of the Delta Rule, which is reported in Algorithm 8. Possible termination conditions of this algorithm are:

- the output of the neuron approximates the target value in a satisfactory way for each training instance (observation), or
- a previously fixed maximum number of iterations (which is a parameter of the algorithm) has been performed.

Algorithm 8: Pseudocode of the Delta Rule for ANNs composed of one neuron, using the mean square error and a sigmoid activation function.

Initialize all the weights $w_0, w_1, ..., w_n$ with random values;

while (**not** termination condition) **do**

> Select an input vector $\mathbf{x}_j$ from the training set, and calculate the corresponding output value y_j of the neuron, using Equation (7.3). Let d_j be the expected output (target), that is associated to $\mathbf{x}_j$ in the training set;
>
> **if** (y_j does not approximate d_j is a satisfactory way) **then**
>
> > for all $i = 0, 1, .., n$, modify the weight w_i as follows:
> > $w_i = w_i + \eta \, (d_j - y_j) \, y_j \, (1 - y_j) \, x_i$;
>
> **end**

end

Also, remark that, contrarily to what typically happens for the Perceptron, the output of the activation function in the Delta Rule (sigmoid in this case) is a continuous value. So, our objective is that this value approximates the target "in a satisfactory way", rather than being exactly identical to the target. In general, the definition of "satisfactory" is defined by means of a previously chosen error threshold ε_{train}. In this way, for a given training instance j, y_j is considered to approximate "in a satisfactory way" the corresponding target d_j if and only if: $|d_j - y_j| \leq \varepsilon_{train}$.

Last but not least, remark that also ADALINE neurons have a threshold connection, exactly as in the case of the Perceptron (it was not represented in Figure 7.11 for simplicity). Using the same notation as for the Perceptron, the weight of the threshold connection is called w_0, and the corresponding input, x_0, is constantly equal to 1. In the continuation, we present a simulation of the Delta Rule algorithm on a simple numeric example.

Example – Application of the Delta Rule

Let us consider the following "toy" training set:

(x_1, x_2)	d
$(-2, 6)$	1
$(6, 2)$	1
$(-4, 1)$	0
$(-10, 4)$	0

The objective of this example is to simulate some steps of the Delta Rule algorithm, using this training set. Intuitively, this training set represents a simple classification problem, whose objective is to find a model able to classify observations $(-2, 6)$ and $(6, 2)$ into one class (labelled as 1) and observations $(-4, 1)$ and $(-10, 4)$ into

another class (labelled as 0). Notice that this training set is completely equivalent
to the one that we have studied as an example of the functioning of the Perceptron
learning rule, in Section 7.1. The only difference between that training set and this
one is in the target values, which were -1 and 1 in Section 7.1, and are 0 and 1 here.
This is due to the fact that the Perceptron, in the example of Section 7.1, was using
the "step" activation function, whose possible output values are -1 and 1, while
the Delta Rule here will use the sigmoid activation function, which has asymptotes
at 0 and 1. One should remember that, in real classification datasets, target values
have the aspect of class labels. When we need to replace those labels using numeric
values (as is the case with ANNs), we should do it consistently with the possible
outputs of the system.

The first step of the Delta Rule is the weights initialization. This is typically
done randomly. Let us assume, for instance, that these values are (exactly as in the
example that we have studied in Section 7.1 for the Perceptron):

$$w_1 = 1, \quad w_2 = 2, \quad w_0 = -12$$

Furthermore, let us suppose that we keep the learning rate constant (and let that
constant be equal to $\eta = 1.0$), let us consider a sigmoid activation function, and
let us consider, as the maximum acceptable error for each training observation,
$\varepsilon_{train} = 0.01$.

Now, let us assume that we select the first observation (first line) in the dataset
(i.e., $\mathbf{x}_1 = (-2,6)$). Let us calculate the output of the neuron for this observation (all
the calculations will be truncated at the second decimal digit from now on):

$$y_1 = f(w_0 + w_1 x_1 + w_2 x_2) = f(-12.0 + 1.0 \cdot (-2.0) + 2.0 \cdot 6.0) = f(-2)$$
$$= \frac{1}{1 + e^{-2}} \approx 0.88$$

The corresponding target d_1 is equal to 1.0, so y_1 does not approximate d_1 in a
satisfactory way. This means that the weights need to be updated. Applying Equation (7.6), we have:

$$w_0 = w_0 + \eta (d_1 - y_1) y_1 (1 - y_1) x_0$$
$$= -12.0 + 1.0 \cdot 0.22 \cdot 0.88 \cdot 0.22 \cdot 1.0 \approx -11.96$$
$$w_1 = w_1 + \eta (d_1 - y_1) y_1 (1 - y_1) x_1 = 1.0 + 1.0 \cdot 0.22 \cdot 0.88 \cdot 0.22 \cdot 1.0 \approx 1.04$$
$$w_2 = w_2 + \eta (d_1 - y_1) y_1 (1 - y_1) x_2 = 2.0 + 1.0 \cdot 0.22 \cdot 0.88 \cdot 0.22 \cdot 2.0 \approx 2.09$$

Let us now assume that, for the next iteration, we select the same training observation: (i.e., $\mathbf{x}_1 = (-2,6)$). Let us calculate the output of the neuron, using the updated
values of the weights:

$$y_1 = f(w_0 + w_1 x_1 + w_2 x_2) = f(-11.96 + 1.04 \cdot (-2.0) + 2.09 \cdot 6.0) = f(-1.5) =$$
$$= \frac{1}{1 + e^{-1.5}} \approx 0.18$$

The reader is now invited to notice that the output, which was equal to 0.12 at the first step, is now closer to the corresponding target (i.e., $d_1 = 1.0$). Iterating the process, the output should approximate the target in a satisfactory way (i.e., with a difference smaller than or equal to $\varepsilon_{train} = 0.01$), in approximately 20 time steps.

The objective of this example was to convince the reader that:

- the Delta Rule is a simple way of implementing gradient descent, fast and easy to execute (in particular when the used activation function is the sigmoid); and
- gradient descent actually works, in the sense that, at every step, the output is closer to the target than previously.

However, as mentioned in Section 7.1, the problem studied in this example is linearly separable. So, as Theorem 7.4 tells us, the error surface is unimodal (no local minima exist on that surface, except for the globally optimal solution). So, if we choose an appropriate learning rate η, decreasing the error at each step will bring us arbitrarily close to the target. But if the problem was nonlinearly separable, as we already know, the error surface may contain local optima. The problem will be studied at the end of the next section, whose objective is to present the Backpropagation learning rule.

7.3 Backpropagation

The Backpropagation learning rule [Haykin, 1998] extends the Delta Rule to multi-layer feedforward ANNs. It is probably the most common learning rule for multi-layer ANNs. The basic idea is that the errors of the *output neurons* are *propagated backwards* to the *hidden neurons*. In other words, the error of a hidden neuron is defined as the sum of all the errors of all the output neurons to which it is directly connected. Backpropagation can be applied to networks with any number of layers, but, keeping in mind the Universal Approximation Theorem (Theorem 7.3), in this section we restrict our study to networks with just one hidden layer. This allows us to keep a simpler and more compact notation. The task of extending the study to networks with more than one hidden layer is left as an exercise. Furthermore, in this section, we will consider networks in which each neuron has a sigmoidal activation function. Besides allowing the Universal Approximation Theorem to hold, since it is a nonlinear function, sigmoid has also another interesting advantage that we will discover in this section. The task of extending the study to the case of other activation functions is also left as an exercise.

Backpropagation is composed of one *forward step* and one *backward step*. In the forward step, the weights of the connections remain unchanged and the outputs of the network are calculated, propagating the inputs through all the neurons of the network. At this point, the error of each output neuron is calculated. The backward step consists in the modification of the weights of each connection. This calculation is made in the following way:

- for the output neurons, the modification is done by means of the Delta Rule;
- for the hidden neurons, the modification is done by *propagating backwards* the error of the output neurons: the error of each hidden neuron is considered to be equal to the sum of all the errors of the neurons of the subsequent layer.

As for the Delta Rule, the weights **w** of the connections in the network are updated using the formula:

$$\mathbf{w} = \mathbf{w} + \Delta\mathbf{w} \tag{7.7}$$

where:

$$\Delta\mathbf{w} = -\eta \frac{\partial E}{\partial \mathbf{w}} \tag{7.8}$$

In other words, to calculate $\Delta\mathbf{w}$, we start from gradient descent. Backpropagation distinguishes the cases of update of the weights of the connections entering the output neurons and of the ones entering the hidden neurons. These two different cases are presented in the next two sections, respectively.

Before going into the details of the mathematical steps that will allow us to obtain the Backpropagation algorithm, it is appropriate to fix the following terminology/notation:

- Let p be the number of inputs of the network, and let the input units be $IN_1, IN_2, ..., IN_p$;
- For each $i = 1, 2, ..., p$, let x_i be an input value that is fed to input unit IN_i (remark that x_i is the *ith* component of an input vector, coming from the training set);
- Let n be the number of neurons in the unique hidden layer (hidden neurons from now on), and let the hidden neurons be $HN_1, HN_2, ..., HN_n$;
- For each $j = 1, 2, ..., n$, let z_j be the output calculated by neuron HN_j and let HE_j be the partial error of hidden neuron HN_j;
- Let m be the number of neurons in the output layer (output neurons from now on), and let the output neurons be $ON_1, ON_2, ..., ON_m$;
- For each $k = 1, 2, ..., m$, let y_k be the output calculated by neuron ON_k (remark that y_k is the *kth* component of the output of the network) and let OE_k be the partial error of output neuron ON_k (remark that OE_k is the *kth* component of the global error made by the network on a particular input observation);
- For each $i = 1, 2, ..., p$, and for each $j = 1, 2, ..., n$ let HW_{ij} be the weight of the connection joining the input unit IN_i to the hidden neuron HN_j (a generic synapse in the hidden layer);
- For each $j = 1, 2, ..., n$, and for each $k = 1, 2, ..., m$, let OW_{jk} be the weight of the connection joining the hidden neuron HN_j to the output neuron ON_k (a generic synapse in the output layer).

This terminology is simplified by Figure 7.12, where input units, hidden and output neurons and weights, along with their indexes, have been represented in the schema of a feedforward, two-layer ANN architecture. In this terminology, input units have

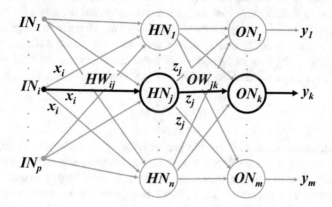

Fig. 7.12 The architecture of a feedforward, two-layer ANN, with the notation used in the development of the Backpropagation algorithm

been indicated using the symbol *IN* (which stands for *IN*put); hidden neurons have been indicated using the symbol *HN* (which stands for *Hidden Neuron*); output neurons have been indicated using the symbol *ON* (which stands for *Output Neuron*); weights of the synapses entering the hidden neurons (also called weights of the hidden layer from now on) have been indicated using the symbol *HW* (which stands for *Hidden Weight*); weights of the synapses entering the output neurons (also called weights of the output layer from now on) have been indicated using the symbol *OW* (which stands for *Output Weight*); errors of the output units have been indicated using the symbol *OE* (which stands for *Output Error*); and finally, errors of the hidden units have been indicated using the symbol *HE* (which stands for *Hidden Error*). For the sake of clarity, in Sections 7.3.1 and 7.3.2:

- character i will *only* be used to index input units;
- character j *only* to index hidden neurons; and
- character k *only* to index output neurons.

Last but not least, we point out that, as for the previously studied types of ANN, also for feedforward multilayer ANNs all neurons have a threshold connection, with input value constantly equal to 1 (not represented in Figure 7.12 for simplicity). The weight of the threshold connection needs to be updated, just like any other weight in the network. Consistently with the previously used notation, for each $j = 1, 2, ..., n$, the weight of the threshold connection entering neuron HN_j will be referred to using the notation HW_{0j}, and for each $k = 1, 2, ..., m$, the weight of the threshold connection entering neuron ON_k will be referred to using the notation OW_{0k}. This notation will prevent us from having to distinguish between connections joining different units and threshold connections.

Before studying how the weights of the different synapses can be updated, let us briefly discuss the concept of *partial error* of a neuron. For output neurons, the concept is straightforward: given that the expected output is known for those neurons, the partial error is simply a quantification of the distance between calculated and expected outputs. Concerning hidden neurons, as mentioned above, the partial error is equal to the sum of the errors of the output neurons. In other words, for each $j = 1, 2, ..., n$, we define the partial error of neuron HN_j as:

$$HE_j = \sum_{k=1}^{m} OE_k \tag{7.9}$$

Notice that, in our formalization, the partial error of all the hidden neurons is the same, because there is complete interconnection between subsequent levels of the network. In other words, a synapse exists between each hidden neuron and each output neuron. The generalization of Backpropagation to networks with missing connections is left as an exercise.

7.3.1 Weights Update – Output Layer

The objective of this part of the study is to find an efficient way of updating the weights OW_{jk} of the synapses that join hidden neurons HN_j to output neurons ON_k (synapses that enter the output neurons). For those types of weights, Equation (7.7) turns into:

$$OW_{jk} = OW_{jk} + \Delta OW_{jk} \tag{7.10}$$

and Equation (7.8) turns into:

$$\Delta OW_{jk} = -\eta \frac{\partial OE_k}{\partial OW_{jk}} \tag{7.11}$$

In order to simplify Equation (7.11), let us now decompose the output of neuron ON_k, and its partial error, into the following parts:

- Let v_k be the weighted sum of the values entering neuron ON_k; in other words: $v_k = \sum_{j=0}^{n} OW_{jk} \cdot z_j$. Notice that, analogously to the previous sections, from now on, by definition, we will consider $z_0 = 1$, which will allow us to treat the threshold connection like all the other connections entering the neuron;
- Let y_k be the output of neuron ON_k, in other words: $y_k = f(v_k)$, where f is the activation function of neuron ON_k (notice that the symbol f does not have any index because, in our particular case, we are assuming that all the neurons in the network have the same activation function);

- Let e_k be defined as: $e_k = d_k - y_k$, where d_k is the expected output (i.e., the target value) for neuron ON_k. Notice that e_k is the basis for calculating the partial error OE_k made by neuron ON_k. The value of OE_k depends on the particular metric we use to express the error. Possible examples are: $OE_k = |e_k|$, $OE_k = e_k^2$, etc.

This decomposition of the output and partial error of ON_k is graphically represented in Figure 7.13, where f represents the activation function of ON_k and OE_k the partial error function. Using this decomposition, Equation (7.11) can be rewritten as:

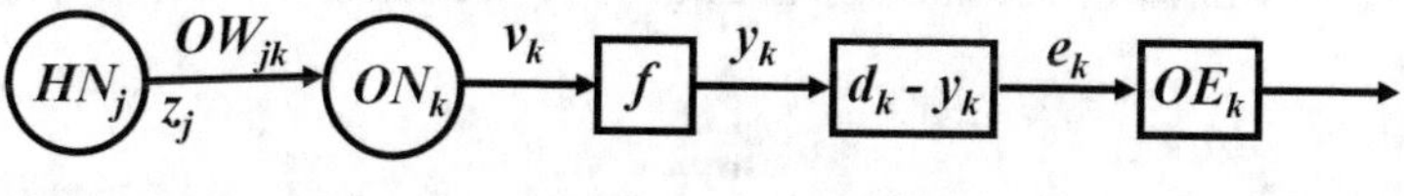

Fig. 7.13 A section of Figure 7.12, reporting only a generic hidden neuron HN_j, with its output z_j, a generic output neuron ON_k, and the synapse between the two, with its weight OW_{jk}. The output and partial error of ON_k have been decomposed into various factors that are useful to simplify Equation (7.11)

$$\Delta OW_{jk} = -\eta \cdot \frac{\partial OE_k}{\partial e_k} \cdot \frac{\partial e_k}{\partial y_k} \cdot \frac{\partial y_k}{\partial v_k} \cdot \frac{\partial v_k}{\partial OW_{jk}} \tag{7.12}$$

The idea now is to consider this new expression, and simplify each term, one by one. Before starting this simplification process, let us fix one further notation: given a function $\phi(x)$, from now on we will use notation $\phi'(x)dx$ as a synonym of $\frac{\partial \phi}{\partial x}$, to indicate the (first) derivative of function ϕ with respect to variable x.

Let us now start the process of simplification of Equation (7.12), by simplifying its first term, i.e.:

$$\frac{\partial OE_k}{\partial e_k} \tag{7.13}$$

To make this simplification, we need to express the partial error OE_k as a function of e_k. In other words, we need to choose the metric to express the error. Even though the process is general, and can be applied in principle with any type of metric, in this section we choose the square error. In other words, we define:

$$OE_k = \frac{1}{2} \sum_{k=1}^{m} e_k^2 \tag{7.14}$$

Notice that, in Equation (7.14), we have added an unconventional multiplicative term $\frac{1}{2}$. This was done purely for simplifying the mathematical calculations. More usual multiplicative terms would have been 1, if the chosen metric is the square error, or $\frac{1}{m}$, if the chosen metric is the mean square error. But using those multiplicative terms would force us to carry with us a multiplication by a constant, until the final development of Equation (7.12). That would not change the qualitative effect of the final algorithm that will be developed, and would only represent a further burden for our notation. For this reason, we decided to avoid multiplications by constants and obtain a more compact formulation. So, now, plugging Equation (7.14) into Equation (7.13), we obtain:

$$\frac{\partial OE_k}{\partial e_k} = \left[\frac{1}{2} e_k^2\right]' de_k = e_k \qquad (7.15)$$

Let us now simplify the second term in Equation (7.12), i.e.:

$$\frac{\partial e_k}{\partial y_k}$$

From the definition of e_k, we obtain:

$$\frac{\partial e_k}{\partial y_k} = \left[d_k - y_k\right]' dy_k = -1 \qquad (7.16)$$

It is worth noticing that Equation (7.12) has a negative sign on the right-hand side of the symbol of equality, coming from the definition of gradient descent (i.e., from the fact that the search proceeds in the direction of the negative gradient of the error function). The result of Equation (7.16) will be useful to remove that negative sign in the final formulation, turning it into a positive one.

Let us now simplify the third term in Equation (7.12), i.e.:

$$\frac{\partial y_k}{\partial v_k}$$

Given that, by definition, $y_k = f(v_k)$, we have:

$$\frac{\partial y_k}{\partial v_k} = f'(v_k) dv_k \qquad (7.17)$$

For the moment, we are not able to further simplify Equation (7.17), because the activation function f has not been specified yet. Further simplifications are possible for some particular activation functions. For instance, later in this Section we will obtain a simplification in the case that f is the sigmoid function.

Finally, let us simplify the fourth term in Equation (7.12), i.e.:

$$\frac{\partial v_k}{\partial OW_{jk}}$$

Replacing v_k with its definition, we obtain:

$$\frac{\partial v_k}{\partial OW_{jk}} = \left[OW_{0k} \cdot z_0 + OW_{1k} \cdot z_1 + \ldots + OW_{jk} \cdot z_j + \ldots + OW_{nk} \cdot z_n \right]' dOW_{jk} = z_j$$

$$(7.18)$$

Finally, substituting Equations (7.15), (7.16), (7.17) and (7.18) into Equation (7.12), we obtain:

$$\Delta OW_{jk} = \eta \cdot e_k \cdot [f'(v_k) \, dv_k] \cdot z_j \qquad (7.19)$$

Equation (7.19) represents a general formula for updating the weights of the output layer. Clearly, the derivative of the activation function (i.e., the term $f'(v_k) \, dv_k$) is not helpful for automating the calculation. However, if we use the sigmoid as an activation function then Equation (7.19) can become very handy and appropriate for automation. In fact, given the sigmoid function f, defined as:

$$f(x) = \frac{1}{1+e^{-x}}$$

If we calculate the derivative of f, we obtain:

$$f'(x)dx = \frac{e^{-x}}{(1+e^{-x})^2} = \frac{1}{1+e^{-x}} \cdot \frac{e^{-x}}{1+e^{-x}} =$$
$$\frac{1}{1+e^{-x}} \cdot \left[1 - \frac{1}{1+e^{-x}} \right] = f(x) \cdot [1 - f(x)]$$

In other words, it is possible to express the derivative of the sigmoid function as a (simple) function of the sigmoid itself. Using the adopted notation, we can write:

$$f'(v_k) \, dv_k = f(v_k) \cdot [1 - f(v_k)]$$

And remembering that, by definition of y_k, we have $y_k = f(v_k)$, we can write:

$$f'(v_k) \, dv_k = y_k \cdot (1 - y_k) \qquad (7.20)$$

Substituting Equation (7.20) into Equation (7.19), we obtain the formula for updating the weights of the output layer, in the case that the output neurons use the sigmoid activation function:

$$\Delta OW_{jk} = \eta \cdot e_k \cdot y_k \cdot (1 - y_k) \cdot z_j$$

or, replacing e_k by its definition:

$$\Delta OW_{jk} = \eta \cdot (d_k - y_k) \cdot y_k \cdot (1 - y_k) \cdot z_j \qquad (7.21)$$

As expected, Equation (7.21) is completely equivalent to Equation (7.6), except for the different notation used. In fact, output neurons update weights using the Delta Rule.

The reader is now invited to have a close look at Equation (7.21), and recognize that the result of this equation can be calculated in a very simple way, since all the terms involved in it are known. Specifically:

- η is a parameter of the algorithm (the learning rate), and so it is known at learning time;
- d_k is the expected output of an output neuron, and so this information is included in the (supervised) training set at our disposal;
- y_k is the calculated output of an output neuron, and it can be obtained once the weights have a value, simply by propagating the inputs throughout the whole network;
- z_j is the output of a hidden neuron, which can also be calculated, once the weights have a value, in the process of propagating the inputs throughout the whole network.

In other words, whenever a network has some initial weights, and it is evaluated, we immediately have available all the terms that allow us to calculate ΔOW_{jk}, applying Equation (7.21).

Before passing to the analysis of the modification of the weights of the hidden layer, it is worth pointing out that we have just discovered the second important positive aspect of using the sigmoid activation function: it allows us to avoid calculating derivatives, thus making the modification of the weights simple, and easy to automate. We recall that the first important characteristic that we have already studied, is that, it being a nonlinear function, if we use the sigmoid as an activation function then the Universal Approximation Theorem holds, allowing us to use only one layer of hidden neurons.

We finally rewrite Equation (7.21) in a form that will be particularly useful when we write the pseudocode of the Backpropagation algorithm (in Section 7.3.3):

$$\Delta OW_{jk} = \eta \cdot \beta_k \cdot z_j \qquad (7.22)$$

where:

$$\beta_k = (d_k - y_k) \cdot y_k \cdot (1 - y_k)$$

In other words, we have isolated the product of all the terms that are relative to the kth output neuron, giving it the name β_k.

7.3.2 Weights Update – Hidden Layer

Let us now observe Figure 7.14, containing the needed elements to obtain an equation for the update of the weights HW_{ij} of the hidden layer. The figure shows a

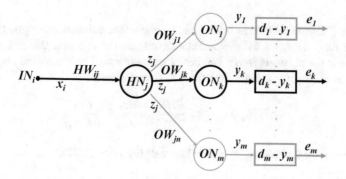

Fig. 7.14 A section of Figure 7.12, reporting only a generic input unit IN_i of the ANN, a generic hidden neuron HN_j and the m output neurons $ON_1, ON_2, ..., ON_m$ with their respective calculated output values $y_1, y_2, ..., y_m$ and partial errors $e_1, e_2, ..., e_m$

generic input unit IN_i, a generic hidden neuron HN_j, with the weight HW_{ij} of the connection joining them. It also shows, for each $k = 1, 2, ..., m$, the output neuron ON_k, with its corresponding calculated output y_k, and error component e_k. Shown in the figure are also the *ith* component x_i of an actual input observation that is fed into the network through input unit IN_i, and the output calculated by neuron HN_j, called z_j. In this section, z_j will be defined as:

$$z_j = f(u_j) \tag{7.23}$$

where f is the activation function of neuron HN_j and u_j is defined as follows:

$$u_j = \sum_{i=0}^{p} HW_{ij} \cdot x_i \tag{7.24}$$

Notice that, in Equation (7.24), the summation is calculated over all inputs (we recall that index i is used to indicate the generic input). In synthesis, u_j represents, for the hidden neurons, what variable v_k represented for output neurons in Section 7.3.1: the weighted sum of the values entering into a neuron via its input connections. Finally, notice that, analogously to what we have already done previously, for each input observation, we define: $x_0 = 1$. This allows us to treat the threshold connection of neuron HN_j like any of its other connections.

As for the output neurons, also for the hidden neurons, the starting point is given by the gradient descent formulation, shown in Equation (7.7) and Equation (7.8). In the specific case of hidden neurons, Equation (7.7) turns into:

$$HW_{ij} = HW_{ij} + \Delta HW_{ij} \tag{7.25}$$

and Equation (7.8) turns into:

$$\Delta HW_{ij} = -\eta \frac{\partial HE_j}{\partial HW_{ij}} \tag{7.26}$$

Equation (7.26) will be transformed into a simpler formulation, by applying several mathematical steps. As for the output neurons, also in this case the first step is to decompose the equation into a number of terms that will be simplified one by one. More specifically, we rewrite Equation (7.26) as follows:

$$\Delta HW_{ij} = -\eta \cdot \frac{\partial HE_j}{\partial z_j} \cdot \frac{\partial z_j}{\partial u_j} \cdot \frac{\partial u_j}{\partial HW_{ij}} \tag{7.27}$$

Let us begin by developing the second term of Equation (7.27), i.e.:

$$\frac{\delta z_j}{\delta u_j}$$

Applying the definition of z_j, given in Equation (7.23), we have:

$$\frac{\delta z_j}{\delta u_j} = \frac{\delta f(u_j)}{\delta u_j} = f'(u_j) \, du_j \tag{7.28}$$

Similarly to what happened for the output neurons, this equation is not further simplified for the moment. However, when a particular activation function is chosen, it is possible to obtain a much more manageable form. In particular, the equation obtained for the sigmoid activation function will be discussed later in this section.

Now, let us develop the third term of Equation (7.27), i.e.:

$$\frac{\partial u_j}{\partial HW_{ij}}$$

Taking into account the definition of u_j given in Equation (7.24), we have:

$$\frac{\partial u_j}{\partial HW_{ij}} = \left[HW_{0j} \cdot x_0 + HW_{1j} \cdot x_1 + \ldots + HW_{ij} \cdot x_i + \ldots + HW_{pj} \cdot x_p \right]' dHW_{ij} = x_i \tag{7.29}$$

In fact, the derivative is performed with respect to variable HW_{ij}, and all other terms in the summation are constant.

Finally, let us develop the first term of Equation (7.27), i.e.:

$$\frac{\partial HE_j}{\partial z_j} \tag{7.30}$$

In this case, we have to remember that Backpropagation makes the assumption that the partial error of the hidden neurons is equal to the sum of the partial errors of the output neurons to which they are directly connected. Using this assumption, HE_j was defined in Equation (7.9), which we repeat here for convenience:

$$HE_j = \sum_{k=1}^{m} OE_k$$

Plugging this definition into Equation (7.30), we obtain:

$$\frac{\partial HE_j}{\partial z_j} = \frac{\partial(\sum_{k=1}^{m} OE_k)}{\partial z_j}$$

and using the notion that the derivative of a sum is equal to the sum of the derivatives, we can write:

$$\frac{\partial HE_j}{\partial z_j} = \sum_{k=1}^{m} \frac{\partial OE_k}{\partial z_j} \tag{7.31}$$

But Equation (7.31) can be rewritten as:

$$\frac{\partial HE_j}{\partial z_j} = \sum_{k=1}^{m} \left(\frac{\partial OE_k}{\partial e_k} \cdot \frac{\partial e_k}{\partial v_k} \cdot \frac{\partial v_k}{\partial z_j} \right) \tag{7.32}$$

where, as in Section 7.3.1, $e_k = d_k - y_k$ and $v_k = \sum_{j=0}^{n} OW_{jk} \cdot z_j$.

Let us now develop the first term under summation in Equation (7.32), i.e.:

$$\frac{\partial OE_k}{\partial e_k}$$

This development was already shown in Equation (7.15) of Section 7.3.1. We copy it here for convenience:

$$\frac{\partial OE_k}{\partial e_k} = \left[\frac{1}{2} e_k^2 \right]' de_k = e_k \tag{7.33}$$

Let us now develop the second term under summation in Equation (7.32), i.e.:

$$\frac{\partial e_k}{\partial v_k}$$

Applying the definition of e_k, we have:

$$\frac{\partial e_k}{\partial v_k} = \frac{\partial(d_k - y_k)}{\partial v_k} = \frac{\partial(d_k - f(v_k))}{\partial v_k} = -f'(v_k) \, dv_k \tag{7.34}$$

Also in this case, it is important to remark the negative sign in the result of this development, which we will use to remove the negative sign in Equation (7.27).

Finally, let us develop the third term under summation in Equation (7.32), i.e.:

$$\frac{\partial v_k}{\partial z_j}$$

By replacing v_k with its definition, we obtain:

$$\frac{\partial v_k}{\partial z_j} = \left[OW_{0k} \cdot z_0, OW_{1k} \cdot z_1, ..., OW_{jk} \cdot z_j, ..., OW_{nk} \cdot z_n \right]' dz_j = OW_{jk} \quad (7.35)$$

If we now substitute Equation (7.33), Equation (7.34) and Equation (7.35) into Equation (7.32), we obtain:

$$\frac{\partial HE_j}{\partial z_j} = -\sum_{k=1}^{m} \left(e_k \cdot [f'(v_k) \, dv_k] \cdot OW_{jk} \right) \quad (7.36)$$

Remark that, in Equation (7.36), the summation runs over all output neurons, and OW_{jk} indicates the weight of the synapse joining the *jth* hidden neuron to the *kth* output neuron. This weight has already been updated by the Backpropagation algorithm, as studied in Section 7.3.1.

Joining together all the developments so far, we are finally able to rewrite Equation (7.27). More specifically, if we substitute Equation (7.36), Equation (7.28) and Equation (7.29) into Equation (7.27), we obtain:

$$\Delta HW_{ij} = \eta \cdot \sum_{k=1}^{m} \left(e_k \cdot [f'(v_k) \, dv_k] \cdot OW_{jk} \right) \cdot [f'(u_j) \, du_j] \cdot x_i \quad (7.37)$$

Equation (7.37) corresponds to the general formula for updating the weights of the hidden layer. This formula looks complex and, above all, it seems hard to automate, because of the presence of several activation function derivatives. But, as we studied in Section 7.3.1, the sigmoid activation function has the advantage of having a derivative that can be expressed as a function of the sigmoid itself. So, if f is the sigmoid activation function, Equation (7.37) turns into:

$$\Delta HW_{ij} = \eta \cdot \sum_{k=1}^{m} \left(e_k \cdot f(v_k) \cdot (1 - f(v_k)) \cdot OW_{jk} \right) \cdot f(u_j) \cdot (1 - f(u_j)) \cdot x_i$$

and, given that $e_k = d_k - y_k$, $y_k = f(v_k)$ and $z_j = f(u_j)$, we have:

$$\Delta HW_{ij} = \eta \cdot \sum_{k=1}^{m} \left((d_k - y_k) \cdot y_k \cdot (1 - y_k) \cdot OW_{jk} \right) \cdot z_j \cdot (1 - z_j) \cdot x_i \quad (7.38)$$

The reader is now invited to acknowledge that it is completely possible to automate the calculation of Equation (7.38), since all the elements that appear in it are known:

- η, the learning rate, is a parameter of the algorithm, and so it is known at learning time;
- d_k is the expected output of neuron ON_k, and it is contained in the dataset, so it is known;
- y_k is the calculated output of neuron ON_k, so it is known, since, before updating the weights, the outputs of the network have to be calculated;
- OW_{jk} is a weight of the output layer, and, at the moment of modifying the weights of the hidden layer, it has already been updated, and so its new value is known.
- z_j is the output of hidden neuron HN_j, and so it known, because it has been calculated in the process of calculation of the outputs of the network;
- x_i is the ith component of a training observation, it is contained in the dataset, and so it is known.

Furthermore, we can also observe that the term $(d_k - y_k) \cdot y_k \cdot (1 - y_k)$ has already been found in Section 7.3.1 and, in Equation (7.22), it was called β_k. This allows us to further simplify Equation (7.38) as follows:

$$\Delta HW_{ij} = \eta \cdot \sum_{k=1}^{m} \left(\beta_k \cdot OW_{jk} \right) \cdot z_j \cdot (1 - z_j) \cdot x_i$$

Last but not least, we now rewrite this equation as follows:

$$\Delta HW_{ij} = \eta \cdot \gamma_j \cdot x_i \tag{7.39}$$

where:

$$\gamma_j = z_j \cdot (1 - z_j) \cdot \sum_{k=1}^{m} \left(\beta_k \cdot OW_{jk} \right)$$

The reader is now invited to compare Equation (7.39), for updating the weights of the hidden layer, with Equation (7.22), for updating the weights of the output layer, and recognize that these two equations have a very similar shape. This will allow us to write the pseudocode of the Backpropagation algorithm in a simple way, in the next section.

7.3.3 The Backpropagation Algorithm

The pseudocode for the Backpropagation learning rule, in the case of feedforward ANNs with one hidden layer, is given in Algorithm 9. As for the Delta rule, also in this case the termination condition is:

Termination condition: the expected outputs **d** are approximated "in a satisfactory way" by the calculated outputs **y** for *every* input vector **x** in the training set, or a previously fixed number of iterations has been executed.

As for the Delta Rule, the concept of approximating the target "in a satisfactory way" is defined by setting a threshold ε_{train}, below which the error between calcu-

---

Algorithm 9: Backpropagation learning rule for feedforward ANNs with p input units $IN_1, IN_2, ..., IN_p$, one hidden layer containing n neurons $HN_1, HN_2, ..., HN_n$, and m output neurons $ON_1, ON_2, ..., ON_m$.

$\forall i = 1, 2, ..., p, \forall j = 1, 2, ..., n$, let HW_{ij} be the weight of the synapse joining IN_i to HN_j;

$\forall j = 1, 2, ..., n, \forall k = 1, 2, ..., m$, let OW_{jk} be the weight of the synapse joining HN_j to ON_k;

Initialize all the weights HW_{ij} and OW_{jk} in the network with random values;

while (not termination condition) **do**

     1. Select an input observation $\mathbf{x} = \{x_1, x_2, ..., x_p\}$ from the training set, and let $\mathbf{d} = \{d_1, d_2, ..., d_m\}$ be the expected output – or target – that can be found in the dataset, corresponding to observation $\mathbf{x}$;

     2. *Forward Phase:*
        Calculate the output of the network for input $\mathbf{x}$ by feeding each input value x_i into the corresponding input unit IN_i and propagating them throughout the network. Let $\mathbf{y} = \{y_1, y_2, ..., y_m\}$ be the calculated output of the network and $\mathbf{z} = \{z_1, z_2, ..., z_n\}$ be the calculated outputs of the hidden neurons;

     3. **if** (**y** approximates **d** in a satisfactory way) **then**

        | do nothing and **go to** point 1.;
        end

        else

        Backward Phase:

           3.1. *Weight Update for the Output Layer:*
              for each $k = 1, 2, ..., m$, calculate: $\beta_k = (d_k - y_k) \, y_k \, (1 - y_k)$ and modify the weights of the connections entering ON_k as follows: $OW_{jk} = OW_{jk} + \eta \, \beta_k \, z_j$;

           3.2. *Weight Update for the Hidden Layer:*
              for each $j = 1, 2, ..., n$, calculate: $\gamma_j = z_j \, (1 - z_j) \sum_{k=1}^{m} (\beta_k \, OW_{jk})$ and modify the weights of the connections entering HN_j as follows: $HW_{ij} = HW_{ij} + \eta \, \gamma_j \, x_i$;

        end

end

---

lated and expected outputs is considered "acceptable" or "satisfactory". ε_{train} should be considered as one further parameter of the algorithm. The reader is also invited to observe that, if the condition of Point 3 in Algorithm 9 is satisfied (i.e., **y** approximates **d** in a satisfactory way), the algorithm iterates, by choosing a new input observation **x**. It should be observed that, as for the other studied learning rules, no particular order for selecting the observations is imposed by the algorithm, and choosing a random observation at each step may be an appropriate strategy. Last but not least, the reader is also invited to notice that when the weights of the hidden layer are updated (Point 3.2 of Algorithm 9), β_k and OW_{jk} have already been updated in Point 3.1. So, when these values are used in Point 3.2, the updated values should be considered. Let us now clarify the functioning of Backpropagation with a simple numeric example.

Example of Functioning of Backpropagation

Let us consider the dataset of the XOR problem, which we have already studied, and let us execute some steps of the Backpropagation algorithm on it. The dataset is:

x_1	x_2	d
1	1	0
-1	-1	0
-1	1	1
1	-1	1

It should be noticed that the possible target values are 0 and 1 (and not -1 and 1, as previously) because the activation function that will be used in this example is the sigmoid, which has asymptotes at 0 and 1[1]. Given that the problem is not linearly separable, it is appropriate to use a network with at least one hidden layer. In order to keep the calculations as simple as possible, let us consider the network represented in Figure 7.15, where all the notations used in the previous sections have been respected. Notice that, while the number of input units and output neurons is

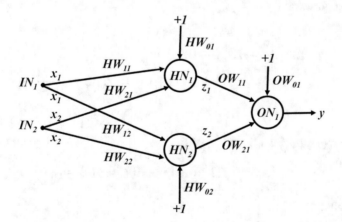

Fig. 7.15 The architecture of the feedforward ANN used in the example of Section 7.3.3

given by the definition of the problem (in fact, the dataset has two input variables

---

[1] Remember that, in real data, the target of a classification problem is expressed in terms of two or more class labels. If, as in our case, it has to be transformed into numeric values, it should be done at our convenience, taking into account the particular algorithm used.

and one target value), the number of hidden layers and the number of neurons in each one of these layers are parameters. Other parameters that need to be set are the learning rate η and the admissible error ε_{train}. To make calculations simpler, let us consider $\eta = 1$, and let us also assume $\varepsilon_{train} = 0.01$. With these settings, we are now ready to begin the simulation of the execution of the algorithm.

The first step of Backpropagation is the random initialization of all the weights in the network. Let us assume, for instance:

- $HW_{01} = 10$, $HW_{11} = 9$, $HW_{12} = 10$, $HW_{21} = 7$, $HW_{22} = 9$, $HW_{02} = -10$;
- $OW_{01} = -5$, $OW_{11} = 11$, $OW_{21} = -10$.

We now need to select an input observation $\mathbf{x} = \{x_1, x_2\}$ and, for that observation, execute the *Forward Phase* of the algorithm, consisting in the calculation of the output, propagating the inputs throughout the whole network. Let us assume, for simplicity, that the first chosen observation is also the first one that appears in the training set. So, the first chosen observation is:

$$\mathbf{x} = \{1, 1\}$$

Propagating the inputs throughout the whole network, in this case, means to calculate the output of neurons HN_1 and HN_2 (called z_1 and z_2, respectively), and use them to calculate the output of neuron ON_1 (i.e., y), which actually corresponds to the output of the network. Given the actual values of the weights and the input vector $\mathbf{x}$, and remembering that f is the sigmoid activation function, the calculations are straightforward:

$$z_1 = f(x_1 \cdot HW_{11} + x_2 \cdot HW_{21} + HW_{01}) =$$
$$f(1 \cdot 9 + 1 \cdot 7 + 10) = f(26) = \frac{1}{1+e^{-26}} \approx 0.999$$

$$z_2 = f(x_1 \cdot HW_{12} + x_2 \cdot HW_{22} + HW_{02}) =$$
$$f(1 \cdot 10 + 1 \cdot 9 - 10) = f(9) = \frac{1}{1+e^{-9}} \approx 0.999$$

And, finally:

$$y = f(z_1 \cdot OW_{11} + z_2 \cdot OW_{21} + OW_{01}) =$$
$$f(0.999 \cdot 11 - 0.999 \cdot 10 - 5) = f(-4.0009) \approx 0.01797$$

y was supposed to be an approximation of $d = 0$, with a maximum admissible error of $\varepsilon_{train} = 0.01$. Clearly, the current value of y does not approximate d in a satisfactory way. For this reason, it is now necessary to execute the *Backward Phase* of the algorithm, which consists in the modification of the weights. This phase begins with the modification of the weights entering the output neuron (weights of the output layer). We have:

$$OW_{11} = OW_{11} + \eta \, \beta_1 \, z_1, \quad \text{where: } \beta_1 = (d - y) \, y \, (1 - y)$$

Replacing the variables with their current values, we have:

$$\beta_1 = (0 - 0.01797) \cdot 0.01797 \cdot (1 - 0.01797) \approx -0.000284$$

And so:

$$OW_{11} \approx 11 - 1 \cdot 0.000284 \cdot 0.999 \approx 10.999$$

And analogously for the other weights:

$$OW_{21} = OW_{21} + \eta \, \beta_1 \, z_2 \approx -10 - 1 \cdot 0.000284 \cdot 0.999 \approx -10.00028$$

and:

$$OW_{01} = OW_{01} + \eta \cdot \beta_1 \cdot 1 \approx -5 - 1 \cdot 0.000284 \approx -5.00028$$

Using these new weights, we can now modify the weights of the hidden layer:

$$HW_{11} = \eta \, \gamma_1 \, x_1, \quad \text{where: } \gamma_1 = z_1 \, (1 - z_1) \, \beta_1 \, OW_{11}$$

Replacing the variables with their current values, we have:

$$\gamma_1 = 0.999 \cdot (1 - 0.999) \cdot (-0.000284 \cdot 10.999) \approx 0$$

and so, HW_{11} remains practically the same, i.e.:

$$HW_{11} = 9$$

Analogous calculations can be done for all the other weights of the hidden layer, and they lead to the conclusion that all of them remain practically unchanged (calculations are left as an exercise). So, at the end of the backward phase, we have the following new weights:

- $HW_{01} = 10$, $HW_{11} = 9$, $HW_{12} = 10$, $HW_{21} = 7$, $HW_{22} = 9$, $HW_{02} = -10$;
- $OW_{01} = -5.00028$, $OW_{11} = 10.999$, $OW_{21} = -10.00028$.

At this point, a new iteration of the Backpropagation algorithm should begin, with the selection of a new input observation **x**. For simplicity, let us assume that, in this particular case, the selected observation is the same one that was chosen at the previous step, i.e.:

$$\mathbf{x} = \{1,1\}$$

Iterating the *Forward Step*, we have (calculations are left as an exercise):

$$z_1 \approx 0.999, \quad z_2 \approx 0.999$$

as was expected because the weights of the hidden layer practically did not change. Using these results, we have:

$$y = f(z_1 \cdot OW_{11} + z_2 \cdot OW_{21} + OW_{01}) \approx$$
$$f(0.999 \cdot 10.999 - 0.999 \cdot 10.00028 - 5.00028) \approx f(-4.002) \approx 0.01794$$

We now point out that, at the previous iteration, the calculated output was 0.01797. Remembering that the target that needs to be approximated is equal to 0, it is clear that, even though slightly, the calculated output has approached the target.

The calculations involved in this example were reported here only with the purpose of clarifying with a numeric test case the functioning of the algorithm. They have, by no means, to be interpreted as calculations that have to be made manually. Nevertheless, several elements should be retained from this example: first of all, the reader should notice that the calculations, although they may seem complex, can be completely automated. Also, it is not difficult to convince oneself that they can be rather efficient, since they only consist of sums, subtractions and multiplications of known values. Secondly, from this example one should understand that Backpropagation, although usually rather slow, is an effective algorithm, able to reduce the error, with slow steps, towards zero.

7.3.4 Parameters of Backpropagation and Discussion

Now that we have been able to obtain an efficient algorithm for training feedforward multilayer ANNs, let us discuss how to set some important parameters of these networks and one of the best-known issues of these networks: overfitting.

Learning Rate η

The parameter η has an influence on the speed of learning of an ANN. In particular:

- If η is too small, the learning of the network can be slow.
- If η is too big, the network can be "unstable" (in other words,"oscillations" can happen around the optimal value of the vector of weights).

Sorensen [Sorensen, 1994] proposes to begin the algorithm with a relatively "large" value (whose magnitude is problem dependent), and to gradually decrease the value of η during the execution of the algorithm, in a similar way to what happens to the control parameter of the Simulated Annealing (see Section 2.6 of Chapter 2). In this way, for a vast set of applications, we can control (or even eliminate) the risk of having numerous oscillations around the optimal value of the weights.

Momentum α

In spite of all the achievements obtained so far, another problem remains: it is still possible that the Backpropagation algorithm, as it has been presented so far, gets stuck in a *local minimum* on the error surface. In fact, as previously studied, if the problem is not linearly separable, the surface of the error function can be multi-modal, i.e., several local minima can exist. Backpropagation, like the Delta Rule, is nothing but a convenient way of expressing the gradient descent formulation. As such, also Backpropagation, like the Delta Rule, allows us to decrease the error at each step, but may get trapped in a local minimum of the error surface. To reduce the risk of getting trapped in a local minimum, the Delta Rule and Backpropagation can be modified by inserting a parameter called the *momentum* α. If we decide to use momentum, the modifications of the weights are updated as follows: Equation (7.22) becomes:

$$\Delta OW_{jk} = \eta \cdot \beta_k \cdot z_j + \alpha \cdot \Delta OW_{jk} \tag{7.40}$$

and Equation (7.39) becomes:

$$\Delta HW_{ij} = \eta \cdot \gamma_j \cdot x_i + \alpha \cdot \Delta HW_{ij} \tag{7.41}$$

By its very definition, the momentum α is such that $0 \leq |\alpha| < 1$. The value of the momentum is typically a *random number*, chosen to escape from local minima with a given probability [Sorensen, 1994].

Local Minima and Hidden Neurons

Sometimes, another way of reducing the risk of getting stuck in local minima of the error surface consists in augmenting the *number* of hidden neurons. But it has also been experimentally shown that, in some cases, if this number is too high, the risk of getting stuck in local minima can increase instead of decreasing [Sorensen, 1994]. To find the right number of hidden neurons to solve a problem is often an empirical task, based on experience and on the knowledge that we have of the problem. Often, some preliminary experiments are needed to find the right number. A little help (which, however, is often not enough to relieve us from a preliminary experimental phase of parameter tuning) is given later in this book: a heuristic formula that binds the dimension of the training set, the number of hidden neurons, the total number of connections of the network and the average admissible error.

Number of Vectors in the Training Set

To obtain a good generalization from ANNs, we have to take into account that:

- If the training set is too big, there can be a risk of *overfitting* (i.e., the network is too specialized for the training data).
- If the training set is too small, there can be a risk of *underfitting* (i.e., the network does not learn enough).

In the case of a network with only one level of hidden neurons, some studies have been done regarding the suitable training set size to use to solve a problem [Baum and Haussler, 1989]. This study reports that:

- if we denote by ε the average of the admissible errors between outputs and targets on test data, and the average error of the network on the training set is smaller than $\varepsilon/2$,
- if we denote by M the number of hidden neurons and by W the total number of connections in the network,

then an appropriate number of training vectors is given by:

$$\text{Training set size} = K = O(\frac{W}{\varepsilon} \; ln(\frac{M}{\varepsilon})) \tag{7.42}$$

Number of Layers and Number of Neurons

In a large proportion of practical cases, the surface of the error function contains a finite number of discontinuities and thus *one* layer of hidden neurons is sufficient to approximate the target function with arbitrary precision, provided that the activation functions of the hidden neurons are nonlinear (Universal Approximation Theorem [Hartman et al., 1990, Hornik et al., 1989], see Theorem 7.3). However, finding the right number of neurons to allocate in the hidden layer is still an open problem. Also for this parameter, we have to take into account that:

- If it is too big, we can have the risk of overfitting.
- If it is too small, we can have the risk of underfitting.

Generally, the error rates on the training set and on the test set change, during the learning phase and with the number of hidden neurons, as idealized in Figure 7.16. Our objective is to find the number of hidden units M that is able to minimize the error on the test set. To find this value is not easy, because it depends on the problem, but Equation (7.42) can be helpful. Often, only practice can help and it is necessary to perform a set of experiments to look for the suitable value M for the application at hand.

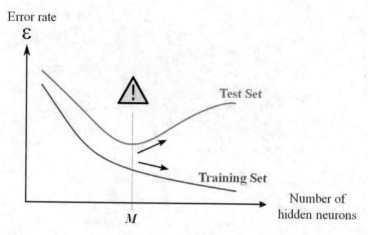

Fig. 7.16 Typical error rates on the training set and on the test set as the number of hidden units changes

7.4 Recursive Neural Networks

The difference between a feedforward ANN and a Recursive (or Cyclic) ANN is that in the feedforward ANNs (as we have studied so far) the information always goes in one direction: from the inputs to the outputs. On the other hand, in cyclic ANNs, we can have information flows in the opposite direction, thus creating loops [Jain and Medsker, 1999, Chinea, 2009]. Examples of known cyclic ANNs are: Jordan Networks [Wysocki and Lawrynczuk, 2015], Elman Networks [Elman, 1990], Hopfield Networks [Ansari and Hou, 1997] and Boltzmann Machines [Hinton, 2010]. Only Jordan Networks will be (briefly) considered in this book. The interested reader is referred to the previously cited sources for a deeper presentation of cyclic ANNs.

Jordan networks are an extension of feedforward ANNs. In this kind of networks, output units are connected "backwards" at the input level by means of a set of further units called *state units*. There are as many state units as output units. Each state unit, exactly like each input unit, is connected to the units of the first hidden layer. The architecture of a Jordan network can be represented as in Figure 7.17. Learning in Jordan networks happens between input units plus state units and hidden units, and between hidden units and output units. The used learning rule is Backpropagation. The weights of the connections between output units and state units (the "backward" connections) are not modified during learning and remain constantly equal to 1. In other words, output values at a given time t simply join the input values at time $t+1$. A typical application of Jordan networks is classification using time series datasets.

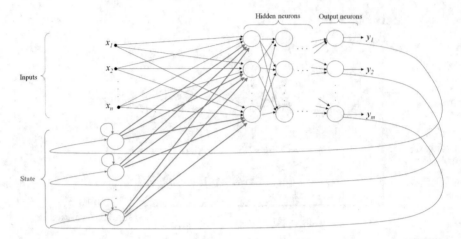

Fig. 7.17 The architecture of a Jordan ANN

Chapter 8
Genetic Programming

GAs, studied in Chapter 3, are capable of solving many problems and simple enough to allow for solid theoretical studies. Nevertheless, the representation of individuals that characterizes GAs (i.e., the fact that individuals in GAs must be strings of a previously fixed length) can be a limitation for a wide set of applications. In these cases, the most natural representation for a solution is a hierarchical computer program, rather than a string of characters of a fixed length. For example, strings of a static length do not readily support the hierarchical organization of tasks into subtasks typical of computer programs, they do not provide any convenient way of incorporating iteration and recursion, and so on. But above all, GA representation schemes do not have any dynamic variability: the initial selection of string length limits in advance the number of internal states of the system and limits what the system can learn.

This lack of representation power (already recognized in [De Jong, 1988]) is overcome by Genetic Programming (GP) [Koza, 1992]. As with GAs, GP belongs to the field of Evolutionary Computation, but contrarily to GAs, GP operates with general hierarchical computer programs. In other words, GP manages a population of computer programs. These programs are typically initialized randomly, and then evolved, using an algorithm that is inspired by the Theory of Evolution of Charles Darwin, with the objective of automatically discovering programs that are appropriate for solving the problem at hand. So, GP is a method for automatically generating a program that solves a problem, starting from the high-level specifications of the problem itself and, in general, without any intervention from a human programmer. As studied in the previous chapters, data models are particular computer programs, and, as such, GP can be seen as a Machine Learning method. Even though every programming language (e.g., Pascal, Fortran, C, etc.) is capable of expressing and executing general computer programs, Koza chose the *LISP* (*LISt Processing*) language to code GP individuals. The reasons for this choice can be summarized as follows:

- Both programs and data have the same form in LISP, so it is possible and convenient to treat a computer program as data in the genetic population.

© Springer Nature Switzerland AG 2023
L. Vanneschi and S. Silva, *Lectures on Intelligent Systems*, Natural Computing Series,
https://doi.org/10.1007/978-3-031-17922-8_8

- This common form of programs and data is a parse tree and this allows us in a simple way to decompose a structure into substructures (subtrees) to be manipulated by the genetic operators.
- LISP facilitates the programming of structures whose size and shape change dynamically and the handling of hierarchical structures.
- Many programming tools were commercially available for LISP.

In other words, GP, as originally defined by Koza, considers individuals as LISP-like tree structures. These structures are perfectly capable of capturing all the fundamental properties of modern programming languages. GP using this representation is called *tree-based GP*[1]. The tree-based representation of genomes, although the oldest and most commonly used, is not the only one that has been employed in GP. In particular, in recent decades, growing attention has been dedicated by researchers to linear genomes [Brameier and Banzhaf, 2001], graph genomes [Miller, 2001], stack-based [Spector and Robinson, 2002] and grammar-based GP [O'Neill and Ryan, 2003].

This chapter is structured as follows: Section 8.1 introduces the main definitions and characteristics of GP and of its operators, including specifications of its typical behaviors and an example of a simple run, described step by step. Section 8.2 presents the most significant theoretical studies that have been performed in GP, known as schema theory. Section 8.3 describes some common typical problems of GP, or GP benchmarks, while Section 8.4 briefly describes some of the current challenges and open issues in GP. Finally, Sections 8.5 and 8.6 present two of the most recent and promising developments of GP.

8.1 The GP Process

In synthesis, the GP paradigm breeds computer programs to solve problems by executing the following steps:

1. Generate an initial population of computer programs (or individuals).
2. Iteratively perform the following steps until the termination criterion has been satisfied:

   2.1. Execute each program in the population and assign it a fitness value according to how well it solves the problem.
   2.2. Create a new population by applying the following operations:
   2.2.1. Probabilistically select a set of computer programs to be reproduced, on the basis of their fitness (selection).
   2.2.2. Copy some of the selected individuals, without modifying them, into the new population (replication[2]).

---

[1] Of course, modern tree-based GP is implemented in languages like C, C++, Java or Python, rather than LISP.

[2] Originally called reproduction in [Koza, 1992]

    2.2.3. Create new computer programs by genetically recombining randomly chosen parts of two selected individuals (crossover).

    2.2.4. Create new computer programs by substituting randomly chosen parts of some selected individuals with new randomly generated ones (mutation).

    2.2.5. Between the old and new programs, select the ones that will form the new population (survival).

3. The best computer program that appears in any generation is designated as the result of the GP process at that generation. This result may be a solution (or an approximate solution) to the problem.

The attentive reader will not have failed to recognize clear similarities between the general functioning of GAs (presented in Chapter 3) and that of GP. The high-level algorithm is actually extremely similar, with the only major difference typically being that, in GP, the individuals resulting from the application of one genetic operator are not used as input for another genetic operator. In other words, crossover and mutation are not applied sequentially. More specifically, mutation is not applied to the offspring generated by crossover. Instead, some selected individuals undergo crossover, some of them mutation and some of them replication, according to fixed probabilities that are parameters of the algorithm. This is justified by the fact that, as we will study later in this chapter, GP genetic operators are more "disruptive" than those of GAs, and thus applying more than one operator would risk generating individuals that are too different from their parents. Besides this, the different representation of the individuals evolving in the population makes GP deeply different from GAs in its dynamics and interpretation. In the following sections, each part of the GP process is analyzed in detail, specifying the differences and similarities between GP and GAs.

8.1.1 Representation of GP Individuals

In tree-based GP, the set of all the possible structures that can be generated is the set of all the possible trees that can be built recursively from a set of function symbols $\mathscr{F} = \{f_1, f_2, \ldots, f_n\}$ (also called primitive functions, and used to label internal tree nodes) and a set of terminal symbols $\mathscr{T} = \{t_1, t_2, \ldots, t_m\}$ (used to label tree leaves). This potentially infinite search space is usually limited in size, by restricting it to only those trees whose depth is less than or equal to a previously fixed parameter d[3]. Each element in the function set $\mathscr{F}$ takes a fixed number of arguments, specifying its *arity*. Functions may include arithmetic operations ($+$, $-$, $*$, etc.), other mathematical functions (such as `sin`, `cos`, `log`, `exp`), Boolean operations (such as AND, OR, NOT), conditional operations (such as `If-Then-Else`), iterative operations (such as `While-Do`) and/or any other domain-specific functions that may

---

[3] We recall that the *depth* of a tree is defined as the longest possible path from the root of the tree to one of its leaves.

be defined. Each terminal is typically either a variable or a constant, defined on the problem domain.

Example 8.1. Given the following sets of functions and terminals:

$$\mathscr{F} = \{+, -\}, \quad \mathscr{T} = \{x, 1\}$$

a legal GP individual is represented in Figure 8.1.

Fig. 8.1 A tree that can be built with the sets $\mathscr{F} = \{+, -\}$ and $\mathscr{T} = \{x, 1\}$

This tree can also be represented by the following LISP-like S-expression (for a definition of LISP S-expressions see, for instance, [Koza, 1992]):

$$(+ x (- x 1))$$

which is the prefix notation representation for expression $x + (x - 1)$.

Closure and Sufficiency of Function Set and Terminal Set. The function and terminal sets should be chosen so as to verify the requirements of *closure* and *sufficiency*. The closure property requires that each of the functions in the function set be able to accept, as its arguments, any value and data type that may possibly be returned by any function in the function set and any value and data type that may possibly be assumed by any terminal in the terminal set. In other words, each function should be well defined for any combination of arguments that it may encounter. The reason why this property must be verified is clearly that programs must be executed in order to assign them a fitness, and a failure in one of the executions of one of the programs composing the population would lead either to a failure of the whole GP system or to the generation of unpredictable results. The function and terminal sets of the previous example clearly satisfy the closure property. The following ones, for instance, don't satisfy this property:

$$\mathscr{F} = \{*, /\}, \quad \mathscr{T} = \{x, 0\}$$

In fact, each evaluation of an expression containing an operation of division by zero would cause an error. In order to use division, but avoid this type of problem, this operation is usually modified in order to verify the closure property (see Section 8.3.1). Respecting the closure property in real-life applications is not always straightforward, since the use of many different data types could be necessary. A common example is a mix of Boolean and numeric functions: function sets could exist composed of Boolean functions (*AND, OR, ...*), arithmetic functions (+, −,

$*, /, \ldots$), comparison functions ($>, <, =, \ldots$), conditionals (*IF THEN ELSE*), etc. and one might want to evolve expressions such as:

$$IF \ ((x > 10*y) \ AND \ (y > 0)) \ THEN \ z + y \ ELSE \ z*x$$

In such cases, introducing typed functions into the GP genome can help to force the closure property to be verified. GP in which each node carries its type as well as the types it can call, thus forcing functions calling it to cast the argument into the appropriate type, is called *strongly typed GP* [Banzhaf et al., 1998]. Using types might make even more sense in GP than with a human programmer, since a human programmer has a mental model of what needs to be done, whereas the GP system is completely random in its initialization and variation phases. Furthermore, type checking reduces the search space, which is likely to facilitate the search.

The sufficiency property requires that the set of terminals and the set of functions be capable of expressing a solution to the problem. For instance, the function and terminal sets of the previous example verify the sufficiency property if the problem at hand is an arithmetic one. It does not verify this property, for instance, if the problem faced is a logic one. For many domains, the requirements for sufficiency in the function and terminal sets are not clear and the definition of appropriate sets depends on the experience and the knowledge of the problem of the GP designer.

8.1.2 Initialization of a GP Population

Initialization of the population is the first step of the evolution process. It consists in the creation of the program structures that will later be evolved. The most common initialization methods in tree-based GP are the *grow* method, the *full* method and the *ramped half-and-half* method [Koza, 1992]. These methods will be explained in the following paragraphs, where the set of function symbols composing the trees will be denoted by $\mathscr{F}$, the set of terminal symbols by $\mathscr{T}$ and the maximum depth allowed for the trees by d.

Grow initialization. When the grow method is employed, each tree of the initial population is built using the following algorithm:

- a random symbol is selected with uniform probability from $\mathscr{F}$ to be the root of the tree;
- let n be the arity of the selected function symbol. Then n nodes are selected with uniform probability from the set $\mathscr{F} \cup \mathscr{T}$ to be its sons;
- for each function symbol between these n nodes, the method is recursively applied, i.e., its sons are selected from the set $\mathscr{F} \cup \mathscr{T}$, unless this symbol has a depth equal to $d - 1$. In the latter case, its sons are selected from $\mathscr{T}$.

In other words, the root is selected with uniform probability from $\mathscr{F}$, so that no tree composed of a single node is created initially (even though, in some implementations, trees composed of one single node can be admitted in the initial population).

Nodes with depths between 1 and $d - 1$ are selected with uniform probability from $\mathscr{F} \cup \mathscr{T}$, but once a branch contains a terminal node, that branch has ended, even if the maximum depth d has not been reached. Finally, nodes at depth d are chosen with uniform probability from $\mathscr{T}$. Since the incidence of choosing terminals from $\mathscr{F} \cup \mathscr{T}$ is random throughout initialization, trees initialized using the grow method are likely to have irregular shape, i.e., to contain branches of various different lengths.

Full initialization. Full initialization works like grow initialization, with the difference that, instead of selecting nodes from $\mathscr{F} \cup \mathscr{T}$, the full method chooses only function symbols (i.e., symbols in $\mathscr{F}$) until a node is at a depth equal to $d - 1$. Then it chooses only terminals (i.e., symbols in $\mathscr{T}$). The result is that every branch of the tree goes to the full maximum depth.

Ramped half-and-half initialization. As first noted by Koza [Koza, 1992], a population initialized with the above two methods may be composed of trees that are too similar to each other. In order to increase population diversity, the ramped half-and-half technique has been developed. Let d be the maximum-depth parameter. The population is divided equally among individuals to be initialized with trees having maximum depths equal to 1, 2, ..., $d - 1$, d. For each depth group, half of the trees are initialized with the full technique and half with the grow technique.

8.1.3 Fitness Evaluation

Each program in the population is assigned a fitness value, representing its ability to solve the problem. This value is calculated by means of some well-defined explicit procedure. The two fitness measures most commonly used in GP are raw fitness and standardized fitness. They are described below.

Raw Fitness. Raw fitness, as defined by Koza, is "the measurement of fitness that is stated in the natural terminology of the problem itself". In other words, raw fitness is the most simple and natural way to calculate the ability of a program to solve a problem. For example, if the problem consists in driving a robot to make it pick up the maximum possible number of objects contained in a room, the raw fitness of a program that drives the robot could be the number of objects effectively picked up after its execution.

Often, but not always, raw fitness is calculated over a set of *fitness cases*. A fitness case corresponds to a representative situation in which the ability of a program to solve a problem can be evaluated. For example, consider the problem of generating an arithmetic expression that approximates a polynomial, like for instance $x^4 + x^3 + x^2 + x$, over the set of natural numbers smaller than 10. Then, a fitness case is one of those natural numbers. Suppose $x^2 + 1$ to be one expression to evaluate, then we say that $2^2 + 1 = 5$ is the value assumed by this expression over the fitness case

2. Raw fitness is then defined as the sum of the distances over all fitness cases between values returned by perfect solutions and values returned by individuals to be evaluated. Formally, the raw fitness f_R of an individual i, calculated over a set of N fitness cases, can be defined as:

$$f_R(i) = \sum_{j=1}^{N} |S(i,j) - C(j)|^k$$

where $S(i,j)$ is the value returned by the evaluation of individual i over fitness case j, $C(j)$ is the correct value for fitness case j and $k \in \mathbb{N}$.

Fitness cases are typically a small sample of the entire domain space and they form the basis for generalizing the results obtained to the entire domain space. The choice of how many fitness cases to use, and which ones, is often crucial and it may depend on the available data, on the experience of the GP designer and her knowledge of the problem.

Standardized Fitness. Standardized fitness restates the raw fitness so that a lower numerical value is always a better value. For cases in which lesser values of raw fitness are better, it can happen that standardized fitness equals raw fitness. In many cases, it is convenient and desirable to make the best value of standardized fitness equal zero. If not already the case, this can be achieved by subtracting or adding a constant. If, for a particular problem, a greater value of raw fitness is better, and the maximum possible value of raw fitness f_R^{max} is known, standardized fitness f_S of an individual i can be defined as:

$$f_S(i) = f_R^{max} - f_R(i)$$

where $f_R(i)$ is the raw fitness of i.

8.1.4 Selection

As pointed out in Chapter 3, selection depends on the phenotype of the individuals, while the genetic operators depend on their genotype. Given that what makes a difference between GP and GAs is the genotype, i.e., the structures representing the individuals evolving in the population, the selection operators of GP are identical to those of GAs. In particular, GP can be implemented using fitness proportionate selection (roulette wheel), ranking selection and tournament selection. The interested reader is referred to Section 3.1 for a presentation of these selection algorithms. In GP, tournament selection is the most common choice. Numerous other selection algorithms have been developed for GP, such as tournaments that select parents based on more than one criterion [Luke and Panait, 2002] (which allows the implementation of pseudo-multiobjective evolution), and lexicase selection [Helmuth et al., 2015] (which maintains higher levels of population diversity, a desirable property for solving most problems), just to name a few.

8.1.5 Genetic Operators

Given that GP differs from GAs in the genotype of the individuals evolving in the population, new genetic operators of crossover and mutation have to be defined for GP. The standard GP crossover and mutation are presented in the continuation.

Crossover. The crossover (sexual recombination) operator creates variation in the population by producing new offspring that consist of parts taken from each parent. The two parents, which will be called T_1 and T_2, are chosen by means of a selection algorithm. Standard GP crossover [Koza, 1992] begins by independently selecting one random point in each parent (it will be called the crossover point for that parent). The crossover fragment for a particular parent is the subtree rooted at the node lying underneath the crossover point. The first offspring is produced by deleting the crossover fragment of T_1 from T_1 and inserting the crossover fragment of T_2 at the crossover point of T_1. The second offspring is produced in a symmetric manner. Figure 8.2 shows an example of standard GP crossover.

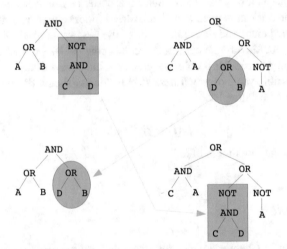

Fig. 8.2 An example of standard GP crossover. Crossover fragments are marked by gray shapes

Because entire subtrees are swapped and because of the closure property of the functions, crossover always produces syntactically legal programs, regardless of the selection of parents or crossover points.

It is important to remark that in cases where a terminal and/or the root of one parent are located at the crossover point, generated offspring could have considerable depths. This may be one possible cause of the phenomenon of *bloat*, i.e., progressive growth of the code size of individuals in the population, which will be discussed later. For this reason, many variants of the standard GP crossover have been proposed in the literature. The most common ones consist in assigning different probabilities of being chosen as crossover points to the various parents' nodes, depending on the depth level at which they are situated. In particular, it is very common to assign low probability of being selected as crossover points to the root and the leaves, so as to limit the influence of degenerative phenomena like the ones described above. Another different kind of GP crossover is *one-point crossover*, introduced in [Poli and Langdon, 1998a]. It deserves to be mentioned for the importance it has had in the development of a solid GP theory (see Section 8.2).

Mutation. Mutation is asexual, i.e., it operates on only one parental program. Standard GP mutation, often called *subtree* mutation, begins by choosing a point at random, with uniform probability distribution, within the selected individual. This point is called the mutation point. Then, the subtree laying below the mutation point is removed and a new randomly generated subtree is inserted at that point. Figure 8.3 shows an example of standard GP mutation.

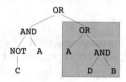

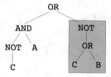

Fig. 8.3 An example of standard GP mutation

This operation, as is the case for standard crossover, is controlled by a parameter that specifies the maximum depth allowed and limits the size of the newly created subtree that is to be inserted. Nevertheless, the depth of the generated offspring can be considerably larger than that of the parent.

As for crossover, many variants of standard GP mutation have been developed too. The most commonly used are aimed at limiting the probability of selecting the root and/or the leaves of the parent as mutation points. A special mention is deserved by *point mutation* [Poli and Langdon, 1997], which exchanges a single node with a random node of the same arity, for the importance it has had in GP theory (see Section 8.2). Other commonly used variants of GP mutation are: *permutation* (or *swap* mutation), which exchanges two arguments of a node, and *shrink mutation*, which generates a new individual from a parent's subtree.

8.1.6 Survival

Once the offspring are created, the new population may completely replace the previous one, or there may be a selection of which individuals survive, among the old and new populations. Like in GAs, also in GP it is common to use some form of *elitism*, in which the best k individuals among old and new are copied unchanged into the next population, guaranteeing their survival. This parameter k is the size of the elite, and to turn off elitism one simply has to set $k = 0$. Again, like in GAs, the genetic operator of replication, described above, also represents a soft form of elitism, as it also (probabilistically) promotes the survival of the best individuals into the next population.

8.1.7 GP Parameters

Once the GP user has decided the set of functions $\mathscr{F}$ and the set of terminals $\mathscr{T}$ used to represent potential solutions of a given problem, and once the exact implementation of the genetic operators to employ has been chosen, still some parameters that characterize evolution need to be set. A list comprising some of these parameters is the following one:

- Population size.
- Population initialization algorithm.
- Selection algorithm.
- Crossover type and rate.
- Mutation type and rate.
- Maximum tree depth.
- Elitism.
- Stopping criteria.

Some of these choices arrive with more parameters to set, for example, tournament selection requires choosing the tournament size, and elitism requires choosing the elite size and the replication rate, the same way it did in GAs. The importance of parameter setting in EAs is a controversial issue. For instance, some work suggests that EAs are mostly insensitive to parameter choices [Sipper et al., 2018], while others seem to have a different opinion, at least for some versions of GP [Trujillo et al., 2020]. In general, much of what GP researchers know about parameter setting is empirical and based on experience.

Besides these parameters, an array of different implementation choices may result in wildly different evolutionary dynamics and capabilities. Like in GAs, also in GP we may have a steady-state instead of generational implementation, or a multi-objective approach, just to name a few. Specific to GP, we may have different bloat control methods, of which the maximum tree depth is one of the simplest, and we may have Automatically Defined Functions (ADFs) or other modular structures, just to name a few. The usefulness of ADFs has been shown by Koza in [Koza, 1994], later followed by other modular constructs [Koza et al., 1999], all aimed at allowing a high degree of code reusability inside GP individuals.

8.1.8 An Example Run

A very simple example GP run is discussed here. The problem to be solved is the even parity 2 problem, and it consists in finding a Boolean function of two Boolean arguments that returns *true* if an even number of its arguments are true and *false* otherwise (a generalization called the even parity k problem will be defined later in this chapter). Let A and B be the names of the two arguments; a Boolean function $f(A,B)$ perfectly solving this problem must respect the truth table in Table 8.1. Every line of

A	B	$f(A,B)$
false	false	true
false	true	false
true	false	false
true	true	true

Table 8.1 Truth table of the optimal individual for the even parity 2 problem

this table represents a fitness case. For every Boolean function of arguments A and B, its raw fitness is defined as the number of hits over all the fitness cases. Since the maximum raw fitness value, in this case, is equal to 4, we define the standardized fitness as equal to 4 minus the raw fitness. In this way, an optimal solution has a standardized fitness equal to 0 and the worst individuals have a standardized fitness equal to 4.

Let the following set of GP parameters be used: population size of 4 individuals, tournament selection of size 2, crossover rate equal to 50%, mutation rate equal to 25% and replication rate equal to 25%, maximum tree depth equal to 4 and ramped half-and-half initialization.[4] Let individuals be built with the set of functions $\mathscr{F} = \{and, or, not\}$ and the set of terminals $\mathscr{T} = \{A, B\}$.

The process begins with the generation of the initial population by the ramped half-and-half technique. Since the maximum tree depth is 4 and the population size is 4, the initial population will probably be composed of one individual of depth 1, one individual of depth 2, one individual of depth 3 and one individual of depth 4. Let the individuals composing the initial population be the following ones (prefix expressions instead of tree representations are given for the sake of simplicity):

1. $T_1 = not(A)$
2. $T_2 = or(and(A,B), and(A,A))$
3. $T_3 = and(and(A,B), or(A,A))$

---

[4] The reader is warned that these parameters are unrealistic and have been used for the sake of simplicity, just to show a first example of a GP run.

4. $T_4 = not(or(B,not(or(A,B))))$

The following steps consist in evaluating the fitness of all the individuals composing the population. Truth tables of individuals T_1, T_2, T_3, T_4 are shown in Figure 8.4, tables (a) through (d), respectively. Let f_R be the raw fitness and f_S be the standardized

A	B	T_1
false	false	true
false	true	true
true	false	false
true	true	false
	(a)	

A	B	T_2
false	false	false
false	true	false
true	false	true
true	true	true
	(b)	

A	B	T_3
false	false	false
false	true	false
true	false	false
true	true	true
	(c)	

A	B	T_4
false	false	false
false	true	false
true	false	true
true	true	false
	(d)	

Fig. 8.4 (a) Truth table of individual $not(A)$; (b) Truth table of individual $or(and(A,B),and(A,A))$; (c) Truth table of individual $and(and(A,B),or(A,A))$; (d) Truth table of individual $not(or(B,not(or(A,B))))$

fitness. From these tables, the following fitness values can be calculated:

1. $f_R(T_1) = 2 \rightarrow f_S(T_1) = 2$
2. $f_R(T_2) = 2 \rightarrow f_S(T_2) = 2$
3. $f_R(T_3) = 3 \rightarrow f_S(T_3) = 1$
4. $f_R(T_4) = 1 \rightarrow f_S(T_4) = 3$

Given the rates of replication, crossover and mutation, one individual will probably be selected for replication, two individuals for crossover and one for mutation. Let the tournament selection be first applied between T_1 and T_4. T_1 has a better fitness value and thus T_1 is reproduced, i.e., copied as it is into the new population. Analogously, let the two individuals chosen with the tournament technique for crossover be T_2 and T_3 and let

$$T_5 = and(and(A,B),and(A,A)), \quad T_6 = or(and(A,B),or(A,A))$$

be the two offspring to be inserted into the new population. Finally, let T_2 be the individual selected for mutation and let:

$$T_7 = or(and(A,B),and(A,not(B)))$$

be the generated offspring. Then, the new population is:

1. $T_1 = not(A)$

2. $T_5 = and(and(A,B), and(A,A))$
3. $T_6 = or(and(A,B), or(A,A))$
4. $T_7 = or(and(A,B), and(A, not(B)))$

At this point, the process is iterated on this new population. Truth tables analogous to the ones of Figure 8.4 could be written for T_1, T_5, T_6 and T_7. These tables would allow one to calculate the following values of standardized fitness:

1. $f_S(T_1) = 2$
2. $f_S(T_5) = 1$
3. $f_S(T_6) = 2$
4. $f_S(T_7) = 2$

Let T_6 be the individual selected for replication. Let T_1 and T_7 be the individuals selected for crossover and let

$$T_8 = A, \quad T_9 = or(and(A,B), and(not(A), not(B)))$$

be the offspring to be inserted into the new population. Finally, let T_5 be the individual selected for mutation and let

$$T_{10} = and(and(A,B), B)$$

be the generated offspring. Then, the new population is:

1. $T_6 = or(and(A,B), or(A,A))$
2. $T_8 = A$
3. $T_9 = or(and(A,B), and(not(A), not(B)))$
4. $T_{10} = and(and(A,B), B)$

Iterating the process, and thus evaluating the fitness of all the individuals in the new population, T_9 is discovered to have a standardized fitness equal to 0, and thus it is an optimal solution. This leads the process to stop and to return T_9 as a solution to the given problem.

An important remark can be made on this example: consider, for instance, individual T_6: $or(and(A,B), or(A,A))$. This expression is clearly equivalent to $or(and(A,B), A)$ (in the sense that these two expressions have identical truth values). From this consideration, it is straightforward to deduce that GP individuals are not necessarily (and in general *are not*) in their most natural form. If the final user needs to have solutions in such a form, a *simplification* phase is necessary. The steps that enable simplification of the structure of solutions are often called *rewrite steps*. This phase clearly depends on the type of language used to code GP individuals and it cannot be generalized.

8.2 GP Theory

After reading the introduction to GP given in Section 8.1, one question may naturally arise: why should GP work at all? This question can be made more precise by splitting it into the following ones: why should the iterative GP process allow the building of solutions of better and better fitness? And why should it find a solution that is satisfactory for a given problem? Or even better: what is the probability of improving the fitness of solutions through the GP generations? What is the probability of finding a satisfactory solution for a given problem? The attempt to answer these questions has been an important research challenge in the GP field since its early years. The discussion contained in this section is inspired by the one in [Langdon and Poli, 2002], where Langdon and Poli offer a complete and detailed discussion of GP theory.

Being able to answer the above questions surely implies a deep understanding of what happens inside a GP population through the generations. One may think of somehow visualizing a population on a Cartesian plane. In this way, one would often find that initially the population looks like a cloud of randomly scattered points but that, through the generations, this cloud "moves" in the search space, following a well-defined trajectory. This representation would probably provide interesting information about the dynamics regulating the GP process. But, since GP is a stochastic technique, in different runs different trajectories would be observed. Moreover, it is normally impossible to visualize a search space, given its high dimensionality and complexity. Thus, one may think of recording some numerical values concerning individuals of a population through the generations and of calculating statistics on them. These numerical values may be the average fitness of the individuals, the length of the individuals, differences between parent and offspring fitness and so on. Nevertheless, given the complexity of a GP system and its numerous degrees of freedom, any number of these statistical descriptors would be able to capture only a tiny fraction of the system's characteristics.

For these reasons, the only way to understand the behavior of a GP system appears to be the definition of precise mathematical models. Theoretical studies on GAs have already been discussed in Section 3.4, where the GAs Schema Theorem was presented. Those studies have inspired the formulation of a theory for GP. This theory, consisting of a rigorous probabilistic model for GP systems, can be considered as the foundation of GP theory. This section is not intended to explain this complex subject in detail, but just to give a simple introduction.

Early GP Schema Theorems. Schema theory for GP had a slow start, one of the difficulties being that the variable-size tree structure makes it harder to develop a definition of schema. Koza [Koza, 1992] was the first one to address schema theory in GP. However, his arguments are informal and only hint at the existence of building blocks in GP. The first mathematical formulation of a schema theorem for GP is due to Altenberg [Altenberg, 1994a]. He defined a schema as a subexpression and supplied equations for the proportion of a certain individual in the population at a certain generation and the probability that crossover picks up a certain expression from a randomly chosen program at a certain generation.

A formalization of a schema theorem for GP more similar to Holland's one for GAs is due to O'Reilly [O'Reilly and Oppacher, 1995]. Similarly to what happens for GAs, she defines a schema using a "don't care symbol" that allows us to define an order and a length for schemata. She estimates the probability of disruption of schemata by the maximum probability of disruption $P_d(H,t)$, producing the following schema theorem:

$$E[m(H,t+1)] \geq m(H,t) \frac{f(H,t)}{\overline{f}(t)} (1 - p_c P_d(H,t))$$

where $f(H,t)$ is the mean fitness of all instances of schema H and $\overline{f}(t)$ is the average fitness in the population at generation t. The disadvantage of using the maximum probability is that it may produce a very conservative measure of the number of schemata at a given generation. Moreover, the maximum probability of disruption varies with the size of a given schema and makes it very difficult to predict which schemata will tend to multiply in the population and why.

Other interesting schema theorem formulations for GP are due to Whigham [Whigham, 1996], who produced a schema theorem for a GP system based on context-free grammars, Rosca [Rosca, 1997] and Poli and Langdon [Poli and Langdon, 1998b], who gave a pessimistic lower bound (approximation) on the expected number of copies of a schema in the next generation. Next, schema theorems that give an exact expected number, rather than a bound, will be considered.

Exact GP Schema Theorem. The development of an exact and general schema theory for GP is due to Poli and colleagues [Langdon and Poli, 2002]. Syntactically, a schema is a tree with some "don't care" nodes (labelled with the symbol "=") which represent exactly one node (primitive function or terminal). Semantically, a schema represents all programs that match its size, shape and defining nodes (i.e., nodes that are not "don't care").

In addition to the definition of schema, exact GP schema theory is based on the concept of *hyperschema* and *variable-arity hyperschema* (VA hyperschema). A hyperschema is a tree composed of internal nodes from the set $\mathscr{F} \cup \{=\}$ and leaves from $\mathscr{T} \cup \{=,\#\}$, where the "#" symbol stands for any valid subtree. A VA hyperschema is a tree composed of internal nodes from the set $\mathscr{F} \cup \{=,\#\}$ and leaves from the set $\mathscr{T} \cup \{=,\#\}$, where the "=" "don't care" symbol stands for exactly one node, the terminal "#" stands for any valid subtree, while the function "#" stands for exactly one function of arity not smaller than the number of subtrees connected to it. If a function symbol "#" is matched by a function of greater arity than the number of subtrees connected to it, then some arguments of that function are left unspecified.

Many formulations of exact schema theorems for GP have been developed, depending on the type of genetic operators used (one-point crossover, point mutation, standard crossover, etc.), and on whether each member of the population (*microscopic* schema theorems) or average population properties (*macroscopic* schema theorems) have to be considered. One of the most general forms of exact schema theorem for GP is probably the following.

Theorem 8.1 (Macroscopic Exact GP Schema Theorem for Standard Crossover).

Let selection and standard crossover be the genetic operators used by a GP system and let:

- $\alpha(H,t)$ *be the probability that the individuals produced by selection and crossover at generation t match schema H (also called total schema transmission probability for schema H).*
- p_{xo} *be the crossover rate.*
- $p(H,t)$ *be the probability of selecting an individual matching schema H to be a parent at generation t.*
- $G_1, G_2, \ldots$ *be all the possible program shapes (i.e., all the schemata of fixed size and shape, including only "=" symbols).*
- $N(K)$ *be the number of nodes in schema K.*
- $U(H,i)$ *be the hyperschema representing all the trees that match the portion of schema H above crossover point i; in other words $U(H,i)$ is the hyperschema obtained by replacing the subtree below crossover point i with a "#" node in H.*
- $L(H,i,j)$ *be the VA hyperschema representing all the trees that match the portion of schema H below crossover point i, but where the matching portion is rooted at some arbitrary node j.*

Then the following equality holds:

$$\alpha(H,t) = (1 - p_{xo})\, p(H,t) +$$
$$p_{xo} \sum_{k,l} \frac{1}{N(G_k)N(G_l)} \sum_{i \in H \cap G_k} \sum_{j \in G_l} p(U(H,i) \cap G_k, t)\, p(L(H,i,j) \cap G_l, t)$$

$$(8.1)$$

An even more general formulation of the exact schema theorem exists. It holds for *any* type of subtree-swapping crossover and so it applies, for instance, to Koza's crossover, to one-point crossover and many others. The interested reader can find this formulation in [Poli and McPhee, 2003a, Poli and McPhee, 2003b]. The contribution of GP exact schema theory to the comprehension of GP systems dynamics is undeniable. For instance, in [Langdon and Poli, 2002], Poli and Langdon have performed some experimental analysis based on GP exact schema theory, which has helped in deeply understanding how GP works on some concrete problems.

8.3 GP Benchmarks

GP has been applied to many fields in industry and science and has produced a large amount of results. The attempt to classify all the applications in which GP has been used since its early beginnings is probably hopeless, even though important efforts can be found in [Langdon, 1996, Banzhaf et al., 1998]. In [Koza and Poli, 2003], Koza and Poli state that GP may be especially productive in areas having, among others, some or all of the following characteristics:

- where there is poor understanding of the problem at hand,
- where finding the size and shape of the ultimate solution is a major part of the problem,
- where there are good simulators to test performance of candidate solutions but poor methods to directly obtain good solutions,
- where conventional mathematical analysis does not, or cannot, provide analytic solutions,
- where an approximate solution is acceptable.

One more characteristic can be added here:

- where it is impossible, or difficult, to write an algorithm to solve the problem.

Problems with one or more of these characteristics can, in some sense, be called "typical GP problems". In [Koza, 1992], Koza defines a set of problems that can be considered as belonging to this class and which have the relevant property of being simple to define and suitable for application of GP. For this reason, they have been adopted by the GP research community as a, more or less, agreed upon set of benchmarks. They are introduced in Sections 8.3.1, 8.3.2 and 8.3.3. Of course this list is not exhaustive, and many other benchmarks exist and are used in GP research, but it can be considered a good set of problems to be used by researchers to test their hypotheses, since it is composed of problems of different natures and often showing different behaviors. For a more complete list of GP benchmarks that also contains pointers to freely available data, the reader is referred to [McDermott et al., 2012]. In particular, the first benchmark discussed here (symbolic regression) is a mathematical problem, the second one (even parity k) is a Boolean problem, and the third one (the artificial ant) is a simple application of path planning in artificial intelligence.

8.3.1 Symbolic Regression

We have already introduced symbolic regression in Chapter 5, since it is one of the main types of problem of Machine Learning. However, given the importance that it has in GP, it is appropriate to rediscuss here some of the main characteristics of this type of problem, and present it in the new perspective of GP.

Given a set of vectors $\mathbf{X} = \{\mathbf{x}_1, \mathbf{x}_2, ..., \mathbf{x}_n\}$, where for all $i = 1, 2, ..., n, \mathbf{x}_i \in \mathbb{R}^m$, and a vector $\mathbf{t} = [t_1, t_2, ..., t_n]$, where for all $i = 1, 2, ..., n, t_i \in \mathbb{R}$, a symbolic regression problem can be generally defined as the problem of finding, or approximating, a function $\phi : \mathbb{R}^m \to \mathbb{R}$, also called the target function, such that:

$$\forall i = 1, 2, ..., n : \quad \phi(\mathbf{x}_i) = t_i$$

GP is typically used to solve symbolic regression problems using a set of primitive functions $\mathscr{F}$ that are mathematical functions, for instance the arithmetic functions or others, and a set of terminal symbols $\mathscr{T}$ that contain at least m different real-valued variables, and may also contain any set of numeric constants. In this way, a GP individual (or program) P can be seen as a function that, for each input vector $\mathbf{x}_i$, returns the scalar value $P(\mathbf{x}_i)$. In symbolic regression, to measure the fitness of an individual P any distance metric (or error) between the vector $[P(\mathbf{x}_1), P(\mathbf{x}_2), ..., P(\mathbf{x}_n)]$ and the vector $[t_1, t_2, ..., t_n]$ can be used. As an example, one may use the mean Euclidean distance, or root mean square error, and the fitness $f(P)$ of a GP individual P would be:

$$f(P) = \sqrt{\frac{\sum_{i=1}^{n}(P(\mathbf{x}_i) - t_i)^2}{n}} \tag{8.2}$$

or one may use the Manhattan distance, or absolute error, and in this case the fitness $f(P)$ of a GP individual P is:

$$f(P) = \sum_{i=1}^{n}|P(\mathbf{x}_i) - t_i| \tag{8.3}$$

Using any error measure as fitness, a symbolic regression problem can be seen as a minimization problem, where the optimal fitness value is equal to zero (in fact, any individual with an error equal to zero behaves on the input data exactly like the target function ϕ). As is customary in Machine Learning, the vectors $\mathbf{x}_1, \mathbf{x}_2, ..., \mathbf{x}_n$ are usually called input data, input vectors, training instances or *fitness cases*, while the values $t_1, t_2, ..., t_n$ are usually identified as the corresponding *target values*, or expected output values. $\mathbf{X}$ is usually called the *dataset*. Finally, the values $P(\mathbf{x}_1), P(\mathbf{x}_2), ..., P(\mathbf{x}_n)$ are usually called the *output values* of individual P on the input data.

Example 8.2. Let $\mathbf{X} = \{[3, 12, 1], [5, 4, 2]\}$ and let $\vec{t} = [27, 13]$. For instance, GP individuals may be coded using as primitive functions the set of arithmetic operators $\mathscr{F} = \{+, -, *\}$ and as terminals a set of three real-valued variables (since the input vectors have size equal to 3) $\mathscr{T} = \{k_1, k_2, k_3\}$. In this way, the search space contains all the trees that can be built by composing the symbols in $\mathscr{F}$ and $\mathscr{T}$ (with the only exception that usually a maximum possible depth is imposed on the trees, as previously discussed). Using, for instance, the absolute error, one may calculate the fitness of an individual, for instance:

$$P(k1,k2,k3) = k3 * (k1 - k2)$$

To do that, one has to first calculate the output values of P on the input data. In other words, one has to calculate $P(3,12,1)$ (obtained by substituting the values of the first input vector in the dataset $\mathbf{X}$ for k_1, k_2 and k_3 respectively in the expression of P) and $P(5,4,2)$ (obtained by substituting the values of the second input vector in the dataset $\mathbf{X}$ for k_1, k_2 and k_3 in P). So, the fitness of P is:

$$
\begin{aligned}
f(P) &= |P(3,12,1) - 27| + |P(5,4,2) - 13| \\
&= |(1 * (12 - 3)) - 27| + |(2 * (5 - 4)) - 13| \\
&= |9 - 27| + |2 - 13| = 18 + 11 = 29
\end{aligned}
$$

It is not difficult to realize that, in this example, a global optimum, i.e., an individual that has a fitness equal to zero, is:

$$P_{opt}(k_1,k_2,k_3) = k_1 + 2 * k_2$$

From this, we can see that GP individuals do not have to necessarily use all the variables in $\mathscr{T}$ (for instance, P_{opt} does not use k_3).

In this simple example, only the binary operators of sum, subtraction and multiplication have been used. When division is also used, it is typical to "protect" it in some way from failure in case the denominator is equal to zero. The oldest and most popular method to protect division is to replace it with an operator that is equal to division if the denominator is different from zero and that returns a constant value otherwise [Koza, 1992]. Nevertheless, several more sophisticated methods have been introduced [Keijzer, 2003].

Of course, one of the main requirements for symbolic regression problems is that the evolved models have a good generalization ability (as discussed in Chapter 5).

Symbolic Regression with Synthetic Functions. Symbolic regression has a huge number of real-life applications. Nevertheless, real-world datasets are often very complex, and they may be noisy and contain errors. For this reason, when we want to study the properties of GP and other Machine Learning algorithms, it is often useful to create artificial, or synthetic, datasets with some known properties. A popular way of doing this is to consider a given known target function, and create a dataset that contains some inputs and some corresponding outputs generated by that function. The objective is to test whether GP, and/or other algorithms, are able to find that function, using only the considered points. For instance, one may consider a function (also called a quartic polynomial) like: $f(x) = x^4 + x^3 + x^2 + x$. A dataset could be created by using as input data a set of values for x (say, for instance, the first 100 natural numbers), and as corresponding targets the corresponding values of $f(x)$.

This quartic polynomial is known to be a rather simple function for GP to find. It can be made harder by defining numerical coefficients for the different terms. A large set of other typical synthetic symbolic regression benchmarks can be found in [McDermott et al., 2012].

8.3.2 Boolean Problems

Boolean problems are similar to symbolic regression, with the only difference that both input data and the corresponding targets are Boolean values. Many real-life applications of Boolean problems exist, the most typical ones probably being the automatic synthesis of integrated electric circuits, on which GP reported several practical successes so far [Koza, 1992]. As for symbolic regression, also for Boolean problems it is possible that real-life datasets are too complex to be used when the properties of algorithms need to be investigated. For this reason, it is typical to create artificial, or synthetic, Boolean problems, with known properties, and use them as benchmarks to test the dynamics of GP and other algorithms.

One of the most popular Boolean synthetic problems is the even parity k problem [Koza, 1992]. The goal of this problem is to find a Boolean function of k Boolean arguments that returns *true* if an even number of its Boolean arguments evaluates to true, and that returns *false* otherwise. A very simple case, even parity 2, has already been introduced in Section 8.1.8, where a function perfectly solving this problem has been found. This function is:

$$f(A,B) = or(and(A,B), and(not(A), not(B)))$$

and its truth values for all possible values of its Boolean arguments A and B are represented in Table 8.1. As this table shows, each time an even number (0 or 2, in this case) of arguments is true, f returns true and each time an odd number (1, in this case) of arguments is true, f returns false. In general, the number of fitness cases, i.e., the number of all possible permutations of the values of the k parameters, is 2^k. Fitness is usually computed as 2^k minus the number of hits over the 2^k cases. Thus, a perfect individual has fitness equal to 0, while the worst individuals have fitness equal to 2^k. Unlike what happens in Section 8.1.8, a typical set of functions employed for this problem is $\mathscr{F} = \{nand, nor\}$, while the terminal set is usually composed of k different Boolean variables.

Besides the even parity k problems, other known Boolean GP benchmarks are the h-multiplexer [Koza, 1992] and the FPGA [Vanneschi, 2004].

8.3.3 The Artificial Ant on the Santa Fe Trail

In this problem [Koza, 1992], an artificial ant is placed on a 32×32 toroidal grid. Some of the cells from the grid contain food pellets. The goal is to find a navigation strategy for the ant that maximizes its food intake. The ant starts in the upper left cell of the grid, identified by the coordinates (0, 0), facing east. It has a very limited view of its world. In particular, it has a sensor that can see only a single immediately adjacent cell in the direction the ant is currently facing. Food is placed on the grid according to the "Santa Fe trail", an irregular trail consisting of 89 food pellets. The trail is not straight and continuous, but instead has single gaps, double gaps and triple gaps at corners. Figure 8.5 shows the Santa Fe trail. Food is represented by solid black squares, while gaps are represented by gray squares. Numbers identify key characteristics along the trail, for example the number 3 highlights the first corner, number 11 the first single gap, and so on.

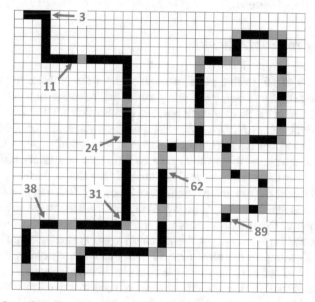

Fig. 8.5 The Santa Fe trail used for the artificial ant problem

The set of terminals used for this problem is usually $\mathcal{T} = \{Right, Left, Move\}$, and corresponds to the actions the ant can perform: rotate to the right by 90°, rotate to the left by 90°, and move forward in the currently facing direction. When the ant moves into a square containing a food pellet, it eats the food (thereby eliminating the pellet from that square and erasing the trail). The set of primitive functions that are typically used for this problem is $\mathcal{F} = \{IfFoodAhead, Progn2, Progn3\}$. *IfFoodAhead* is a conditional branching operator that takes two arguments and executes the first one if and only if a food pellet is present in the case that it is adjacent to the ant in the direction the ant is facing, and the second one otherwise (it represents the information the ant can get by its sensor). *Progn2* and *Progn3* are common LISP operators. *Progn2* takes two arguments and causes the ant to unconditionally execute the first argument, followed by the second one; *Progn3* is analogous, but it takes three arguments, which are executed in an ordered sequence. An individual built with these sets $\mathcal{F}$ and $\mathcal{T}$ can be considered as a "program" that allows the ant to navigate the grid. As fitness function, the total number of food pellets lying on the trail (89) minus the amount of food eaten by the ant in a fixed amount of time is considered. This turns the problem into a minimization one, like the previous ones. Each move operation and each rotate operation is considered to take one time step, and the ant is usually limited to 600 time steps. This timeout limit is sufficiently small to prevent a random walk of the ant to cover all the 1024 squares, and thus eat all the food, before timing out.

8.4 GP Open Issues

8.4.1 GP Problem Difficulty

The capability of GP to find good solutions varies from problem to problem. To convince oneself of this fact, one could perform the following experiment: execute the artificial ant on the Santa Fe trail problem (see Section 8.3.3) for, say, n generations; record the values $f_1, f_2, \ldots, f_n$, where, for each $g = 1, 2, \ldots, n$, f_g is the fitness of the best individual found in the population at generation g. Since GP is based on stochastic operators, these values may be fortuitous and surely lack statistical significance. For this reason, as we have studied for GAs in Section 3.6, it is appropriate to repeat the execution a number of times, say 100, and consider average (or median) results. Thus, let $\overline{f}_g$ be the average of the best fitness values found at generation g over the 100 runs performed and plot on a Cartesian two-dimensional plane the values $\overline{f}_1, \overline{f}_2, \ldots, \overline{f}_n$ (on the ordinates) against generation numbers (on the abscissas). Now, repeat the same process for a symbolic regression problem (see Section 8.3.1), aimed at finding a simple equation, like for instance $x^4 + x^3 + x^2 + x$ (a quartic polynomial). Let the GP parameters used to solve these two different problems be identical (except, of course, for the sets of functions $\mathscr{F}$ and of terminal symbols $\mathscr{T}$). Figure 8.6 shows the results of this experiment, where the set of GP parameters for both problems was the following one: population size of 2500 individuals, ramped half-and-half initialization, tournament selection of size 10, crossover rate equal to 95% (standard GP crossover [Koza, 1992]), mutation rate equal to 0.1% (standard subtree mutation [Koza, 1992]), maximum tree depth for the initialization phase equal to 6, maximum depth for the crossover and mutation phases equal to 17, elitism (with elite size equal to 1). In the case of the symbolic regression problem, 100 equidistant points included in the range $[0, 5]$ have been used as fitness cases. The blue curve represents results of artificial ant and the black one results of symbolic regression. This figure clearly shows that, for the symbolic regression problem, the optimal solution (fitness equal to zero) has been found (or at least appropriately approximated) in all the executed runs before generation 8. This is surely not the case for the artificial ant problem, since the blue curve does not touch the abscissas axis during the first 40 generations. Data not shown here confirm that, even if generations until 500 were considered, still the blue curve would

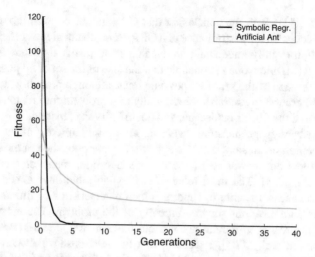

Fig. 8.6 Symbolic regression problem and artificial ant problem. Evolution of best fitness during the first 40 generations. The two curves have been obtained using the same GP parameters (see text) and are averages over 100 independent GP runs

not touch the abscissas axis. Moreover, fewer than 50 runs, over the total 100 runs executed, have led to the discovery of one optimal solution before generation 500 for the artificial ant problem.

These different behaviors are usual in GP, when considering different problems. Thus, the following questions arise naturally: why does it happen? Why are some problems easily solved by GP, while others are so hard? The following observations can be made about the experiment shown in Figure 8.6:

(i) The GP parameters used for the two considered problems are exactly the same.
(ii) The range of all possible fitness values that an individual of the symbolic regression problem can take is much larger than the ones that an individual of the artificial ant can take. In fact, fitness values for the ant problem range from 0 to 89 by definition (since 89 is the number of food pellets on the Santa Fe trail), while the best fitness value in the population at generation 0 for the symbolic regression problem was, on average, around 120 in the experiment shown (see Figure 8.6). Furthermore, the "granularity" in the fitness function is very different: only 90 different fitness values are possible for the ant problem, while fitness is continuous for symbolic regression, and so an infinite number of values are possible.
(iii) Trees in the ant problem can be built using just three primitive functions (*If-FoodAhead*, *Progn2*, *Progn3*), while in the symbolic regression problem, they can be built using four primitive functions ($+$, $-$, $*$ and $//$). Furthermore, arities of the operators are also different: all the operators used for symbolic regression have an arity equal to 2, while two operators used for the ant have an arity equal to 3 and one of them has an arity equal to 2.

Observation (i) leads to the conclusion that GP parameters, even though they can have an influence on the performance of a GP system, do not give a sufficient amount of information to fully understand its dynamics and justify its behavior. Observations (ii) and (iii) allow one to conclude that the size of the set of all possible fitness values and the size of the set of all possible trees, although probably not irrelevant, are not valid criteria to establish the difficulty of a problem for GP. In other words, the structure of the fitness landscape, and not only its size, matters.

Thus, answering the question "what makes a problem easy or hard for GP?" does not seem to be an easy task. Several works were published in the last decade, trying to given an answer to this ambitious question, many of them collected in [Vanneschi, 2004]. The most relevant are arguably the ones aimed at defining mathematical measures able to capture some characteristics of fitness landscapes that can have implications for the difficulty of the problem. The most successful of these measures, even though not without flaws, is the *fitness-distance correlation* [Tomassini et al., 2005], indicating that the relationship between fitness and distance to the goal can give a reliable indication of the hardness of the problem, assuming that the distance is appropriately related to the genetic operators used to evolve [Gustafson and Vanneschi, 2005]. Another measure that can give some useful indications is the *negative slope coefficient* [Vanneschi et al., 2006], based on the concept of *fitness clouds* [Vanneschi et al., 2004].

8.4.2 Premature Convergence or Stagnation

After a certain number of generations, GP populations, as is the case for GAs and any other evolutionary algorithm, tend to contain individuals that are similar, or even identical, to each other. To show this phenomenon, measures analogous to the ones introduced in Section 3.5.1 for GAs can be used. Many reasons can be given for premature convergence. First of all, the selection mechanism acts on phenotypes, thus assigning high probabilities of surviving to only a few good-quality individuals. Secondly, according to schema theory, building blocks tend to multiply in the population, thus introducing similar substructures inside individuals [Langdon and Poli, 2002].

Many techniques have been developed by GP researchers to maintain diversity, both genotypic and phenotypic, inside GP populations (see, for instance, [Ekárt and Németh, 2002]). Although these techniques have often proved very useful to understand why premature convergence happens, their main drawback is generally that they are time consuming, since they demand the calculation of measures like structural distances, entropy or variance, at each generation. This generally causes an increment in the total completion time of GP systems, which may make them unusable in practice (even though efficient methods to approximate diversity measures have been defined [Burke et al., 2002]). Otherwise, new genetic operators, like different kinds of selections, crossovers or mutations, have been defined in order to produce offspring that are as different as possible from their parents, or from the other individuals in the population, by construction. These techniques generally succeed in maintaining diversity inside populations, but substantially change the GP algorithm (in particular the genetic operators used) and thus the behavior of GP systems. [Fernández et al., 2003] demonstrated that parallelizing the GP process, and organizing it into separate and interacting subpopulations, helps to limit premature convergence and its deleterious effects on GP. The migration of candidate solutions from one population to another, in fact, allows individuals having different ancestors, and thus possibly different evolutionary histories and behaviors, to enter converging populations and to inject diversity inside them. Moreover, since (copies of) the fitter individuals of each subpopulation are sent to the other ones, good quality of solutions should be maintained together with diversity (one could informally say that not just "diversity", but "good diversity" is maintained).

8.4.3 The Problem of Bloat

The search space of GP is virtually unlimited and programs tend to grow in size during the evolutionary process. Code growth is a healthy result of genetic operators in search of better solutions, but it also permits the appearance of pieces of redundant code that increase the size of programs without improving their fitness. These "useless" pieces of code are often called *introns*, based on the name given to their biological counterparts. Introns can be roughly divided into two categories: inviable code and unoptimized code (or syntactic/structural and semantic introns [Angeline, 1998, Brameier and Banzhaf, 2003]). The former is code that cannot contribute to the fitness no matter how many changes it suffers, either because it is never executed or because its return value is ignored. The latter is viable code containing redundant elements whose removal would not change the return value [Luke, 2003]. Besides consuming precious time in an already computationally intensive process, redundant code may start growing rapidly, a phenomenon known as bloat [Banzhaf et al., 1998, Chapter 7], [Langdon and Poli, 2002, Chapter 11]. Bloat can be defined as an excess of code growth without a corresponding improvement in fitness. This is a serious and widely studied problem in GP, often being a main cause of stagnation of the evolutionary process.

The different explanations for bloat given through the years are not necessarily contradictory. Some appear to be generalizations or refinements of others, and several most certainly complement each other. An extensive review of the first five theories presented below can be found in [Silva and Costa, 2009]. A detailed explanation of the last theory, Crossover Bias, can be found in [Silva et al., 2012].

Hitchhiking. One of the first explanations for the proliferation of introns among GP programs, advanced by Tackett, was the hitchhiking phenomenon [Tackett, 1994]. This is a common and undesirable occurrence in genetic algorithms where unfit building blocks propagate throughout the population simply because they happen to adjoin highly fit building blocks. According to the hitchhiking explanation, the reason why naturally emerging introns in GP become so abundant is that they, too, are hitchhikers.

Defense Against Crossover. The idea of defense against crossover as being the explanation for bloat has persisted in the literature for a long time [Altenberg, 1994b, Blickle and Thiele, 1994, McPhee and Miller, 1995, Nordin and Banzhaf, 1995, Smith and Harries, 1998]. It is based on the fact that standard crossover is usually very destructive [Banzhaf et al., 1998, Chapter 6], [Nordin and Banzhaf, 1995, Nordin et al., 1996]. In face of a genetic operator that seldom creates offspring better than their parents, particularly in more advanced stages of the evolution, the advantage belongs to individuals that at least have the same fitness as their parents, i.e., those who were created by neutral variations. Introns provide standard crossover and other genetic operators with genetic material where swapping can be performed without harming the effective code, leading to these neutral variations.

Removal Bias. Although supporting the defense against crossover theory, Soule performed additional experiments and concluded that there must be a second cause for code growth, presenting a theory called removal bias [Langdon et al., 1999, Soule and Foster, 1998]. The presence of inviable code provides regions where removal or addition of genetic material does not modify the fitness of the individual. According to removal bias, to maintain fitness the removed branches must be contained within the inviable region, meaning they cannot be deeper than the inviable subtree. On the other hand, the addition of a branch inside an inviable region cannot affect fitness regardless of how deep the new branch is. This asymmetry can explain code growth, even in the absence of destructive genetic operators.

Fitness Causes Bloat. The first theory that does not make introns responsible for bloat was advanced by Langdon and Poli [Langdon, 1998, Langdon and Poli, 1997, Langdon and Poli, 1998, Langdon et al., 1999]. The fitness causes bloat theory basically states that with a representation of variable length there are many different ways to represent the same program, long and short, and a static evaluation function will attribute the same fitness to all, as long as their behavior is the same. Given the inherent destructiveness of crossover, when better solutions become hard to find there is a selection bias towards programs that have the same fitness as their parents. Because there are many more longer ways to represent a program than shorter ways, a natural drift towards longer solutions occurs, causing bloat.

Modification Point Depth. Another explanation for bloat was advanced by Luke and is usually referred to as modification point depth [Luke, 2003]. Confirming previous results [Igel and Chellapilla, 1999], Luke observed that when a genetic operator modifies a parent to create an offspring, the deeper the modification point, the smaller the change in fitness. Once again because of the destructive nature of crossover, small changes will eventually benefit from a selective advantage over large changes, so there is a preference for deeper modification points, and consequently larger trees. Plus, the deeper the modification point, the smaller the branch that is removed, thus creating a removal bias [Soule and Heckendorn, 2002].

Crossover Bias. Dignum and Poli [Dignum and Poli, 2007, Dignum and Poli, 2008, Poli et al., 2007, Poli et al., 2008b] explain code growth in tree-based GP by the effect that standard subtree crossover has on the distribution of tree sizes in the population. The average length of programs in the mating pool does not differ from that of the resultant child population after the application of crossover. However, the length distribution of the child population, under normal GP experimental conditions, is biased towards smaller programs. Smaller programs will be unable to obtain reasonable fitness and will be discarded by selection, hence increasing the average size of programs in the mating pool for the succeeding generation.

Regarding methods for counteracting bloat, they are very numerous, and act at different phases of the evolutionary cycle. For example, when evaluating fitness, the *parametric parsimony pressure* method, e.g., [Zhang and Mühlenbein, 1995] adds a term to the fitness calculation that penalizes larger individuals, while the *Tarpeian* method [Poli, 2003] periodically "kills" a fraction of individuals with above-average size by giving them an extremely bad fitness value; when selecting the parents for breeding, size may also be taken into consideration, either in a true multiobjective setting, e.g., [Bleuler et al., 2001] or using modified size-aware tournaments [Luke and Panait, 2002]; different types of genetic operators have also been developed that counteract bloat, such as *homologous crossover* [Langdon, 1999]; regarding selection for survival, Koza's maximum depth is still the most common method [Koza, 1992], while others include dynamic depth and size limits [Silva and Costa, 2009] and the *operator equalisation* method [Silva and Dignum, 2009]. Other types of methods do not fit into any particular phase of the evolutionary cycle. A taxonomy and survey of most bloat control methods can be found in [Silva et al., 2012].

8.5 Geometric Semantic Genetic Programming

8.5.1 Semantics in Genetic Programming

Geometric Semantic GP (GSGP) is the name we give to GP that uses two novel genetic operators, called geometric semantic operators, instead of the traditional crossover and mutation. These new operators are based on the concept of semantics that is briefly introduced here. As discussed previously, let $\mathbf{X} = \{\mathbf{x}_1, \mathbf{x}_2, ..., \mathbf{x}_n\}$ be the set of input data, or fitness cases, of a supervised learning problem, and $\mathbf{t} = [t_1, t_2, ..., t_n]$ the vector of the respective expected output or target values. Let P be a GP individual (or program). As discussed previously, P can be seen as a function that, for each input vector $\mathbf{x}_i$, returns a value $P(\mathbf{x}_i)$. Following [Moraglio et al., 2012], the *semantics* of P is given by the vector:

$$\mathbf{s}_P = [P(\mathbf{x}_1), P(\mathbf{x}_2), ..., P(\mathbf{x}_n)]$$

In other words, from now on, we indicate with the term semantics the vector of the output values of a GP individual on the input data. Even though the concept of semantics is general, and applies to any type of supervised learning problem, it is particularly intuitive to discuss the case of symbolic regression. So, for simplicity, and without forgetting that it is just a particular case study while the concepts are general, let us assume that the problem at hand is a symbolic regression one. In this case, $sp \in \mathbb{R}^m$, and so sp can be represented as a point in an n-dimensional Cartesian space, which we call *semantic space*. Remark that the target vector **t** itself is a point in the semantic space and, since we are dealing with supervised learning, its exact location is known. What is not known is the tree structure of a GP individual that has **t** as its own semantics. Basically, when working with GP, one may imagine the existence of two different spaces: one that we call genotypic or syntactic space, in which GP individuals are represented by tree structures (or, according to the different type of GP, linear structures, graphs, etc.), and one that we call semantic space, in which GP individuals are represented by their semantics, and thus by points. The situation is exemplified in Figure 8.7, where, for simplicity, the semantic space is represented in two dimensions, which corresponds to the toy case in which only two training instances exist. The figure also shows that to each tree

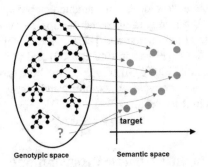

Genotypic space   Semantic space

Fig. 8.7 When we work with GP, we can imagine the existence of two spaces: the genotypic space, in which individuals are represented by their structures, and the semantic space, in which individuals are represented by points, which are their semantics. In the figure, the semantic space is represented in 2D, which corresponds to the unrealistic case in which only two training instances exist

in the genotypic space there corresponds a point in the semantic space. This correspondence is surjective and, in general, not bijective, since different trees can have the same semantics. Once we have the semantics of a GP individual, its fitness can be calculated as the distance between the semantics and the target, using any metric. For instance, Equation (8.2) on page 222 is the mean Euclidean distance between $sp = [P(x_1), P(x_2), ..., P(x_n)]$ and $t = [t_1, t_2, ..., t_n]$, while Equation (8.3) on page 222 is the Manhattan distance between sp and **t**.

Example 8.3. Let us consider the same symbolic regression problem as in Example 8.2 (page 222). In that problem, the set of input data was $X = \{[3, 12, 1], [5, 4, 2]\}$ and the vector of the corresponding target values was $t = [27, 13]$. In that example, we have considered the set of primitive functions $\mathscr{F} = \{+, -, *\}$ and a set of terminals composed of three real-valued variables $\mathscr{T} = \{k_1, k_2, k_3\}$. Also, in that example, we have studied an individual whose expression in infix notation is $P(k1,k2,k3) = k3 * (k1 - k2)$. What is the semantics of this individual?

The semantics of $P(k1,k2,k3) = k3 * (k1 - k2)$, in this case, is a vector of dimension equal to 2, because there are two training instances (the vectors contained in dataset $\mathbf{X}$), where the first component is equal to the evaluation of P on the first input vector and the second component is equal to the evaluation of P on the second input vector. In other words, the first component is obtained by substituting the values 3, 12 and 1 respectively for k_1, k_2 and k_3, and evaluating P. Analogously, the second component is obtained by substituting the values 5, 4 and 2 for k_1, k_2 and k_3. So:

$$\vec{s_P} = [P(3,12,1), P(5,4,2)] = [1*(12-3), 2*(5-4)] = [9,2]$$

Using, for instance, the absolute error between semantics and target, we have that the fitness of P is:

$$f(P) = d([9,2],[27,13]) = |9-27| + |2-13| = 18 + 11 = 29$$

where, in this case, d is the Manhattan distance. Comparing this calculation with that of Example 8.2 (page 222) to calculate the fitness of P, we can clearly see that these two calculations are completely identical.

8.5.2 Similarity Between Semantic Space of Symbolic Regression and Continuous Optimization

The reader is now invited to have a look back at Section 3.7, page 102, where continuous optimization problems were introduced, and geometric genetic operators of GAs were presented for those problems. Let us now consider a particular instance of a continuous optimization problem, with the following characteristics:

- $S = \{\mathbf{v} \in \mathbb{R}^n \mid \forall i = 1, 2, ..., n : v_i \in [\alpha_i, \beta_i]\}$
- $\forall \mathbf{v} \in S: f(\mathbf{v}) = d(\mathbf{v}, \mathbf{t})$
- Minimization problem.

where d is a distance measure (think, for simplicity, of the Euclidean distance, but the reasoning holds also for any other metric), and $\mathbf{t} \in \mathbb{R}^n$ is a predefined, and known, global optimum. In informal terms, solutions of this problem instance are vectors of n real numbers included in a predefined interval, and the fitness of an individual is equal to the distance of that individual to a unique, and known, globally optimal solution. Let us now assume that we are trying to solve this problem with GAs, using geometric mutation (also called box mutation, or ball mutation). As we have studied in Section 3.7, in this situation, the fitness landscape of this problem is unimodal. In other terms, there are no local optima, except for the global optimum. For this reason, the problem is characterized by a very good evolvability. This fact can be easily seen by implementing it. It will not be difficult to verify that, simply applying geometric mutation iteratively, it is possible to find solutions that are arbitrarily close to the global optimum. Just to fix some simple terminology, let a problem with these characteristics be called *CONO*, which stands for *Continuous Optimization with kNown Optimum*. We find this acronym particularly appropriate because the shape of the fitness landscape for this problem is actually a cone[5], where the vertex represents the global optimum. In synthesis:

> IF box mutation is the operator used to explore the search space
> THEN The CONO problem has a unimodal fitness landscape.

Let us now observe the right part of Figure 8.7, showing the semantic space of a symbolic regression problem. In this space, individuals are points and the target is known. It should not be hard to understand that this space is identical to the space of solutions of the CONO problem. This fact has a very important consequence for the solution of symbolic regression problems using GP. Similarly to the above property, we could now write:

> IF we define a GP operator that works like box mutation on the semantic space
> THEN **any** symbolic regression problem has a unimodal fitness landscape.

Let us repeat this property again, but with different words:

> If we are able to define, on the syntax of the GP individuals (i.e., on their tree structure)[6] an operator that has, on the semantic space, the same effect as box mutation, then the fitness landscape is unimodal for any symbolic regression problem.

In other terms, if we were able to define such an operator, then we would be able to map any symbolic regression problem into an instance of the CONO problem that uses box mutation, in the sense that we would be able to perform exactly the same actions in a space (the semantic space of GP) that is identical. As such, we would inherit the same fitness landscape properties, i.e., a unimodal fitness landscape. It is worth stressing here one point:

> This property would hold for any symbolic regression problem, independently of how large or complex the data of the problem are.

Since no locally optimal solution exists (except for the global optima), actually *any* symbolic regression problem could be *easy* to optimize for GP (at least on the training set, where fitness is calculated), including problems characterized by huge amounts of data. This fact would clearly foster GP as a very promising method for facing the new challenges of *Big Data* [Fan and Bifet, 2013].

At this point, beginner readers, for instance students, are invited to stop for a second and reflect on the importance and impact that this would have. For years, one of the main justifications that researchers have given to the limitations of GP was the fact that it was extremely difficult to study its fitness landscapes, because of the

---

[5] The word "cono" actually means cone in several languages of Latin origin, including Italian and Spanish.

[6] How could it be otherwise? GP is working with a population of trees, so the genetic operators can only act on them!

extreme complexity of the genotype/phenotype mapping, and because of the complexity of the neighborhoods induced by GP crossover and mutation. Introducing such an operator, we would not have to worry about this anymore! For any symbolic regression problem, we would have the certainty that the fitness landscape is unimodal, and thus easily evolvable. Furthermore: how many ML methods do you know in which the error surface is guaranteed to be unimodal for any possible application? Saying that this GP system would be the first ML system to induce unimodal error surfaces would probably be inappropriate; it is not impossible that other machine learning systems with this characteristic may have been defined so far. But still, it is absolutely legitimate to say that this characteristic is quite rare in ML, and should give a clear advantage to GP, compared to other well-known systems, at least in terms of evolvability.

All we have to do to obtain such an important result is to define an operator that, acting on trees, has an effect on the semantic space that is equivalent to box mutation. In other words, if we mutate a GP individual P_1, obtaining a new individual P_2, the semantics of P_2 should be like the semantics of P_1 except for a perturbation of its coordinates, whose magnitude is included in a predefined range. This is the objective of geometric semantic mutation, which is defined in the continuation.

8.5.3 Geometric Semantic Mutation

The objective of Geometric Semantic Mutation (GSM) is to generate a transformation on the syntax of GP individuals that has the same effect on their semantics as box mutation. The situation is exemplified in Figure 8.8. More particularly, this

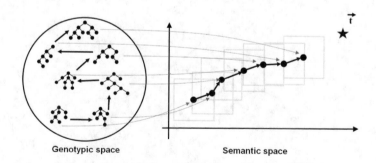

Genotypic space   Semantic space

Fig. 8.8 A simple graphical representation, in the genotypic space, of a chain of solutions $\mathscr{C} = \{s_1, s_2, ..., s_h\}$ where, for each $i = 1, 2, ..., h-1$, s_{i+1} is a neighbor of s_i, and the corresponding points in the semantic space. The known vector of target values is represented in the semantic space by a star

figure represents a chain of possible individuals that could be generated by applying GSM several times, with their corresponding semantics. Given that the semantics of the individuals generated by mutation can be any point inside a box of a given side centered on the semantics itself, GSM has always the possibility of creating an individual whose semantics is closer to the target (represented by a star symbol in the figure). As a direct consequence, the fitness landscape has no locally optimal solutions. Comparing the semantic space of Figure 8.8 with Figure 3.18 (page 103), it should not be difficult to see that if we use GSM, we *are* actually performing a CONO problem with box mutation on the semantic space. The definition of GSM, as given in [Moraglio et al., 2012], is as follows.

Definition 8.1. Geometric Semantic Mutation (GSM). Given a parent function $P : \mathbb{R}^n \rightarrow \mathbb{R}$, geometric semantic mutation with mutation step ms returns the function $P_M = P + ms \cdot (T_{R1} - T_{R2})$, where T_{R1} and T_{R2} are random functions.

It is not difficult to have an intuition of the fact that GSM has the same effect as box mutation on the semantic space. In fact, one should consider that each element of the semantic vector of P_M is a "weak" perturbation of the corresponding element in P's semantics. We informally define this perturbation as "weak" because it is given by a random expression centered at zero (the difference between two random trees). Nevertheless, by changing parameter ms, we are able to tune the "step" of the mutation, and thus the importance of this perturbation. Figure 8.9 gives a visual representation of the tree generated by GSM on a simple example. The tree P that

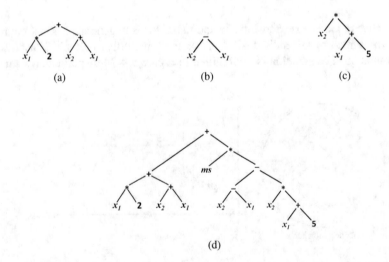

Fig. 8.9 (a) A GP individual P that is going to be mutated; (b) and (c) Two random trees T_{R1} and T_{R2}; (d) The individual P_M generated by geometric semantic mutation.

is mutated is represented in Figure 8.9a. The two used random trees T_{R1} and T_{R2} are shown in Figure 8.9b and Figure 8.9c respectively. Finally, Figure 8.9d shows the resulting tree P_M generated by GSM.

In practice, and in order to make the perturbation even weaker, it is often useful to limit the codomain of the possible outputs of T_{R1} and T_{R2} to a given predefined range. This allows us to better "control" what mutation can do. The typical situation is that T_{R1} and T_{R2} are forced to assume values in $[0, 1]$. This can be done easily, for instance, by "wrapping" T_{R1} and T_{R2} inside a logistic function. In other words, random trees are generated and the logistic is applied to their output before plugging them into P_M. This practice turns out to be extremely important for overfitting control in GSGP, as we will see later.

Before continuing, it is extremely important to stop for a while and convince oneself about the importance of having random *trees/expressions* (like T_{R1} and T_{R2}) in the definition of GSM, instead of just having random constants. The motivation is the following: when we mutate an individual, we want to perturb each coordinate of its semantics by a *different* amount. It is easy to understand why this is important by considering a simple numeric example. Let the semantic of an individual P be, say, $\mathbf{s}_P = [5.6, 9.2]$, and let the target vector be $\mathbf{t} = [9, 10]$ (we are again considering the unrealistic two-dimensional case for simplicity). If we used just random numbers for applying the perturbation, then we would only be able to mutate each one of the coordinates by the same amount. So, if we mutate by, say, 0.5, we obtain a new individual P_M whose semantics is $[6.1, 9.7]$. Even though P_M has a semantics that is closer to the target than P, it should not be difficult to convince oneself that if we iterate mutation, even if we change the size of the perturbation at each step, we will never have any chance of reaching the target. The only possibility that we have to reach the target is to mutate the first coordinate *more* (i.e., by a larger amount) than the second one, simply because the first coordinate of $\mathbf{s}_P$ is further away from the corresponding coordinate of $\mathbf{t}$ than the second coordinate. So, we need a way of doing a perturbation that has to possess the following properties:

- it has to be random;
- it has to be likely to be different for each coordinate;
- it does not have to use any information from the dataset.

By the third point, we mean that the algorithm that makes the perturbation cannot have a form like:

$$\text{"if } (\mathbf{x}_i = ...) \textbf{ then } \text{perturbation} = ..."$$

because in this case the system would clearly overfit the training data: the final individual would actually have a form that is very similar to that of Equation 5.1 (page 118), which was identified as one of the most typical overfitting models, because it simply mimics the data, instead of learning its underlying model.

Under these hypotheses, the only way we could imagine of doing the perturbation was to sum to the value calculated by individual P the value calculated by a random expression. A random expression, in fact, is likely to have different output values for the different fitness cases. Last but not least, the fact that the difference between two random expressions is used ($T_{R1} - T_{R2}$) instead of just one random expression can be justified as follows. Especially in the final part of a GP run, it may happen that some of the coordinates have already been approximated in a satisfactory way, while it is not the case for others. In such a situation, it would be useful to have the possibility of modifying *some* coordinates and *not* modifying (or, which is the same, modifying by an amount equal to zero) others. The difference between two random expressions is a random expression *centered at zero*. This means that its output value is more likely to be equal to zero, or close to zero, than to be equal to any other value. In other words, by using the difference between two random expressions, we are imposing that some coordinates may have a perturbation that is likely to be equal, or at least as close as possible, to zero.

8.5.4 Geometric Semantic Crossover

GP practitioners may be surprised to notice that, so far, basically only mutation has been considered, practically ignoring crossover. Crossover, in fact, is known to be the most powerful genetic operator, at least in standard GP. This section intends to fill this gap, by presenting a Geometric Semantic Crossover (GSC) that can behave, on the semantic space, like geometric crossover of GAs in continuous optimization, defined in Section 3.7. Geometric GAs crossover works by generating one offspring that has, for each coordinate, a linear combination of the corresponding coordinates of the parents with coefficients in $[0, 1]$, whose sum is equal to 1. Under these conditions, the offspring can geometrically be represented as a point that stands in the segment joining the parents. This is the behavior that GSC must have on the semantic space, as exemplified in Figure 8.10. The objective of GSC is to generate

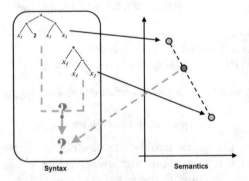

Fig. 8.10 Graphical representation of geometric semantic crossover, in the simple case of two-dimensional semantic space. The offspring generated by this crossover has a semantics that stands in the segment joining the semantics of the parents

the tree structure of an individual whose semantics stands in the segment joining the semantics of the parents. Following [Moraglio et al., 2012], GSC is defined as follows:

Definition 8.2. Geometric Semantic Crossover (GSC). Given two parent functions $T_1, T_2 : \mathbb{R}^n \to \mathbb{R}$, the geometric semantic crossover returns the function $T_{XO} = (T_1 \cdot T_R) + ((1 - T_R) \cdot T_2)$, where T_R is a random function whose output values range in the interval $[0, 1]$.

It is not difficult to see from this definition that T_{XO} has a semantics that is a linear combination of the semantics of T_1 and T_2, with random coefficients included in $[0, 1]$ and whose sum is 1. The fact that we are using a random expression T_R instead of a random number can be interpreted analogously to our explanation of the use of random expressions in GSM. Furthermore, it is worth mentioning that in Definition 8.2 the fitness function is supposed to be the Manhattan distance; if Euclidean distance is used, then T_R should be a random constant instead. The interested user is referred to [Moraglio et al., 2012] for an explanation of this concept. Figure 8.11 gives a visual representation of the tree generated by GSC on a simple example.

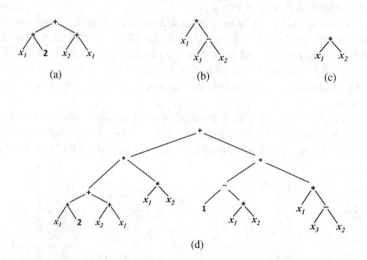

Fig. 8.11 Two parents T_1 and T_2 (plots (a) and (b) respectively), one random tree T_R (plot (c)) and the offspring T_{XO} of the crossover between T_1 and T_2 using T_R (plot (d))

The fact that the semantics of the offspring T_{XO} stands in the segment joining the semantics of the parents T_1 and T_2 has a very interesting consequence: the offspring generated by GSC cannot be worse than the worst of its parents, a property that has already been studied in Section 3.7 for GAs geometric crossover. For a deeper discussion of this property, the reader is referred to [Moraglio, 2008, Moraglio et al., 2012].

8.5.5 Code Growth and New Implementation

Looking at their definition (and at Figures 8.9 and 8.11), it is not hard to see that geometric semantic operators create offspring that contain the complete structure of the parents, plus one or more random trees and some additional arithmetic operators: the size of the offspring is thus clearly much larger than the size of their parents. The rapid growth of the individuals in the population, shown by Moraglio et al. [Moraglio et al., 2012], makes these operators unusable in practice: after a few generations the population becomes unmanageable because the fitness evaluation process becomes unbearably slow. The solution suggested in [Moraglio et al., 2012] consists in performing an automatic simplification step after each generation in which the individuals are replaced by (hopefully smaller) semantically equivalent ones. However, this additional step adds to the computational cost of GP and is only a partial solution to the progressive size growth. Last but not least, depending on the particular language used to code individuals and the used primitives, automatic simplification can be a very hard task.

In this section, we present a novel implementation of GP using these operators that overcomes this limitation, making them efficient without performing any simplification step. This implementation was first presented in [Vanneschi et al., 2013, Castelli et al., 2015]. Although the algorithm is described assuming the representation of the individuals is tree based, the implementation fits any other type of representation.

In a first step, we create an initial population of (typically random) individuals, exactly as in standard GP. We store these individuals in a table (which we call $\mathscr{P}$ from now on) as in the example reported in Figure 8.12a, and we evaluate them. To

Id	Individual
T_1	$x_1 + x_2 x_3$
T_2	$x_3 - x_2 x_4$
T_3	$x_3 + x_4 - 2x_1$
T_4	$x_1 x_3$
T_5	$x_1 - x_3$

(a)

Id	Individual
R_1	$x_1 + x_2 - 2x_4$
R_2	$x_2 - x_1$
R_3	$x_1 + x_4 - 3x_3$
R_4	$x_2 - x_3 - x_4$
R_5	$2x_1$

(b)

Id	Operator	Entry
T_6	crossover	$\langle \text{ID}(T_1), \text{ID}(T_4), \text{ID}(R_1) \rangle$
T_7	crossover	$\langle \text{ID}(T_4), \text{ID}(T_5), \text{ID}(R_2) \rangle$
T_8	crossover	$\langle \text{ID}(T_3), \text{ID}(T_5), \text{ID}(R_3) \rangle$
T_9	crossover	$\langle \text{ID}(T_1), \text{ID}(T_5), \text{ID}(R_4) \rangle$
T_{10}	crossover	$\langle \text{ID}(T_3), \text{ID}(T_4), \text{ID}(R_5) \rangle$

(c)

Fig. 8.12 Illustration of the example described in Section 8.5.5. (a) The initial population P; (b) The random trees used by crossover; (c) The representation in memory of the new population P'

store the evaluations we create a table (which we call $\mathscr{V}$ from now on) containing, for each individual in $\mathscr{P}$, the values resulting from its evaluation on each fitness case (in other words, it contains the semantics of that individual). Hence, with a population of n individuals and a training set of k fitness cases, table $\mathscr{V}$ will be made of n rows and k columns. Then, for every generation, a new empty table $\mathscr{V}'$ is created. Whenever a new individual T must be generated by crossover between selected parents T_1 and T_2, T is represented by a triplet $T = \langle \text{ID}(T_1), \text{ID}(T_2), \text{ID}(R) \rangle$, where R

is a random tree and, for any tree τ, $\text{ID}(\tau)$ is a *reference* (or memory pointer)[7] to τ (using a C-like notation). This triplet is stored in an appropriate structure (which we call $\mathcal{M}$ from now on) that also contains the name of the operator used, as shown in Figure 8.12(c). The random tree R is created, stored in $\mathcal{P}$, and evaluated in each fitness case to reveal its semantics. The values of the semantics of T are also easily obtained, by calculating $(T_1 \cdot R) + ((1 - R) \cdot T_2)$ for each fitness case, according to the definition of geometric semantic crossover, and stored in $\mathcal{V}'$. Analogously, whenever a new individual T must be obtained by applying mutation to an individual T_1, T is represented by a triplet $T = \langle \text{ID}(T_1), \text{ID}(R_1), \text{ID}(R_2) \rangle$ (stored in $\mathcal{M}$), where R_1 and R_2 are two random trees (newly created, stored in $\mathcal{P}$ and evaluated for their semantics). The semantics of T is calculated as $T_1 + ms \cdot (R_1 - R_2)$ for each fitness case, according to the definition of geometric semantic mutation, and stored in $\mathcal{V}'$. At the end of each generation, table $\mathcal{V}'$ is copied into $\mathcal{V}$ and erased. All the rows of $\mathcal{P}$ and $\mathcal{M}$ referring to individuals that are not ancestors[8] of the new population can also be erased. Note that, while $\mathcal{M}$ grows at every generation, by keeping the semantics of the individuals separated we are able to use a table $\mathcal{V}$ whose size is independent of the number of generations. Summarizing, this algorithm is based on the idea that, when semantic operators are used, an individual can be fully described by its semantics (which makes the syntactic component much less important than in standard GP), a concept discussed in depth in [Moraglio et al., 2012]. Therefore, at every generation we update table $\mathcal{V}$ with the semantics of the new individuals, and save the information needed to build their syntactic structures without explicitly building them.

In terms of computational time, it is worth emphasizing that the process of updating table $\mathcal{V}$ is very efficient as it does not require the evaluation of the entire trees. Indeed, evaluating each individual requires (except for the initial generation) constant time, which is independent of the size of the individual itself. In terms of memory, tables $\mathcal{P}$ and $\mathcal{M}$ grow during the run. However, table $\mathcal{P}$ adds a maximum of $2 \times n$ rows per generation (if all new individuals are created by mutation) and table $\mathcal{M}$ (which contains only memory pointers) adds a maximum of n rows per generation. Even if we never erase the "ex-ancestors" from these tables (and never reuse random trees, which is also possible), we can manage them efficiently for several thousands of generations. Let us briefly consider the cost in terms of time and space of evolving a population of n individuals for g generations. At every generation, we need $O(n)$ space to store the new individuals. Thus, we need $O(ng)$ space in total. Since we need to do only $O(1)$ operations for any new individual (since the fitness can be computed using the fitness of the parents), the time complexity is also $O(ng)$. Thus, we have a linear space and time complexity with respect to

---

[7] Simple references to *lookup table* entries can be used in the implementation instead of real memory pointers (see [Vanneschi et al., 2013, Castelli et al., 2015]). This makes the implementation possible also in programming languages that do not allow direct manipulation of memory pointers, for instance Java or MatLab.

[8] The term "ancestors" here is abused slightly to designate not only the parents but also the random trees used to build an individual by crossover or mutation.

population size and number of generations. This computational complexity is very reasonable, and for sure competitive with several other ML systems.

The final step of the algorithm is performed after the end of the last generation. In order to reconstruct the individuals, we may need to "unwind" the compact representation and make the syntax of the individuals explicit. Therefore, despite performing the evolutionary search very efficiently, in the end we may not avoid dealing with the large trees that characterize the standard implementation of geometric semantic operators. However, most probably we will only be interested in the best individual found, so this unwinding (and recommended simplification) process may be required only once, and it is done offline after the run is finished. This greatly contrasts with the solution proposed by Moraglio et al. of building and simplifying *every* tree in the population at each generation online with the search process. If we are not interested in the form of the optimal solution, we can avoid the "unwinding phase" and we can evaluate an unseen input with a time complexity equal to $O(ng)$. In this case the individual is used as a "black box" which, in some cases, may be sufficient. Excluding the time needed to build and simplify the best individual, the proposed implementation allows us to evolve populations for thousands of generations with a considerable speed up with respect to standard GP.

Example 8.4. Let us consider the simple initial population P shown in table (a) of Figure 8.12 and the simple pool of random trees that are added to P as needed, shown in table (b). For simplicity, we will generate all the individuals in the new population (which we call P' from now on) using only crossover, which will require only this small amount of random trees. Besides the representation of the individuals in infix notation, these tables contain an identifier (Id) for each individual ($T_1, ..., T_5$ and $R_1, ..., R_5$). These identifiers will be used to represent the different individuals, and the individuals created for the new population will be represented by the identifiers $T_6, ..., T_{10}$. The individuals of the new population P' are simply represented by the set of entries exhibited in table (c) of Figure 8.12. This table contains, for each new individual, a *reference* to the ancestors that have been used to generate it and the name of the operator used to generate it (either "crossover" or "mutation"). For example, the individual T_6 is generated by the crossover of T_1 and T_4 and using the random tree R_1.

Let us assume that now we want to reconstruct the genotype of one of the individuals in P', for example T_{10}. The tables in Figure 8.12 contain all the information needed to do that. In particular, from table (c) we learn that T_{10} is obtained by crossover between T_3 and T_4, using random tree R_5. Thus, from the definition of geometric semantic crossover, we know that it will have the following structure: $(T_3 \cdot R_5) + ((1 - R_5) \cdot T_4)$. The remaining tables (a) and (b), which contain the syntactic structure of T_3, T_4, and R_5, provide us with the rest of the information we need to completely reconstruct the syntactic structure of T_{10}, which is:

$$((x_3 + x_4 - 2\,x_1) \cdot (2\,x_1)) + ((1 - (2\,x_1)) \cdot (x_1\,x_3))$$

and upon simplification becomes:

$$-x_1 \left(4\,x_1 - 3\,x_3 - 2\,x_4 + 2\,x_1\,x_3\right).$$

8.5.6 Learning and Generalization in Real-Life Applications

The literature reports on various results obtained on several different domains using the implementation of GSGP presented above. In this section, a subset of those results is briefly discussed. The objective of this section is only to give the reader an idea of the quality of the results that can be obtained using GSGP, including a discussion of its generalization ability. We do not intend in any way to be exhaustive about the results that have been obtained. For a deeper review of the literature, the reader is referred to [Vanneschi et al., 2014].

All the applications presented in this section are real-life symbolic regression problems. Table 8.2 summarizes the main characteristics of each one of them. As

Table 8.2 The main characteristics of the test problems used in the experiments presented in this section

Dataset Name (ID)	# Features	# Instances	Objective
%F	241	359	Predicting the value of human oral bioavailability of a candidate new drug as a function of its molecular descriptors
%PPB	626	131	Predicting the value of the plasma protein binding level of a candidate new drug as a function of its molecular descriptors
LD50	626	234	Predicting the value of the toxicity of a candidate new drug as a function of its molecular descriptors
PEC	45	240	Predicting the value of energy consumption in one day as a function of a set of meteorologic data, and other kinds of data, concerning that day
PARK	18	42	Predicting the value of Parkinson's disease severity as a function of a set of the patient's data
CONC	8	1028	Predicting the value of concrete strength as a function of a set of features of concrete mixtures

the table shows, we are using six different problems. The first three of them (%F, %PPB and LD50) are problems in pharmacokinetics and they consist in the prediction of a pharmacokinetic parameter (bioavailability, plasma protein binding level and toxicity, respectively) as a function of some molecular descriptors of a potential new drug. The PEC dataset has the objective of predicting energy consumption in one day as a function of several different types of data relative to the previous days. The PARK dataset contains data about a set of patients with Parkinson's disease and the target value is a quantification of the severity of the disease, according to a standard measure. Finally, the CONC dataset has the objective of predicting concrete strength as a function of a set of parameters that characterize a concrete mixture. For different reasons, all these problems are considered important in their respective domains, and they have been studied so far using several different computational intelligence methods.

The results that have been obtained concerning a comparison between GSGP and standard GP (ST-GP) on these problems are presented in Figure 8.13 (%F, %PPB and LD50 datasets) and Figure 8.14 (PEC, PARK and CONC datasets). The plots in these figures report, for each problem, the results obtained on the training set (leftmost plot) and on the test set (rightmost plot). A detailed discussion of the parameters used in both GP systems in these experiments is beyond the objective of this chapter. What we can generally observe from Figure 8.13 and Figure 8.14 is that GSGP is able to consistently outperform ST-GP both on the training set and on the test set for all the considered problems. Statistical tests also indicated that these differences are statistically significant.

The good results that GSGP has obtained on training data were expected: the geometric semantic operators induce a unimodal fitness landscape, which facilitates evolvability. On the other hand, on a first analysis, it has been a surprise to observe the excellent results that have been obtained on test data. These results even appeared a bit counterintuitive at first sight: we were expecting that the good evolvability on training data would entail an overfitting of those data. However, in order to give an interpretation to the generalization ability of GSGP, one characteristic of geometric semantic operators was realized that was not so obvious previously:

> *the geometric properties of geometric semantic operators hold independently of the data on which individuals are evaluated, and thus they hold also on test data!*

In other words, for instance, geometric semantic crossover produces an offspring that stands between the parents also in the semantic space induced by test data. As a direct implication, following exactly the same argument as Moraglio et al. [Moraglio et al., 2012], each offspring is, in the worst case, not worse than the worst of its parents on the test set. Analogously, as happens for training data, geometric semantic mutation produces an offspring that is a "weak" perturbation of its parent also in the semantic space induced by test data (and the maximum possible perturbation is, again, limited by the *ms* step). The immediate consequence for the behavior of GSGP on test data is that, while geometric semantic operators do not guarantee an improvement in test fitness each time they are applied, they at least guarantee that the possible worsening of the test fitness is bounded (by the test fitness of the worst parent for crossover, and by *ms* for mutation). In other words, *geometric semantic operators help control overfitting*. Of course, overfitting may still happen for GSGP (as happens, in a slight but visible way for instance in plots (d) and (f) of Figure 8.13, reporting the results on %PPB and LD50 respectively), but there are no big "jumps" in test fitness like the ones observed for ST-GP. It is worth remarking that, without the novel implementation presented in Section 8.5.5 that allowed us to use GSGP on these complex real-life problems, this interesting property would probably have remained unnoticed. We also remark that the implementation of GSM described in Section 8.5.3 contains one important de-

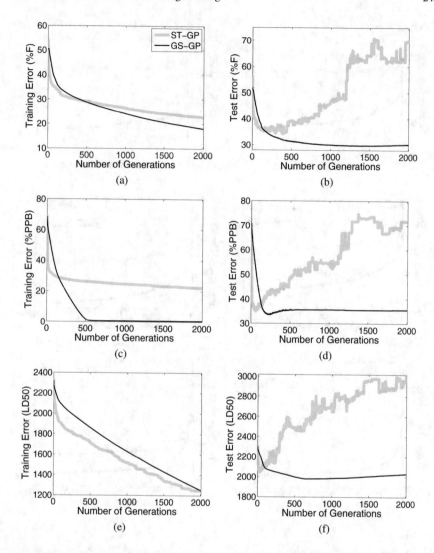

Fig. 8.13 Experimental comparison between standard GP (ST-GP) and Geometric Semantic GP (GS-GP). (a) %F problem, results on the training set; (b) %F problem, results on the test set; (c) %PPB problem, results on the training set; (d) %PPB problem, results on the test set; (e) LD50 problem, results on the training set; (f) LD50 problem, results on the test set

tail that was not in the original implementation of [Moraglio et al., 2012], which is the logistic function applied to the output of each of the random trees. Without this, the perturbation applied to the offspring of GSM would not be bound by the mutation step *ms*. Indeed, Gonçalves et al. [Gonçalves et al., 2015] have discovered that, without these bounds, GSGP overfits very quickly. The same work also proposes

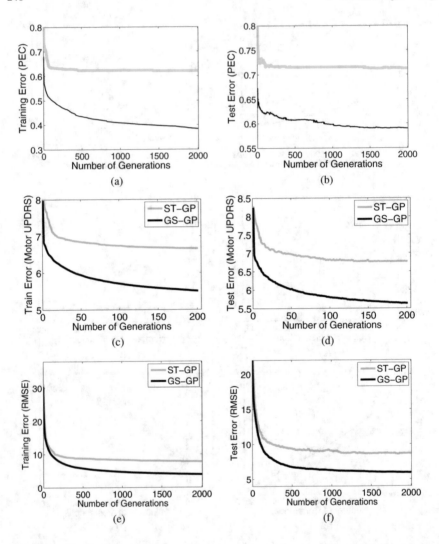

Fig. 8.14 Experimental comparison between standard GP (ST-GP) and Geometric Semantic GP (GS-GP). (a) PEC problem, results on the training set; (b) PEC problem, results on the
test set; (c) PARK problem, results on the training set; (d) PARK problem, results on the test set;
(e) CONC problem, results on the training set; (f) CONC problem, results on the test set

two variants of GSM that deterministically and optimally adapt the mutation step,
obtaining competitive generalization in only one or two generations.

Table 8.3 also reports an experimental comparison between GSGP and a wide set
of nonevolutionary machine learning state-of-the-art methods on the CONC dataset.
Analogous results can be found in the literature also for all the other studied prob-

Table 8.3 An experimental comparison between GSGP (last line), ST-GP (second to last line) and other machine learning strategies on the CONC dataset. The leftmost column contains the name of the method, the middle one the results obtained on the training set at termination, and the rightmost column contains the results obtained on the test set. Root Mean Square Error (RMSE) results are reported

Method	Train	Test
Linear regression	10.567	10.007
Square Regression	17.245	15.913
Isotonic Regression	13.497	13.387
Radial Basis Function Network	16.778	16.094
SVM Polynomial Kernel (1st degree)	10.853	10.260
SVM Polynomial Kernel (2nd degree)	7.830	7.614
SVM Polynomial Kernel (3rd degree)	6.323	6.796
SVM Polynomial Kernel (4th degree)	5.567	6.664
SVM Polynomial Kernel (5th degree)	4.938	6.792
Artificial Neural Networks	7.396	7.512
Standard GP	7.792	8.67
Geometric Semantic GP	3.897	5.926

lems, and they show that GSGP is able to outperform all the other techniques both on training and test data.

8.6 Multiclass GP

Until now, classification has not been discussed in the context of GP. Looking back at Section 8.3.1, pertaining to symbolic regression with GP, it is easy to see why many binary classification problems are solved as if they, too, were regression problems [Espejo et al., 2010].

The definition of a classification problem is very similar to that of a regression problem. Given a set of vectors $\mathbf{X} = \{\mathbf{x}_1, \mathbf{x}_2, ..., \mathbf{x}_n\}$, where for all $i = 1, 2, ..., n, \mathbf{x}_i \in \mathbb{R}^p$, and a categorical vector $\mathbf{y} = [y_1, y_2, ..., y_n]$, where for all $i = 1, 2, ..., n, y_i \in M$, where M is a set of class labels, a classification problem can be generally defined as the problem of finding a mapping $g : \mathbb{R}^p \to M$ such that $\forall i = 1, 2, ..., n : g(\mathbf{x}_i) = y_i$.

All it takes to transform a binary classification problem into a regression problem is to represent the two class labels as numeric expected outputs, e.g., 0 and 1, so that GP can run as usual, using the same function and terminal sets, and the same fitness function that would be used for symbolic regression. With this setting, GP will find a function that outputs values close to 0 for one class, and close to 1 for the other class. In order to obtain class predictions from such a model, a cutoff is applied to the predicted numeric outputs, e.g., 0.5. Predictions below the cutoff are labeled as class A, while predictions above the cutoff are labeled as class B. Figure 8.15 illustrates this setting, where one data point belonging to class B (yellow crosses) would be misclassified as class A (blue circles) because its value is lower than the cutoff.

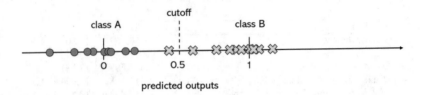

Fig. 8.15 Representation of regression-like binary classification, by transforming class labels A and B into numeric expected outputs 0 and 1, and applying a cutoff of 0.5 to the numeric predicted outputs to obtain label predictions. Class A data points are represented as blue circles, while class B data points are represented as yellow crosses

Another, more relaxed option is to allow complete freedom regarding the predicted output values and use a fitness function that simply rewards the minimization of the overlap between whichever ranges are produced for each class. For future reference, we designate this method as *free_outputs*. We remark that the function evolved to produce the output values is a combination of the p original features of the problem, and as such can be called a hyperfeature. In Figure 8.15 there is no overlap between the ranges of the two classes.

In order to classify unseen data using the *free_outputs* approach, we need more than just the evolved function, or hyperfeature. Just as earlier we needed to know that 0.5 was the cutoff to apply to the predicted outputs, now we also need to know how to cast each predicted output into a class. One option is to, once again, provide a cutoff, this time calculated to maximize the accuracy on the training data. Another simple option is to provide the mean points of each class, so that each unseen data point is assigned to the class with the nearest mean.

What about multiclass classification problems? It is certainly tempting to use the same rationale of transforming class labels into numeric expected outputs and obtaining class predictions by applying multiple cutoffs to the predicted outputs. However, it is too difficult to find a single function that can handle three or more unrelated classes and produce distinct outputs for each one of them. Minimizing the overlap between class ranges is equally difficult. Naturally, it is possible to solve classification problems with GP in a non-regression-like fashion, for example, by using conditional operators to evolve models similar to decision trees, among other options described in [Espejo et al., 2010].

One recent family of methods, here collectively designated as Multiclass GP, takes the *free_outputs* classification method one step further. Instead of evolving a single hyperfeature, it collectively evolves a number of hyperfeatures that effectively produce a mapping between the original p-dimensional feature space and a new q-dimensional hyperfeature space, where q is independent of p and of the number of classes m. Figure 8.16 illustrates a two-dimensional space containing points of three different classes. In this new space, Multiclass GP applies a nearest centroid classifier based on the Mahalanobis distance, using an accuracy-based measure as fitness.

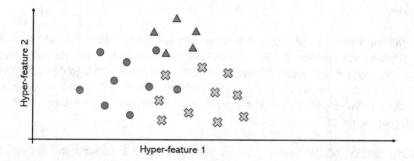

Fig. 8.16 Representation of a two-dimensional hyperfeature space containing data points belonging to three different classes, represented as blue circles, yellow crosses and red triangles

In the remainder of this chapter we will present detailed descriptions of four variants of Multiclass GP, named M2GP, M3GP, eM3GP and M4GP, including results obtained in different classification datasets, whose characteristics are summarized in Table 8.4. We will finish with a discussion regarding the use of Multiclass GP as a feature construction method.

Table 8.4 Datasets used for comparing different Multiclass GP variants. The 'heart' (HRT), 'segment' (SEG), 'vowel' (VOW), 'yeast' (YST) and 'movement-libras' (M-L) datasets can be found at the KEEL repository [Alcala-Fdez et al., 2011], whereas the 'waveform' (WAV) dataset is available at [Bache and Lichman, 2013]. 'IM-3' and 'IM-10' are the satellite imagery datasets used in [Vasconcelos et al., 2015, Batista and Silva, 2020, Batista et al., 2021]

Dataset	HRT	IM-3	WAV	SEG	IM-10	YST	VOW	M-L
Classes	2	3	3	7	10	10	11	15
Features	13	6	40	19	6	8	13	90
Samples	270	322	5000	2310	6798	1484	990	360

8.6.1 M2GP – Multidimensional Multiclass GP

The basic idea of M2GP, originally introduced by [Ingalalli et al., 2014] as Multidimensional Multiclass GP, is to find a transformation such that the transformed data can be grouped in clusters, one cluster per class. As stated earlier, the number of dimensions of the transformed data is independent of the number of dimensions of the original data and of the number of classes. Therefore, it may happen that a high-dimensional dataset containing many classes is easily classified by a low-dimensional clustering, while a low-dimensional dataset with few classes is better classified by a high-dimensional clustering. The components of M2GP that are different from those of a standard GP implementation (Section 8.1) are described below.

Representation. M2GP uses a representation for the solutions that allows them to perform the mapping $k : \mathbb{R}^p \rightarrow \mathbb{R}^q$. The representation is basically the same used for regular tree-based GP, except that the root node of the tree is a dummy node that exists only to define the number of dimensions q of the new space. Each branch stemming directly from the root encodes one hyperfeature that performs the mapping in one of the q dimensions.

Initialization. M2GP trees are initialized using ramped half-and-half skewed to 25% Grow and 75% Full based on the suggestion that a higher proportion of full trees facilitates the initial evolution [Ingalalli et al., 2014]. Below, we explain how to establish the number of branches, i.e., dimensions of the hyperfeature space.

Fitness Evaluation. The truly specialized element of M2GP is the fitness function. Each individual is evaluated in the following way. All the p-dimensional data points of the training set are mapped into the new q-dimensional space (each branch of the tree encodes one of the q dimensions). On this new space, for each of the m classes in the dataset, the covariance matrix and the cluster centroid are calculated from the samples belonging to that class. The Mahalanobis distance between each point and each of the m centroids is calculated. Each point is assigned the class whose centroid is closer. Fitness is the overall accuracy of this classification (the percentage of samples correctly classified).

The Mahalanobis distance between a data point $\mathbf{x}_i$ and the centroid $\mathbf{c}_j$ of the cluster formed by the points of class j is given by

$$D_M = \sqrt{(\mathbf{x}_i - \mathbf{c}_j)\Sigma^{-1}(\mathbf{x}_i - \mathbf{c}_j)},$$

where Σ is the covariance matrix of the points belonging to class j. In M2GP, whenever Σ is not invertible, the Euclidean distance is used instead.

The preference for Mahalanobis instead of Euclidean distance is not a small detail. Initial studies have consistently shown that the distance metric indeed plays a substantial role in the performance of M2GP, especially in higher-dimensional solution spaces [Ingalalli et al., 2014]. Unlike the Euclidean distance, the Mahalanobis distance not only is able to capture the physical distance between the sample and the class clustered data sets, but also considers the statistical correlation between them, thereby reasserting the work of [Shiming Xiang and Zhang, 2008].

Genetic Operators. The genetic operators used by M2GP are the regular subtree crossover and mutation, used in [Ingalalli et al., 2014] with probabilities 0.9 and 0.1, respectively, except that the root of the tree (the dummy node) is never chosen as the crossing or mutation node.

At the end of a run, the solution returned by M2GP is composed not only of the tree of the best individual, but also of the covariance matrices and cluster centroids of each class. In order to classify unseen data, M2GP uses the tree to map the new samples into the new space, and then uses the covariance matrices and the cluster centroids in order to determine the minimum Mahalanobis distance between each sample and each centroid. (Note that the covariance matrices and cluster centroids are not recalculated when classifying new data.)

Choosing the number of dimensions. M2GP is incapable of adding or removing dimensions during the evolution, so the number of dimensions q has to be fixed at the beginning of each run. It is not obvious how to choose this important parameter, as it will naturally depend on the characteristics of each problem, as well as on the other GP settings such as the function and terminal sets. However, [Ingalalli et al., 2014] noticed that the best fitness found on the initial random generation is highly correlated with the best fitness found on the final generation. Therefore, before initiating a run, M2GP chooses q by executing the following procedure:

Initialization:	$q = 1$; create a random initial population where all the individuals have only one branch, and record the fitness of the best individual;
In each iteration:	create a new initial population where all the individuals have $q + 1$ branches; if the fitness of the new best individual is better than the previously recorded one, then $q = q + 1$;
Stop condition:	q was not incremented.

Table 8.5 shows a subset of the results[9] reported in [Ingalalli et al., 2014], comparing the median test accuracy of different methods on the datasets listed in Table 8.4. In most problems, M2GP is surpassed by at least one other method. However, unlike all other methods, M2GP is never the worst method on any of the datasets. Therefore, M2GP appears to be a safe and competitive classifier.

8.6.2 M3GP – M2GP with Multidimensional Populations

As described above, the original M2GP uses a greedy approach to determine how many dimensions the evolved solutions should have. It may happen that, by fixing the number of dimensions at the beginning of the run, the algorithm is prevented from finding better solutions during the search, ones that may use a different number of dimensions. Therefore, a new variant of Multiclass GP, originally presented in [Muñoz et al., 2015], uses additional genetic operators that add, remove and swap dimensions. The result is a population that includes individuals of different dimensions, where natural selection discards the worst ones and naturally leads the search

---

[9] The results reported here are different from [Ingalalli et al., 2014] in two cases:
1) In [Ingalalli et al., 2014] the result of M2GP for WAV was incorrectly reported as 94.8;
2) For reasons stated in [Ingalalli et al., 2014], the results reported for HRT referred to standard GP and not M2GP.

Table 8.5 Comparison between M2GP and state-of-the-art methods. Median test accuracy obtained in 30 runs on the datasets listed in Table 8.4. For each problem, the best results are in bold (more than one means there is no statistically significant difference between their medians). For each problem, a plus sign after the value means the method was significantly better than M2GP, while a minus sign means the method was significantly worse than M2GP. The statistical test used was Kruskal-Wallis with Bonferroni correction at the 0.01 significance level

	HRT	IM-3	WAV	SEG	IM-10	YST	VOW	M-L
SVM	55.6−	93.8	86.3+	55.8−	90.4	41.1−	81.8−	14.4−
J48	79.6	93.8	74.8−	96.1+	94.7+	55.2	75.9−	63.4
RF	80.2	94.8	81.5−	97.3+	96.9+	57.5+	89.4+	71.8+
RS	81.5	92.8	82.2−	96.0	93.9+	56.6	82.8	65.7
MLP	80.2	95.9	83.3−	96.3+	90.2	58.0+	82.5−	75.9+
MCC	84.0+	95.4	86.8+	92.4−	81.8−	58.0+	57.6−	60.6
M2GP	80.2	93.8	84.9	95.6	90.2	53.8	85.9	63.0

towards the ideal number of dimensions. This variant is called M3GP, which stands for M2GP with Multidimensional Populations. In M3GP, the representation of the individuals is the same as in M2GP, as well as the fitness evaluation. The next paragraphs explain how M3GP initializes the population, and describe the new genetic operators it uses, including a pruning operator, and finally explain why these particular aspects make elitism an important factor in M3GP.

Initialization. M3GP starts the evolution with a random population where all the individuals have only one dimension. This ensures that the evolutionary search begins looking for simple, unidimensional solutions, before moving towards higher-dimensional and potentially more complex solutions. To avoid individuals that are too small to be useful, and since M2GP already biased the initial population toward full trees, M3GP uses only the Full initialization method to create all its initial individuals.

Mutation. During the breeding phase, whenever mutation is the chosen genetic operator, M3GP performs one of three actions, with equal probability: 1) standard subtree mutation, taking care not to touch the root node, as in M2GP; 2) adding a randomly created new tree as a new branch of the root node, effectively adding one dimension to the parent tree; 3) randomly removing a complete branch of the root node, effectively removing one dimension from the parent tree. As mentioned above, the initial population only contains unidimensional individuals. From there, the algorithm has to be able to explore several different dimensions. As mutation is the only way of adding or removing dimensions, in M3GP it assumes a high importance and therefore its probability of occurrence is 50% (i.e., 50/3% for each of the three mutation types).

Crossover. Whenever crossover is chosen, M3GP performs one of two actions, with equal probability: 1) standard subtree crossover, avoiding the root node as in M2GP; 2) swapping of dimensions, where a random complete branch of the root node is chosen in each parent, and swapped with each other, effectively swapping dimensions between the parents. The second event is just a particular case of the first, where the crossing nodes are guaranteed to be directly connected to the root node. The probability of occurrence of crossover is 50%, therefore 25% for each of the two crossover types.

Pruning. Mutation, as described above, makes it easy for M3GP to add dimensions to the solutions. However, many times some of the dimensions are useless or even degrade the fitness of the individual, so they would be better removed. Mutation can also remove dimensions but, as described above, it does so randomly and blind to fitness. Instead of making the genetic operators more 'intelligent', M3GP keeps them simple and completely stochastic, while relying on a pruning operator to trim unwanted dimensions. The pruning procedure removes the first dimension and reevaluates the tree. If the fitness improves, the pruned tree replaces the original and goes through pruning of the next dimension. Otherwise, the pruned tree is discarded and the original tree goes through pruning of the next dimension. The procedure stops after pruning the last dimension. Pruning is applied only to the best individual in each generation. Applying it to all the individuals in the population could pose two problems: 1) a significantly higher computational demand, where a considerable amount of effort would be spent on individuals that would still be unfit after pruning; 2) the possibility of causing premature convergence due to excessive removal of genetic material (the same way that code editing has been shown to cause it [Haynes, 1998]. Preliminary experiments in [Muñoz et al., 2015] have revealed that pruning the best individual of each generation shifts the distribution of the number of dimensions to lower values (or prevents it from shifting to higher values so easily) during the evolution, without harming fitness.

Elitism. As mentioned above, in order to explore solutions of different dimensions M3GP relies on mutation to add and remove dimensions from the individuals, with a fairly high probability. It also has to rely on selection to keep the best dimensions in the population and discard the worst ones. The way to do this is by ensuring some elitism in the survival of the individuals from one generation to the next. Unlike M2GP, where elitism was mostly inconsequential to the outcome of the evolution, M3GP cannot afford to lose the best individual of any generation, and therefore always copies it to the next generation. We recall that this individual is already optimized in the sense that it went through pruning.

Table 8.6 shows the results reported in [Silva et al., 2016] comparing the performance of M2GP and M3GP (and eM3GP, to be discussed later) on the datasets listed in Table 8.4, in terms of training and test accuracy, and number of nodes and dimensions of the solutions returned. In training, M3GP surpasses M2GP in all the problems except M-L, where the two methods perform equally well. In test, M3GP is better than or equal to M2GP on all problems except M-L. It is interesting to note that it is on the higher-dimensional problems (except M-L) that M3GP achieves better results than M2GP (the problems are roughly ordered by dimensionality of the data). The M-L exception may have a simple explanation, which is how easily M3GP reaches maximal accuracy on the training set. Both M2GP and M3GP achieve 100% training accuracy, but M3GP does it in only a few generations, producing very small and accurate solutions that barely generalize to unseen data. On the other hand, M2GP does not converge immediately, so in its effort to learn the characteristics of the data it also evolves some generalization ability. Regarding the structure and size of the returned models, M3GP tends to use more dimensions and more nodes than M2GP.

Table 8.6 Comparison between M2GP, M3GP and eM3GP. Median values of training and test accuracy, and number of nodes and dimensions (with minimum and maximum), obtained in 30 runs on the datasets listed in Table 8.4. For each problem, the best fitness results are in bold (more than one means there is no statistically significant difference between their medians). The statistical test used was Friedman with Bonferroni-Holm correction at the 0.05 significance level

	HRT	IM-3	WAV	SEG	IM-10	YST	VOW	M-L
Training fitness								
M2GP	89.4	98.2	87.4	96.8	91.4	62.6	95.9	**100**
M3GP	**94.7**	**99.6**	**90.7**	**98.1**	**93.0**	**68.5**	**100**	**100**
eMeGP	86.7	98.2	81.8	96.1	92.0	61.0	87.8	**100**
Test fitness								
M2GP	**80.2**	93.8	**84.9**	95.6	90.2	53.8	85.9	63.0
M3GP	79.0	**95.4**	**84.3**	95.6	**91.0**	**56.2**	**93.8**	57.1
eM3GP	**80.8**	93.2	81.2	94.7	**90.3**	**56.1**	78.6	**65.1**
Number of nodes								
M2GP	37	24	126	43	117	146	49	33
M3GP	110	66	71	111	239	274	53	13
eM3GP	4	8	3	8	58	14	10	4
Number of dimensions								
M2GP	2.5 *(1-8)*	2 *(1-4)*	5 *(2-10)*	4 *(3-8)*	7 *(4-10)*	5.5 *(1-13)*	9 *(4-18)*	10 *(7-12)*
M3GP	12 *(1-17)*	5 *(2-8)*	31 *(29-37)*	11 *(5-21)*	12 *(11-16)*	13 *(11-18)*	20 *(16-20)*	12 *(10-13)*
eM3GP	1 *(1-4)*	1 *(1-5)*	1 *(1-10)*	6 *(2-10)*	7 *(3-12)*	10 *(1-16)*	4 *(1-14)*	2 *(1-11)*

Table 8.7 shows the results reported in [Silva et al., 2016] comparing the training and test accuracy of different methods on the datasets listed in Table 8.4. In test accuracy, RF was the best method on five datasets, followed by M3GP and MLP, the best methods on four datasets each.

8.6.3 eM3GP – Ensemble M3GP

The eM3GP variant, proposed in [Silva et al., 2016], stands for Ensemble M3GP and was developed in an attempt to avoid two problems observed in M3GP: 1) the occasional degradation of class accuracy on some classes that were previously well classified, caused by the discovery of new best individuals that improve overall accuracy based on other classes; 2) the proliferation of dimensions that happens on some problems, resulting in much larger individuals, but not much fitter, than the ones obtained with M2GP.

Table 8.7 Comparison between M2GP, M3GP, eM3GP and state-of-the-art methods. Median training and test accuracy obtained in 30 runs on the datasets listed in Table 8.4. For each problem, the best results are in bold (more than one means there is no statistically significant difference between their medians). The statistical test used was Friedman with Bonferroni-Holm correction at the 0.05 significance level

	HRT	IM-3	WAV	SEG	IM-10	YST	VOW	M-L
Training fitness								
RF	**98.4**	100	**99.5**	**99.9**	**99.8**	**98.3**	99.9	99.2
RS	88.9	97.1	92.0	98.4	96.3	71.1	97.8	92.3
MLP	**98.4**	98.7	98.5	97.6	91.0	64.6	91.9	91.3
M2GP	89.4	98.2	87.4	96.8	91.4	62.6	95.9	**100**
M3GP	94.7	99.6	90.7	98.1	93.0	68.5	**100**	**100**
eM3GP	86.7	98.2	81.8	96.1	92.0	61.0	87.8	**100**
Test fitness								
RF	80.2	**94.8**	81.5	**97.3**	**96.9**	57.5	89.4	71.8
RS	81.5	92.8	82.2	96.0	93.9	56.6	82.8	65.7
MLP	80.2	**95.9**	83.3	96.3	90.2	**58.0**	82.5	**75.9**
M2GP	80.2	93.8	**84.9**	95.6	90.2	53.8	85.9	63.0
M3GP	79.0	95.4	84.3	95.6	91.0	56.2	**93.8**	57.1
eM3GP	81.4	93.2	81.2	94.7	90.3	56.1	78.6	65.1

Although similar to M3GP is many aspects, eM3GP assumes that a set of transformations, each proving to be good for discriminating a single class, can do a better job than a single transformation used for discriminating all the classes. Therefore, the main differences introduced by eM3GP are the following.

Storing specialized transformations. During an eM3GP run, a catalog of "specialized" transformations is kept, one for each class. When eM3GP begins its search and creates its very first individual, m copies of this transformation are stored as the set of best transformations for each of the m classes of the problem. The numbers of true positives (TP) and false positives (FP) obtained by this transformation on each class are also stored. With every new individual created, the TP and FP numbers are calculated and compared with the stored ones. For each class, if the new individual improves either of these numbers (increases TP or decreases FP) without degrading any of them, then the individual replaces the stored one as the best transformation for this class, while for the other classes the stored transformation remains unaltered. Note that these are not exactly "specialized" transformations, since they are not evolved specifically for binary classification. Note also that, at any given moment, among the m elements of this catalog there may be repeated individuals.

Representation. The individuals of eM3GP are created, recombined and mutated using the same representation and genetic operators as the individuals of M3GP. However, when it's time to use an individual to make a prediction (which is required for measuring its fitness) it acquires an ensemble-like representation. The individual is first replicated in m copies, one per class, and then combined with the catalog of m specialized transformations in an iterative nondeterministic process, with the goal of deciding which transformation (copy of individual or stored specialized transformation) is adopted for each class. First, fitness is measured for the ensemble of m copies of the same transformation. Then, in a random order, the copy of each class is replaced by the corresponding specialized transformation of the catalog, and fitness is measured again. If the replacement improves fitness, it becomes permanent, otherwise it is undone. In the end, among the m components of the final ensemble, there may or may not be a copy of the original individual. However, using only the catalog instead of a combination between individual and catalog proved to be detrimental to fitness [Silva et al., 2016].

Fitness Evaluation. The only difference between the fitness function of eM3GP and that of the previous variants is that the distances to the cluster centroids of each class are measured on the hyperfeature space obtained by the transformation adopted for that class.

Tables 8.6 and 8.7 include the results of eM3GP, together with the results of M2GP and M3GP, comparing them with each other and with other state-of-the-art methods on the datasets listed in Table 8.4. These results were reported in [Silva et al., 2016] and show that, although in most problems eM3GP was not able to surpass the accuracy of M3GP, in many cases a similar accuracy was obtained with much smaller individuals.

8.6.4 M4GP

Unlike the previous variants, which use a tree-based representation for the solutions, M4GP [La Cava et al., 2018, La Cava et al., 2019] uses a stack-based representation. By default, this representation supports multiple outputs, eliminating the need for the dummy root nodes required by the previous variants. M4GP initializes the population with individuals of various sizes and dimensionality, and applies genetic operators that are the stack-based equivalents to those of M3GP. Besides the representation and initialization, M4GP introduces additional differences to the selection of individuals for breeding and for survival. In [La Cava et al., 2019], M4GP with regular tournament selection [Poli et al., 2008a] (M4GP-tn) is compared with a variant that uses lexicase selection [Helmuth et al., 2015] (M4GP-lx) and another one that uses age-fitness Pareto survival [Schmidt and Lipson, 2011] (M4GP-ps). Table 8.8 shows the results[10] of comparing the test accuracy of these three variants of M4GP with the previous variants and the state-of-the-art methods on the datasets listed in Table 8.4. The superiority of M4GP is clear, in particular M4GP-ps.

---

[10] The results reported here are different from [La Cava et al., 2019] on two problems:
1) In the M-L problem (called Movl in [La Cava et al., 2019]) the results of RF, MLP, M2GP and eM3GP were incorrectly reported as 89.4, 82.5, 85.9 and 78.6, respectively;
2) For the YST (Yeast) problem, the result of M4GP-lx was incorrectly indicated as being statistically better than all the others.

Table 8.8 Comparison between M4GP and state-of-the-art methods. Median test accuracy obtained in 30 runs on the datasets listed in Table 8.4. For each problem, the best results are in bold (more than one means there is no statistically significant difference between their medians). The statistical test used was Wilcoxon rank-sum with Holm correction at the 0.01 significance level

	HRT	IM-3	WAV	SEG	IM-10	YST	VOW	M-L
RF	80.2	94.8	81.5	**97.3**	**96.9**	**57.5**	89.4	71.8
RS	81.5	92.8	82.2	96.0	93.9	**56.6**	82.8	65.7
MLP	80.2	95.9	83.3	96.3	90.2	**58.0**	82.5	75.9
SVM	55.6	93.8	86.3	55.8	90.4	41.1	81.8	14.4
M2GP	80.2	93.8	84.9	95.6	90.2	53.8	85.9	63.0
M3GP	79.0	95.4	84.3	95.6	91.0	**56.2**	93.8	57.1
eM3GP	80.9	93.3	81.2	94.7	90.3	56.2	78.6	65.2
M4GP-lx	85.2	**97.9**	85.3	**96.6**	90.7	**58.9**	95.6	73.1
M4GP-ps	**90.1**	**97.9**	**87.1**	96.1	89.8	**58.9**	97.5	**80.1**
M4GP-tn	87.7	**97.9**	86.0	95.1	89.6	**56.8**	96.0	**76.9**

8.6.5 Multiclass GP and Feature Construction

As stated above, a GP system that evolves combinations of the original features of a problem is actually building hyperfeatures, and therefore doing feature construction[11]. Of course the same can be said about other learners, but the fact that GP does not impose restrictions on the form of the allowed combinations makes it particularly adequate for knowledge discovery through feature construction, something that has been recognized since the early days of GP (e.g., [Bensusan and Kuscu, 1996]). The Multiclass GP variants described above further increase the potential of GP for feature construction. Although a nearest centroid classifier has been used in all variants, it can be easily replaced by any other classifier, naturally transforming the system into a powerful wrapper-like[12] or embedded method. Some recent publications, and references therein, highlight the potential of such systems for both classification and regression tasks [Muñoz et al., 2019, Muñoz et al., 2020, Cava and Moore, 2020, Batista and Silva, 2020, Batista et al., 2021].

Besides feature construction, M3GP has also been the inspiration for ensemble construction, in a system where regular trees are evolved by the standard genetic operators and, at the same time, forests are evolved by adding, deleting and swapping trees, using the same specialized operators as M3GP [Rodrigues et al., 2020].

---

[11] Also called feature learning, feature induction, feature extraction and feature discovery, among others, all part of the general concept of feature engineering (see Chapter 5).

[12] Normally, wrapper methods only do feature selection, but here both selection and construction can occur as a result of the same process.

Chapter 9
Bayesian Learning

Bayesian learning [Tipping, 2004, Barber, 2012] is the name commonly used to identify a set of computational methods for supervised learning based on Bayes' Theorem. Broadly speaking, Bayes' Theorem deals with the modification of our perception of the probability of an event, as a consequence of the occurrence of one or more facts. For instance, what probability are you assigning to the event "somebody stole my car" at the moment? Of course, this can depend on many different factors, but on a normal day, one may argue that that probability is generally rather low. Now, imagine that you go looking for your car, and the car is not in the place where you remember that you parked it. What is now the probability of the event "somebody stole my car"? The fact that the car is not where it was parked clearly changes the probability that it was stolen. This property is general: the realization of some events can modify the probability of others. This property can be exploited to tackle Machine Learning tasks, for instance classification: data, interpreted as events, can be used to change the probability that a given observation belongs to a given class. Before studying this mechanism in detail, let us first present Bayes' Theorem and its most immediate use in Machine Learning.

9.1 Bayes' Theorem and Machine Learning

Let A and B be two events, and $P(A)$ and $P(B)$ their respective probabilities (sometimes called marginal probabilities). Also, let $P(A|B)$ be the conditional probability of event A, or likelihood of event A, knowing that B is true. Analogously, let $P(B|A)$ be the probability of event B being true given that event A is true. Bayes' Theorem can be enunciated as follows.

Theorem 9.1. *(Bayes' Theorem)*

$$P(A|B) = \frac{P(B|A)\,P(A)}{P(B)}$$

© Springer Nature Switzerland AG 2023
L. Vanneschi and S. Silva, *Lectures on Intelligent Systems*, Natural Computing Series,
https://doi.org/10.1007/978-3-031-17922-8_9

Proof. Directly from the definition of conditional probability, we have:

$$P(A|B) = \frac{P(A,B)}{P(B)}$$

where $P(A,B)$ is the probability of both events A and B happening (in other references sometimes denoted by $P(A \cap B)$). From the previous equation, we can write:

$$P(A,B) = P(A|B)\,P(B)$$

However, given that $P(A,B) = P(B,A)$, we have:

$$P(A|B)\,P(B) = P(B|A)\,P(A)$$

From which follows the thesis immediately.

$\square$

The formula might look complicated, but it is actually quite user friendly: all we need to do is plug three ingredients into the formula, and this allows us to have an updated probability, based on new information. $P(A|B)$ is often called the *posterior probability*, in the sense that it quantifies the "new" probability of A, after we have received the information that B has happened.

As puzzling as it may seem at first sight, this simple theorem of probability calculus can be very important for Machine Learning. In fact, let us assume, for instance, that we want to tackle a classification task. In other terms, we have a dataset D, and we receive a new (unseen) observation, on which we need to predict the class label. Let us assume, for simplicity, that the task is binary classification, i.e., classification into two possible classes C_1 and C_2. Then, we have two different possible hypotheses:

- The new observation belongs to class C_1 (let us call this hypothesis h_1);
- The new observation belongs to class C_2 (let us call this hypothesis h_2).

We can use Bayes' Theorem to make this classification. Remember that we have some facts that we can observe, and it is based on those facts that we do the classification. Now, let us ask to ourselves, what is the information (i.e., the facts!) that we normally use to generate a classifier? The answer is straightforward: the data! All the information we need is in D, which we consider the training set. So, all we have to do is to calculate the probability that h_1 is true after having observed D, and the probability that h_2 is true after having observed D. If the former is larger than the latter, then the new observation will be categorized into class C_1, otherwise into class C_2. Applying Bayes' Theorem directly, we have:

$$P(h_1|D) = \frac{P(D|h_1) \cdot P(h_1)}{P(D)}, \qquad P(h_2|D) = \frac{P(D|h_2) \cdot P(h_2)}{P(D)}$$

Remark that we just have to compare $P(h_1|D)$ to $P(h_2|D)$. In order to understand which one of the two is larger, we do not have to calculate them exactly. To make this comparison, we can observe that the quantity at the denominator, i.e., $P(D)$, is the same in both formulas, and thus it does not have any influence on the comparison. So, we can simply "ignore it". So, in practice, what we have to do is just to calculate $P(D|h_1) \cdot P(h_1)$ and $P(D|h_2) \cdot P(h_2)$. If the former is larger than the latter, then the new observation will be categorized into class C_1, otherwise into class C_2.

Let us give the name *maximum a posteriori* hypothesis h_{MAP} to the hypothesis that has the maximum probability, among h_1 and h_2, *after* having observed our data D (i.e., "*a posteriori*"), and let H be the space of all possible hypotheses (in our case: $H = \{h_1, h_2\}$). We have:

$$h_{MAP} = \underset{h \in H}{\textbf{argmax}} \; P(D|h) \cdot P(h)$$

Let us see how this result can be calculated in practice, using a simple example.

Example 9.1. Let us consider a medical diagnosis problem, in which there are only two alternative hypotheses; given a particular patient and a particular disease:

- the patient has the disease;
- the patient does not have the disease.

The available data is from a particular laboratory test, with two possible outcomes: *positive* or *negative*. We have prior knowledge that, over the entire population of people, only 0.8% have this disease. Furthermore, we know that the lab test is an imperfect indicator of the disease: the test returns a correct positive result in 98% of the cases in which the disease is actually present, and a correct negative result in 97% of the cases in which the disease is actually not present. We can summarize the situation like this:

$P(\text{disease}) = 0.008$ $P(\text{not disease}) = 0.992$
$P(\text{positive test} \mid \text{disease}) = 0.98$ $P(\text{negative test} \mid \text{disease}) = 0.02$
$P(\text{positive test} \mid \text{not disease}) = 0.03$ $P(\text{negative test} \mid \text{not disease}) = 0.97$

Suppose we now observe a new patient, for whom the lab test returns a positive result. Should we diagnose the patient as having the disease?

According to the previous discussion, we have to understand whether $P(\text{disease} \mid \text{positive test})$ is larger than $P(\text{not disease} \mid \text{positive test})$ or the other way around. Applying Bayes' Theorem, we have to respectively calculate $P(\text{positive test} \mid \text{disease}) \cdot P(\text{disease})$ and $P(\text{positive test} \mid \text{not disease}) \cdot P(\text{not disease})$ and see which one of the two is the largest. We have all the quantities we need, so we can do it:

$$P(\text{disease} \mid \text{positive test}) = P(\text{positive test} \mid \text{disease}) \cdot P(\text{disease})$$
$$= 0.98 \cdot 0.008 = 0.0078$$

$$P(\text{not disease} \mid \text{positive test}) = P(\text{positive test} \mid \text{not disease}) \cdot P(\text{not disease})$$
$$= 0.03 \cdot 0.992 = 0.0298$$

So, the maximum *a posteriori* hypothesis h_{MAP} is:

$$h_{MAP} = \text{not disease}$$

A bit surprisingly, we must conclude that, even though the lab test was positive, the most probable hypothesis is still that the patient does *not* have the disease. It is important to remark that in Bayesian inference, the hypotheses are not completely accepted or rejected, but rather become more or less probable as more data is observed.

9.2 Naïve Bayes

Naïve Bayes is the simplest classifier based on Bayesian inference. It uses a *very* restrictive (and often false!) hypothesis: that all the variables in the dataset are independent of each other. Despite its simplicity and this restrictive hypothesis, Naïve Bayes has been shown to often have a very good classification performance; in some domains, even comparable with or better than that of Artificial Neural Networks (discussed in Chapter 7) and Decision Trees (discussed in Chapter 6).

Let us assume that we have a classification dataset with n variables (features), and let us assume that we receive a new observation, which we want to classify. Of course, the observation will have the form:

$$a_1, a_2, ..., a_n$$

i.e., n values, one for each variable. The space of our hypotheses H is now characterized by k hypotheses, where k is the number of classes in our dataset/problem:

- the new observation belongs to class C_1;
- the new observation belongs to class C_2;
- ...
- the new observation belongs to class C_k;

Analogously to the previous example, of all the hypotheses in the space H, we have to find the most probable, the maximum *a posteriori* hypothesis h_{MAP}. In other words, we want to find:

$$h_{MAP} = \underset{h \in H}{\textbf{argmax}}\, P(h|a_1, a_2, ..., a_n)$$

Applying Bayes' Theorem:

$$P(h|a_1, a_2, ..., a_n) = \frac{P(a_1, a_2, ..., a_n|h) \cdot P(h)}{P(a_1, a_2, ..., a_n)}$$

As previously remarked, for all hypotheses $h \in H$ the denominator $P(a_1, a_2, ..., a_n)$ is the same. So, this denominator is irrelevant for deciding what is the maximum *a posteriori* hypothesis, and it can be removed. So, we can conclude that:

$$h_{MAP} = \underset{h \in H}{\textbf{argmax}} \, P(a_1, a_2, ..., a_n | h) \cdot P(h)$$

where:

- $P(h)$ is easy to estimate for the various $h \in H$. We simply have to count the frequency with which the target value h occurs in the training data. In other words, for each class, we have to count the number of observations labeled with that class and divide it by the total number of observations.

- $P(a_1, a_2, ..., a_n | h)$ is instead very hard to estimate for the different $h \in H$ (even its intuitive meaning is arguably very hard to understand). But we can easily transform it into something that is very easy to calculate, making the very restrictive assumption, typical of the Naïve Bayes method, that the attribute values are conditionally independent, given the target value.

So, now our objective is to transform the term $P(a_1, a_2, ..., a_n | h)$ into an expression that is easy to calculate using the dataset. If we make the previously mentioned assumption of independence of the attribute values, we can write:

$$P(a_1, a_2, ..., a_n | h) = P(a_1 | h) \cdot P(a_2 | h) \cdot ... \cdot P(a_n | h) = \prod_{i=1}^{n} P(a_i | h)$$

For each $i = 1, 2, ..., n$ and for each $h \in H$, $P(a_i | h)$ can be easily calculated. Simply, for each class, we have to count the proportion of observations labeled with that class in which the *ith* attribute has exactly the value a_i. The next example should clarify.

Example 9.2. Let us recall the dataset reported in Table 6.1, on page 149, whose objective was to categorize days into two classes, to predict whether a given person would play tennis or not. The dataset is repeated here for the sake of convenience:

Day	Outlook	Temperature	Humidity	Wind	PlayTennis
D1	Sunny	Hot	High	Weak	No
D2	Sunny	Hot	High	Strong	No
D3	Overcast	Hot	High	Weak	Yes
D4	Rain	Mild	High	Weak	Yes
D5	Rain	Cool	Normal	Weak	Yes
D6	Rain	Cool	Normal	Strong	No
D7	Overcast	Cool	Normal	Strong	Yes
D8	Sunny	Mild	High	Weak	No
D9	Sunny	Cool	Normal	Weak	Yes
D10	Rain	Mild	Normal	Weak	Yes
D11	Sunny	Mild	Normal	Strong	Yes
D12	Overcast	Mild	High	Strong	Yes
D13	Overcast	Hot	Normal	Weak	Yes
D14	Rain	Mild	High	Strong	No

Let us now assume that we want to classify the following new (unseen) observation:

$$\alpha = <\text{Outlook} = \text{sunny}, \text{Temperature} = \text{cool}, \text{Humidity} = \text{high}, \text{Wind} = \text{strong}>$$

Of course, the space of hypotheses H is:

- h_1: observation α belongs to class "Yes";
- h_2: observation α belongs to class "No";

Following the previous reasoning, in order to find the maximum *a posteriori* hypothesis h_{MAP}, we have to understand which one of the following two quantities is the bigger one:

- $P(\text{Outlook} = \text{sunny}, \text{Temperature} = \text{cool}, \text{Humidity} = \text{high}, \text{Wind} = \text{strong} \mid \text{class} = \text{Yes}) \cdot P(\text{class} = \text{Yes})$
- $P(\text{Outlook} = \text{sunny}, \text{Temperature} = \text{cool}, \text{Humidity} = \text{high}, \text{Wind} = \text{strong} \mid \text{class} = \text{No}) \cdot P(\text{class} = \text{No})$

If we accept the hypothesis of independence of the single variables (which is clearly not true in this example), this is equivalent to understanding which one of the following quantities is the bigger:

- $h_1 \rightarrow P(\text{Outlook} = \text{sunny} \mid \text{class} = \text{Yes}) \cdot P(\text{Temperature} = \text{cool} \mid \text{class} = \text{Yes}) \cdot P(\text{Humidity} = \text{high} \mid \text{class} = \text{Yes}) \cdot P(\text{Wind} = \text{strong} \mid \text{class} = \text{Yes}) \cdot P(\text{class} = \text{Yes})$

- $h_2 \rightarrow P(\text{Outlook} = \text{sunny} \mid \text{class} = \text{No}) \cdot P(\text{Temperature} = \text{cool} \mid \text{class} = \text{No}) \cdot P(\text{Humidity} = \text{high} \mid \text{class} = \text{No}) \cdot P(\text{Wind} = \text{strong} \mid \text{class} = \text{No}) \cdot P(\text{class} = \text{No})$

The good news is that all the quantities above can be calculated using only the training set. Starting by saying that, in general, a computer will be able to calculate all these quantities incomparably faster than we can do it manually, let us make the effort of calculating all these quantities manually in this example, so that it can be completely clear what each one of these quantities exactly represents. In the following pointed list, for each one of the quantities, we describe how we can calculate it using the training set, and then we give the result.

- $P(\text{class} = \text{Yes}) = \frac{\#\text{observations in which class is Yes}}{\text{Total } \#\text{observations}} = 9/14 \approx 0.64$

- $P(\text{class} = \text{No}) = \frac{\#\text{observations in which class is No}}{\text{Total } \#\text{observations}} = 5/14 \approx 0.36$

- $P(\text{Outlook} = \text{sunny} \mid \text{class} = \text{Yes}) = \frac{\#\text{observations where class is Yes and Outlook is sunny}}{\text{Total } \#\text{observations where class is Yes}} = 2/9 \approx 0.22$

- $P(\text{Temperature} = \text{cool} \mid \text{class} = \text{Yes}) = \frac{\#\text{observations where class is Yes and Temperature is cool}}{\text{Total } \#\text{observations where class is Yes}} = 3/9 \approx 0.33$

- $P(\text{Humidity} = \text{high} \mid \text{class} = \text{Yes}) = \frac{\#\text{observations where class is Yes and Humidity is high}}{\text{Total } \#\text{observations where class is Yes}} = 3/9 \approx 0.33$

- $P(\text{Wind} = \text{strong} \mid \text{class} = \text{Yes}) = \frac{\#\text{observations where class is Yes and Wind is strong}}{\text{Total } \#\text{observations where class is Yes}} = 3/9 \approx 0.33$

- $P(\text{Outlook} = \text{sunny} \mid \text{class} = \text{No}) = \frac{\#\text{observations where class is No and Outlook is sunny}}{\text{Total } \#\text{observations where class is No}} = 3/5 = 0.6$

- $P(\text{Temperature} = \text{cool} \mid \text{class} = \text{No}) = \frac{\#\text{observations where class is No and Temperature is cool}}{\text{Total } \#\text{observations where class is No}} = 1/5 = 0.2$

- $P(\text{Humidity} = \text{high} \mid \text{class} = \text{No}) = \frac{\#\text{observations where class is No and Humidity is high}}{\text{Total } \#\text{observations where class is No}} = 4/5 \approx 0.8$

- $P(\text{Wind} = \text{strong} \mid \text{class} = \text{No}) = \frac{\#\text{observations where class is No and Wind is strong}}{\text{Total } \#\text{observations where class is No}} = 3/5 \approx 0.6$

We are now able to calculate the *a posteriori* probability of the two hypotheses:

- $h_1 \rightarrow P(\text{class} = \text{Yes} \mid \text{Outlook} = \text{sunny}, \text{Temperature} = \text{cool}, \text{Humidity} = \text{high}, \text{Wind} = \text{strong}) = 0.64 \cdot 0.22 \cdot 0.33 \cdot 0.33 \cdot 0.33 \approx 0.005$

- $h_2 \rightarrow P(\text{class} = \text{No} \mid \text{Outlook} = \text{sunny}, \text{Temperature} = \text{cool}, \text{Humidity} = \text{high}, \text{Wind} = \text{strong}) = 0.36 \cdot 0.6 \cdot 0.2 \cdot 0.8 \cdot 0.6 \approx 0.02$

The *a posteriori* probability of event h_2 is larger than that of event h_1. The conclusion is that we classify (unseen) instance α into class "No", meaning that our prediction is that the person will *not* play tennis on that day.

In [Domingos and Pazzani, 1996], Domingos and Pazzani show that the prediction made by Naïve Bayes can be optimal even if the attributes are not independent of each other, thus highlighting the excellent performance often obtained by Naïve Bayes, despite its simplicity.

9.3 Beyond Naïve Bayes: Hints on Bayesian Networks

Despite the excellent performance reported in the literature for many real-life applications, and despite the findings in [Domingos and Pazzani, 1996], which mitigate the negative effects of the hypothesis of independence of the variables, it is undeniable that this hypothesis can represent a limitation for Naïve Bayes in some scenarios, particularly when complex relationships of interdependency between variables are a fact. In those situations, more sophisticated paradigms, able to capture variable interdependencies, may be needed. One of these formalisms is *Bayesian Networks* (BNs). A BN is a graph that allows us to represent and reason about an uncertain domain. The vertices (nodes) in BNs represent a set of random variables, $X = X_1, ..., X_i, ..., X_n$, from the domain, for instance the variables in a dataset. The edges (links) connecting pairs of nodes, $X_i \rightarrow X_j$, represent the direct dependencies between variables. The only constraint on the structure allowed for a BN is that there must not be any directed cycles: you cannot return to a node simply by following directed edges. So, BNs are directed acyclic graphs.

One first observation that could be made is that Naïve Bayes is also a (particular) BN. The characteristic of a graph representing Naïve Bayes is that it only has one edge for each input variable, joining the variable itself to the target variable. For instance, a BN modeling a problem like the one discussed in Example 9.2 could be represented as in Figure 9.1. The interpretation is that, in the model used for the

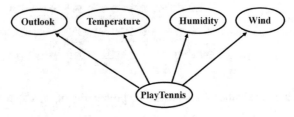

Fig. 9.1 The structure of the "naïve" Bayesian network of Example 9.2

problem of Example 9.2, the target variable PlayTennis is (of course) dependent on all the input variables[1] and there is no interdependence between any of the other variables. So, BNs are a formalism that also includes Naïve Bayes as a particular(ly simple) case.

Let us now consider a problem that can be modeled with a BN of a different shape compared to the one shown in Figure 9.1. This problem will be characterized by known variable interdependencies, and thus it will not be appropriate to model it using Naïve Bayes. A deliberately simple example is discussed.

Example 9.3. Let us study two events that can cause grass to be wet: the fact that a sprinkler is active and the fact that it is raining. Both these effects can cause grass to be wet, but still they are not mutually independent: in fact, one may reasonably imagine that when it rains, the sprinkler is not active. So, the fact of a sprinkler being active or not depends on whether it is raining or not. This situation can be modeled with the Bayesian network shown in Figure 9.2. Three Boolean variables are present in this BN: Wet Grass, Sprinkler and Rain. Variable Sprinker is dependent on variable Rain, while variable Wet Grass is dependent on both Sprinkler and Rain. A graph like the one in Figure 9.2 represents only a part of the definition of a BN, that is its *topology* (i.e., the way its vertices are connected by edges). For

---

[1] An effective feature selection algorithm should, in fact, remove possible variables on which the target does not depend, in the preprocessing phase.

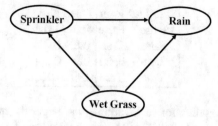

Fig. 9.2 The topology of the Bayesian network used in Example 9.3

the definition to be complete, the relationships between connected nodes have to be quantified. This is done by specifying a conditional probability distribution for each node, and, for the case of discrete variables as in this example, this can be done by means of conditional probability tables (CPTs). For instance, let us assume that the vertex representing variable Sprinkler is associated with the following CPT:

Rain	True	False
False	0.4	0.6
True	0.01	0.99

This table expresses the probability of variable Sprinkler being true or false, depending on the possible values of the variable Rain, on which it depends. The interpretation of this CPT is:

- If it is not raining (Rain = False), then the probability of the sprinkler being active (Sprinkler = True) is 0.4 and inactive (Sprinkler=False) is 0.6;
- If it is raining (Rain = True), then the probability of the sprinkler being active (Sprinkler = True) is 0.01 and inactive (Sprinkler=False) is 0.99.

Notice that, in general, a CPT is associated to *each* variable in the system, even if the variable does not depend on any other. In that case, the CPT simply contains the *a priori* probabilities for that variable. This is the case, in this example, for variable Rain. Its CPT is supposed to contain the probability of raining or not raining for an average day. So, the CPT of variable Rain may look like the following table:

True	False
0.2	0.8

Last but not least, the CPT of variable Wet Grass contains an entry for each possible combination of the variables it depends on. Let us assume that the CPT of variable Wet Grass, in our case, is:

Sprinkler	Rain	True	False
False	False	0.0	1.0
False	True	0.8	0.2
True	False	0.9	0.1
True	True	0.99	0.01

As it is easy to understand, for each variable, the larger the number of variables it depends on, the bigger the CPT. The BN can now be completely defined, as in Figure 9.3. Figure 9.3 is identical to Figure 9.2, except that in Figure 9.3 the vertices

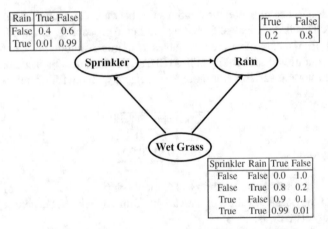

Fig. 9.3 The complete definition of the Bayesian network used in Example 9.3

have been annotated with the CPT of the corresponding variable. It should not be difficult to convince oneself that, usually, the CPTs are part of (or can be extracted from) the definition of the problem. For instance, if we have a supervised dataset, once the topology of the network has been defined (and this can be done manually, or by means of specific algorithms, as we will discuss in the continuation), the CPTs can usually be calculated directly from the dataset with simple counting operations, similar, for instance, to the ones that have allowed us to calculate probabilities $P(\text{Outlook} = \text{sunny} \mid \text{class} = \text{Yes})$ or $P(\text{Outlook} = \text{sunny} \mid \text{class} = \text{No})$ in Example 9.2.

Looking at the definition of a BN like the one in Figure 9.3, it is also not difficult to understand that BNs are a construct that allows for more general computations than the "simple" prediction of a class label for a given target variable. More specifically, using BNs it is possible to estimate the probability of *any* variable having any of its possible values, given actual values of any of the others.

Just as an example, let us now calculate the probability that it is raining (Rain=True), knowing that the grass is wet (Wet Grass = True). From now on, for simplicity, variable Wet Grass will be abbreviated as G, Rain as R, Sprinkler as S. Furthermore, for any variable β, $\beta = \text{True}$ will be abbreviated by simply writing β, while $\beta =$ False will be represented using the notation $\neg\beta$. So, the probability we want to estimate is: $P(R|G)$. Directly from the definition of conditional probability, we have:

$$P(R|G) = \frac{P(G,R)}{P(G)} \tag{9.1}$$

The right part of Equation (9.1) can be transformed, obtaining:

$$P(R|G) = \frac{P(G,S,R) + P(G,\neg S,R)}{P(G,S,R) + P(G,S,\neg R) + P(G,\neg S,R) + P(G,\neg S,\neg R)} \tag{9.2}$$

Now, remembering that, for the definition of joint probability, for each triple of events A, B and C we have:

$$P(A,B,C) = P(A|B,C)\,P(B|C)\,P(C) \tag{9.3}$$

we can transform each term of Equation (9.2) into a form that is similar to Equation (9.3), and then calculate its value using the values in the CPTs.

Let us begin with term $P(G,S,R)$. From Equation (9.3), we have:

$$P(G,S,R) = P(G|S,R)\,P(S|R)\,P(R) \tag{9.4}$$

But each term on the left-hand side of Equation (9.4) can be extracted directly from the CPTs. So, Equation (9.4) becomes:

$$P(G,S,R) = P(G|S,R)\,P(S|R)\,P(R) = 0.99 \cdot 0.01 \cdot 0.2 = 0.00198 \tag{9.5}$$

Analogously, for the other terms in Equation (9.2), we have:

$$P(G,\neg S,R) = P(G|\neg S,R)\,P(\neg S|R)\,P(R) = 0.8 \cdot 0.99 \cdot 0.2 = 0.1584 \tag{9.6}$$
$$P(G,S,\neg R) = P(G|S,\neg R)\,P(S|\neg R)\,P(\neg R) = 0.9 \cdot 0.4 \cdot 0.8 = 0.288 \tag{9.7}$$
$$P(G,\neg S,\neg R) = P(G|\neg S,\neg R)\,P(\neg S|\neg R)\,P(\neg R) = 0.0 \cdot 0.6 \cdot 0.8 = 0.0 \tag{9.8}$$

Finally, substituting Equations (9.5), (9.6), (9.7) and (9.8) into Equation (9.2), we obtain:

$$P(R|G) = \frac{0.00198 + 0.1584}{0.00198 + 0.288 + 0.1584 + 0.0} \approx 0.3577 \tag{9.9}$$

So, we can conclude that, if the grass is wet, the *a posteriori* probability that it is raining is approximately equal to 35%.

Fixing some values of some variables and, with that information, calculating the probability that another variable has some value is a task that is left as an exercise. For instance, analogously to what happens for Naïve Bayes, to predict a class label in a binary classification task, one may calculate the probability of a variable having a value and the probability of the same variable having the other possible value in the same conditions. The higher of these two probabilities is finally the one that directs our decision on the predicted class label. Interestingly, as we have seen in this example, when we use BNs, we do not need an unseen observation to be "complete" (i.e., all the variables to have a value) to calculate the probability of a possible prediction outcome. For instance, here we have calculated the probability that it is raining, knowing that the grass is wet, without having any information on whether the sprinkler is active or not.

In the process discussed in the above example, all the steps were formal, except for one, which still appears to be quite heuristic: the determination of the BN topology. There are basically two ways of building the topology of a BN: a manual construction or an automatic design (so called "topology learning").

Manual construction of a Bayesian network assumes prior expert knowledge of the underlying domain. In particular, the variable interdependencies must be known. However, in some cases, the task of manually defining the topology of the network is too complex for humans. In those cases, one may try to employ algorithms that have the objective of inferring the topology directly from the data. The interested reader is referred to [Singh and Valtorta, 1995, Chen, 2016] for surveys and discussions on existing algorithms. Even though research on this subject is still ongoing, interesting results have been recently obtained, among others, in [Wu et al., 2001, Beretta et al., 2018].

Chapter 10
Support Vector Machines

Let us imagine a linearly separable training data set, characterized by only two class labels. In such a situation, the binary classification task can be accomplished by determining a linear separator for the training points. Given that an infinite number of possible linear separators exist in general, methods such as the Perceptron algorithm find just any of the existing separators, while other methods search for the "best" linear separator, according to some criterion. Support Vector Machines (SVMs) aim to find a decision surface that is maximally far away from any data point, with the objective of maximizing classification accuracy and robustness, and generalization ability. In this chapter, SVMs are first introduced for binary classification and for linearly separable problems. Then, the concepts are extended to nonlinearly separable problems and multiclass classification.

10.1 Binary Classification, Linearly Separable Problems

Let us define a binary classification problem as the task of separating a set of *positive* samples (instances labeled with $+$) from a set of *negative* samples (instances labeled with $-$), and let us assume that the problem is linearly separable. The situation is represented in Figure 10.1(a) for the elementary case of two-dimensional data. Observing the figure, it is clear that several separating straight lines exist. Assuming that you were allowed to choose one to perform the classification, which one would you choose? It is intuitive that it is not such a good idea to have a straight line that is too close to positive or negative examples. In fact, data might be affected by noise, so the position of points may be imprecise and thus a line that is too close to a point may not be accurate. Furthermore, unseen points are generally different from the training ones, and a straight line that is too close to training points may fail to correctly classify unseen ones. On the other hand, a straight line like the dashed one pictured in Figure 10.1(a), that is neither too close to the positive examples nor to the negative ones, looks like a more appropriate choice. Informally, we could say that the best line may be the one that has the property of standing in the middle of

© Springer Nature Switzerland AG 2023
L. Vanneschi and S. Silva, *Lectures on Intelligent Systems*, Natural Computing Series,
https://doi.org/10.1007/978-3-031-17922-8_10

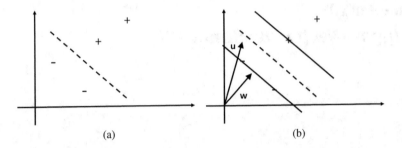

Fig. 10.1 A simple linearly separable, binary classification problem in two dimensions

the "widest street" that separates the negative examples from the positive examples. The distance from the decision surface to the closest data point determines what we call the *margin*, or *gutter*, of the classifier. Thus, the best line is the one that maximizes the distance between the line itself and the margins. Margins are shown with solid lines in Figure 10.1(b). The approach of SVMs is informally called the "widest street" approach, because the three parallel straight lines in Figure 10.1(b) vaguely resembles a street. This method of construction necessarily means that the decision function for an SVM is fully specified by a (usually small) subset of the data, which defines the position of the separator. These points are referred to as the *support vectors* (the points intercepting the margins in Figure 10.1(b)). Other data points play no part in determining the decision surface that is chosen.

Now imagine that we have a vector (like **w** in Figure 10.1(b)) of any length, constrained to be perpendicular to the median line of our street. Imagine that we also have some unknown and a vector (like **u** in the figure) pointing to it. We want to understand whether that unknown is on the right side of the street or on the left side of the street. What we must do to answer the question is to project that vector **u** onto **w**, which is perpendicular to the street. Remembering that the projection of a vector onto another can be expressed as a function of the "dot product" of the two vectors, we could now measure whether $\mathbf{w} \cdot \mathbf{u}$ is greater than or equal to some given constant, or, without loss of generality, for a given constant b:

$$\mathbf{w} \cdot \mathbf{u} + b \geq 0$$

If this expression is true, then our unknown point is a positive example, otherwise it is a negative example. So, this is the shape of our decision rule. The problem is that we do not know what constant b and what vector **w** to use. All we know is that **w** has to be perpendicular to the median line of the street, but so far it can be of any length. So, we do not have enough constraints to fix a particular b or a particular **w** yet. What we need is some constraint in such a way that we are actually able to calculate a **w** and a b. One assumption we could make is that, if we take that vector **w** and we multiply it for a training positive example $\mathbf{x}_+$, then this product must be grater than or equal to 1:

$$\mathbf{w} \cdot \mathbf{x}_+ + b \geq 1 \tag{10.1}$$

In other words, an unknown point can be anywhere in the street, but if it is a positive sample, then we are going to assume that the decision function returns a value that is greater than or equal to 1. Likewise, for a negative example $\mathbf{x}_-$, we will assume that our decision function will have to return a value that is equal to or less than -1:

$$\mathbf{w} \cdot \mathbf{x}_- + b \leq -1 \tag{10.2}$$

In other words, we are imposing a separation of -1 to +1 for all the training samples. So, now we could just try to solve the system formed by Equations (10.1) and (10.2), in order to find a $\mathbf{w}$ and a b that guarantees this kind of separation for all the training samples.

In order to make the system more manageable, we now introduce a variable y_i such that $y_i = +1$ for positive samples and $y_i = -1$ for negative samples. Multiplying both previous equations by y_i brings the two equations to be the same, in fact we obtain:

$$y_i(\mathbf{w} \cdot \mathbf{x}_+ + b) \geq 1$$
$$y_i(\mathbf{w} \cdot \mathbf{x}_- + b) \geq 1$$

So, now we can say that, for any training sample $\mathbf{x_i}$, whether it is positive or negative, we have:

$$y_i(\mathbf{w} \cdot \mathbf{x_i} + b) - 1 \geq 0 \tag{10.3}$$

Now, we can imagine that we make one more assumption, i.e., for every $\mathbf{x_i}$ in the gutter:

$$y_i(\mathbf{w} \cdot \mathbf{x_i} + b) - 1 = 0 \tag{10.4}$$

In other words, the result of this equation will be exactly equal to zero for the points circled in red in Figure 10.2(a), and greater than zero for the points circled in blue in the same figure. The points in the gutter, the ones circled in red, are what we call

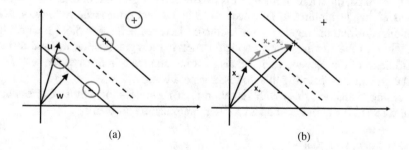

(a)   (b)

Fig. 10.2 Support vectors and separations, for the same problem as in Figure 10.1

the *support vectors*, and are the only training points we use to build our classifier. Our objective is to maximize the distance between the two gutters of the street, so, let us try to express that distance. To do this, let us consider a positive example $\mathbf{x}_+$

and a negative example $\mathbf{x}_-$, and let us consider the difference between vectors $\mathbf{x}_+$ and $\mathbf{x}_-$. Vectors $\mathbf{x}_+$ and $\mathbf{x}_-$ are shown in black, while their difference is shown in red in Figure 10.2(b). If we only had a unit vector normal to the median line of the street, like the one shown in green in Figure 10.2(b), then we could consider the "dot product" (i.e., the scalar product) between that unit vector and the difference between $\mathbf{x}_+$ and $\mathbf{x}_-$, and that would be the width of the street. But, one of our first assumptions was that $\mathbf{w}$ is normal to the median line of the street. So, we could say that the width of the street is equal to:

$$width = (\mathbf{x}_+ - \mathbf{x}_-) \cdot \frac{\mathbf{w}}{||\mathbf{w}||} \tag{10.5}$$

In fact, $\frac{\mathbf{w}}{||\mathbf{w}||}$ is a unit vector and, given that $\mathbf{w}$ is normal to the median line of the street, also $\frac{\mathbf{w}}{||\mathbf{w}||}$ is normal to the median line of the street.

Now, from Equation (10.4), which constraints the samples in the line of the gutter, we have that, for positive samples, $y_i = 1$, and thus:

$$\mathbf{w} \cdot \mathbf{x}_+ = 1 - b$$

So, from the previous observation, and with analogous reasoning for a negative example that stands in the gutter, we can develop Equation (10.5), obtaining:

$$width = (\mathbf{x}_+ - \mathbf{x}_-) \cdot \frac{\mathbf{w}}{||\mathbf{w}||} = \frac{\mathbf{x}_+ \cdot \mathbf{w} - \mathbf{x}_- \cdot \mathbf{w}}{||\mathbf{w}||} = \frac{1 - b + 1 + b}{||\mathbf{w}||}$$

This allows us to rewrite the Equation (10.5) as:

$$width = \frac{2}{||\mathbf{w}||} \tag{10.6}$$

In other words, the width of the street is maximized if $\frac{||\mathbf{w}||}{2}$ is minimized, or, in other words, if $||\mathbf{w}||$ is minimized. The reader is invited to notice the analogy between this minimization and the regularization methods discussed in Section 5.6. Maximizing the width of the street, we are implicitly applying a regularization method to the coefficients of the decision rule. This is a further argument in favor of the selection of the maximum separating line, to foster generalization.

Joining Equation (10.4) with Equation (10.6), we are now able to express the final standard formulation of an SVM as a minimization problem:

Find $\mathbf{w}$ and b, such that:

- $\frac{1}{2} \mathbf{w}^T \cdot \mathbf{w}$ is minimized,
- under the constraint: $y_i(\mathbf{w}^T \cdot \mathbf{x_i} + b) - 1 = 0$.

So, the problem is now reduced to the optimization of a quadratic function, subject to linear constraints. Quadratic optimization problems are a standard, well known class of mathematical optimization problems, and many algorithms exist for solving them. We could in principle build an SVM using standard quadratic programming, but much recent research was devoted to studying the particular structure of the kind of quadratic problem that emerges from an SVM. As a result, there are more complex, but much faster and more scalable, methods for building SVMs. The details of the mathematical derivation of such methods are beyond the scope of the book. However, it is interesting to understand the shape of the solution of such an optimization problem. The solution involves constructing a dual problem, where a Lagrange multiplier α_i is associated with each constraint $y_i(\mathbf{w}^T \cdot \mathbf{x_i} + b) \leq 1$ in the primal problem:

Find $\alpha_1, \alpha_2, ..., \alpha_N$, such that:

- $\sum_i \alpha_i - \dfrac{1}{2} \sum_i \sum_j \alpha_i\, \alpha_j\, y_i\, y_j\, \mathbf{x_i}^T \cdot \mathbf{x_j}$ is maximized,
- under the constraint: $\sum_i \alpha_i y_i = 0$,
- and: $\alpha_i \geq 0$ for all $i = 1, 2, ..., N$.

The solution is of the form:

- $\mathbf{w} = \sum_i \alpha_i\, y_i\, \mathbf{x_i}$
- $b = y_k - \mathbf{w}^T \cdot \mathbf{x_k}$, for any $\mathbf{x_k}$ such that $\alpha_k \neq 0$

In the solution, most of the α_i are equal to zero. Each α_i that is different from zero indicates that the corresponding $\mathbf{x_i}$ is a support vector. The classification function is then:

$$f(\mathbf{x}) = \text{sign}\left(\sum_i \alpha_i\, y_i\, \mathbf{x_i}^T \cdot \mathbf{x} + b \right) \tag{10.7}$$

As we can see, the most expensive calculations are the dot products between the unseen point $\mathbf{x}$ and the support vectors $\mathbf{x_i}$. This makes SVM particularly efficient in terms of computational speed, compared to several other Machine Learning systems. In the continuation, we see a numeric example for a very simple case study.

Example 10.1. Let us consider the extremely simple binary classification task represented in Figure 10.3, where only three training instances are present, one of which, i.e., $(2,3)$, is a positive example and the other two, i.e., $(1,1)$ and $(2,0)$, are negative examples. The maximum margin weight vector $\mathbf{w}$ will be parallel to the shortest line connecting points of the two classes, that is, the line between $(1,1)$ and $(2,3)$. So, the support vectors are $(1,1)$ and $(2,3)$ and the optimal decision surface is orthogonal to the line joining them. Let us now use the following equation to calculate weight vector $\mathbf{w}$:

$$\mathbf{w} = \sum_i \alpha_i\, y_i\, \mathbf{x_i} \tag{10.8}$$

where:

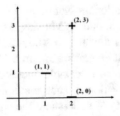

Fig. 10.3 Graphical representation of the simple data used in Example 10.1

- $\alpha_i > 0$ for the support vectors, and $\alpha_i = 0$ for the other points that are not support vectors. In some way, we could informally say that the task of the α_is is to let only support vectors participate in the summation, and give a different positive "weight" in the summation to each support vector;
- $y_i = 1$ for the positive example $(2,3)$, and $y_i = -1$ for the negative example $(1,1)$

So, Equation (10.8) can rewritten as follows:

$$\mathbf{w} = \alpha_1 \cdot (2,3) - \alpha_2 \cdot (1,1) \tag{10.9}$$

Furthermore, if we consider the constraint:

$$\sum_i \alpha_i y_i = 0$$

then we have:

$$\alpha_1 - \alpha_2 = 0$$

In other words, α_1 and α_2 are identical. Let their value be equal to a. In other words:

$$\alpha_1 = \alpha_2 = a$$

Thus, Equation (10.9) becomes:

$$\mathbf{w} = a \cdot (2,3) - a \cdot (1,1) = (2a,3a) - (a,a) = (a,2a)$$

So, using the two support vectors, we have that the following two equations must be satisfied:

$$a + 2a + b = -1 \quad \text{(using point } (1,1)) \tag{10.10}$$

and:

$$2a + 6a + b = 1 \quad \text{(using point } (2,3)) \tag{10.11}$$

Form Equation (10.11), we obtain:

$$b = 1 - 8a \tag{10.12}$$

Substituting Equation (10.12) in Equation (10.10), we have:

$$a + 2a + 1 - 8a = -1$$

That is:

$$a = \frac{2}{5}$$

and so:

$$b = 1 - 8\,\frac{2}{5} = -\frac{11}{5}$$

In conclusion, we have:

$$\mathbf{w} = (\frac{2}{5}, \frac{4}{5}) \quad \text{and} \quad b = -\frac{11}{5}$$

and the equation of the optimal separating hyperplane is:

$$g(x_1, x_2) = \frac{2}{5}x_1 + \frac{4}{5}x_2 - \frac{11}{5}$$

which is equivalent to:

$$g(x_1, x_2) = x_1 + 2x_2 - 5.5$$

Last but not least, we can calculate the width of the margin. Knowing that:

$$width = \frac{2}{||\mathbf{w}||}$$

we have:

$$width = \frac{2}{\sqrt{4/25 + 16/25}} = \frac{2}{\sqrt{20/5}} = \frac{5}{\sqrt{5}} = \sqrt{5}$$

10.2 Soft Margin Classification

The examples considered so far are extremely simple, and they have a property that is very rarely satisfied: points belonging to the two classes are very well separated. In reality, problems are often not linearly separable, and one possible reason is the presence of "noise" in data, that can make, for instance, one or more positive points appear inside the "cloud" of negative examples and/or vice versa. When the number of points that do not respect the linear separation is "limited", the standard approach is to allow the fat decision margin to make a few mistakes; in other words, some points (outliers or noisy examples) are left inside or on the wrong side of the margin. We then pay a cost for each misclassified example, which depends on how far it is from meeting the margin requirement given in Equation (10.3). To implement this, we introduce so-called *slack variables* ξ_i. The situation is shown for a simple two-dimensional case in Figure 10.4. In simple words, the value of a slack variable is

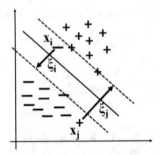

Fig. 10.4 Points x_i and x_j are the wrong side of the margin. The values of their respective slack variables are ξ_i and ξ_j

the distance of a misclassified example to the correct gutter. A value different from zero for ξ_i allows x_i to not meet the margin requirement at a cost proportional to the value of ξ_i. The formulation of the SVM optimization problem with slack variables is:

Find w, b and ξ_i such that:

- $\frac{1}{2} \mathbf{w}^T \mathbf{w} + C \sum_i \xi_i$ is minimized,
- under the constraint that, for all $\{x_i, y_i\}$: $y_i(\mathbf{w}^T \mathbf{x_i} + b) \geq 1 - \xi_i$,

where C is a new parameter of the algorithm that, consistently with the discussion in Section 5.6, we call the *regularization term*. In fact, C helps to control overfitting: as C becomes large, it is unattractive to not respect the data at the cost of reducing the geometric margin; when it is small, it is easy to account for some data points with the use of slack variables and to have a fat margin placed, capturing the majority of the data. The optimization problem is now to trade off how fat it can make the margin versus how many points are misclassified. The margin can be less than 1 for a point x_i by setting $\xi_i > 0$, but then one pays a penalty of $C\xi_i$ in the minimization for having done that. The sum of the ξ_is gives an upper bound for the training error. The dual problem for soft margin classification becomes:

Find $\alpha_1, \alpha_2, ..., \alpha_N$, such that:

- $\sum_i \alpha_i - \frac{1}{2} \sum_i \sum_j \alpha_i \alpha_j y_i y_j \mathbf{x_i}^T \cdot \mathbf{x_j}$ is maximized,
- under the constraint: $\sum_i \alpha_i y_i = 0$,
- and: $0 \leq \alpha_i \leq C$ for all $i = 1, 2, ..., N$.

Neither the slack variables ξ_i nor Lagrange multipliers for them appear in the dual problem. All we are left with is the constant C bounding the possible size of the

Lagrange multipliers for the support vector data points. As before, the points x_i with α_i different from zero will be the support vectors. The solution of the dual problem is of the form:

- $w = \sum_i \alpha_i \, y_i \, x_i$
- $b = y_k \, (1 - \xi_k) - w^T \cdot x_k$, for any $k = \text{argmax}_k \alpha_k$

Again, w is not needed explicitly for classification, which can be done in terms of dot products between points as in Equation (10.7). If the problem is nonlinearly separable, or with small margin, then every data point which is misclassified, or within the margin, will have a nonzero α_i. If this set of points becomes large, then the calculations can become rather slow.

10.3 Multiclass Classification

SVMs are, by their very nature, binary classifiers. If the task consists in partitioning data into h classes, with $h > 2$, one common technique is to build h "one-versus-rest" (also called "one-versus-all") classifiers. In other words, we select one class C_1, and we generate a binary classifier partitioning data into observations categorized as belonging to C_1 and "others". Then we select another class C_2, and we repeat the process using only the data that were *not* categorized as belonging to C_1. The process is iterated until all h classes have been selected. On unseen data, it is customary to choose the class which classifies the unseen datum with greatest margin. Another strategy is to build a set of "one-versus-one" classifiers, considering all pairwise combinations of class labels, and to choose the class that is selected by the most classifiers. While this involves building $h \times (h-1)/2$ different classifiers, the time for training each classifier may be smaller, since the training data set for each classifier is smaller (only the data labeled with the two classes we are considering are needed). Besides these two simple methods for using SVMs for multiclass classification, other methods, possibly more "elegant", but more complex, have been defined. These methods are beyond the scope of this book. The interested reader is referred to [Mayoraz and Alpaydin, 1999, Chih-Wei Hsu and Chih-Jen Lin, 2002].

10.4 Nonlinearly Separable Problems: the Kernel Trick

So far, we have studied SVMs for linearly separable problems, possibly with a few exceptions or some noise. In order to understand the idea that is at the base of the use of SVMs for nonlinearly separable problems, let us consider an example like the one represented in Figure 10.5(a). Even though the points can be represented along just one dimension, the reader can agree that no linear function can separate

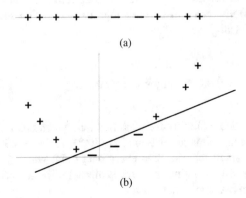

Fig. 10.5 (a): representation of the points for a nonlinearly separable problem; (b): projections of the points on a higher-dimensional feature space, by means of a quadratic function. The mapped problem is now linearly separable

the positive examples from the negative examples. One way to solve this problem is to map the data on to a higher-dimensional space, and then to use a linear classifier in the higher-dimensional space. For example, Figure 10.5(b) shows that a linear separator can classify the data if we use a quadratic function to map the data into two dimensions (and several other types of transformations could be imagined, besides the quadratic one). The general idea is to map the original feature space to some higher-dimensional feature space, where the training set is linearly separable. Of course, this needs to be done in a way that preserves relevant dimensions of relatedness between data points, so that the resultant classifier should still have generalization ability. SVMs provide an efficient way of doing this mapping to a higher-dimensional space, which is referred to as *the kernel trick*. As we have studied so far, the SVM linear classifier relies on a dot product between data point vectors. Let $K(\mathbf{x_i}, \mathbf{x_j}) = \mathbf{x_i}^T \mathbf{x_j}$. Then the classifier we have seen so far is:

$$f(\mathbf{x}) = \text{sign} \left(\sum_i \alpha_i \, y_i \, K(\mathbf{x_i}, \mathbf{x}) + b \right) \tag{10.13}$$

Now, assume we map every data point into a higher-dimensional space via some transformation $\Phi : \mathbf{x'} \to \phi(\mathbf{x'})$. Then the dot product becomes $\phi(\mathbf{x_i})^T \phi(\mathbf{x_j})$. If it turned out that this dot product could be computed simply and efficiently in terms of the original data points, then we would not have to apply the mapping Φ. Instead, we could simply compute the quantity $K(\mathbf{x_i}, \mathbf{x_j}) = \phi(\mathbf{x_i})^T \phi(\mathbf{x_j})$, and then use the function's value in Equation (10.13). A kernel function K is such a function that corresponds to a dot product in some expanded feature space.

Even though several types of kernels can be defined, the vast majority of work with kernels uses one of two families of functions of two vectors, which we define below, and which define valid kernels. The two commonly used families of kernels are polynomial kernels and radial basis functions. Polynomial kernels are of the form:

$$K(\mathbf{x},\mathbf{z}) = (1+\mathbf{x}^T\mathbf{z})^d$$

The case of $d = 1$ is a linear kernel, which corresponds to SVMs, as they were studied in the previous sections (with the only, minor, difference that constant 1 changes the threshold). The case of $d = 2$ gives a quadratic kernel, and is very commonly used. The most common form of radial basis function is a Gaussian distribution, calculated as:

$$K(\mathbf{x},\mathbf{z}) = e^{-(\mathbf{x}-\mathbf{z})^2/(2\sigma^2)}$$

Beyond these two families, there has been interesting work developing other kernels, some of which gave promising experimental results. Interestingly, other Machine Learning algorithms, for instance Genetic Programming, can also be used to automatically generate appropriate kernels for SVMs [Sullivan and Luke, 2007].

Chapter 11
Ensemble Methods

Ensemble ML methods build predictive models by inducing several different predictors, called base predictors or base learners. Typically, a base predictor is a very simple model that is not meant to work on its own. The predictions of such simple models are normally not much better than random guesses, which is why they are called weak learners. It is through the aggregation of the different answers from the various base learners that ensemble learning builds strong learners that produce accurate predictions.

Different ensemble methods may use different types of base learners (decision trees, neural networks, etc., or even a mix of several types), different ways of obtaining a diverse set of learners from the same original dataset, and different ways of aggregating their outputs into a single prediction. Some of the first attempts at building ensembles used decision trees as base learners (e.g., [Kwok and Carter, 1990]) and the most powerful ensemble methods available today still maintain that preference. In this chapter we will focus on some of the most relevant methods, covering Random Subspaces (RS), Random Forests (RF), Adaptive Boosting (AdaBoost) and Gradient Boosting (GB). All of them use decision trees as base learners, but they use different methods to obtain the different learners and/or to aggregate their predictions.

It should be clear why the base learners that compose an ensemble must be different from one another. If they all produced the same predictions when faced with a dataset, then the aggregation of their outputs would not be different from the output of any one taken separately. The strength of an ensemble, in ML and in many other aspects outside of computation and artificial intelligence, is the diversity of opinions, in this case predictions. Therefore, it is not surprising that, in order to induce an ensemble model, each base predictor must learn from a different version or subset of the original data.

The next three sections will describe the different processes that may take part in inducing an ensemble model: bootstrapping, aggregating and boosting. The last two sections will describe how to put these elements together in building specific ensembles of different types, first RF and RS, and then AdaBoost and GB.

© Springer Nature Switzerland AG 2023
L. Vanneschi and S. Silva, *Lectures on Intelligent Systems*, Natural Computing Series,
https://doi.org/10.1007/978-3-031-17922-8_11

11.1 Bootstrapping

Bootstrapping is a name believed to have its origins in the eighteenth or nineteenth century, when it meant to pull oneself up by the bootstraps, i.e., an impossible task. Nowadays, it means to achieve something by using your own resources without external help.

In ML, bootstrapping [Efron, 1982, Efron and Tibshirani, 1993] is a sampling method for obtaining different sets of data from a single original dataset. The default method is based on random sampling with replacement, i.e., elements are picked from the original dataset one by one, each time with exactly the same probability as any other element. These picked elements then form what is called a bootstrapped dataset, which can be smaller than, equal to, or even larger than the original dataset. Given the randomness of the process, it is normal that some elements appear more than once in the same bootstrapped dataset and that some of the original elements do not appear in any of the bootstrapped datasets. The distribution of each bootstrapped dataset is expected to be approximately the same as the distribution of the original dataset. Variants of the default bootstrapping may assign different probabilities of being picked to different elements of the original dataset, taking into account particular distributions or known correlations in the data.

The number of bootstrapped datasets, as well as their size, is chosen according to the needs and limitations. The most common reason for using bootstrapping is the need to have a number of datasets with some diversity among them, and the limitation of not having enough data to simply split the original dataset into large enough parts. In ensemble methods, bootstrapping is used for obtaining different datasets for the base predictors to learn from.

11.2 Aggregating

Another key element of ensemble learning is the aggregation of predictions [Breiman, 1996]. Although each base learner is trained on a different dataset and will probably output a different prediction for each data point it is asked to predict, the prediction returned by the ensemble should not be ambiguous. Therefore, all the predictions of the different base learners must be aggregated into a single answer. This may be obtained by a simple majority vote (for classification) or average (for regression), or by more complex schemes involving the weighting of the different answers or even the application of an ML algorithm to learn the best combination of answers (a process known as stacking [Wolpert, 1992]).

Applying aggregation to the predictions from learners trained on bootstrapped datasets is generally called bagging (bootstrap aggregating) [Breiman, 1996]. Although in the ML literature the term is used freely to designate different variants of the original approach, it is normally associated with the parallel independent training of different base learners, followed by majority voting. On the other hand, boosting (next section) is associated with the sequential training of learners where each depends on the answers of the previous ones.

11.3 Boosting

When the term boosting was initially used in ML [Kearns, 1988], it referred to the general idea of combining simple (weak) classifiers in order to obtain better (strong) classifiers. Nowadays, boosting refers specifically to the process of building an ensemble by adding weak learners sequentially, always forcing the next learner to pay more attention to the errors of the previous ones. This can be done in different ways, giving rise to different algorithms.

The first boosting algorithm [Schapire, 1990] was used for classification and had only three base learners. The first learner could see all the training data; the second learner was trained with a subset where half of the data points had been misclassified by the first learner; the third learner was given only the data points where the two first learners disagreed, if any. Therefore, the different learners were trained on different subsets of the original data, based on previous errors and disagreements. The predictions of this small ensemble were obtained by aggregating the predictions of the three learners by simple majority voting.

Today, the most popular boosting methods take into consideration not only the previous errors but also their magnitude. Adaptive boosting achieves this by reweighting the samples or resampling the data based on the amount of error of the previous learners, while gradient boosting relies on iteratively fitting the next learners to the errors themselves, in a gradient descent manner (see Section 7.2).

11.4 Bagging Methods

The two methods described in this section fall into the bagging category, where the base learners can be trained in parallel and independently of one another.

11.4.1 Random Subspaces

Originally developed for classification, the method called Random Subspaces (RS) [Ho, 1998b] trains each weak learner (decision tree) on a small random subset of the original features of the problem. Therefore, each tree sees all the training samples, but only a few dimensions of the original complete feature space. Furthermore, each tree is given as many split nodes as needed to achieve 100%

accuracy[1] on the training set, but once again, this training set is a projection onto the lower-dimensional subspace of selected features, so this decision tree is still a weak learner on the original complete feature space. The aggregation is done by majority voting, or by averaging the numerical predictions when RS is applied to regression problems. The method has been used with several different types of base learners (e.g., KNN [Ho, 1998a]) and has been the target of various improvements, particularly in what concerns the choice of the subspaces (e.g., [Bryll et al., 2003, Tian and Feng, 2021]).

11.4.2 Random Forests

Random Forests (RF) [Breiman, 2001] also generate each decision tree in a subset of the available features. More specifically, following the idea of random split selection [Dietterich, 2000], only a random subset of features is considered each time a decision node is created during the tree induction process. Furthermore, as in the bagging method [Breiman, 1996], in RF each decision tree is induced on a different bootstrapped training set. The combination of randomly selecting both features and observations resulted in one of the most successful ensemble methods today. Simple majority voting or averaging (for classification or regression, respectively) is used for aggregating the predictions.

11.5 Boosting Methods

The two methods described in this section fall into the boosting category, where the base learners are created sequentially, each forced to pay more attention to the predictive errors made by the previous learners.

11.5.1 Adaptive Boosting

Originally developed for binary classification, Adaptive Boosting (AdaBoost) [Freund and Schapire, 1997, Freund and Schapire, 1996] was the first widely used boosting system. The trees that compose it are typically so shallow that they are called tree stumps.

In the beginning of the model induction process, all the N samples of the training data have equal weight: $w_i = 1/N, i = 1, 2, ..., N$. Once the first tree is created ($m = 1$), its error err_m is measured as the sum of the weights of the wrongly classified sam-

---

[1] From [Ho, 1998b], "When two samples cannot be distinguished by the selected features, there will be ambiguities, but if no decision is forced in such cases, this does not introduce errors".

ples[2], and the weight of this tree is calculated as: $\alpha_m = 1/2 \times \log((1 - err_m)/err_m)$. This means that if the error of the tree is small (large), its weight is a positive (negative) value; if its predictions are close to random, its weight is appropriately close to 0. Once the first tree is created, the sample weights are modified such that the wrongly classified ones become more important: $new\_w_i = w_i \exp(\alpha_m)$. In the same proportion, the correctly classified ones become less important: $new\_w_i = w_i \exp(-\alpha_m)$. The weights are then normalized to sum 1 again, and the next tree is created considering the new normalized weights.

Dealing with weighted samples may not be a trivial task for some types of base learners, and even simple ones like trees require modified criteria for the decision nodes. Therefore, an alternative is to use the weights to build a boostrapped dataset where each sample is selected with probability equal to its weight. This results in a dataset where previously mispredicted samples will appear more often, and the next base learner can then be created considering all the bootstrapped samples equally important. Once complete, the ensemble performs predictions by aggregating the responses of all its base learners by voting weighted by the learner weights α_m.

Simple and powerful, AdaBoost is still a very popular and successful boosting method. Many improved AdaBoost variants have been developed, not only for binary classification but also for other ML tasks such as regression and multiclass classification, as well as for semi-supervised learning [Ferreira and Figueiredo, 2012].

11.5.2 Gradient Boosting

Gradient Boosting (GB) [Friedman, 2000, Friedman, 2002, Friedman et al., 2000] is a general method for minimizing the error of the ensemble model, and as such can be considered to be a generalization of AdaBoost. It defines boosting as a numerical problem and approximates the solution using gradient descent. In GB, each weak learner added to the ensemble minimizes the error of the strong learner. Instead of trying to fit the samples, it fits the errors themselves; instead of each learner having a weight on the aggregated prediction, all learners are weighted by the same factor, normally called the learning rate (or shrinkage factor). The following description explains the basics of GB for regression. The additional steps and modifications for classification are described later. Both types use regression trees (see Section 6.2) as base learners.

The first learner is simply a constant (which can be regarded as a leaf of a tree), normally calculated as the average of the observed values (on the training set) of the dependent variable, i.e., the variable we want to predict. This average will be the predicted value for all the observations. The differences between observed and predicted values, called residuals[3], are calculated for each observation. The next

---

[2] All weights being equal, this is a simple accuracy measure.

[3] The term pseudo-residuals is more correct because the expression that calculates the residuals is the derivative of the gradient function, and different gradient functions may not result in true residuals.

weak learner is created to fit these residuals, and its predictions are weighted by the learning rate, a constant between 0 and 1. The new residuals are calculated as the difference between the observed values (the same ones as before) and the predicted values (the new predictions made by the partial ensemble built so far). Except for the first weak learner, which produces a single value, the predictions of all other learners are weighted by the learning rate in both the complete ensemble and all the partial ensembles in between.

For classification, GB becomes slightly more complicated, since the gradient function must be differentiable even when dealing with categories. The learners are induced and added to the ensemble (as before, weighted by the learning rate) in a continuous space defined by log-likelihood values obtained from the values of the residuals. At the same time, the log-likelihood values need to be converted into probabilities (with the logistic function, or softmax for multiclass problems) whenever predictions are needed for calculating residuals or for performing classifications. Many concepts of Logistic Regression (see Section 5.7.3) are used when doing classification with GB.

One particular GB method has gained extreme popularity, Extreme Gradient Boosting, better known as XGBoost [Chen and Guestrin, 2016]. Besides the techniques already implemented in GB to minimize overfitting, such as the use of the learning rate, limitations on the maximum depth of the trees, and pruning, XGBoost takes further actions towards good generalization: a regularization similar to [Johnson and Zhang, 2014] and feature subsampling as in the RS and RF methods. Other tweaks of XGBoost are focused on the type of regression trees used and are aimed at running the algorithm with large and potentially sparse datasets and/or in distributed computation environments.

Chapter 12
Unsupervised Learning: Clustering Algorithms

Most unsupervised learning performs clustering. A well-known exception is auto-encoder neural networks, which learn how to code the input data into a (typically) lower-dimensional representation. However, although autoencoders are normally categorized under unsupervised learning, they use the input data itself as the expected output, and therefore can also be regarded as supervised learning. We do not cover autoencoders or any other unsupervised method whose goal is not to split the data into different groups.

Clustering algorithms group the data according to the similarities between the observations, based on a distance metric, without knowledge of the class labels. The groups formed are called *clusters*. Clustering is useful for exploring and getting to know the data. It can and should be used as a preprocessing step for other methods, even when the class labels are known. For example, the cluster labels can be added to the data as an additional feature, or the observations belonging to different clusters can be handled separately, even by different classification algorithms, depending on the characteristics of each cluster. Clustering is an essential part of most semisupervised learning methods. It can also help in the detection of outliers.

Clustering is usually said to find the "natural" splitting of the data. In a two-dimensional, or even three-dimensional feature space, humans are extremely good at this task, and so they are also capable of quickly evaluating the quality of a clustering. However, in higher-dimensional feature spaces, the observations can no longer be easily visualized. With the multitude of clustering algorithms available nowadays, the challenge then becomes to choose the one that produces the best clustering. In times of big data, it is also vital to guarantee that it can perform the clustering in a reasonable amount of time and without exhausting all the available computer memory.

In the next sections, we will cover three main types of clustering: hierarchical, centroid-based and density-based. We leave out other, less common types, such as distribution-based and grid-based clustering. We also leave out biclustering and soft clustering algorithms. We show step-by-step running examples of the different algorithms, discuss the setting of their parameters, and suggest a few methods for evaluating the results.

© Springer Nature Switzerland AG 2023
L. Vanneschi and S. Silva, *Lectures on Intelligent Systems*, Natural Computing Series,
https://doi.org/10.1007/978-3-031-17922-8_12

12.1 Hierarchical Clustering

Hierarchical clustering gets its name from the multilevel organization of clusters it forms. Nonhierarchical clustering is often called flat clustering. Hierarchical clustering can be done by an agglomerative or divisive process. Agglomerative is, by far, the most common choice, a bottom-up approach where initially every data point is a cluster, and at each step the two closest clusters are joined together, normally until only one cluster exists.

Hierarchical agglomerative

Initialization:	each observation is a cluster;
In each iteration:	the two closest clusters are joined together;
Stop condition:	only one cluster exists.

Other stop criteria may be used, based on the number of clusters already formed and/or the distance between them. However, these decisions are usually taken only after the complete hierarchy has been formed and analysed.

Regardless of the distance metric used, the distance between two clusters can be calculated in several different ways, some of the most common being:

- Single-linkage: shortest distance found between any two elements belonging to different clusters. This option is prone to the chaining effect (see 12.1.2), where clusters far apart are connected to each other;
- Complete-linkage: longest distance instead of shortest. This option is prone to the crowding effect, where clusters are very close to each other;
- Average-linkage: group average, the most common being the average distance between all the pairs of elements belonging to different clusters. This is a balanced option, albeit more computationally intensive.

Other common options are only meaningful when using Euclidean distance, such as:

- Centroid-linkage: distance between cluster centroids;
- Ward's linkage: different related metrics based on the original work of Ward [Ward, 1963], e.g., the squared distance between cluster centroids, multiplied by a factor (usually called the minimum variance method).

Contrary to the agglomerative process, the divisive option is a top-down approach that starts with only one cluster containing all data points, and at each step splits one cluster in two, normally until all the clusters are singletons and cannot be further split.

Hierarchical divisive outer loop

Initialization:	only one cluster exists, including all the observations;
In each iteration:	split one cluster in two;
Stop condition:	only singleton clusters exist.

Once again, other stop criteria may be used, but the decisions regarding which clusters to consider are normally taken after building and analysing the complete hierarchy. Depending on the stop criteria, the order in which the clusters are split may become relevant, in which case the cluster to split in each iteration should be the most disperse one, according to some measure of variability.

Divisive hierarchical clustering is rarely used because it is computationally more expensive than the agglomerative approach. Given the unfeasability of trying every possible split to decide which one is the best, the divisive approach often requires heuristics to decide how to split each cluster. One possibility is to use a flat clustering algorithm to perform each split, for example K-Means (described in 12.2). Here we adopt the simple divisive method by [MacNaughton-Smith et al., 1964], presented in [Kaufman and Rousseeuw, 1990] as producing good results within a reasonable amount of computational time. According to this method, the most disperse cluster is the one containing the largest pairwise distance, and the splitting of a cluster C is done by iteratively moving elements from C to a new cluster $NewC$, as follows.

Hierarchical divisive inner loop – split cluster

Initialization:	$NewC$ is empty.
In each iteration:	**1.** for each element in C, calculate average distance to the other elements in C;
	2. choose element i with largest average distance to the others, $avgC$;
	3. calculate average distance between i and the elements in $NewC$, $avgNewC$ (0 if $newC$ is empty);
	4. if $avgC > avgNewC$ move i from C to $NewC$.
Stop condition:	no element was moved in the last iteration.

Intuitively, an element of C moves to the new cluster $NewC$ if it is on average closer to the elements of $NewC$ than to the remaining elements of C.

Agglomerative and divisive approaches may produce different hierarchies of clusters from the same data. From the way they are designed, agglomerative is better at recognizing small clusters, while divisive is better at recognizing large ones. Both share the problem that the decisions taken at each step cannot be reverted in subsequent steps, but the divisive approach benefits from seeing the global distribution of the data, which may help in taking better initial decisions.

Agglomerative hierarchical clustering is a deterministic process, except when two or more pairs of clusters are at exactly the same distance, in which case the choice of which to merge should be random. Divisive hierarchical clustering may also choose randomly if faced with the same problem, but it may also be a completely stochastic process, depending on the procedure used for splitting the clusters.

Hierarchical clustering does not scale well with the size of the data, meaning that for large datasets a standard implementation will probably take an unreasonable amount of time to run and/or exhaust the computer memory due to the size of the distance matrix.

Hierarchical clustering provides a structured view of the clusters in a tree-like plot called a *dendrogram*. In a dendrogram, the pairs of clusters are connected by lines whose height (or length, depending on plot orientation) represents the distance between them (or difference in variance, with Ward's linkage). The dendrogram provides valuable information regarding the spatial arrangement of the data points. Because it allows visualization of the distances within and between clusters, regardless of the distance metric or the dimensionality of the feature space, it assists in the difficult task of deciding in how many clusters the data should be grouped. The dendrogram is normally "cut" where the links between the clusters are longer, meaning that these clusters are farther apart from each other, according to the linkage option used. After completing this task, it is common to disregard the hierarchical distances and retain only the flat partitioning of the data.

Table 12.1 shows a dataset with six observations, each described by four features. Next, we present three examples of hierarchical clustering on this small dataset, with step-by-step building of the clusters and dendrogram, using different splitting approaches (agglomerative and divisive), distance metrics (Euclidean and Manhattan) and linkage options (average and single).

12.1.1 Example 1 – Agglomerative Hierarchical Clustering, Euclidean Distance, Average Linkage

In this example, we perform agglomerative hierarchical clustering of the data in Table 12.1, using Euclidean distance and average linkage.

Table 12.1 Dataset with six observations and four features. We will freely use the term Obs followed by a number to identify either an observation or a cluster containing only that observation

	Feature 1	Feature 2	Feature 3	Feature 4
Observation 1	6	0	0	1
Observation 2	0	0	1	0
Observation 3	4	0	0	0
Observation 4	8	0	1	1
Observation 5	2	1	0	1
Observation 6	8	0	0	1

We begin with six clusters identified as Obs1, Obs2, Obs3, Obs4, Obs5, Obs6. In each iteration, in order to merge the two closest clusters, we need to known the pairwise distances between all the clusters, calculated according to the distance and linkage choices.

Iteration 1:

Distance between clusters Obs1 and Obs2:
$$d(Obs1,Obs2) = \sqrt{(6-0)^2 + (0-0)^2 + (0-1)^2 + (1-0)^2} = \sqrt{36+0+1+1} = \sqrt{38} \approx 6.2$$

Distance between clusters Obs1 and Obs3:
$$d(Obs1,Obs3) = \sqrt{(6-4)^2 + (0-0)^2 + (0-0)^2 + (1-0)^2} = \sqrt{4+0+0+1} = \sqrt{5} \approx 2.2$$

(...)

Notice that the linkage option is irrelevant so far, as all the clusters still have only one element each.

Distance matrix:

	Obs1	Obs2	Obs3	Obs4	Obs5	Obs6
Obs1		6.16	2.24	2.24	4.12	2.00
Obs2	6.16		4.12	8.06	2.65	8.12
Obs3	2.24	4.12		4.24	2.45	4.12
Obs4	2.24	8.06	4.24		6.16	1.00
Obs5	4.12	2.65	2.45	6.16		6.08
Obs6	2.00	8.12	4.12	1.00	6.08	

Clusters Obs4 and Obs6 are the closest clusters (distance 1.00), so they are merged in a single cluster identified as Obs4+Obs6. We now have five clusters: Obs1, Obs2, Obs3, Obs4+Obs6, Obs5.

The dendrogram is initialized like this, connecting Obs4 to Obs6 at height 1.00:

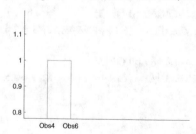

Iteration 2:

Distance between clusters Obs1 and Obs4+Obs6:
$$(d(Obs1,Obs4) + d(Obs1,Obs6))/2 = (2.24 + 2.00)/2 = 2.12$$

Distance between clusters Obs2 and Obs4+Obs6:
$$(d(Obs2,Obs4) + d(Obs2,Obs6))/2 = (8.06 + 8.12)/2 = 8.09$$

(...)

Distance matrix:

	Obs1	Obs2	Obs3	Obs4+Obs6	Obs5
Obs1		6.16	2.24	2.12	4.12
Obs2	6.16		4.12	8.09	2.65
Obs3	2.24	4.12		4.18	2.45
Obs4+Obs6	2.12	8.09	4.18		6.12
Obs5	4.12	2.65	2.45	6.12	

Clusters Obs1 and Obs4+Obs6 are the closest clusters (distance 2.12), so they are merged in a single cluster identified as Obs1+Obs4+Obs6, and we now have four clusters, Obs1+Obs4+Obs6, Obs2, Obs3, Obs5. The dendrogram now connects Obs1 to Obs4+Obs6 at height 2.12, like this:

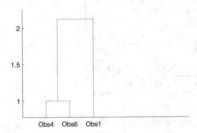

Iteration 3:

Distance between clusters Obs1+Obs4+Obs6 and Obs2:
$(d(Obs1, Obs2) + d(Obs4, Obs2) + d(Obs6, Obs2))/3 = (6.16 + 8.06 + 8.12)/3 \approx 7.45$

Distance between clusters Obs1+Obs4+Obs6 and Obs3:
$(d(Obs1, Obs3) + d(Obs4, Obs3) + d(Obs6, Obs3))/3 = (2.24 + 4.24 + 4.12)/3 \approx 3.53$

(...)

Distance matrix:

	Obs1+Obs4+Obs6	Obs2	Obs3	Obs5
Obs1+Obs4+Obs6		7.45	3.53	5.45
Obs2	7.45		4.12	2.65
Obs3	3.53	4.12		2.45
Obs5	5.45	2.65	2.45	

Clusters Obs3 and Obs5 are the closest clusters (distance 2.45), so they are merged as Obs3+Obs5, and we now have three clusters. The dendrogram now shows a connection between Obs3 and Obs5 at height 2.45, like this:

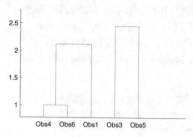

Iteration 4:

Distance between clusters Obs1+Obs4+Obs6 and Obs3+Obs5:
$(d(Obs1, Obs3) + d(Obs1, Obs5) + d(Obs4, Obs3) + d(Obs4, Obs5) + d(Obs6, Obs3) +$
$+d(Obs6, Obs5))/6 = (2.24 + 4.12 + 4.24 + 6.16 + 4.12 + 6.08)/6 \approx 4.49$

Distance between clusters Obs2 and Obs3+Obs5:
$(d(Obs2, Obs3) + d(Obs2, Obs5))/2 = (4.12 + 2.65)/2 \approx 3.39$

(...)

Distance matrix:

	Obs1+Obs4+Obs6	Obs2	Obs3+Obs5
Obs1+Obs4+Obs6		7.45	4.49
Obs2	7.45		3.39
Obs3+Obs5	4.49	3.39	

Clusters Obs2 and Obs3+Obs5 are merged and the dendrogram connects them at height 3.39:

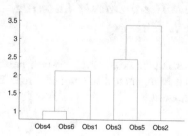

Iteration 5:

Distance between clusters Obs1+Obs4+Obs6 and Obs2+Obs3+Obs5:

$(d(Obs1, Obs2) + d(Obs1, Obs3) + d(Obs1, Obs5) + d(Obs4, Obs2) + d(Obs4, Obs3) +$
$+ d(Obs4, Obs5) + d(Obs6, Obs2) + d(Obs6, Obs3) + d(Obs6, Obs5))/9$
$= (6.16 + 2.24 + 4.12 + 8.06 + 4.24 + 6.16 + 8.12 + 4.12 + 6.08)/9 \approx 5.48$

Distance matrix:

	Obs1+Obs4+Obs6	Obs2+Obs3+Obs5
Obs1+Obs4+Obs6		5.48
Obs2+Obs3+Obs5	5.48	

The two clusters are merged and connected in the dendrogram at height 5.48. The clustering algorithm has reached its stop condition.

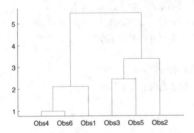

The dendrogram is a faithful representation of the clustering process we just saw, clearly suggesting the existence of two clusters with three elements each, where one of the clusters contains two elements that are very similar (cluster Obs1+Obs4+Obs6, with Obs4 and Obs6 connected at very low height) and the other cluster is more disperse (cluster Obs2+Obs3+Obs5, with higher connections). A horizontal cut at distance 4, for example, would establish these two clusters.

12.1.2 Example 2 – Agglomerative Hierarchical Clustering, Manhattan Distance, Single Linkage

Using the same dataset as the previous example (Table 12.1), we now perform agglomerative hierarchical clustering using Manhattan distance and single linkage, showing all the steps and the final dendrogram.

Iteration 1:

Distance between clusters Obs1 and Obs2:

$d(Obs1, Obs2) = |6 - 0| + |0 - 0| + |0 - 1| + |1 - 0| = 6 + 0 + 1 + 1 = 8$

Distance between clusters Obs1 and Obs3:

$d(Obs1, Obs3) = |6-4| + |0-0| + |0-0| + |1-0| = 2+0+0+1 = 3$

(...)

Distance matrix:

	Obs1	Obs2	Obs3	Obs4	Obs5	Obs6
Obs1		8	3	3	5	2
Obs2	8		5	9	5	10
Obs3	3	5		6	4	5
Obs4	3	9	6		8	1
Obs5	5	5	4	8		7
Obs6	2	10	5	1	7	

Clusters Obs4 and Obs6 are, once again, the closest clusters (distance 1), so they are merged.

Iteration 2:

Distance between clusters Obs1 and Obs4+Obs6:

$min(d(Obs1, Obs4), d(Obs1, Obs6)) = min(3, 2) = 2$

Distance between clusters Obs2 and Obs4+Obs6:

$min(d(Obs2, Obs4), d(Obs2, Obs6)) = min(9, 10) = 9$

(...)

Distance matrix:

	Obs1	Obs2	Obs3	Obs4+Obs6	Obs5
Obs1		8	3	2	5
Obs2	8		5	9	5
Obs3	3	5		5	4
Obs4+Obs6	2	9	5		7
Obs5	5	5	4	7	

Clusters Obs1 and Obs4+Obs6 are the closest clusters (distance 2), so they are merged. So far, the process is obtaining the same clustering as the previous example, with practically the same distances, despite using different distance and linkage options.

Iteration 3:

Distance between clusters Obs1+Obs4+Obs6 and Obs2:
$min(d(Obs1, Obs2), d(Obs4, Obs2), d(Obs6, Obs2)) = min(8, 9, 10) = 8$

Distance between clusters Obs1+Obs4+Obs6 and Obs3:
$min(d(Obs1, Obs3), d(Obs4, Obs3), d(Obs6, Obs3)) = min(3, 6, 5) = 3$

(...)

Distance matrix:

	Obs1+Obs4+Obs6	Obs2	Obs3	Obs5
Obs1+Obs4+Obs6		8	3	5
Obs2	8		5	5
Obs3	3	5		4
Obs5	5	5	4	

Clusters Obs1+Obs4+Obs6 and Obs3 are the closest clusters (distance 3), so they are merged. This differs from what we obtained in the previous example.

Iteration 4:

Distance between clusters Obs1+Obs3+Obs4+Obs6 and Obs2:
$min(d(Obs1, Obs2), d(Obs3, Obs2), d(Obs4, Obs2), d(Obs6, Obs2)) = min(8, 5, 9, 10) = 5$

(...)

Distance matrix:

	Obs1+Obs3+Obs4+Obs6	Obs2	Obs5
Obs1+Obs3+Obs4+Obs6		5	4
Obs2	5		5
Obs5	4	5	

Clusters Obs1+Obs3+Obs4+Obs6 and Obs5 are the closest clusters (distance 4), so they are merged.

Iteration 5:

Distance between clusters Obs1+Obs3+Obs4+Obs5+Obs6 and Obs2:
$min(d(Obs1, Obs2), d(Obs3, Obs2), d(Obs4, Obs2), d(Obs5, Obs2), d(Obs6, Obs2)) =$

$$= min(8,5,9,5,10) = 5$$

Distance matrix:

	Obs1+Obs3+Obs4+Obs5+Obs6	Obs2
Obs1+Obs3+Obs4+Obs5+Obs6		5
Obs2	5	

The two clusters are merged (distance 5) and the process reaches its stop condition, with the final dendrogram:

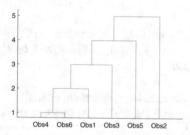

This dendrogram is very different from the one obtained in the first example, showing only a sequential joining of elements to the same cluster. This is known as the chaining effect, and is fairly common with single linkage. In some cases the chaining effect may be useful for recognizing elongated clusters (as illustrated in Section 12.4), but in this case it produced a useless result. Manhattan distance with average linkage would have produced basically the same dendrogram as the first example, in the previous section.

12.1.3 Example 3 – Divisive Hierarchical Clustering, MacNaughton-Smith et al. Method

Using the same dataset as the previous examples (Table 12.1), we now perform divisive hierarchical clustering using the MacNaughton-Smith et al. [MacNaughton-Smith et al., 1964] splitting method, based on Euclidean distance.

We begin with only one cluster containing all six observations. In each iteration, we choose to split the most disperse cluster, defined as the one with the largest pairwise distance between its elements. All pairwise Euclidean distances can be found in the first distance matrix of Example 1 in 12.1.1.

Iteration 1:

The most disperse cluster is the only one that exists, containing the largest pairwise distance of 8.12, between Obs2 and Obs6.

C is Obs1+Obs2+Obs3+Obs4+Obs5+Obs6;
$NewC$ is empty.

Iteration 1.1:

Average distance between Obs1 and the remaining observations in C:
$(d(Obs1, Obs2) + d(Obs1, Obs3) + d(Obs1, Obs4) + d(Obs1, Obs5) + d(Obs1, Obs6))/5$
$= (6.16 + 2.24 + 2.24 + 4.12 + 2.00)/5 \approx 3.35$

Average distance between Obs2 and the remaining observations in C:
$(d(Obs2, Obs1) + d(Obs2, Obs3) + d(Obs2, Obs4) + d(Obs2, Obs5) + d(Obs2, Obs6))/5$
$= (6.16 + 4.12 + 8.06 + 2.65 + 8.12)/5 \approx 5.82$

(...)

Average distances:

Obs1	3.35
Obs2	5.82
Obs3	3.43
Obs4	4.34
Obs5	4.29
Obs6	4.26

Obs2 is at the largest average distance (5.82) from the other observations in C, so it is moved to $NewC$.

C is Obs1+Obs3+Obs4+Obs5+Obs6;
$NewC$ is Obs2.

Iteration 1.2:

Average distance between Obs1 and the remaining observations in C:
$(d(Obs1, Obs3) + d(Obs1, Obs4) + d(Obs1, Obs5) + d(Obs1, Obs6))/4 \approx 2.65$

(...)

Average distances:

Obs1	2.65
Obs3	3.26
Obs4	3.41
Obs5	4.70
Obs6	3.30

Obs5 is at the largest average distance (4.70) from the other observations in C. The average of distances between Obs5 and the observations in $NewC$ (2.65) is smaller, so Obs5 is moved to $NewC$.

C is Obs1+Obs3+Obs4+Obs6;
$NewC$ is Obs2+Obs5.

Iteration 1.3:

Average distances:

Obs1	2.16
Obs3	3.53
Obs4	3.24
Obs6	2.37

Obs3 is at the largest average distance (3.53) from the other observations in C. The average of distances between Obs3 and the observations in $NewC$ (3.29) is smaller, so Obs3 is moved to $NewC$.

C is Obs1+Obs4+Obs6;
$NewC$ is Obs2+Obs3+Obs5.

Iteration 1.4:

Average distances:

Obs1	2.12
Obs4	1.62
Obs6	1.50

Obs1 is at the largest average distance (2.12) from the other observations in C.

The average of distances between Obs1 and the observations in *NewC* (4.17) is larger, so no observation is moved and the stop condition (of the inner loop) has been reached.

We now have two clusters, Obs1+Obs4+Obs6 and Obs2+Obs3+Obs5.

Iteration 2:

The most disperse cluster is Obs2+Obs3+Obs5, with the largest pairwise distance (4.12, between Obs2 and Obs3) higher than the largest pairwise distance in Obs1+Obs4+Obs6 (2.24, between Obs1 and Obs4).

C is Obs2+Obs3+Obs5;
NewC is empty.

Iteration 2.1:

Average distances:	
Obs2	3.39
Obs3	3.29
Obs5	2.55

Obs2 is at the largest average distance (3.29) from the other observations in *C*, so it is moved to *NewC*.

C is Obs3+Obs5;
NewC is Obs2.

Iteration 2.2:

Average distances:	
Obs3	2.45
Obs5	2.45

Obviously the two distances are the same, and smaller than the distance to the only element in *NewC*, therefore no observation is moved and we stop the inner loop.

We now have three clusters: Obs1+Obs4+Obs6, Obs2, Obs3+Obs5.

Iteration 3:

The most disperse cluster is Obs3+Obs5, with the distance 2.45 between Obs3 and Obs5. With only two elements, the cluster is trivially split in two.

We now have four clusters: Obs1+Obs4+Obs6, Obs2, Obs3, Obs5.

Iteration 4:

The most disperse cluster is Obs1+Obs4+Obs6, the only one remaining that can still be split (distance 2.24 between Obs1 and Obs4).

C is Obs1+Obs4+Obs6;
$NewC$ is empty.

Iteration 4.1:

Average distances:	
Obs1	2.12
Obs4	1.62
Obs6	1.50

Obs1 is at the largest average distance (2.12) from the other observations in C, so it is moved to $NewC$.

C is Obs4+Obs6;
$NewC$ is Obs1.

Iteration 4.2:

Average distances:	
Obs4	1.00
Obs6	1.00

The two distances are the same, and smaller than the distance to the only element in *NewC*, therefore no observation is moved and we stop the inner loop.

We now have five clusters: Obs1, Obs4+Obs6, Obs2, Obs3, Obs5.

Iteration 5:

The most disperse cluster is Obs4+Obs6, the only one remaining that can still be split (distance 1.00 between Obs4 and Obs6). With only two elements, the cluster is trivially split in two.

We now have six clusters, each one containing only one observation.

The dendrogram obtained is the same as the final dendrogram of Example 1 (Section 12.1.1). However, as in [Kaufman and Rousseeuw, 1990], now the height of the connections is the largest pairwise distance inside the cluster.

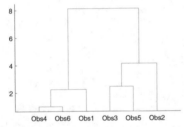

Cutting this dendrogram at height 6, for example, would result in the same two clusters found in the first example.

12.2 Centroid-Based Clustering

K-Means is probably the best-known clustering algorithm. It relies on the notion of *centroid* to assign each observation to a cluster. The centroid of a cluster is a point that represents the average element of that cluster. Its coordinates in the feature space are the mean values of the respective features of all the observations that belong to the cluster.

After placing a predefined number of random points in the feature space, representing the centroids of hypothetical clusters, K-Means repeatedly assigns each observation to the nearest centroid and then relocates the centroids based on these assignments, until none of the assignments changes. This process minimizes intra-cluster variance, i.e., the sum of squared Euclidean distances between the centroid and the elements of the cluster. It does not guarantee to find the global optimum.

K-Means	
Initialization:	k random points are placed in the n-dimensional feature space, representing the centroids of the k clusters to form.
In each iteration:	**1. assignment step:** each observation is assigned to its nearest centroid;
	2. update step: the location of the k centroids is updated according to the new assignments (if new assignments are different from old ones).
Stop condition:	none of the assignments changed in the last iteration.

The stop condition above is the ideal situation when the algorithm converges to a stable set of clusters. However, in practice there must be a maximum number of iterations after which the process stops, to avoid excessive running times due to slow convergence. Convergence may even be impossible because, as in hierarchical clustering, sometimes a random decision is needed when there is more than one right choice. In the case of K-Means, this happens whenever an observation is at the exact same distance from more than one centroid.

Regardless of this occasional nondeterministic behavior, K-Means is a stochastic algorithm because of its random initialization. Different initial centroids may result in wildly different clusterings of the same data, and some of these clusterings may be very low quality due to an unfortunate choice of the initial random centroids. One such example is illustrated in Figure 12.1, where the final clustering completely fails to describe the real distribution of the data. In order to mitigate this problem, the initial points should be well spread in the feature space. One such alternative initialization, called *k-means++*, does exactly this. Unlike in normal initialization, the initial centroids are chosen among the points of the dataset. The first centroid is chosen randomly, and each of the others is chosen with probability proportional to its distance from the closest centroid already chosen. It is possible for a cluster to find itself without any assigned data point, which may suggest a bad location of the initial centroids. If this happens often, it may even suggest a wrong choice of k, the number of clusters to form.

Concerning the number of clusters k, the main handicap of K-Means is the need to choose this important setting before running the algorithm. Without *a priori* knowledge about the data, this may be a guessing game. It may be useful to run hierarchical clustering on at least a subset of the data, in an attempt to visualize the "natural" number of clusters in the dendrogram, or at least a good approximation. A trial-and-error procedure may then be adopted, where different settings of k are used, and the quality of each clustering is measured to help the decision. Some implementations of K-Means do this automatically. Either way, it is always a good idea to run K-Means several times, and choose the best clustering according to some evaluation measure. Section 12.6 will briefly describe some possible ways to evaluate the quality of a clustering.

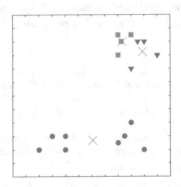

Fig. 12.1 Example of a poor clustering. The centroids are the crosses.

By the very definition of cluster centroid, K-Means assumes that clusters are (hyper)spherical, and is meant to be used with Euclidean distance (although some variants, like the Mahalanobis distance, are also meaningful). For different distance metrics, the related K-Medoids algorithm should be used instead. In K-Medoids, each cluster is represented by a *medoid*, a point from the dataset whose average distance to the other elements of the same cluster is minimal. K-Medoids minimizes the sum of pairwise distances between the medoid and the other elements of the cluster, and also does not guarantee convergence to a global optimum. Other algorithms produce clustering results very similar to those of K-Means. In Section 12.5 we will take a brief look at clustering with unsupervised neural networks.

Table 12.2 shows a dataset with 10 observations, each described by two features. Figure 12.2 represents this dataset as a scatter plot. We invite the reader to observe the distribution of the data points and picture a few alternative clusterings of this data. Next, we present one example of K-Means clustering of this dataset with $k = 3$, with step-by-step assignments and updates. Then we illustrate the effect that random initializations have on the quality of the clusters formed, with $k = 2, 3, 4$. Finally, we perform a small study of the effect that different initializations (normal and k-means++) have on the diversity and distribution of the clusterings obtained, with $k = 3$.

12.2.1 Example – K-Means Clustering, $k = 3$

In this example, we perform K-Means clustering of the data in Table 12.2, using $k = 3$.

We begin with three random points within the boundaries of the feature space, representing the centroids: $c1 = (4.5, 5.5), c2 = (2.0, 3.0), c3 = (5.0, 4.0)$.

Table 12.2 Dataset with 10 observations and two features. We will freely use the term Obs followed by a number to identify either an observation or a cluster containing only that observation

	Feature 1	Feature 2
Observation 1	2.0	3.5
Observation 2	2.5	3.0
Observation 3	2.0	4.0
Observation 4	2.5	3.5
Observation 5	3.0	5.0
Observation 6	4.0	4.0
Observation 7	4.0	3.0
Observation 8	3.5	2.5
Observation 9	3.5	4.5
Observation 10	5.0	6.0

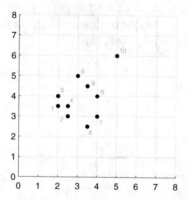

Fig. 12.2 Representation of the data points in Table 12.2

Iteration 1:

Assignment step:

Euclidean distance between Obs1 and $c1$:
$$d(Obs1, c1) = \sqrt{(2.0 - 4.5)^2 + (3.5 - 5.5)^2}$$

(...)

Distances between observations and centroids, with minimum distances in bold, and graphical representation of assigned points and centroid locations:

		$c1$ (4.5,5.5)	$c2$ (2.0,3.0)	$c3$ (5.0,4.0)
Obs1	(2.0,3.5)	3.20	**0.50**	3.04
Obs2	(2.5,3.0)	3.20	**0.50**	2.69
Obs3	(2.0,4.0)	2.92	**1.00**	3.00
Obs4	(2.5,3.5)	2.83	**0.71**	2.55
Obs5	(3.0,5.0)	**1.58**	2.24	2.24
Obs6	(4.0,4.0)	1.58	2.24	**1.00**
Obs7	(4.0,3.0)	2.55	2.00	**1.41**
Obs8	(3.5,2.5)	3.16	**1.58**	2.12
Obs9	(3.5,4.5)	**1.41**	2.12	1.58
Obs10	(5.0,6.0)	**0.71**	4.24	2.00

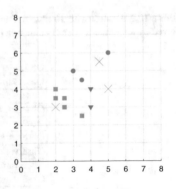

Update step:
$$c1 = ((3.5+3.0+5.0)/3, (4.5+5.0+6.0)/3) = (11.5/3, 15.5/3) = (3.8, 5.2)$$
$$c2 = ((2.0+2.5+2.0+2.5+3.5)/5, (3.5+3.0+4.0+3.5+2.5)/5) = (2.5, 3.3)$$
$$c3 = ((4.0+4.0)/2, (4.0+3.0)/2) = (4.0, 3.5)$$

Iteration 2:

Assignment step:

		$c1$ (3.8,5.2)	$c2$ (2.5,3.3)	$c3$ (4.0,3.5)
Obs1	(2.0,3.5)	2.48	**0.54**	2.00
Obs2	(2.5,3.0)	2.56	**0.30**	1.58
Obs3	(2.0,4.0)	2.16	**0.86**	2.06
Obs4	(2.5,3.5)	2.14	**0.20**	1.50
Obs5	(3.0,5.0)	**0.82**	1.77	1.80
Obs6	(4.0,4.0)	1.22	1.66	**0.50**
Obs7	(4.0,3.0)	2.21	1.53	**0.50**
Obs8	(3.5,2.5)	2.72	1.28	**1.12**
Obs9	(3.5,4.5)	**0.76**	1.56	1.12
Obs10	(5.0,6.0)	**1.44**	3.68	2.69

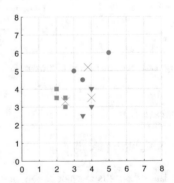

Update step:
$$c1 = (3.8, 5.2) \text{ (no change)}$$
$$c2 = ((2.0+2.5+2.0+2.5)/4, (3.5+3.0+4.0+3.5)/4) = (2.3, 3.5)$$
$$c3 = ((4.0+4.0+3.5)/3, (4.0+3.0+2.5)/3) = (3.8, 3.2)$$

Iteration 3:

Assignment step:

	c1 (3.8,5.2)	c2 (2.3,3.5)	c3 (3.8,3.2)
Obs1 (2.0,3.5)	2.48	**0.30**	1.82
Obs2 (2.5,3.0)	2.56	**0.54**	1.32
Obs3 (2.0,4.0)	2.16	**0.58**	1.97
Obs4 (2.5,3.5)	2.14	**0.20**	1.33
Obs5 (3.0,5.0)	**0.82**	1.66	1.97
Obs6 (4.0,4.0)	1.22	1.77	**0.82**
Obs7 (4.0,3.0)	2.21	1.77	**0.28**
Obs8 (3.5,2.5)	2.72	1.56	**0.76**
Obs9 (3.5,4.5)	**0.76**	1.56	1.33
Obs10 (5.0,6.0)	**1.44**	3.68	3.05

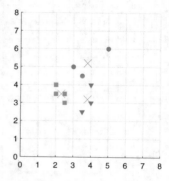

Cluster assignments did not change, so the process reaches its stop condition.

Final centroids:
$c1 = (3.8, 5.2)$
$c2 = (2.3, 3.5)$
$c3 = (3.8, 3.2)$

12.2.2 The Effect of Stochastic Initialization

Figure 12.3 shows examples of different clusterings of the data in Table 12.2 obtained with the K-Means algorithm with normal random initialization of centroids and different settings for the number of clusters ($k = 2, 3, 4$). The purpose is to illustrate the large differences in the quality of the different clusterings obtained. We use our own (necessarily subjective) judgment to qualify each clustering as 'good' or 'bad'. For $k = 3$, the good and bad clusterings are the same as clusterings 9 and 7 (respectively) in the top plot of Figure 12.4 (k-means++ initialization) and the same as clusterings 7 and 5 in the bottom plot of the same figure (random initialization). Therefore, the clusterings qualified as bad appeared more often than the ones qualified as good.

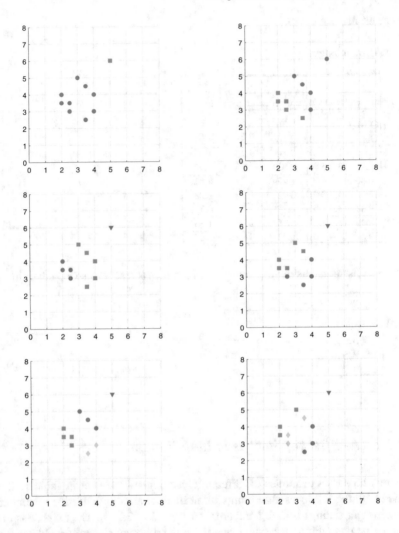

Fig. 12.3 Examples of good (left) and bad (right) clusterings performed by K-Means with $k = 2$ (top), $k = 3$ (middle) and $k = 4$ (bottom)

12.2.3 Random Versus K-means++ Initialization with $k = 3$

Still using the 10 data points in Table 12.2, we have run K-Means with $k = 3$ one thousand times with random initialization, and one thousand times with k-means++ initialization, in order to observe the diversity and distribution of the resulting clusterings. With 10 points, there are 120 possible initializations with k-means++. Given the relative distance between the data points, some combinations of initial centroids are much more probable than others, so it is expected that some final cluster assignments will appear much more often than others. In our experiments, the 10 points clustered 1000 times (with k-means++) produced 20 different clusterings, with a strong preference for a particular clustering that appeared more than 200 times, while eight other clusterings appeared more than 50 times each (Figure 12.4, top). With random initialization instead of k-means++, there is more freedom in the choice of the initial centroids, and an even higher diversity of clusterings was obtained (close to 30), but the preferences are more concentrated on a small group of clusterings, with two appearing more than 200 times each, another appearing more than 150 times, and only one other that appeared more than 50 times (Figure 12.4, bottom).

The most preferred clustering with k-means++ initialization is the same as one of the two most preferred clusterings with random initialization (Figure 12.5, most preferred clustering on the left). This clustering is therefore the most common clustering found by K-Means in this dataset, and yet it is found only 23% of the time with k-means++ initialization and 20% of the time with random initialization. The other most preferred clustering with random initialization (Figure 12.5, on the right) is one of the second most preferred clusterings with k-means++ initialization, found 12% of the time.

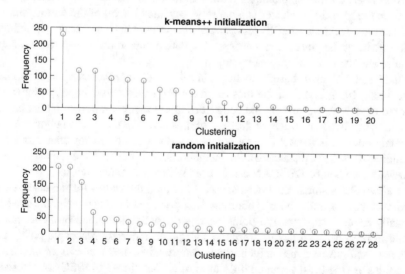

Fig. 12.4 Frequency of different clusterings in 1000 trials of K-Means, with k-means++ initialization (top) and random initialization (bottom). The numbers do not identify the same clusterings in both plots

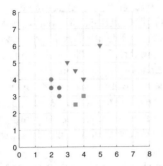 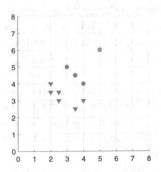

Fig. 12.5 The two most common clusterings found with random initialization of K-Means. The clustering on the left is also the most commonly found with k-means++ initialization

12.3 Density-Based Clustering

Density-based clustering emulates human intuition when forming clusters. It is based on the idea that a cluster is a densely populated region of the feature space, separated from other clusters by less populated regions. This imposes no restrictions on the shape of the clusters, and accepts that data points in the sparse regions may be noise and therefore may remain unclustered.

DBSCAN (Density-based spatial clustering of applications with noise) [Ester et al., 1996] is one of the most used density-based clustering algorithms. In order to explain it, we rely on the concept of *dense neighborhood* of a data point, defined by the two parameters of the algorithm, ε and *minPoints*. The neighborhood of a data point A is the set of data points at a distance no greater than ε from A (including A itself, at distance 0); this neighborhood is dense if it contains at least *minPoints* data points. DBSCAN can be used with any distance metric.

In a two-dimensional Euclidean space, ε is called the *radius* (of the circle centered at A that delimits the neighborhood). A point with a dense neighborhood is normally called a *core point*; a point inside a dense neighborhood of a core point is said to be *density reachable* from the core point; a density reachable point that does not itself have a dense neighborhood is normally called a *border point*. These definitions are the most common ones in most explanations of DBSCAN, but they are not needed for our explanation of the algorithm.

DBSCAN involves two nested loops. The outer loop cycles through all data points, skipping the ones already assigned to a cluster, and calls the inner loop to form a new cluster for each unassigned data point that has a dense neighborhood. Points without a dense neighborhood are temporarily marked as noise, and later they can be assigned a cluster or permanently remain as noise.

DBSCAN outer loop

Initialization:	no clusters exist; *points-to-visit* = all data points.
In each iteration:	**1.** choose next unassigned data point from *points-to-visit* and find its neighborhood; **2.** if the neighborhood is dense, form new cluster, otherwise mark point as noise.
Stop condition:	all unassigned data points in *points-to-visit* have been visited.

Intuitively, the outer loop finds all the dense regions in the feature space, while the inner loop forms a new cluster with each of them. A new cluster begins with a single data point, and then recursively grows by adding the points in its dense neighborhood, and points in their respective dense neighborhoods, and so on, until no more dense neighborhoods are reachable.

DBSCAN inner loop – form new cluster

Initialization:	the data point A (from outer loop) is assigned to a new cluster C; *neighbors-to-visit* = all unassigned points in the dense neighborhood of A;
In each iteration:	**1.** choose one unassigned point from *neighbors-to-visit* (in no particular order) and assign it to cluster C; **2.** if point was not noise, find its neighborhood, otherwise skip the next step; **3.** if neighborhood is dense, add all its unassigned neighbors to *neighbors-to-visit*.
Stop condition:	all data points in *neighbors-to-visit* have been assigned.

Together, the two parameters of DBSCAN, ε and *minPoints*, determine the density of points that is needed for a region to be considered part of a cluster, instead of remaining as noise. Although a very successful algorithm, DBSCAN poses the problem of choosing parameter values that produce a meaningful clustering, a similar problem to choosing the number of clusters in K-Means. Once again, hierarchical clustering may be helpful for visualizing the structure of the data and apprehending the distances between data points, a valuable aid in estimating the size and density of the clusters. Another problem is that different clusters may have different densities, and therefore it may be impossible for DBSCAN to recognize them all using any single choice of parameters.

Some alternatives to DBSCAN address this problem. The OPTICS (Ordering points to identify the clustering structure) [Ankerst et al., 1999] algorithm is closely related to DBSCAN, but instead of assigning points to clusters, it orders them by a particular *reachability distance* criterion. The ordered points can reveal a hierarchy of clusters when visualized in a plot called a *reachability plot*. OPTICS relies on the value of the minimum radius that includes *minPoints* data points. Because this value may be different for each data point, it can detect clusters of different densities. Furthermore, the usefulness of the reachability plot is not seriously affected by the parameter settings. In the limit, ε can be very large and *minPoints* can be very small, and the OPTICS algorithm may still reveal a decent clustering. Hierarchical DBSCAN (HDBSCAN) [Campello et al., 2013] also builds a hierarchy of clusters in dealing with clusters of different densities. It replaces the ε parameter by a more intuitive one, that is the minimum cluster size (in terms of number of elements). Unlike OPTICS, it automatically chooses the best clustering based on the hierarchy.

DBSCAN is a deterministic algorithm, although it may produce slightly different results if the ordering of the data points is changed. In the example we show next, where we apply DBSCAN to the 10 data points of Table 12.2 using *minPoints* = 3 and ε = 1, all the 3,628,800 possible orderings of the 10 data points result in the exact same clustering. We also show the DBSCAN results on the same data when using different settings.

12.3.1 *Example – DBSCAN Clustering, minPoints* = 3 *and* ε = 1

In this example, we apply DBSCAN to the data in Table 12.2, with the settings *minPoints* = 3 and ε = 1. We begin with no clusters formed (Figure 12.6a), and all points yet to be visited:

points-to-visit = {Obs1, Obs2, ..., Obs10}.

Iteration 1:

Choose next unassigned data point from *points-to-visit*: Obs1.
Neighborhood of Obs1 is all points at distance $\leq \varepsilon$ from Obs1.
Neighborhood of Obs1 = {Obs1, Obs2, Obs3, Obs4}.

Number of points in neighborhood is 4, therefore $\geq$ *minPoints*.
Neighborhood is dense, so form a new cluster:

Assign Obs1 to new cluster C1 (Figure 12.6b, C1 points represented as red circles). The neighbors to visit are all unassigned points in the (dense) neighborhood of Obs1:

neighbors-to-visit = {Obs2, Obs3, Obs4}.

Iteration 1.1:

Choose one unassigned point from *neighbors-to-visit*: Obs2.
Assign Obs2 to cluster C1 (Figure 12.6c).

Obs2 was not previously marked as noise, so find its neighborhood.
Neighborhood of Obs2 = {Obs1, Obs2, Obs3, Obs4}.

Number of points in neighborhood is $\geq$ *minPoints*.
Neighborhood is dense, so add all its unassigned points to *neighbors-to-visit*

$$neighbors\text{-}to\text{-}visit = \{Obs2, Obs3, Obs4\} \cup \{Obs3, Obs4\} =$$
$$= \{Obs2, Obs3, Obs4\}.$$

Iteration 1.2:

Choose one unassigned point from *neighbors-to-visit*: Obs3.
Assign Obs3 to cluster C1 (Figure 12.6d).

Obs3 was not previously marked as noise, so find its neighborhood.
Neighborhood of Obs3 = {Obs1, Obs2, Obs3, Obs4}.

Number of points in neighborhood is $\geq$ *minPoints*.
Neighborhood is dense, so add all its unassigned points to *neighbors-to-visit*

$$neighbors\text{-}to\text{-}visit = \{Obs2, Obs3, Obs4\} \cup \{Obs4\} = \{Obs2, Obs3, Obs4\}.$$

Iteration 1.3:

Choose one unassigned point from *neighbors-to-visit*: Obs4.
Assign Obs4 to cluster C1 (Figure 12.6e).

Obs4 was not previously marked as noise, so find its neighborhood.
Neighborhood of Obs4 = {Obs4, Obs1, Obs2, Obs3}.

Number of points in neighborhood is $\geq$ *minPoints*.
Neighborhood is dense, so add all its unassigned points to *neighbors-to-visit*

$$neighbors\text{-}to\text{-}visit = \{Obs2, Obs3, Obs4\} \cup \{\} = \{Obs2, Obs3, Obs4\}.$$

All data points in *neighbors-to-visit* have been assigned, therefore cluster C1 is formed.

Iteration 2:

Choose next unassigned data point from *points-to-visit*: Obs5.
Neighborhood of Obs5 = {Obs5, Obs9}.

Number of points in neighborhood is 2, therefore < *minPoints*.
Neighborhood is not dense, so Obs5 is marked as noise (Figure 12.6f, noise points represented as open circles).

Iteration 3:

Choose next unassigned data point from *points-to-visit*: Obs6.
Neighborhood of Obs6 = {Obs6, Obs7, Obs9}.

Number of points in neighborhood is 3, therefore ≥ *minPoints*.
Neighborhood is dense, so form a new cluster:

Assign Obs6 to new cluster C2 (Figure 12.6g, C2 points represented as green squares). The neighbors to visit are all unassigned points in the (dense) neighborhood of Obs6:

   neighbors-to-visit = {Obs7, Obs9}.

Iteration 3.1:

Choose one unassigned point from *neighbors-to-visit*: Obs7.
Assign Obs7 to cluster C2 (Figure 12.6h).

Obs7 was not previously marked as noise, so find its neighborhood.
Neighborhood of Obs7 = {Obs6, Obs7, Obs8}.

Number of points in neighborhood is ≥ *minPoints*.
Neighborhood is dense, so add all its unassigned points to *neighbors-to-visit*

neighbors-to-visit = {Obs7, Obs9} ∪ {Obs8} = {Obs7, Obs8, Obs9}.

Iteration 3.2:

Choose one unassigned point from *neighbors-to-visit*: Obs8.
Assign Obs8 to cluster C2 (Figure 12.6i).

Obs8 was not previously marked as noise, so find its neighborhood.
Neighborhood of Obs8 = {Obs7, Obs8}.

Number of points in neighborhood is < *minPoints*.
Neighborhood is not dense, therefore do nothing.

neighbors-to-visit = {Obs7, Obs8, Obs9} (unchanged).

Iteration 3.3:

Choose one unassigned point from *neighbors-to-visit*: Obs9.
Assign Obs9 to cluster C2 (Figure 12.6j).

Obs9 was not previously marked as noise, so find its neighborhood.
Neighborhood of Obs9 = {Obs5, Obs6, Obs9}.

Number of points in neighborhood is ≥ *minPoints*.
Neighborhood is dense, so add all its unassigned points to *neighbors-to-visit*

neighbors-to-visit = {Obs7, Obs8, Obs9} ∪ {Obs5} =
= {Obs5, Obs7, Obs8, Obs9}.

Iteration 3.4:

Choose one unassigned point from *neighbors-to-visit*: Obs5.
Assign Obs5 to cluster C2 (Figure 12.6k).

Obs5 was previously marked as noise, therefore do nothing else.
neighbors-to-visit = {Obs5, Obs7, Obs8, Obs9} (unchanged).

All data points in *neighbors-to-visit* have been assigned, therefore cluster C2 is formed.

Iteration 4:

Choose next unassigned data point from *points-to-visit*: Obs10.
Neighborhood of Obs10 = {Obs10}.

Number of points in neighborhood is 1, therefore $< minPoints$.
Neighborhood is not dense, so Obs10 is marked as noise (Figure 12.6l).

All data points in *points-to-visit* have been visited, therefore the process stops. Obs10 remains unassigned to any cluster.

12.3.2 DBSCAN Clustering with Different Settings

In Figure 12.7 we show the clusterings obtained by DBSCAN when using $\varepsilon = 0.75$ and *minPoints* $= 3$ (left), and when using $\varepsilon = 0.75$ and *minPoints* $= 2$ (right).

Notice how decreasing the radius of the neighborhood (ε) prevents additional points from being assigned to a cluster (left), and how decreasing the number of points required for a dense neighborhood allows the formation of an additional cluster (right).

12.4 Hierarchical Clustering Versus K-Means and DBSCAN

Here we observe how hierarchical clustering behaves with the 10 data points of Table 12.2, and how its hierarchy of clusters compares with the results obtained by K-Means and DBSCAN.

Figure 12.8 shows the dendrograms produced by agglomerative hierarchical clustering with single linkage (left) and with average linkage (right), both using Euclidean distance. The dendrogram on the left is a good example of how single linkage is useful for identifying elongated clusters (also notice the many mergings done at the same distance). The hierarchy it shows is a faithful representation of what was observed in the examples of DBSCAN clustering, with the first four points forming an obvious first cluster, then the next five points forming one or two clusters, and finally the last point appearing to be an outlier. The dendrogram on the right also shows a hierarchy where the first four points form an obvious cluster, and the last point appears isolated. However, the five points in the middle now form two well-separated clusters that do not merge. If this dendrogram is cut such that four clusters

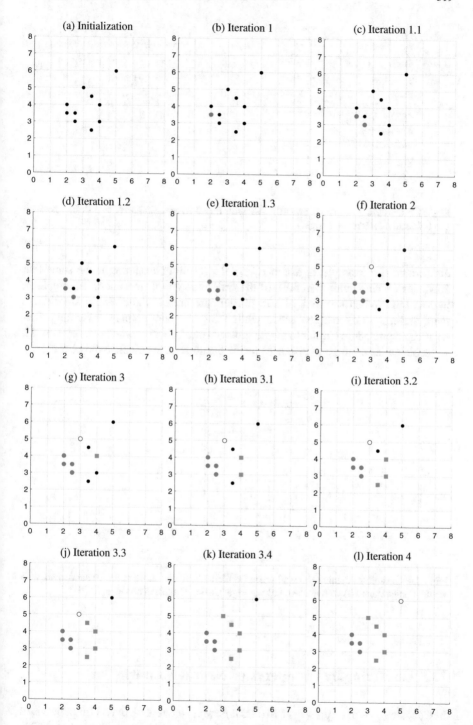

Fig. 12.6 All steps of DBSCAN applied to the data in Table 12.2, with parameters $\varepsilon = 1$ and $minPoints = 3$

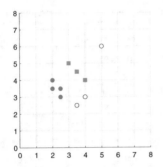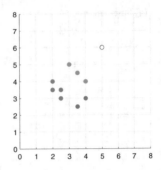

Fig. 12.7 Clusterings obtained by DBSCAN with $\varepsilon = 0.75$ and *minPoints* $= 3$ (left), and with $\varepsilon = 0.75$ and *minPoints* $= 2$ (right)

are formed (for example, at distance 1.5), the resulting clustering is the same that K-Means obtains more than 50% of the time with $k = 4$ (the one in Figure 12.3, bottom left). When we think of how clusters are built in the different algorithms, these findings make complete sense: while DBSCAN adds points to a forming cluster using a procedure similar to single linkage (most obvious when *minPoints* $= 1$), K-Means relies on average distances inside the clusters to calculate the centroids.

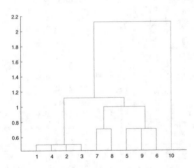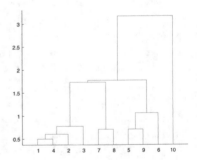

Fig. 12.8 Clusterings obtained by agglomerative hierarchical clustering of the 10 data points with single linkage (left) and with average linkage (right), using Euclidean distance

12.5 Clustering by Unsupervised Neural Networks

In Chapter 7, we have presented Artificial Neural Networks (ANNs) for supervised learning, and in particular for classification tasks. Now we study the use of ANNs for unsupervised learning, specifically for clustering tasks. Several ANNs perform unsupervised learning. In this book, we study:

- Competitive Learning Neural Networks (CLNNs);
- Kohonen neural networks (or Self-Organizing Maps – SOMs).

Given that SOMs can be seen as an extension of CLNNs, our analysis begins with a presentation of CLNNs. For a deeper look at both these types of ANNs, the reader is referred to the book [Kohonen et al., 2001].

12.5.1 Competitive Learning Neural Networks

The architecture of CLNNs is shown in Figure 12.9, where the number of inputs n is equal to the number of input variables, or features, of the data, while the number of output neurons m is equal to the number of clusters into which we want to group the data. As in K-Means, this number has to be known *a priori*.

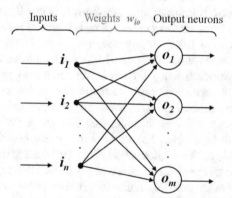

Fig. 12.9 The architecture of a Competitive Learning Neural Network (CLNN)

The functioning of a CLNN is very simple: whenever an input vector $\mathbf{x}$ is presented to the network, the network elects a *winner* among the output neurons. The network works in such a way that input vectors $\mathbf{x}$ belonging to the same cluster will produce the same output neuron as winner. The winner output neuron is decided in the following way: for each output neuron o, let $\mathbf{w}_o$ be the vector of the weights of the connections that enter o. For a given input vector $\mathbf{x}$, the output neuron k that is defined as the winner is the output neuron for which the distance (typically the Euclidean distance) of the weight vector $\mathbf{w}_k$ to the input vector $\mathbf{x}$ is minimal. In other words, an output neuron k is chosen as the winner if, for all output neurons o:

$$\|\mathbf{w}_k - \mathbf{x}\| \leq \|\mathbf{w}_o - \mathbf{x}\|$$

As is customary for any ANN, also for CLNNs the learning phase corresponds to a phase in which the weights of the synapses are modified. In particular, once the winner k has been chosen, only the weights of the connections entering k are modified, and they are modified in such a way that they get *even closer* to the input vector $\mathbf{x}$:

$$\mathbf{w}_k(t+1) = \mathbf{w}_k(t) + \eta\left(\mathbf{x}(t) - \mathbf{w}_k(t)\right)$$

where η is a learning rate constant similar to the one used by the other types of ANN that we have studied so far. In simple words, the neuron whose weights are closest to the input vector is chosen as winner, and its weights are further shifted towards the input vector itself.

CLNNs are one of the few ANNs for which a random initialization of the weights is inconvenient. It is not difficult to convince oneself of the reason why this is the case, if we reflect on the very functioning of the algorithm: in the end, we want the final weights to "resemble" (or if you prefer, to represent) input data. In particular, there should be a pattern of similarity in the final configuration of the net between the weights of the connection entering one neuron and the data belonging to the cluster that neuron represents. So, instead of beginning with random values, which would probably be rather different from the input data, and similarly to what we have already seen for other clustering algorithms, it is usually more convenient to select a subset of the input vectors $\{\mathbf{x}_1, \mathbf{x}_2, ..., \mathbf{x}_M\}$, where M is the number of output neurons and, for each $i = 1, 2, ..., M$, we assign $\mathbf{w}_i$ to the vector $\mathbf{x}_i$. But what input data should we choose for the initialization? It is not hard to understand that, in order to boost the network efficiency, the ideal situation would be if we were able to initialize each weight vector with one observation belonging to a different cluster. This action would be equivalent to already categorizing correctly those observations at the initialization step, relieving the algorithm from the job of finding the correct cluster for those input data. Given that we are dealing with an unsupervised learning problem, and so we do not have information about the labels of the observations, we need to approximate this situation as much as possible. Thinking that data coming from different clusters are probably rather diverse compared to each other, a common practice is to chose the M input vectors with the maximum diversity for the initialization of the weights, hoping that each one of those vectors will belong to a different cluster (notice the similarity to the k-means++ initialization, Section 12.2). This method is clearly more convenient than selecting M random input vectors with uniform distribution, because, for instance, if a high number of input vectors belonging to the same cluster exist, we risk selecting M observations belonging to the same cluster.

Figure 12.10 shows on a Cartesian plane (for simplicity we use a two-dimensional plane) the typical situation after the learning of a CLNN: at the end of the learning phase the weight vectors (represented by colored shapes in the figure) should represent the centroids of the various clusters (the training set points are represented by noncolored shapes in the figure). This result is no different from what would be obtained with K-Means. In fact, both CLNNs and SOMs perform a type of centroid-based clustering.

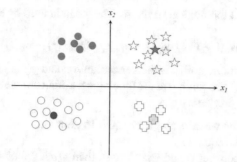

Fig. 12.10 A visualization of the typical situation after the learning of a CLNN: the weight vectors (represented as colored shapes here) approximate the centroids of the clusters

12.5.2 Self-Organizing Maps

Kohonen networks, or Self-Organizing Maps (SOMs), can be seen as an extension of the CLNNs described above. The main difference between SOMs and CLNNs is that in SOMs the output neurons are organized in a *topological structure* that is often a two-dimensional grid. In this way, it is possible to identify a neighborhood for the output neurons. The architecture of a SOM is shown in Figure 12.11.

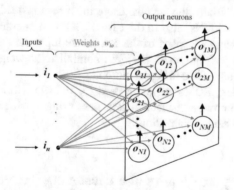

Fig. 12.11 The architecture of a Self-Organizing Map (SOM)

A SOM works in such a way that input vectors that are "close to each other" (in terms of Euclidean distance) will choose as winners output neurons that are "close to each other" (in the output neurons topology). Given an input vector, a winner output neuron is decided exactly as for CLNNs: the winner is the output neuron for which the distance between the vector of the weights of the entering connections and the input vector is minimal. The difference between SOMs and CLNNs is in the way weights are updated: in SOMs not only the weights of the connections entering the winner neuron are updated, but also the weights of all the other connections, and the *strength* of the modification is as large as the output neuron is near to the winner neuron in the output topological structure. The formula used by SOMs for updating weights is:

$$\mathbf{w}_o(t+1) = \mathbf{w}_o(t) + \eta \ g(o,k) \ (\mathbf{x}(t) - \mathbf{w}_o(t))$$

where o is any output neuron, k is the winner neuron and $g(o,k)$ is a function of the distance of neuron k to neuron o in the topological output structure. Function g must have the following properties:

- If the distance between o and k is equal to zero (i.e., $o = k$), then the value of $g(o,k)$ must be equal to 1.
- If the distance between o and k is "large", then $g(o,k)$ must be "small" (almost equal to 0).
- g must be monotonically decreasing.

In other words, if a neuron o is "far" from the winner neuron k in the topological output structure, then its weights do not have to be updated, or have to be updated only by a minimal amount. Neuron weights have to be modified more and more strongly as the neurons are nearer and nearer to the winner neuron in the output topology. An example of a g function is, for instance, the following Gaussian function:

$$g(o,k) = e^{-d(o,k)}$$

where $d(o,k)$ is the (Euclidean) distance between neuron o and neuron k in the output topology. As in CLNNs, and with exactly the same motivation, also in SOMs it is convenient to initialze the weights using input data instead of random values. Furthermore, as in CLNNs, also in the case of SOMs it is convenient, in order to maximize the convergence speed of the net, to use input data that are as different from each other as possible, in an attempt to initialize the weights of each neuron using a vector belonging to a different cluster.

Besides clustering, SOMs are often used for transformations (mapping) of n-dimensional data into two-dimensional data, preserving topological properties (useful, for instance, in data visualization).

12.6 Evaluating the Quality of a Clustering

The quality of a clustering can be evaluated using extrinsic or intrinsic criteria. Extrinsic criteria rely on external information that was not made available during the clustering process, for example, information regarding the intended structure of the clustering, such as the class of each observation. However, in a truly unsupervised setting, we must rely on intrinsic criteria that only use internal information about the clustering itself. Different intrinsic criteria exist, each reflecting a particular aspect that may be important for the quality of a clustering. The choice of which one to use may depend on the meaning of the data and the purpose of clustering it. When in doubt, different criteria should be used, and their evaluation scores compared.

It is important to choose criteria that are suited to the method used for performing the clustering. As an example, clusterings performed by K-Means should be evaluated with criteria that rely on Euclidean distance, centroids, diameters and related concepts, and not on something else that K-Means does not optimize. On the other hand, if appropriate criteria always return bad scores, regardless of the parametrization of K-Means, this may suggest the data does not contain spherical clusters, and therefore a different clustering algorithm should be used. Many times, evaluation of a clustering serves the sole purpose of choosing good parameters for the algorithm, notably the number of clusters. Next, we describe some common evaluation indices, also called validity indices, and some methods for decision making when it comes to choosing the best clustering.

12.6.1 Evaluation Criteria

All evaluation indices are based on the general idea that data points should be close to other points of the same cluster, and far from points of other clusters. Although these notions of *close* and *far* can be based on any type of similarity measure, normally they rely on conventional distance metrics. Most indices may not be appropriate for dealing with arbitrarily shaped clusters, or noisy unclustered data points like the ones that DBSCAN can identify.

Davies-Bouldin Index

The Davies-Bouldin index (DB) [Davies and Bouldin, 1979] measures the average similarity between each cluster and its most similar cluster (where k is the number of clusters):

$$DB = \frac{1}{k} \sum_{i=1}^{k} \max_{j, j \neq i} \{R_{ij}\}$$

R_{ij}, the similarity between two clusters C_i and C_j, is calculated as the ratio between the within-cluster dispersion of both clusters ($S_i + S_j$) and the distance between their centroids c_i and c_j ($d(c_i, c_j)$):

$$R_{ij} = \frac{S_i + S_j}{d(c_i, c_j)}$$

S_i, the dispersion within a cluster C_i, is the average distance between each of the N_i points of the cluster and the cluster centroid c_i:

$$S_i = \frac{1}{N_i} \sum_{x \in C_i} d(x, c_i)$$

The Davies-Bouldin index returns lower (better) scores when the clusters are less disperse and farther away from each other. The minimum score is zero. This index is only meaningful for convex clusters in Euclidean space.

Calinski-Harabasz Index

The Calinski-Harabasz index (CH) [Caliński and Harabasz, 1974], also called the 'variance ratio criterion', was initially developed as a grouping criterion to ensure that both agglomerative and divisive approaches to hierarchical clustering always produced the same results. This index is the ratio of overall between-cluster variance (SS_B) to overall within-cluster variance (SS_W), each normalized by its degrees of freedom (where N is the total number of points in the dataset):

$$CH = \frac{SS_B/(k-1)}{SS_W/(N-k)}$$

SS_B, the overall between-cluster variance, is defined as the sum of squared distances between each cluster centroid c_i and the centroid of the entire dataset c ($d^2(c_i,c)$), weighted by the number of points in the respective cluster (N_i):

$$SS_B = \sum_{i=1}^{k} N_i d^2(c_i,c)$$

SS_W, the overall within-cluster variance, is the sum of squared distances between each point in the dataset and the centroid c_i of the respective cluster C_i:

$$SS_W = \sum_{i=1}^{k} \sum_{x \in C_i} d^2(x,c_i)$$

The Calinski-Harabasz index returns higher (better) scores when the clusters are more dense and farther apart from each other. The score can be arbitrarily large. Like the DB index, it is also more appropriate for spherical clusters in Euclidean space.

Dunn index

The Dunn index (D) [Dunn, 1973] is the ratio of the minimum between-cluster distance to the maximum within-cluster distance. The between-cluster distance can be expressed in several different ways, most commonly as the minimum (single linkage) or maximum (complete linkage) distance between any two points of different clusters, or the distance between the two centroids. The within-cluster distance can also be expressed in different ways, such as the maximum distance between any two points of the cluster, the average of all pairwise distances within the cluster, or the average distance between the cluster points and the centroid. All these possibilities, along with possible different metrics for calculating the distances, give rise to a family of Dunn indices.

Here, we adopt the common formulation of between-cluster distance as the minimum Euclidean distance between any two points of the different clusters, and within-cluster distance as the maximum Euclidean distance between any two points of the cluster:

$$D = \frac{\min_{1 \leq i < j \leq k}\{\min_{x \in C_i, y \in C_j} d(x,y)\}}{\max_{1 \leq m \leq k}\{\max_{x,y \in C_m} d(x,y)\}}$$

The Dunn indices return higher (better) scores when all clusters are compact and well distanced from one another. It takes only one very disperse cluster, or two badly separated clusters, to obtain a low score. Like the previous indices, the Dunn indices are best suited for evaluating convex clusters.

S_Dbw index

The S_Dbw index [Halkidi and Vazirgiannis, 2001] is the sum of within-cluster scatter and between-cluster density:

$$S\_Dbw = Scat + Dens\_bw$$

The within-cluster scatter is obtained by measuring the scattering within each cluster as the norm of vector $\sigma(V_i)$, then averaging for all clusters, and finally normalizing by the norm of vector $\sigma(V)$:

$$Scat = \frac{1}{k} \frac{\sum_{i=1}^{k} ||\sigma(V_i)||}{||\sigma(V)||}$$

where $\sigma(V) = (\sigma(V_1), \ldots, \sigma(V_p))$ is a vector with the standard deviations of the p features for all the points of the dataset, and $\sigma(V_i)$ is the same thing, but only for the points belonging to cluster i. The norm $||X||$ is the Euclidean norm calculated as $\sqrt{X^T X}$, and the standard deviation $\sigma(X)$ is calculated as

$$\frac{1}{N} \sqrt{\sum_{i=1}^{N} (x_i - \mu)^2}$$

where N is the number of elements in vector X and μ is the mean of vector X.

The between-cluster density is the average of the density of points between pairs of clusters in relation to the density of the points within the clusters:

$$Dens\_bw = \frac{2}{k(k-1)} \sum_{i=1}^{k} \left(\sum_{j=i+1}^{k} \frac{density(u_{ij})}{max\{density(c_i), density(c_j)\}} \right)$$

where u_{ij} is the middle point between centroids c_i and c_j of a pair of clusters. $Dens\_bw$ is lower than 1 if, for each (unordered) pair of clusters, the density of points around at least one of their centroids is higher than the density around the middle point between the centroids. The density around a cluster centroid c is the number of points belonging to cluster C that are at a distance from c lower than the average standard deviation of clusters, $stdev$:

$$density(c) = \sum_{x \in C} f(x, c)$$

where

$$f(x, c) = \begin{cases} 1, & \text{if } d(x,c) < stdev \\ 0, & \text{otherwise} \end{cases}$$

and

$$stdev = \frac{1}{k} \sqrt{\sum_{i=1}^{k} ||\sigma(V_i)||}$$

The density around the middle point u_{ij} is the number of points belonging to either C_i or C_j that are at a distance from u_{ij} lower than $stddev$:

$$density(u_{ij}) = \sum_{x \in C_i \cup C_j} f(x, u_{ij})$$

S_Dbw assumes that all the feature vectors are scaled to (approximately) the same range. It returns lower (better) scores when both the scattering inside clusters and the density of points between clusters (in relation to the density inside clusters) are low. Although it uses the concept of density, which makes it seem more appropriate for evaluating clusterings made by DBSCAN, S_Dbw also relies on centroids and convex clusters.

Silhouette index

A popular tool for evaluating a clustering is the *silhouette plot* [Rousseeuw, 1987] and the index (S) [Kaufman and Rousseeuw, 1990] that is calculated from the same data used to build the plot.

For each data point i, a silhouette coefficient $(s(i))$ is calculated. This coefficient is the mean distance between i and the other points of the same cluster $(a(i))$ subtracted from the smallest mean distance between i and the points of each of the other clusters $(b(i))$, normalized by the maximum between the two:

$$s(i) = \frac{b(i)-a(i)}{max\{a(i),b(i)\}}$$

with $a(i) = \frac{1}{n_i-1} \sum_{j \in C_i, j \neq i} d(i,j)$

and $b(i) = \min_{1 \leq j \leq k} \{ \frac{1}{n_j} \sum_{j \in C_j} d(i,j) \} \}$

where n_j is the number of elements in cluster C_j.

A high coefficient means the point is close to the other points of its own cluster, and far from the points of the other clusters. The maximum value is 1. Negative values indicate points that are assigned to the wrong cluster, while values around 0 suggest the presence of overlapping clusters. By convention, points that form singleton clusters also receive the value 0.

The silhouette plot is a horizontal bar plot where each bar represents the coefficient of a data point. The bars are grouped by cluster, and inside each group they are ordered by descending coefficient value, top to bottom. Particularly in large datasets, this plot effectively draws a silhouette where the quality of the clustering can be quickly assessed. Figure 12.12 shows the silhouette plots obtained for the $k = 4$ clusterings represented in Figure 12.3, good-4 on the left and bad-4 on the right.

Different indices can be calculated by aggregating the $s(i)$ values in different ways, for example, the mean coefficient per cluster, and the mean of all the cluster means. However, the most common silhouette index is simply the mean of the $s(i)$ values of all the n points of the dataset:

$$S = \frac{1}{n} \sum_{i=1}^{n} s(i)$$

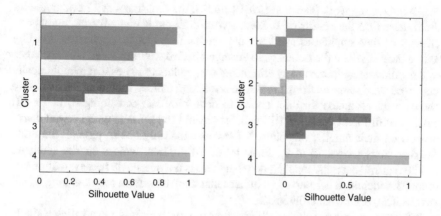

Fig. 12.12 Silhouette plots of the good-4 (left) and bad-4 (right) clusterings represented in Figure 12.3

12.6.2 Decision Making

Table 12.3 contains the scores obtained by the previously discussed five evaluation indices when applied to the clusterings of Figure 12.3 (which were qualitatively classified as good or bad, for $k = 2, 3, 4$). The best score obtained by each index is marked in bold. The score for bad-3 with S_Dbw is undetermined because the density of two or more clusters is zero. Although there is no agreement on whether good-2 or good-4 is the best clustering, all the indices agree on clusterings that were qualified as good. Obviously, these are hand-picked examples where the differences between good and bad are large, and therefore easily caught by most indices. In real-life examples, however, deciding which is the best clustering is seldom an easy task, and the difficulty may start with the choice of an evaluation index.

Table 12.3 Scores obtained by different evaluation indices for the six clusterings of Figure 12.3. The clusterings are named 'good-k' and 'bad-k', according to their qualitative evaluation and their number of clusters k. Upwards/downwards arrows after the name of each index mean that the higher/lower the score, the better. In bold is the best score obtained with each index. The S_Dbw score for bad-3 is undetermined because the density of two or more clusters is zero

	Davies-Bouldin ↓	Calinski-Harabasz ↑	Dunn ↑	S_Dbw ↓	Silhouette ↑
good-2	**0.33**	6.80	**0.83**	0.39	0.72
good-3	0.77	7.76	0.44	0.35	0.53
good-4	0.45	**16.50**	0.71	**0.25**	**0.75**
bad-2	0.92	6.80	0.22	1.72	0.48
bad-3	0.89	7.14	0.28	–	0.44
bad-4	1.39	5.40	0.28	0.41	0.20

An interesting work [Liu et al., 2010] studied the robustness of 11 evaluation indices, based on the results of K-Means with different settings for the number of clusters k when applied to synthetic data containing specific challenges. Starting with a dataset where the points were arranged in five well-separated clusters, some of the indices were immediately eliminated for producing scores that monotonically improved as k increased from 2 to 9. The remaining indices, including the five listed above, were evaluated for their ability to deal with data containing (i) noise, (ii) clusters of different densities, (iii) subclusters and (iv) clusters with skewed distributions on their number of points. S_Dbw was the only one to pass all the tests. Another study [Arbelaitz et al., 2013] tested 30 different indices on 720 synthetic and 20 real-life datasets. It concluded that there is not one single best evaluation criterion, but identified a group of 10 indices that tend to perform better, among which are DB, CH, S_Dbw and Silhouette.

Whatever indices are chosen, their scores are rarely used for evaluating a single clustering in absolute terms. Instead, they are normally used to compare the relative quality of clusterings obtained with different settings, in order to choose the best parameters for the clustering algorithm. Take, as an example, the choice of the number of clusters k in the K-Means algorithm. The evaluation indices are used to evaluate clusterings with different settings of k, and then their scores are compared in order to choose the ideal number of clusters. A popular method to help make this decision is the Elbow method, described below. The cross-validation method, so popular in supervised learning but almost forgotten in clustering, can also help in making such decisions, as described afterwards.

Elbow method

The Elbow method relies on the visual interpretation of a plot, which we call the Elbow plot, where the scores obtained for the different parametrizations of the clustering algorithm are connected by lines. Figure 12.13 shows two such plots, each obtained with a different evaluation index (DB on the left, CH on the right). The parameter being studied is the number of clusters (between 2 and 7) of the K-Means algorithm (with k-means++ initialization) applied to the 10 data points represented in Figure 12.2. Given the stochastic nature of K-Means, each score in the plot is the average of the scores of one thousand independent runs of the algorithm.

The goal of the Elbow method is to find the point in the plot where the slope of the line changes (the elbow point), identifying the number of clusters above which there seems to be little or no advantage in considering an additional cluster. Indices like DB and CH do tend to continually improve the score as the number of clusters increases, and therefore the change in slope may not be sharp. In both our example plots, it is easy to recognize the changing slope at $k = 4$, but in complex real-life data it may be difficult to recognize the elbow, or to choose between different possible elbows. Using more than one evaluation criterion may help achieve a consensus regarding this decision.

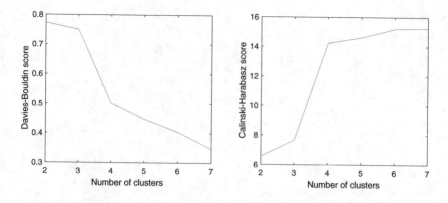

Fig. 12.13 Elbow plots using the scores from the DB index (left) and CH index (right)

Cross-validation

Although not common practice, unsupervised learning should use cross-validation to make sure that the decisions made on a given dataset (let us call it training data) would be appropriate for a different set of points coming from the same distribution, but never seen during the decision-making process (test data).

In the example above, of choosing the number of clusters based on evaluation indices, this means that the choice of k on the training data should be such that the scores obtained on the test set are similar to the ones observed on the training set. In practical terms, the chosen elbow point on the training data should not be very different from the one that would be chosen on the test data, even if that means choosing an elbow that is not exactly the best on training.

Splitting the available data into training and test should not be considered a hindrance, but rather an advantage, as this means having twice the number of votes to support a decision that may not be obvious.

References

[Aarts and Korst, 1989] Aarts, E. and Korst, J. (1989). *Simulated Annealing and Boltzmann Machines: A Stochastic Approach to Combinatorial Optimization and Neural Computing*. John Wiley & Sons, Inc.

[Agarap, 2018] Agarap, A. F. (2018). Deep learning using rectified linear units (ReLU). *ArXiv*, abs/1803.08375.

[Albert and Andreson, 1984] Albert, A. and Andreson, J. A. (1984). On the existence of maximum likelihood estimates in logistic regression models. *Biometrika*, 71(1):1–10.

[Alcala-Fdez et al., 2011] Alcala-Fdez, J., Fernandez, A., Luengo, J., Derrac, J., Garcia, S., Sanchez, L., and Herrera, F. (2011). KEEL data-mining software tool: Data set repository, integration of algorithms and experimental analysis framework. *Journal of Multiple-Valued Logic and Soft Computing 17:2-3, 255-287.*

[Altenberg, 1994a] Altenberg, L. (1994a). Emergent phenomena in genetic programming. In Sebald, A. V. and Fogel, L., editors, *Proceedings of the Third Annual Conference on Evolutionary Programming*, pages 233–241. World Scientific.

[Altenberg, 1994b] Altenberg, L. (1994b). *The Evolution of Evolvability in Genetic Programming*, page 47–74. MIT Press, Cambridge, MA, USA.

[Angeline, 1998] Angeline, P. J. (1998). A historical perspective on the evolution of executable structures. *Fundam. Informaticae*, 35(1-4):179–195.

[Ankerst et al., 1999] Ankerst, M., Breunig, M. M., Kriegel, H.-P., and Sander, J. (1999). OPTICS: Ordering points to identify the clustering structure. In *Proceedings of the 1999 ACM SIGMOD International Conference on Management of Data*, SIGMOD '99, page 49–60. Association for Computing Machinery.

[Ansari and Hou, 1997] Ansari, N. and Hou, E. (1997). *Hopfield Neural Networks*, pages 27–45. Springer, Boston, MA.

[Antoniou and Lu, 2007] Antoniou, A. and Lu, W.-S. (2007). *Practical Optimization: Algorithms and Engineering Applications*. Springer, 1st edition.

[Applegate et al., 2007] Applegate, D. L., Bixby, R. E., Chvatal, V., and Cook, W. J. (2007). *The Traveling Salesman Problem: A Computational Study (Princeton Series in Applied Mathematics)*. Princeton University Press, Princeton, NJ, USA.

© Springer Nature Switzerland AG 2023
L. Vanneschi and S. Silva, *Lectures on Intelligent Systems*, Natural Computing Series,
https://doi.org/10.1007/978-3-031-17922-8

[Arbelaitz et al., 2013] Arbelaitz, O., Gurrutxaga, I., Muguerza, J., Pérez, J. M., and Perona, I. (2013). An extensive comparative study of cluster validity indices. *Pattern Recogn.*, 46(1):243–256.

[Archetti et al., 2007] Archetti, F., Lanzeni, S., Messina, E., and Vanneschi, L. (2007). Genetic programming for computational pharmacokinetics in drug discovery and development. *Genetic Programming and Evolvable Machines*, 8(4):413–432.

[Auger and Teytaud, 2010] Auger, A. and Teytaud, O. (2010). Continuous lunches are free plus the design of optimal optimization algorithms. *Algorithmica*, 57(1):121–146.

[Bache and Lichman, 2013] Bache, K. and Lichman, M. (2013). UCI Machine Learning Repository, University of California, Irvine, School of Information and Computer Sciences. *http://archive.ics.uci.edu/ml.*

[Baker, 1985] Baker, J. E. (1985). Adaptive selection methods for genetic algorithms. In *Proceedings of the 1st International Conference on Genetic Algorithms*, pages 101–111, USA. L. Erlbaum Associates Inc.

[Banzhaf et al., 1998] Banzhaf, W., Nordin, P., Keller, R. E., and Francone, F. D. (1998). *Genetic Programming, An Introduction*. Morgan Kaufmann, San Francisco, CA.

[Barber, 2012] Barber, D. (2012). *Bayesian Reasoning and Machine Learning*. Cambridge University Press, USA.

[Batista et al., 2021] Batista, J. E., Cabral, A. I. R., Vasconcelos, M. J. P., Vanneschi, L., and Silva, S. (2021). Improving land cover classification using genetic programming for feature construction. *Remote Sensing*, 13(9).

[Batista and Silva, 2020] Batista, J. E. and Silva, S. (2020). Improving the detection of burnt areas in remote sensing using hyper-features evolved by M3GP. In *IEEE Congress on Evolutionary Computation, CEC 2020, Glasgow, United Kingdom, July 19-24, 2020*, pages 1–8. IEEE.

[Baum and Haussler, 1989] Baum, E. B. and Haussler, D. (1989). What size net gives valid generalization? *Neural Comput.*, 1(1):151–160.

[Benjamini, 1988] Benjamini, Y. (1988). Opening the box of a boxplot. *The American Statistician*, 42(4):257–262.

[Bensusan and Kuscu, 1996] Bensusan, H. and Kuscu, I. (1996). Constructive induction using genetic programming. In *Evolutionary Computing and Machine Learning Workshop (ICML-96)*. Morgan Kaufmann.

[Beretta et al., 2018] Beretta, S., Castelli, M., Gonçalves, I., Henriques, R., and Ramazzotti, D. (2018). Learning the structure of Bayesian networks: A quantitative assessment of the effect of different algorithmic schemes. *Complexity*, 2018:12 pages. Article ID 1591878.

[Berger, 2017] Berger, D. (2017). Introduction to binary logistic regression and propensity score analysis. Available online: *https://www. researchgate.net/publication/320505159_Introduction_ to_Binary_Logistic_Regression_and_Propensity_Score_ Analysis.*

[Bethke, 1980] Bethke, A. D. (1980). *Genetic Algorithms as Function Optimizers.* PhD thesis, University of Michigan.

[Bhandari et al., 1994] Bhandari, D., Pal, N. R., and Pal, S. K. (1994). Directed mutation in genetic algorithms. *Information Sciences*, 79(3):251–270.

[Bleuler et al., 2001] Bleuler, S., Brack, M., Thiele, L., and Zitzler, E. (2001). Multiobjective genetic programming: reducing bloat using SPEA2. In *Proceedings of the 2001 Congress on Evolutionary Computation (IEEE Cat. No.01TH8546)*, volume 1, pages 536–543.

[Blickle and Thiele, 1994] Blickle, T. and Thiele, L. (1994). Genetic programming and redundancy. In *Genetic Algorithms within the Framework of Evolutionary Computation (Workshop at KI-94)*, pages 33–38.

[Brameier and Banzhaf, 2001] Brameier, M. and Banzhaf, W. (2001). A comparison of linear genetic programming and neural networks in medical data mining. *IEEE Transactions on Evolutionary Computation*, 5(1):17–26.

[Brameier and Banzhaf, 2003] Brameier, M. and Banzhaf, W. (2003). Neutral variations cause bloat in linear GP. In Ryan, C., Soule, T., Keijzer, M., Tsang, E. P. K., Poli, R., and Costa, E., editors, *Genetic Programming, 6th European Conference, EuroGP 2003, Essex, UK, April 14-16, 2003. Proceedings*, volume 2610 of *Lecture Notes in Computer Science*, pages 286–296. Springer.

[Bratton and Blackwell, 2008] Bratton, D. and Blackwell, T. (2008). A simplified recombinant PSO. *Journal of Artificial Evolution and Applications*. Issue S1, Article no. 14.

[Breiman, 1996] Breiman, L. (1996). Bagging predictors. *Machine Learning*, 24(2):123–140.

[Breiman, 2001] Breiman, L. (2001). Random forests. *Mach. Learn.*, 45(1):5–32.

[Breiman et al., 1984] Breiman, L., Friedman, J. H., Olshen, R. A., and Stone, C. J. (1984). *Classification and Regression Trees.* Wadsworth and Brooks, Monterey, CA.

[Bryll et al., 2003] Bryll, R., Gutierrez-Osuna, R., and Quek, F. (2003). Attribute bagging: improving accuracy of classifier ensembles by using random feature subsets. *Pattern Recognition*, 36(6):1291–1302.

[Burke et al., 2002] Burke, E., Gustafson, S., Kendall, G., and Krasnogor, N. (2002). Advanced population diversity measures in genetic programming. In Merelo, J. J., Adamidis, P., Beyer, H. G., Fernández-Villacanas, J.-L., and Schwefel, H.-P., editors, *Parallel Problem Solving from Nature - PPSN VII*, volume 2439 of *Lecture Notes in Computer Science*, pages 341–350. Springer.

[Cagnoni et al., 2008] Cagnoni, S., Vanneschi, L., Azzini, A., and Tettamanzi, A. G. B. (2008). A critical assessment of some variants of particle swarm optimization. In Giacobini, M., Brabazon, A., Cagnoni, S., Di Caro, G. A., Drechsler, R., Ekárt, A., Esparcia-Alcázar, A. I., Farooq, M., Fink, A., McCormack, J., O'Neill, M., Romero, J., Rothlauf, F., Squillero, G., Uyar, A. Ş., and Yang, S., editors, *Applications of Evolutionary Computing*, pages 565–574. Springer.

[Caliński and Harabasz, 1974] Caliński, T. and Harabasz, J. (1974). A dendrite method for cluster analysis. *Communications in Statistics-Simulation and Computation*, 3(1):1–27.

[Campello et al., 2013] Campello, R. J. G. B., Moulavi, D., and Sander, J. (2013). Density-based clustering based on hierarchical density estimates. In Pei, J., Tseng, V. S., Cao, L., Motoda, H., and Xu, G., editors, *Advances in Knowledge Discovery and Data Mining*, pages 160–172. Springer.

[Castelli et al., 2015] Castelli, M., Silva, S., and Vanneschi, L. (2015). A C++ framework for geometric semantic genetic programming. *Genetic Programming and Evolvable Machines*, 16(1):73–81.

[Cava and Moore, 2020] Cava, W. G. L. and Moore, J. H. (2020). Learning feature spaces for regression with genetic programming. *Genet. Program. Evolvable Mach.*, 21(3):433–467.

[Černý, 1985] Černý, V. (1985). Thermodynamical approach to the traveling salesman problem: An efficient simulation algorithm. *Journal of Optimization Theory and Applications*, 45(1):41–51.

[Chen and Guestrin, 2016] Chen, T. and Guestrin, C. (2016). XGBoost: A scalable tree boosting system. In *Proceedings of the 22nd ACM SIGKDD International Conference on Knowledge Discovery and Data Mining, KDD '16*, New York, NY, USA. Association for Computing Machinery.

[Chen et al., 2010] Chen, W., Zhang, J., Chung, H. S. H., Zhong, W., Wu, W., and Shi, Y. (2010). A novel set-based particle swarm optimization method for discrete optimization problems. *IEEE Transactions on Evolutionary Computation*, 14(2):278–300.

[Chen, 2016] Chen, Y. (2016). *Structure Discovery in Bayesian Networks: Algorithms and Applications*. PhD thesis, Iowa State University, USA.

[Cheung et al., 2014] Cheung, N. J., Ding, X., and Shen, H. (2014). Optifel: A convergent heterogeneous particle swarm optimization algorithm for Takagi–Sugeno fuzzy modeling. *IEEE Transactions on Fuzzy Systems*, 22(4):919–933.

[Chib and Greenberg, 1995] Chib, S. and Greenberg, E. (1995). Understanding the Metropolis-Hastings algorithm. *The American Statistician*, 49(4):327–335.

[Chih-Wei Hsu and Chih-Jen Lin, 2002] Chih-Wei Hsu and Chih-Jen Lin (2002). A comparison of methods for multiclass support vector machines. *IEEE Transactions on Neural Networks*, 13(2):415–425.

[Chinea, 2009] Chinea, A. (2009). Understanding the principles of recursive neural networks: A generative approach to tackle model complexity. In Alippi, C., Polycarpou, M., Panayiotou, C., and Ellinas, G., editors, *Artificial Neural Networks – ICANN 2009*, pages 952–963. Springer.

[Clerc, 2004] Clerc, M. (2004). *Discrete Particle Swarm Optimization, illustrated by the Traveling Salesman Problem*, pages 219–239. Springer.

[Coello Coello et al., 2006] Coello Coello, C. A., Lamont, G. B., and Van Veldhuizen, D. A. (2006). *Evolutionary Algorithms for Solving Multi-Objective Problems (Genetic and Evolutionary Computation)*. Springer.

[Cohen et al., 2018] Cohen, G., Sapiro, G., and Giryes, R. (2018). DNN or k–NN: That is the generalize vs. memorize question. *ArXiv*, abs/1805.06822.

[Czepiel, 2002] Czepiel, S. (2002). Maximum likelihood estimation of logistic regression models: Theory and implementation. Available at https://czep.net/stat/mlelr.pdf.

[Darwin, 1859] Darwin, C. (1859). *On the Origin of Species by Means of Natural Selection.* John Murray.

[Davies and Bouldin, 1979] Davies, D. L. and Bouldin, D. W. (1979). A cluster separation measure. *IEEE Trans. Pattern Anal. Mach. Intell.*, 1(2):224–227.

[De Jong and Spears, 1992] De Jong, K. and Spears, W. (1992). A formal analysis of the role of multipoint crossover in genetic algorithms. *Annals of Mathematics and Artificial Intelligence - AMAI*, 5:1–26.

[De Jong, 1988] De Jong, K. A. (1988). Learning with genetic algorithms: an overview. *Machine Learning*, 3:121–138.

[De Maesschalck et al., 2000] De Maesschalck, R., Jouan-Rimbaud, D., and Massart, D. (2000). The Mahalanobis distance. *Chemometrics and Intelligent Laboratory Systems*, 50(1):1–18.

[Deb et al., 2002] Deb, K., Pratap, A., Agarwal, S., and Meyarivan, T. (2002). A fast and elitist multiobjective genetic algorithm: NSGA-II. *Trans. Evol. Comp*, 6(2):182–197.

[Demuth et al., 2014] Demuth, H. B., Beale, M. H., De Jess, O., and Hagan, M. T. (2014). *Neural Network Design.* Martin Hagan, USA, 2nd edition.

[Dietterich, 2000] Dietterich, T. G. (2000). An experimental comparison of three methods for constructing ensembles of decision trees: Bagging, boosting, and randomization. *Mach. Learn.*, 40(2):139–157.

[Dignum and Poli, 2007] Dignum, S. and Poli, R. (2007). Generalisation of the limiting distribution of program sizes in tree-based genetic programming and analysis of its effects on bloat. In *Proceedings of the 9th Annual Conference on Genetic and Evolutionary Computation, GECCO '07*, pages 1588–1595. Association for Computing Machinery.

[Dignum and Poli, 2008] Dignum, S. and Poli, R. (2008). Crossover, sampling, bloat and the harmful effects of size limits. In O'Neill, M., Vanneschi, L., Gustafson, S., Esparcia Alcázar, A. I., De Falco, I., Della Cioppa, A., and Tarantino, E., editors, *Genetic Programming*, pages 158–169. Springer.

[Dodge, 2008] Dodge, Y. (2008). *Kolmogorov–Smirnov Test*, pages 283–287. Springer.

[Domingos and Pazzani, 1996] Domingos, P. M. and Pazzani, M. J. (1996). Simple Bayesian classifiers do not assume independence. In Clancey, W. J. and Weld, D. S., editors, *Proceedings of the Thirteenth National Conference on Artificial Intelligence and Eighth Innovative Applications of Artificial Intelligence Conference, AAAI 96, IAAI 96, Portland, Oregon, USA, August 4-8, 1996, Volume 2*, page 1386. AAAI Press / The MIT Press.

[Dubitzky et al., 2006] Dubitzky, W., Granzow, M., and Berrar, D. P. (2006). *Fundamentals of Data Mining in Genomics and Proteomics.* Springer.

[Dunn, 1973] Dunn, J. C. (1973). A fuzzy relative of the isodata process and its use in detecting compact well-separated clusters. *Journal of Cybernetics*, 3(3):32–57.

[Efron, 1982] Efron, B. (1982). *The Jackknife, the Bootstrap and other resampling plans.* Number 38 in Regional Conference Series in Applied Mathematics. Society for Industrial and Applied Mathematics, Philadelphia, Pa.

[Efron and Tibshirani, 1993] Efron, B. and Tibshirani, R. J. (1993). *An Introduction to the Bootstrap*. Number 57 in Monographs on Statistics and Applied Probability. Chapman & Hall/CRC, Boca Raton, Florida, USA.

[Eiben and Smith, 2015] Eiben, A. E. and Smith, J. E. (2015). *Introduction to Evolutionary Computing*. Springer, 2nd edition.

[Ekárt and Németh, 2002] Ekárt, A. and Németh, S. Z. (2002). Maintaining the diversity of genetic programs. In Foster, J. A., Lutton, E., Miller, J., Ryan, C., and Tettamanzi, A. G. B., editors, *Genetic Programming, Proceedings of the 5th European Conference, EuroGP 2002*, volume 2278 of *LNCS*, pages 162–171, Kinsale, Ireland. Springer.

[Elman, 1990] Elman, J. L. (1990). Finding structure in time. *Cognitive Science*, 14(2):179 – 211.

[Espejo et al., 2010] Espejo, P. G., Ventura, S., and Herrera, F. (2010). A survey on the application of genetic programming to classification. *IEEE Transactions on Systems, Man, and Cybernetics, Part C (Applications and Reviews)*, 40(2):121–144.

[Ester et al., 1996] Ester, M., Kriegel, H.-P., Sander, J., and Xu, X. (1996). A density-based algorithm for discovering clusters in large spatial databases with noise. In *Proceedings of the Second International Conference on Knowledge Discovery and Data Mining*, pages 226–231. AAAI Press.

[Fan and Bifet, 2013] Fan, W. and Bifet, A. (2013). Mining big data: Current status, and forecast to the future. *SIGKDD Explor. Newsl.*, 14(2):1–5.

[Fernández et al., 2003] Fernández, F., Tomassini, M., and Vanneschi, L. (2003). An empirical study of multipopulation genetic programming. *Genetic Programming and Evolvable Machines*, 4(1):21–52.

[Ferreira and Figueiredo, 2012] Ferreira, A. J. and Figueiredo, M. A. T. (2012). *Boosting Algorithms: A Review of Methods, Theory, and Applications*, pages 35–85. Springer, Boston, MA.

[Fischer, 2019] Fischer, J. (2019). The Boltzmann constant for the definition and realization of the Kelvin. *Annalen der Physik*, 531(5):1800304.

[Freund and Schapire, 1996] Freund, Y. and Schapire, R. E. (1996). Experiments with a new boosting algorithm. In *Proceedings of the Thirteenth International Conference on Machine Learning, ICML '96*, page 148–156, San Francisco, CA, USA. Morgan Kaufmann Publishers Inc.

[Freund and Schapire, 1997] Freund, Y. and Schapire, R. E. (1997). A decision-theoretic generalization of on-line learning and an application to boosting. *Journal of Computer and System Sciences*, 55(1):119–139.

[Friedman et al., 2000] Friedman, J., Hastie, T., and Tibshirani, R. (2000). Additive Logistic Regression: a Statistical View of Boosting. *The Annals of Statistics*, 38(2).

[Friedman, 2000] Friedman, J. H. (2000). Greedy function approximation: A gradient boosting machine. *Annals of Statistics*, 29:1189–1232.

[Friedman, 2002] Friedman, J. H. (2002). Stochastic gradient boosting. *Comput. Stat. Data Anal.*, 38(4):367–378.

[Gabriel, 2016] Gabriel, J. (2016). *Artificial Intelligence: Artificial Intelligence for Humans*. CreateSpace Independent Publishing Platform, USA, 1st edition.

[Garey and Johnson, 1990] Garey, M. R. and Johnson, D. S. (1990). *Computers and Intractability; A Guide to the Theory of NP-Completeness*. W. H. Freeman & Co.

[Garg, 2016] Garg, H. (2016). A hybrid PSO–GA algorithm for constrained optimization problems. *Applied Mathematics and Computation*, 274:292 – 305.

[Goldberg, 1989] Goldberg, D. E. (1989). *Genetic Algorithms in Search, Optimization and Machine Learning*. Addison-Wesley.

[Golub and Reinsch, 1970] Golub, G. H. and Reinsch, C. (1970). Singular value decomposition and least squares solutions. *Numer. Math.*, 14(5):403–420.

[Gonçalves et al., 2015] Gonçalves, I., Silva, S., and Fonseca, C. M. (2015). On the generalization ability of geometric semantic genetic programming. In Machado, P., Heywood, M. I., McDermott, J., Castelli, M., García-Sánchez, P., Burelli, P., Risi, S., and Sim, K., editors, *Genetic Programming - 18th European Conference, EuroGP 2015, Copenhagen, Denmark, April 8-10, 2015, Proceedings*, volume 9025 of *Lecture Notes in Computer Science*, pages 41–52. Springer.

[Gustafson and Vanneschi, 2005] Gustafson, S. and Vanneschi, L. (2005). Operator-based distance for genetic programming: Subtree crossover distance. In Keijzer, M., Tettamanzi, A., Collet, P., van Hemert, J., and Tomassini, M., editors, *Genetic Programming*, pages 178–189. Springer.

[Halkidi and Vazirgiannis, 2001] Halkidi, M. and Vazirgiannis, M. (2001). Clustering validity assessment: Finding the optimal partitioning of a data set. In *Proceedings of the 2001 IEEE International Conference on Data Mining*, ICDM '01, pages 187–194, USA. IEEE Computer Society.

[Hall et al., 2009] Hall, M., Frank, E., Holmes, G., Pfahringer, B., Reutemann, P., and Witten, I. H. (2009). The WEKA data mining software: an update. *SIGKDD Explorations*, 11(1):10–18.

[Hartman et al., 1990] Hartman, E., Keeler, J. D., and Kowalski, J. M. (1990). Layered neural networks with Gaussian hidden units as universal approximations. *Neural Computation*, 2:210–215.

[Haykin, 1998] Haykin, S. (1998). *Neural Networks: A Comprehensive Foundation*. Prentice Hall PTR, Upper Saddle River, NJ, USA, 2nd edition.

[Haynes, 1998] Haynes, T. (1998). Collective adaptation: The exchange of coding segments. *Evol. Comput.*, 6(4):311–338.

[Helmuth et al., 2015] Helmuth, T., Spector, L., and Matheson, J. (2015). Solving uncompromising problems with lexicase selection. *IEEE Transactions on Evolutionary Computation*, 19(5):630–643.

[Hinton, 2010] Hinton, G. (2010). Boltzmann machines. *Encyclopedia of Machine Learning*, pages 132–136. Springer.

[Ho, 1998a] Ho, T. K. (1998a). Nearest neighbors in random subspaces. In Amin, A., Dori, D., Pudil, P., and Freeman, H., editors, *Advances in Pattern Recognition*, pages 640–648, Berlin, Heidelberg. Springer.

[Ho, 1998b] Ho, T. K. (1998b). The random subspace method for constructing decision forests. *IEEE Transactions on Pattern Analysis and Machine Intelligence*, 20(8):832–844.

[Holland, 1975] Holland, J. H. (1975). *Adaptation in Natural and Artificial Systems*. The University of Michigan Press, Ann Arbor, Michigan.

[Hornik et al., 1989] Hornik, K., Stinchcombe, M., and White, H. (1989). Multilayer feedforward networks are universal approximators. *Neural Netw.*, 2(5):359–366.

[Hutter et al., 2019] Hutter, F., Kotthoff, L., and Vanschoren, J. (2019). *Automated Machine Learning: Methods, Systems, Challenges*. Springer, 1st edition.

[Igel and Chellapilla, 1999] Igel, C. and Chellapilla, K. (1999). Investigating the influence of depth and degree of genotypic change on fitness in genetic programming. In *Proceedings of the 1st Annual Conference on Genetic and Evolutionary Computation - Volume 2, GECCO '99*, pages 1061–1068, San Francisco, CA, USA. Morgan Kaufmann Publishers Inc.

[Ingalalli et al., 2014] Ingalalli, V., Silva, S., Castelli, M., and Vanneschi, L. (2014). A multi-dimensional genetic programming approach for multi-class classification problems. In Nicolau, M., Krawiec, K., Heywood, M. I., Castelli, M., García-Sánchez, P., Merelo, J. J., Rivas Santos, V. M., and Sim, K., editors, *Genetic Programming*, pages 48–60. Springer.

[Jain and Medsker, 1999] Jain, L. C. and Medsker, L. R. (1999). *Recurrent Neural Networks: Design and Applications*. CRC Press, Inc., Boca Raton, FL, USA, 1st edition.

[James, 2003] James, G. M. (2003). Variance and bias for general loss functions. *Mach. Learn.*, 51(2):115–135.

[Jarboui et al., 2008] Jarboui, B., Damak, N., Siarry, P., and Rebai, A. (2008). A combinatorial particle swarm optimization for solving multi-mode resource-constrained project scheduling problems. *Applied Mathematics and Computation*, 195(1):299 – 308.

[Johnson and Zhang, 2014] Johnson, R. and Zhang, T. (2014). Learning nonlinear functions using regularized greedy forest. *IEEE Transactions on Pattern Analysis and Machine Intelligence*, 36(5):942–954.

[Kagalkar and Raghuram, 2020] Kagalkar, A. and Raghuram, S. (2020). CORDIC based implementation of the Softmax activation function. In *2020 24th International Symposium on VLSI Design and Test (VDAT)*, pages 1–4. IEEE.

[Katoch et al., 2021] Katoch, S., Chauhan, S. S., and Kumar, V. (2021). A review on genetic algorithm: Past, present, and future. *Multimedia Tools and Applications*, 80:8091–8126.

[Kaufman and Rousseeuw, 1990] Kaufman, L. and Rousseeuw, P. J. (1990). *Finding Groups in Data: An Introduction to Cluster Analysis*. John Wiley.

[Keane, 1995] Keane, M. (1995). *The Essence of the Law of Large Numbers*, pages 125–129. Springer, Boston, MA.

[Kearns, 1988] Kearns, M. (1988). Thoughts on hypothesis boosting. Project for Ron Rivest's Machine Learning course at MIT.

[Keijzer, 2003] Keijzer, M. (2003). Improving symbolic regression with interval arithmetic and linear scaling. In Ryan, C., Soule, T., Keijzer, M., Tsang, E., Poli, R., and Costa, E., editors, *Genetic Programming*, pages 70–82. Springer.

[Kelleher et al., 2015] Kelleher, J. D., Namee, B. M., and D'Arcy, A. (2015). *Fundamentals of Machine Learning for Predictive Data Analytics: Algorithms, Worked Examples, and Case Studies.* The MIT Press.

[Kennedy, 2010] Kennedy, J. (2010). Particle swarm optimization. *Encyclopedia of Machine Learning*, pages 760–766. Springer.

[Kennedy and Eberhart, 1995] Kennedy, J. and Eberhart, R. C. (1995). Particle swarm optimization. In *Proceedings of the IEEE International Conference on Neural Networks*, pages 1942–1948.

[Kennedy and Eberhart, 1997] Kennedy, J. and Eberhart, R. C. (1997). A discrete binary version of the particle swarm algorithm. In *1997 IEEE International Conference on Systems, Man, and Cybernetics. Computational Cybernetics and Simulation*, volume 5, pages 4104–4108.

[Kirkpatrick et al., 1983] Kirkpatrick, S., Gelatt, C. D., and Vecchi, M. P. (1983). Optimization by simulated annealing. *Science*, 220(4598):671–680.

[Klema and Laub, 1980] Klema, V. and Laub, A. (1980). The singular value decomposition: Its computation and some applications. *IEEE Transactions on Automatic Control*, 25(2):164–176.

[Kochenderfer and Wheeler, 2019] Kochenderfer, M. J. and Wheeler, T. A. (2019). *Algorithms for Optimization.* The MIT Press.

[Kohonen et al., 2001] Kohonen, T., Schroeder, M. R., and Huang, T. S. (2001). *Self-Organizing Maps.* Springer, 3rd edition.

[Koza, 1992] Koza, J. R. (1992). *Genetic Programming: On the Programming of Computers by Means of Natural Selection.* MIT Press, Cambridge, MA, USA.

[Koza, 1994] Koza, J. R. (1994). *Genetic Programming II.* The MIT Press, Cambridge, Massachusetts.

[Koza et al., 1999] Koza, J. R., Bennett F. H. III, Andre, D., and Keane, M. A. (1999). *Genetic Programming III: Darwinian Invention and Problem Solving.* Morgan Kaufmann, San Francisco, CA.

[Koza and Poli, 2003] Koza, J. R. and Poli, R. (2003). A genetic programming tutorial. In Burke, E., editor, *Introductory Tutorials in Optimization, Search and Decision Support.* Chapter 8. http://www.genetic-programming.com/jkpdf/burke2003tutorial.pdf.

[Krink and Løvbjerg, 2002] Krink, T. and Løvbjerg, M. (2002). The lifecycle model: Combining particle swarm optimisation, genetic algorithms and hill-climbers. In Guervós, J. J. M., Adamidis, P., Beyer, H.-G., Schwefel, H.-P., and Fernández-Villacañas, J.-L., editors, *Parallel Problem Solving from Nature — PPSN VII*, pages 621–630. Springer.

[Kwok and Carter, 1990] Kwok, S. W. and Carter, C. (1990). Multiple decision trees. In *Proceedings of the Fourth Annual Conference on Uncertainty in Artificial Intelligence*, UAI '88, page 327–338, NLD. North-Holland Publishing Co.

[La Cava et al., 2018] La Cava, W., Silva, S., Danai, K., Spector, L., Vanneschi, L., and Moore, J. H. (2018). A multidimensional genetic programming approach for identifying epistatic gene interactions. In *Proceedings of the Genetic and Evolutionary Computation Conference Companion - GECCO '18*, pages 23–24, Kyoto, Japan. ACM Press.

[La Cava et al., 2019] La Cava, W., Silva, S., Danai, K., Spector, L., Vanneschi, L., and Moore, J. H. (2019). Multidimensional genetic programming for multiclass classification. *Swarm and Evolutionary Computation*, 44:260–272.

[Landis and Koch, 1977] Landis, J. R. and Koch, G. G. (1977). The measurement of observer agreement for categorical data. *Biometrics*, 33(1).

[Langdon, 1998] Langdon, W. (1998). The evolution of size in variable length representations. In *1998 IEEE International Conference on Evolutionary Computation Proceedings. IEEE World Congress on Computational Intelligence (Cat. No.98TH8360)*, pages 633–638.

[Langdon, 1996] Langdon, W. B. (1996). A bibliography for genetic programming. In Angeline, P. J. and Kinnear, K. E. Jr., editors, *Advances in Genetic Programming 2*, chapter B, pages 507–532. MIT Press, Cambridge, MA, USA.

[Langdon, 1999] Langdon, W. B. (1999). Size fair and homologous tree genetic programming crossovers. In Banzhaf, W., Daida, J., Eiben, A. E., Garzon, M. H., Honavar, V., Jakiela, M., and Smith, R. E., editors, *Proceedings of the Genetic and Evolutionary Computation Conference*, volume 2, pages 1092–1097, Orlando, Florida, USA. Morgan Kaufmann.

[Langdon and Poli, 1997] Langdon, W. B. and Poli, R. (1997). Fitness causes bloat. In Chawdhry, P. K., Roy, R., and Pant, R. K., editors, *Soft Computing in Engineering Design and Manufacturing*, pages 13–22. Springer.

[Langdon and Poli, 1998] Langdon, W. B. and Poli, R. (1998). Fitness causes bloat: Mutation. In Banzhaf, W., Poli, R., Schoenauer, M., and Fogarty, T. C., editors, *Genetic Programming*, pages 37–48. Springer.

[Langdon and Poli, 2002] Langdon, W. B. and Poli, R. (2002). *Foundations of Genetic Programming*. Springer, Berlin.

[Langdon et al., 1999] Langdon, W. B., Soule, T., Poli, R., and Foster, J. A. (1999). *The Evolution of Size and Shape*, pages 163–190. MIT Press, Cambridge, MA, USA.

[Lehman and Stanley, 2011] Lehman, J. and Stanley, K. O. (2011). *Novelty Search and the Problem with Objectives*, pages 37–56. Springer.

[Liu et al., 2010] Liu, Y., Li, Z., Xiong, H., Gao, X., and Wu, J. (2010). Understanding of internal clustering validation measures. In *Proceedings of the 2010 IEEE International Conference on Data Mining, ICDM '10*, pages 911–916, USA. IEEE Computer Society.

[Lovric, 2011] Lovric, M., editor (2011). *International Encyclopedia of Statistical Science*. Springer.

[Luke, 2003] Luke, S. (2003). Modification point depth and genome growth in genetic programming. *Evol. Comput.*, 11(1):67–106.

[Luke and Panait, 2002] Luke, S. and Panait, L. (2002). Fighting bloat with nonparametric parsimony pressure. In Guervós, J. J. M., Adamidis, P., Beyer, H.-G., Schwefel, H.-P., and Fernández-Villacañas, J.-L., editors, *Parallel Problem Solving from Nature — PPSN VII*, pages 411–421. Springer.

[MacNaughton-Smith et al., 1964] MacNaughton-Smith, P., Williams, W. T., Dale, M. B., and Mockett, L. G. (1964). Dissimilarity analysis: a new technique of hierarchical sub-division. *Nature*, 202(4936):1034–1035.

[Martello and Toth, 1990] Martello, S. and Toth, P. (1990). *Knapsack Problems: Algorithms and Computer Implementations*. John Wiley & Sons, Inc.

[Massey, 1951] Massey, F. J. (1951). The Kolmogorov-Smirnov test for goodness of fit. *Journal of the American Statistical Association*, 46(253):68–78.

[Mayoraz and Alpaydin, 1999] Mayoraz, E. and Alpaydin, E. (1999). Support vector machines for multi-class classification. In Mira, J. and Sánchez-Andrés, J. V., editors, *Engineering Applications of Bio-Inspired Artificial Neural Networks*, pages 833–842. Springer.

[McCandlish, 2011] McCandlish, D. (2011). Visualizing fitness landscapes. *Evolution; International Journal of Organic Evolution*, 65:1544–58.

[McDermott et al., 2012] McDermott, J., White, D. R., Luke, S., Manzoni, L., Castelli, M., Vanneschi, L., Jaskowski, W., Krawiec, K., Harper, R., De Jong, K., and O'Reilly, U.-M. (2012). Genetic programming needs better benchmarks. In *Proceedings of the 14th Annual Conference on Genetic and Evolutionary Computation, GECCO '12*, pages 791–798. Association for Computing Machinery.

[McPhee and Miller, 1995] McPhee, N. F. and Miller, J. D. (1995). Accurate replication in genetic programming. In Eshelman, L. J., editor, *Proceedings of the 6th International Conference on Genetic Algorithms, Pittsburgh, PA, USA, July 15-19, 1995*, pages 303–309. Morgan Kaufmann.

[Miller, 2001] Miller, J. (2001). What bloat? Cartesian genetic programming on Boolean problems. In Goodman, E. D., editor, *2001 Genetic and Evolutionary Computation Conference Late Breaking Papers*, pages 295–302, San Francisco, California, USA.

[Minsky and Papert, 1988] Minsky, M. L. and Papert, S. A. (1988). *Perceptrons: Expanded Edition*. MIT Press, Cambridge, MA, USA.

[Miranda and Fonseca, 2002] Miranda, V. and Fonseca, N. (2002). EPSO-Evolutionary particle swarm optimization, a new algorithm with applications in power systems. In *IEEE/PES Transmission and Distribution Conference and Exhibition*, volume 2, pages 745–750 vol.2.

[Mitchell, 1997] Mitchell, T. M. (1997). *Machine Learning*. McGraw-Hill, Inc., 1st edition.

[Moraglio, 2008] Moraglio, A. (2008). *Towards a geometric unification of evolutionary algorithms*. PhD thesis, University of Essex, Colchester, UK.

[Moraglio et al., 2012] Moraglio, A., Krawiec, K., and Johnson, C. (2012). Geometric semantic genetic programming. In Coello Coello, C. A., Cutello, V., Deb, K., Forrest, S., Nicosia, G., and Pavone, M., editors, *Parallel Problem Solving from Nature - PPSN XII*, volume 7491 of *Lecture Notes in Computer Science*, pages 21–31. Springer.

[Muñoz et al., 2015] Muñoz, L., Silva, S., and Trujillo, L. (2015). M3GP – multiclass classification with GP. In Machado, P., Heywood, M. I., McDermott, J., Castelli, M., García-Sánchez, P., Burelli, P., Risi, S., and Sim, K., editors, *Genetic Programming*, pages 78–91, Cham. Springer.

[Muñoz et al., 2020] Muñoz, L., Trujillo, L., and Silva, S. (2020). Transfer learning in constructive induction with genetic programming. *Genet. Program. Evolvable Mach.*, 21(4):529–569.

[Muñoz et al., 2019] Muñoz, L., Trujillo, L., Silva, S., Castelli, M., and Vanneschi, L. (2019). Evolving multidimensional transformations for symbolic regression with M3GP. *Memetic Comput.*, 11(2):111–126.

[Niknam and Amiri, 2010] Niknam, T. and Amiri, B. (2010). An efficient hybrid approach based on PSO, ACO and k-means for cluster analysis. *Applied Soft Computing*, 10(1):183–197.

[Nobile et al., 2012] Nobile, M. S., Besozzi, D., Cazzaniga, P., Mauri, G., and Pescini, D. (2012). A GPU-based multi-swarm PSO method for parameter estimation in stochastic biological systems exploiting discrete-time target series. In Giacobini, M., Vanneschi, L., and Bush, W. S., editors, *Evolutionary Computation, Machine Learning and Data Mining in Bioinformatics*, pages 74–85. Springer.

[Nordin and Banzhaf, 1995] Nordin, P. and Banzhaf, W. (1995). Complexity compression and evolution. In Eshelman, L. J., editor, *Proceedings of the 6th International Conference on Genetic Algorithms, Pittsburgh, PA, USA, July 15-19, 1995*, pages 310–317. Morgan Kaufmann.

[Nordin et al., 1996] Nordin, P., Francone, F., and Banzhaf, W. (1996). *Explicitly Defined Introns and Destructive Crossover in Genetic Programming*, pages 111–134. MIT Press, Cambridge, MA, USA.

[Norouzi et al., 2012] Norouzi, M., Fleet, D. J., and Salakhutdinov, R. (2012). Hamming distance metric learning. In *Proceedings of the 25th International Conference on Neural Information Processing Systems, NIPS '12 - Volume 1*, pages 1061–1069, USA. Curran Associates Inc.

[O'Neill and Ryan, 2003] O'Neill, M. and Ryan, C. (2003). *Grammatical evolution - Evolutionary automatic programming in an arbitrary language*, volume 4 of *Genetic Programming*. Kluwer.

[O'Reilly and Oppacher, 1995] O'Reilly, U.-M. and Oppacher, F. (1995). The troubling aspects of a building block hypothesis for genetic programming. In Whitley, L. D. and Vose, M. D., editors, *Foundations of Genetic Algorithms (FOGA 1995)*, pages 73–88. Morgan Kaufmann.

[Pedersen and Chipperfield, 2010] Pedersen, M. and Chipperfield, A. (2010). Simplifying particle swarm optimization. *Applied Soft Computing*, 10(2):618–628.

[Pedregosa et al., 2011] Pedregosa, F., Varoquaux, G., Gramfort, A., Michel, V., Thirion, B., Grisel, O., Blondel, M., Prettenhofer, P., Weiss, R., Dubourg, V., et al. (2011). Scikit-learn: Machine learning in Python. *Journal of Machine Learning Research*, 12(Oct):2825–2830.

[Pitzer and Affenzeller, 2012] Pitzer, E. and Affenzeller, M. (2012). *A Comprehensive Survey on Fitness Landscape Analysis*, pages 161–191. Springer.

[Poli, 2003] Poli, R. (2003). A simple but theoretically-motivated method to control bloat in genetic programming. In Ryan, C., Soule, T., Keijzer, M., Tsang, E., Poli, R., and Costa, E., editors, *Genetic Programming, Proceedings of the 6th*

European Conference, EuroGP 2003, volume 2610 of *LNCS*, pages 200–210, Essex. Springer.

[Poli and Langdon, 1997] Poli, R. and Langdon, W. B. (1997). Genetic programming with one-point crossover and point mutation. Technical Report CSRP-97-13, University of Birmingham, UK.

[Poli and Langdon, 1998a] Poli, R. and Langdon, W. B. (1998a). Genetic programming with one-point crossover. In Chawdhry, P. K., Roy, R., and Pant, R. K., editors, *Second On-line World Conference on Soft Computing in Engineering Design and Manufacturing*, pages 23–27. Springer.

[Poli and Langdon, 1998b] Poli, R. and Langdon, W. B. (1998b). Schema theory for genetic programming with one-point crossover and point mutation. *Evolutionary Computation*, 6(3):231–252.

[Poli et al., 2007] Poli, R., Langdon, W. B., and Dignum, S. (2007). On the limiting distribution of program sizes in tree-based genetic programming. In Ebner, M., O'Neill, M., Ekárt, A., Vanneschi, L., and Esparcia-Alcázar, A. I., editors, *Genetic Programming*, pages 193–204. Springer.

[Poli et al., 2008a] Poli, R., Langdon, W. B., and McPhee, N. F. (2008a). *A Field Guide to Genetic Programming*. Lulu Enterprises, UK Ltd.

[Poli and McPhee, 2003a] Poli, R. and McPhee, N. F. (2003a). General schema theory for genetic programming with subtree swapping crossover: Part I. *Evolutionary Computation*, 11(1):53–66.

[Poli and McPhee, 2003b] Poli, R. and McPhee, N. F. (2003b). General schema theory for genetic programming with subtree swapping crossover: Part II. *Evolutionary Computation*, 11(2):169–206.

[Poli et al., 2008b] Poli, R., McPhee, N. F., and Vanneschi, L. (2008b). The impact of population size on code growth in GP: Analysis and empirical validation. In *Proceedings of the 10th Annual Conference on Genetic and Evolutionary Computation, GECCO '08*, page 1275–1282. Association for Computing Machinery.

[Quinlan, 1986] Quinlan, J. R. (1986). Induction of decision trees. *Machine Learning*, 1(1):81–106.

[Quinlan, 1993] Quinlan, J. R. (1993). *C4.5 Programs for Machine Learning*. Morgan Kaufmann, California.

[Rao and Fung, 2008] Rao, R. B. and Fung, G. (2008). On the dangers of cross-validation. An experimental evaluation. In *Proceedings of the SIAM International Conference on Data Mining, SDM 2008, April 24-26, 2008, Atlanta, Georgia, USA*, pages 588–596. SIAM.

[Rashid, 2016] Rashid, T. (2016). *Make Your Own Neural Network*. CreateSpace Independent Publishing Platform, USA, 1st edition.

[Rey and Neuhäuser, 2011] Rey, D. and Neuhäuser, M. (2011). *Wilcoxon-Signed-Rank Test*, pages 1658–1659. Springer.

[Reynolds, 1987] Reynolds, C. W. (1987). Flocks, herds and schools: A distributed behavioral model. In *Proceedings of the 14th Annual Conference on Computer Graphics and Interactive Techniques, SIGGRAPH '87*, pages 25–34, New York, NY, USA. Association for Computing Machinery.

[Rodrigues et al., 2020] Rodrigues, N. M., Batista, J. E., and Silva, S. (2020). Ensemble genetic programming. In Hu, T., Lourenço, N., Medvet, E., and Divina, F., editors, *Genetic Programming - 23rd European Conference, EuroGP 2020, Held as Part of EvoStar 2020, Seville, Spain, April 15-17, 2020, Proceedings*, volume 12101 of *Lecture Notes in Computer Science*, pages 151–166. Springer.

[Rokach and Maimon, 2014] Rokach, L. and Maimon, O. (2014). *Data Mining With Decision Trees: Theory and Applications*. World Scientific Publishing Co., Inc., River Edge, NJ, USA, 2nd edition.

[Rosca, 1997] Rosca, J. P. (1997). Analysis of complexity drift in genetic programming. In Koza, J. R., Deb, K., Dorigo, M., Fogel, D. B., Garzon, M., Iba, H., and Riolo, R. L., editors, *Genetic Programming 1997: Proceedings of the Second Annual Conference*, pages 286–294, Stanford University, CA, USA. Morgan Kaufmann.

[Rosenblatt, 1958] Rosenblatt, F. (1958). The perceptron: A probabilistic model for information storage and organization in the brain. *Psychological Review*, 65:386–408.

[Rousseeuw, 1987] Rousseeuw, P. J. (1987). Silhouettes: A graphical aid to the interpretation and validation of cluster analysis. *Journal of Computational and Applied Mathematics*, 20:53 – 65.

[Roy et al., 2011] Roy, R., Dehuri, S., and Cho, S. B. (2011). A novel particle swarm optimization algorithm for multi-objective combinatorial optimization problem. *Int. J. Appl. Metaheuristic Comput.*, 2(4):41–57.

[Rudin, 1986] Rudin, W. (1986). *Principles of Mathematical Analysis*. McGraw–Hill.

[Rudolph, 1997] Rudolph, G. (1997). *Convergence properties of evolutionary algorithms*. Kovac.

[Russell and Norvig, 2009] Russell, S. and Norvig, P. (2009). *Artificial Intelligence: A Modern Approach*. Prentice Hall Press, Upper Saddle River, NJ, USA, 3rd edition.

[Samuel, 1959] Samuel, A. L. (1959). Some studies in machine learning using the game of checkers. *IBM Journal of Research and Development*, 3(3):210–229.

[Schaffer, 1985] Schaffer, J. D. (1985). Multiple objective optimization with vector evaluated genetic algorithms. In *Proceedings of the 1st International Conference on Genetic Algorithms*, page 93–100, USA. L. Erlbaum Associates Inc.

[Schapire, 1990] Schapire, R. E. (1990). The strength of weak learnability. *Machine Learning*, 5(2):197–227.

[Schmidt and Lipson, 2011] Schmidt, M. and Lipson, H. (2011). *Age-Fitness Pareto Optimization*, pages 129–146. Springer.

[Shalev-Shwartz and Ben-David, 2014] Shalev-Shwartz, S. and Ben-David, S. (2014). *Understanding Machine Learning: From Theory to Algorithms*. Cambridge University Press.

[Sharma et al., 2020] Sharma, S., Sharma, S., and Athaiya, A. (2020). Activation functions in neural networks. *International Journal of Engineering Applied Sciences and Technology*, 04:310–316.

[Shiming Xiang and Zhang, 2008] Shiming Xiang, F. N. and Zhang, C. (2008). Learning a Mahalanobis distance metric for data clustering and classification. *Pattern Recognition*, 41(2):3600–3612.

[Silva and Costa, 2009] Silva, S. and Costa, E. (2009). Dynamic limits for bloat control in genetic programming and a review of past and current bloat theories. *Genetic Programming and Evolvable Machines*, 10(2):141–179.

[Silva and Dignum, 2009] Silva, S. and Dignum, S. (2009). Extending operator equalisation: Fitness based self adaptive length distribution for bloat free GP. In Vanneschi, L., Gustafson, S., Moraglio, A., De Falco, I., and Ebner, M., editors, *Genetic Programming*, pages 159–170. Springer.

[Silva et al., 2012] Silva, S., Dignum, S., and Vanneschi, L. (2012). Operator equalisation for bloat free genetic programming and a survey of bloat control methods. *Genetic Programming and Evolvable Machines*, 13(2):197–238.

[Silva et al., 2016] Silva, S., Muñoz, L., Trujillo, L., Ingalalli, V., Castelli, M., and Vanneschi, L. (2016). *Multiclass Classification Through Multidimensional Clustering*, pages 219–239. Springer, Cham.

[Singh and Valtorta, 1995] Singh, M. and Valtorta, M. (1995). Construction of Bayesian network structures from data: A brief survey and an efficient algorithm. *International Journal of Approximate Reasoning*, 12(2):111 – 131.

[Sipper et al., 2018] Sipper, M., Fu, W., Ahuja, K., and Moore, J. H. (2018). Investigating the parameter space of evolutionary algorithms. *BioData Min.*, 11(1):2:1–2:14.

[Smith and Harries, 1998] Smith, P. W. H. and Harries, K. (1998). Code growth, explicitly defined introns, and alternative selection schemes. *Evol. Comput.*, 6(4):339–360.

[Sorensen, 1994] Sorensen, O. (1994). *Neural Networks in Control Applications*. Aalborg Universitetsforlag. PhD thesis.

[Soule and Foster, 1998] Soule, T. and Foster, J. (1998). Removal bias: a new cause of code growth in tree based evolutionary programming. In *1998 IEEE International Conference on Evolutionary Computation Proceedings. IEEE World Congress on Computational Intelligence (Cat. No.98TH8360)*, pages 781–786.

[Soule and Heckendorn, 2002] Soule, T. and Heckendorn, R. B. (2002). An analysis of the causes of code growth in genetic programming. *Genetic Programming and Evolvable Machines*, 3(3):283–309.

[Spector and Robinson, 2002] Spector, L. and Robinson, A. J. (2002). Genetic programming and autoconstructive evolution with the Push programming language. *Genet. Program. Evolvable Mach.*, 3(1):7–40.

[Stadler, 2002] Stadler, P. F. (2002). *Fitness landscapes*, pages 183–204. Springer.

[Styer, 2019] Styer, D. (2019). Entropy as disorder: History of a misconception. *The Physics Teacher*, 57(7):454–458.

[Sullivan and Luke, 2007] Sullivan, K. M. and Luke, S. (2007). Evolving kernels for support vector machine classification. In *Proceedings of the 9th Annual Conference on Genetic and Evolutionary Computation, GECCO '07*, pages 1702–1707. Association for Computing Machinery.

[Tackett, 1994] Tackett, W. A. (1994). *Recombination, Selection, and the Genetic Construction of Computer Programs*. PhD thesis, University of Southern California, Department of Electrical Engineering Systems, USA.

[Tettamanzi and Tomassini, 2001] Tettamanzi, A. and Tomassini, M. (2001). *Soft Computing: Integrating Evolutionary, Neural and Fuzzy Systems*. Springer.

[Tian and Feng, 2021] Tian, Y. and Feng, Y. (2021). RaSE: Random subspace ensemble classification. *J. Mach. Learn. Res.*, 22:45:1–45:93.

[Tipping, 2004] Tipping, M. E. (2004). *Bayesian Inference: An Introduction to Principles and Practice in Machine Learning*, pages 41–62. Springer.

[Tomassini et al., 2005] Tomassini, M., Vanneschi, L., Collard, P., and Clergue, M. (2005). A study of fitness distance correlation as a difficulty measure in genetic programming. *Evolutionary Computation*, 13(2):213–239.

[Trujillo et al., 2020] Trujillo, L., González, E. Á., Galván, E., Tapia, J. J., and Ponsich, A. (2020). On the analysis of hyper-parameter space for a genetic programming system with iterated F-Race. *Soft Comput.*, 24(19):14757–14770.

[Vanneschi, 2004] Vanneschi, L. (2004). *Theory and Practice for Efficient Genetic Programming*. PhD thesis, Faculty of Sciences, University of Lausanne, Switzerland.

[Vanneschi et al., 2013] Vanneschi, L., Castelli, M., Manzoni, L., and Silva, S. (2013). A new implementation of geometric semantic GP and its application to problems in pharmacokinetics. In *Proceedings of the 16th European Conference on Genetic Programming, EuroGP 2013*, volume 7831 of *LNCS*, pages 205–216. Springer.

[Vanneschi et al., 2014] Vanneschi, L., Castelli, M., and Silva, S. (2014). A survey of semantic methods in genetic programming. *Genetic Programming and Evolvable Machines*, 15(2):195–214.

[Vanneschi et al., 2004] Vanneschi, L., Clergue, M., Collard, P., Tomassini, M., and Vérel, S. (2004). Fitness clouds and problem hardness in genetic programming. In Deb, K., editor, *Genetic and Evolutionary Computation – GECCO 2004*, pages 690–701. Springer.

[Vanneschi et al., 2011] Vanneschi, L., Dodecasa, D., and Mauri, G. (2011). A comparative study of four parallel and distributed PSO methods. *New Generation Computing*, 29(1):129–161.

[Vanneschi et al., 2006] Vanneschi, L., Tomassini, M., Collard, P., and Vérel, S. (2006). Negative slope coefficient: A measure to characterize genetic programming fitness landscapes. In Collet, P., Tomassini, M., Ebner, M., Gustafson, S., and Ekárt, A., editors, *Genetic Programming*, pages 178–189. Springer.

[Vasconcelos et al., 2015] Vasconcelos, M., Cabral, A., Melo, J., Pearson, T., Pereira, H., Cassamá, V., and Yudelman, T. (2015). Can blue carbon contribute to clean development in West–Africa? The case of Guinea–Bissau. *Mitigation and Adaptation Strategies for Global Change*, 20(8):1361–1383.

[Vassilev et al., 2003] Vassilev, V. K., Fogarty, T. C., and Miller, J. F. (2003). *Smoothness, Ruggedness and Neutrality of Fitness Landscapes: from Theory to Application*, pages 3–44. Springer.

[Vlack, 2008] Vlack, L. H. V. (2008). *Elements of Materials Science and Engineering*. Pearson Education, New Delhi, 6th. edition.

[Ward, 1963] Ward, J. H. (1963). Hierarchical grouping to optimize an objective function. *Journal of the American Statistical Association*, 58(301):236–244.

[Whigham, 1996] Whigham, P. A. (1996). *Grammatical Bias for Evolutionary Learning*. PhD thesis, School of Computer Science, University College, University of New South Wales, Australian Defence Force Academy, Canberra, Australia.

[Wolpert, 1992] Wolpert, D. H. (1992). Stacked generalization. *Neural Networks*, 5:241–259.

[Wolpert, 1996] Wolpert, D. H. (1996). The lack of a priori distinctions between learning algorithms. *Neural Computation*, 8(7):1341–1390.

[Wolpert and Macready, 1997] Wolpert, D. H. and Macready, W. G. (1997). No free lunch theorems for optimization. *Trans. Evol. Comp*, 1(1):67–82.

[Wu et al., 2001] Wu, X., Lucas, P., Kerr, S., and Dijkhuizen, R. (2001). Learning Bayesian-network topologies in realistic medical domains. In Crespo, J., Maojo, V., and Martin, F., editors, *Medical Data Analysis*, pages 302–307. Springer.

[Wysocki and Lawrynczuk, 2015] Wysocki, A. and Lawrynczuk, M. (2015). Jordan neural network for modelling and predictive control of dynamic systems. In *2015 20th International Conference on Methods and Models in Automation and Robotics (MMAR)*, pages 145–150.

[Zhang and Mühlenbein, 1995] Zhang, B.-T. and Mühlenbein, H. (1995). Balancing accuracy and parsimony in genetic programming. *Evol. Comput.*, 3(1):17–38.

[Zhang and Xie, 2003] Zhang, W.-J. and Xie, X.-F. (2003). DEPSO: hybrid particle swarm with differential evolution operator. In *SMC'03 Conference Proceedings. 2003 IEEE International Conference on Systems, Man and Cybernetics. Conference Theme - System Security and Assurance (Cat. No.03CH37483)*, volume 4, pages 3816–3821.

[Zitzler and Thiele, 1999] Zitzler, E. and Thiele, L. (1999). Multiobjective evolutionary algorithms: a comparative case study and the strength Pareto approach. *IEEE Transactions on Evolutionary Computation*, 3(4):257–271.

Printed in the United States
by Baker & Taylor Publisher Services